Johannes H. Birringer

Marlowe's »Dr Faustus« and »Tamburlaine«
Theological and Theatrical Perspectives

Verlag Peter Lang
FRANKFURT AM MAIN · BERN · NEW YORK

CIP-Kurztitelaufnahme der Deutschen Bibliothek

Birringer, Johannes H.:
Marlowe's "D[octo]r Faustus" and "Tamburlaine" :
theolog. and theatr. perspectives / Johannes
H. Birringer. - Frankfurt am Main ; Bern ; New
York : Lang, 1984.
　(Trierer Studien zur Literatur ; Bd. 10)
　ISBN 3-8204-5421-7
NE: GT

ISSN 0721-4294
ISBN 3-8204-5421-7
© Verlag Peter Lang GmbH, Frankfurt am Main 1984
Alle Rechte vorbehalten.
Nachdruck oder Vervielfältigung, auch auszugsweise, in allen Formen
wie Mikrofilm, Xerographie, Mikrofiche, Mikrocard, Offset verboten.
Druck und Bindung: Weihert-Druck GmbH, Darmstadt

Marlowe's "Dr Faustus" and "Tamburlaine"

Trierer Studien zur Literatur

Unter Mitarbeit von Karl-Heinz Bender, Wolfgang Düsing, Karl Eibl, Karl Hölz, Walter Pache, Herbert Zirker
Herausgegeben von JÖRG HASLER, BERNHARD KÖNIG, LOTHAR PIKULIK

Bd./Vol. 10

Verlag Peter Lang
FRANKFURT AM MAIN · BERN · NEW YORK

To my Mother and Father

CONTENTS

PREFACE ... 9

CHAPTER ONE:
1. "Theo-Dramatism" and the Myth of the Trespass ... 15
2. A Note on the Texts ... 38

CHAPTER TWO:
1. Macbeth and "Horrible Imaginings" ... 45
2. Faustus' Rhetoric of Aspiration ... 63
3. Extravagant Heroism: The Advent of Tamburlaine ... 78

CHAPTER THREE:
Endless Strife: Performances of Power ... 109

CHAPTER FOUR:
Faustus' Upward Fall: Theology in Marlowe's Drama ... 151

CHAPTER FIVE:
Choreography in the Damnation Scene ... 199

CHAPTER SIX:
The End of Every Art: Faustus' Dialectic of Self-Reprobation ... 221

CHAPTER SEVEN:
Magic Circles ... 259

CHAPTER EIGHT:
Tragedy of the Mind: Faustus and his Covenant ... 285

CHAPTER NINE:
In the "Suburbs of Hell" ... 327

EPILOGUE:
The Faustian Ethos: "Desperate Enterprise"? ... 377

BIBLIOGRAPHY ... 387

INDEX ... 399

PREFACE

The abundant and conflicting interpretations of Christopher Marlowe's plays have often led readers to conclude that he lacked complete control of his dramatic material and struggled to give expression to heightened imaginative impulses which surfaced as disturbingly in his works as they apparently dominated his aggressive personality and beliefs. There is some evidence, apart from his poems and plays themselves, for an extraordinary intensity in Marlowe's short and turbulent life, with the dangerous blasphemies, the nearly overt homosexuality, the quarrels and arrests, the mysterious stint as a double agent in Walsingham's secret service - signs of a wilful courting of disaster not very different from that depicted in his stage heroes. Marlowe's personal investment with his protagonists' compulsive rebelliousness has often been taken for granted, and what nowadays is disparagingly called "romantic" criticism began fairly early with Robert Greene's allusion to "that Atheist Tamburlaine" and his later admonition of the atheist Marlowe.

The ingenuity and excitement of Marlowe's literary creations, on the other hand, have never been questioned even though some critics (including T.S. Eliot) thought it necessary to declare the "immaturity" of his intellectual fervour responsible for what they found wanting in form. If we start from the generally acknowledged assumption, however, that his reputation was based on the exciting verbal power and richly imaginative poetry of his drama, that his plays were the first in English theatre to almost literally overwhelm his audience with the "mighty line" (the immensely flexible, spacious blank-verse measure which was to become the magic key for all later accomplishments in Elizabethan drama), then we approach the rather problematic question of how, precisely, form and content are related in Marlowe's provocative plays. That his two early and most popular plays, *Tamburlaine the Great*, Part 1 and Part 2, as well as the somewhat later *Doctor Faustus* (certainly his best known play today), had a sensational and disturbing effect on the original audience can be judged from the flood of rather curious imitations and parodies that followed the advent of *Tamburlaine* in 1587, and from the host of allusions that we encounter in other texts through the following years. The most immediate response to the plays' verbal challenge among Marlowe's fellow playwrights betrays uneasiness, envy, and outrage. It ought to be emphasized that the complaints put forth by Greene and others were of course addressed to the ideas, the fantasies of ambition and power and their implications for the new heroic and tragic drama Marlowe wrote. But primarily they were directed against the *style*, the bold and unprecedented poetics of hyperbole as well as the spectacular dramaturgy, with which Marlowe caught and manipulated the imaginations of his audience.

I proceed from the working assumption that by attending to the specifics of Marlowe's dramatic style, to the verbal and visual rhetoric of his plays, we shall be in a better position to interpret their dramatic significance and historical particularity. We shall also be able to gain new perspectives on the vexing question of what kind of theological concepts and religious statements the plays represent - a question that has troubled critics ever since Marlowe's infamous reputation as an "atheist" and cynical iconoclast had begun to take shape. In responding to Tamburlaine's and Faustus' dazzling projections of imaginative freedom with outrage and dismay, those contemporaries of Marlowe who thought that the plays were full of intolerable attacks on conventional morality already paved the way for modern scholarship's obsession with the problem of his "orthodoxy." In this respect, Marlowe criticism has proved more disturbing than helpful over the past decades, and one can only be perplexed by the confusion that has arisen since the "romantic" critics, on the one hand, have passionately embraced Marlowe's heterodoxy, and the moralizing critics, on the other hand, have uncovered sound Christian doctrines and received ideas about ethics and about human nature which, supposedly held by Marlowe himself, constituted the basic conviction behind the plays.

Most recent scholarship, while certainly increasing our knowledge of the Elizabethan context and extending our appreciation of Marlowe's likely dependence on pageant, morality play, romance, the Scriptures, iconography, stage conventions, and so forth, seems to complicate the issue of Marlowe's conscious or unconscious choices rather than clarify it. The Marlowe who has emerged during the last decade is certainly even more exciting, even more challenging; a wide range of tones has been found in his generically unstable plays, and he even begins to look - quite fashionably - like a sardonic, maliciously enigmatic ironist.

In view of the multiplicity of interpretations, a new approach that takes account of the plays' apparent inconsistencies and contradictions seems well worth risking. The aim of this study is to present, as briefly and as cogently as I can, a way of looking at Marlowe's most important plays (*Dr Faustus*; *Tamburlaine* Part 1 and Part 2) in terms of the various ways in which each embodies a specific dramatic style and rhetorical mode, employs them as vehicles for an imaginative projection, and relates to its audience. In practice, this enquiry has involved two closely related but separable sets of questions. Those in the first set are designed to clarify what we mean when we talk about Marlowe's subversiveness or the apparently unstable use of theological and ethical criteria in his plays. The orthodoxy of the basic premises in *Dr Faustus* has been argued so extensively and exasperatingly that I am particularly interested in following the discernible trends in Marlowe's "Calvinist" dramaturgy - a dramaturgy which seems all the more surprising if we see it in juxtaposition to the uniquely anti-conventional conception of the *Tamburlaine* plays.

The second set of questions is self-evident; I believe that it makes little sense to talk about ideas, themes, and ethical purport in Marlovian drama without recognizing the plays themselves as distinct experiments in form. Most critical commentaries on his work have tended to disregard or underplay the performance dynamics of Marlowe's theatre and concentrated, instead, on the thinking he brings to bear on his heroes' daring adventures. I venture to balance our critical estimate of Marlowe by focussing on a theatrical perspective from which to view his major plays and from which to relate the most immediate effects as well as

the overall significance of a particular dramatic style to its
ethical and philosophical purports. If the following chapters
are an imperfect attempt to trace the entire range of Marlowe's
capacities as a poet-dramatist, I hope, at least, to have chosen
a method and a critical idiom which can help us to gain a more
complete understanding of the dynamic mechanisms that operate in
the play-in-performance, create its form and intent, and determine
its interaction with the audience.

I wish to thank the many people and institutions that have contributed to my work on Marlowe at various stages of its evolution.
I first read the drama of Marlowe, Shakespeare, and their contemporaries with Professor Jörg Hasler at the University of Trier.
That experience and, especially, his insistent and inspiring demonstration of the role of the theatrical element in dramatic
texts eventually led me to undertake this study and to focus less
extensively on the theological concepts in Marlowe than originally
intended. Professor Hasler not only supervised my first post-
graduate research, but has given me unfailing guidance and patient
encouragement over the years. To him I owe an especially large
debt, and I can only hope that I shall remain worthy of his continued influence on my work. I also owe thanks to his colleague,
Professor Walter Pache, for the interest and spontaneous concern
he showed in examining these pages.

I am grateful to the Konrad Adenauer Foundation for the privilege
of a research scholarship which enabled me to spend a year at St
John's College, Cambridge. It was no doubt the beauty and serenity
of Cambridge and the invaluable advice and support of Mr Leo
Salingar which helped me to overcome initial problems. I am also
grateful to Dr Lisa Jardine for her criticism of early drafts.

My transfer to Yale, in 1980, was assisted by a grant from the
German Academic Exchange Service. With the assistance of the Graduate School and the German Department at Yale I was able to complete the manuscript. During my stay there I benefited immeasur-
ably from the tireless, painstaking, and challenging criticism of
Professor George K. Hunter. His kind interest in my project proved

a source of constant inspiration. My special thanks also to Professors Eugene Waith, John Hollander, Thomas Greene, Conrad Russell, and Harold Bloom for helpful advice and encouragement.

The staffs of the Corpus Christi College Library, the Beinecke Rare Book Collection, and of the University libraries at Trier, Cambridge, and Yale were always more helpful than they had to be. I should also mention the actual productions of Marlowe's plays which I was able to see in Great Britain and the United States; to these theatrical experiences I owe more suggestions than can be adequately acknowledged in footnotes.

A more personal debt is owed to the kindness of many friends who have been firm supporters; among them, Günter Radden, Peter Mitchell, Kathy Garnsworthy, Kathleen Anderson, David Caton, and Lorna Martens must be mentioned.

And, finally, not the least of my gratitude is due to my parents, who throughout my life showed me their unusual patience, love, and understanding, and to the equally enthusiastic and long-suffering Christina Marie Re, without whom the final stages of my work could not have been accomplished.

I am grateful to the editors of *Trierer Studien zur Literatur* for including this book in the series.

New Haven, Connecticut
November 1982

Chapter One

1. "THEO-DRAMATISM" AND THE MYTH OF THE TRESPASS

The dramatic possibilities of the theme of ambition and aspiration are numerous. We tend to be fascinated by the strong performance of a self that can project its overpowering desires and tell them in its own voice. The voice that asserts the self must be a voice of power because it is always already engaged in a struggle or competition with the Other, seeking to impose itself upon or defend itself against some reality conceived as exterior to it.

This struggle to realize and elevate the self, whether or not we want to regard it as an *essentially* proud and ambitious undertaking, is perforce an *evolving* - hence performative - act of self-interpretation and a re-vision of the external. Active self-interpretation is a privilege of those central characters we call heroes, and with regard to the peculiar dynamics of the theatre this implies that the protagonist is seen to control or take overt responsibility for the way in which the plot advances and in which voice is translated into action. If we say that expression of desire, as discourse and action, shapes the specific role which the strong individual character embodies, we already become involved in a larger set of questions concerning the meaning of "role" and the power and possibilities of language in its relation to an existing (anterior) order or system of values. And if we approach poetic drama as a type of literary discourse, we are of course prompted to ask how far the forms of discourse as well as of dramatic expression can be placed within a genre or tradition which could be seen as a kind of container of a known order showing the moral, psychological, and conceptual functioning of the individual in it.

In other words, if we tried to locate representations of the self in heroic and tragic drama, would we not inevitably encounter the central character circumscribed by a web of "textual" relationships, orders of meaning, social bonds? Can we say that Hamlet's encounter with the Ghost, Macbeth's response to the Witches' prophecy, or Faustus' reading of the Bible constitute highly "textualized" moments in which the protagonist's discourse inevitably gets caught up in a play of relations which can point to meanings that are larger than the individual, beyond his control or understanding? To follow this line of argument, the concept of self – and thus the notion of character – seems to be intrinsically connected with the performance, successful or failed, of wilful discourse as a means of creating meaning and of denying the authority of the Other, the cause-effect structure of influence, and the power of a context that subsumes the individual and restricts the possibility of maintaining differences.

The traditional assumption that plot moves character towards a goal or that the protagonist embodies theme becomes even less trustworthy if we consider the fact that heroism and distinct individuality in the drama of the Tudor period are a matter of the functioning of discourse, of the power of poetry itself. Seen from this perspective, the arrival of Marlowe's *Tamburlaine* upon the Elizabethan stage can be said to mark the emergence of a poetics more radical than the Sidneys and Jonsons of Marlowe's age would have ever thought possible, and Sidney's overtly conventional didacticism (in the *Apology*) could very well serve to illustrate the distance between his moral theory of poetry and the violent, disruptive rhetoric of *self*-consciousness we find sealed upon the wild imaginings of Marlowe's rebellious heroes.

A new and considerably more interesting "defence" of poetic power has been presented to us in the writings of Harold Bloom since *The Anxiety of Influence* (1973). Although Bloom's formal model of the "revisionary ratios," or system of tropes and defences that structure intra-poetic and interpoetic relations, seems too limited for a discussion of dramatic poetry, it is worth pondering on his claim that anxiety in poems is meaningful in itself and needs to be read "antithetically," i.e. not as a representation that refers to an object world but metaphorically as the work of an Oedipal struggle between the belated poet and the "pre-emptive force of another imagination."[1] In this theory, tropes are not simply understood as impersonal linguistic processes within the rhetorical structure of a text but as figures of will and expressions of the creative struggle for identity. Echoing Hazlitt's illuminating remarks about the blood-stained language of power in Shakespeare's *Coriolanus*, Bloom celebrates the intense energies that can be felt in a truly agonistic language of desire, possession, and rivalry.

Although the intertextuality in which I am interested is of a different kind, the assertion of an individual voice and will can certainly be regarded as the most dynamic and spectacular component of the theatre Marlowe created, and it opens up further questions about the role of the protagonist that I have already referred to in the beginning. If the hero's enunciative power marks the representation of possessive individualism, we still have to ask ourselves what kind of representation is involved and through which particular conflicts individualism becomes manifest. The latter question, I believe, is intrinsically connected with the former and is likely to have had serious implications for the conception of heroic and tragic drama in the Renaissance. What I propose to examine, then, is the form and expression Marlowe found for those new ideas about the self in the Renaissance that critics commonly take for granted when they speak about the soaring humanist ambitions embodied in Faustus and Tamburlaine. Cultural theorists who explore the transformation of the medieval ethos into the modern ethos tend to quote a few Marlovian lines out of context in order to support their claim that Marlowe's protagonists reflect the characteristic restlessness, aesthetic sensitivity, power-hunger, and acquisitive energy which marked the beginning of the new "Faustian culture."[2]

---

1 Harold Bloom, *A Map of Misreading* (New York: Oxford Univ.Press, 1975), pp. 68f.
2 See, for example, T.K. Seung, *Cultural Thematics: The Formation of the Faustian Ethos* (New Haven: Yale Univ. Press, 1976), esp. pp. ix-xii; 237-59.

One is on safer ground in contemplating whether the mode and style, or linguistic convention, that could be taken as the embodiment of a new form of sensibility indeed help to clarify the astonishing intellectual, ethical, and philosophical changes that were taking place. It has often been underestimated how important the Renaissance infatuation with language and style actually was. In the period we are concerned with, literature was frankly rhetorical, and interpretation arrived at describing the moral effect of a particular text by beginning with its verbal techniques. We only have to remember E.K., the editor/commentator supplied for Spenser's *The Shepheardes Calender*. E.K. is mainly interested in the linguistic value and rhetorical organization of the text. He annotates particularly successful rhetorical moments; he elucidates the text by quoting other texts, classical antecedents, contemporary dictionaries and handbooks; moral meanings are then linked up with the rhetorical ones. In a similar way, Lyly's *Euphues* is almost entirely preoccupied with its own self-conscious stylistic excess.

Michel Foucault has tried to explain these features of Renaissance culture by describing the ways in which the entire world was seen as a *text* which could only be elucidated by reference to other texts.[3] In the universe that Foucault describes, knowledge is endless and endlessly verbal but its acquisition is also forever deferred, in spite of the lists and compendiums that are provided for the systematic exploration of the "prose of the world." One could extend this argument into the radical conclusion that the principal difficulty confronted by the writer of the period is that of transforming his basic rhetorical skills into his *own* discourse or, simply, of creating meaning. Must we not assume, however, that this search for a new meaning is highly problematic, considering those tendencies in the thought of the period that

---

3   Michel Foucault, *The Order of Things* (1966;rpt. New York: Random House, Vintage Books, 1970); for a discussion of the issues that I introduced above, see esp. pp. 17-44. For "further reading" I suggest Jonathan Goldberg's new book: *Endlesse Worke* (Baltimore: Johns Hopkins Univ. Press, 1981).

posit separation and differentiation - the category of the individual - as the central epistemological dilemma which the subject faces in its relation to the other (another person or object; the universe)? If we think of Ficino's and Campanella's, or even Bruno's, descriptions of the desire of the mind to merge with the universe and to transcend the gaps between the self and the other, the Finite and the Infinite, the optimism that inspires such an ethos of universal immediacy tends to confuse the issue even more because the principle of mental freedom that underlies it is meant to demarcate an integrity which can never be filled in a universe in which boundaries are always dissolving.[4] The conception of the sovereign individual as the agent of universal immediacy is perhaps best expressed in Pico della Mirandola's "Oration on the Dignity of Man." Pico ventures to define man as the unique substance of unlimited power, ranging from the earthly to the heavenly; and this power also includes the potential to master infinite reality through finite human language.

One may call Pico's vision, namely the epistemological *and* ontological immediacy between God and creatures, between the supernatural and the natural orders, a daring act of the finite human soul to reach out toward and grasp the "unknowing darkness"[5] of the infinite. But it does not resolve the dualistic tension that

---

4   For the central issues in Renaissance philosophical speculation about the subject-object problem, see Ernst Cassirer, *The Individual and the Cosmos in Renaissance Philosophy*, trans. Mario Domandi (1927;rpt. Philadelphia: Univ. of Philadelphia Press, 1963) and *The Renaissance Philosophy of Man*, ed. Ernst Cassirer et al.(Chicago: Univ. of Chicago Press, 1948). See also Harry Berger, Jr., "The Ecology of the Mind," *CentR*, 8 (1964), 409-34, and Thomas Greene, "The Flexibility of the Self in Renaissance Literature," in *The Discipline of Criticism*, ed. Peter Demetz, Thomas Greene, and Lowry Nelson, Jr. (New Haven: Yale Univ. Press, 1968), pp. 241-64.
5   I have adopted the expression from Bonaventure ("The Journey of the Mind of God," in *The Works of Bonaventure*, trans. José de Vinck [Paterson,N.J.: St.Anthony Guild, 1960-70], I, 58)in order to draw attention to the dialectical relationship that seems to exist between Pico's overtly Neo-Platonic logic of continuity, which can be traced back to the medieval mystic immanentism of a Bonaventure or a Pseudo-Dionysius, and the more influential Augustinian logic of discontinuity with its

lies at the centre of all post-Thomistic theology and metaphysics. On the contrary, the tension is necessary as long as the humanistic ideal - man as the unique substance of unlimited power - is to be upheld. Pico's ideal is expressed in his reinterpretations of Genesis, and his deliberate "misreading" of that text is of course already a transgression of the normative formulations of Christian exegesis. More interestingly, what he spells out, in God's speech to Adam, is a celebration of the fact that man was created after the universe had already been complete and, therefore, not fixed and limited like the angels or the beasts but free to roam the universe (at least) in his mind.

What is also implied, however, is the rather traumatic recognition that the indeterminate self is essentially alienated, split off from the universe. The self is thus established as intrinsically unstable and unlocated, displaced, so to speak, into a "play-within-the-play" in which its desire for fulfilment (at-one-ment) must confront and avoid the obliterative force of that fulfilment (*self*-destruction in the union with God) - a fully dramatic plot-situation, one might argue, in which the action of the individual is always "framed" by a particular logic or structure of relations.

The story is paradigmatic. The immediacy between the self and an all-powerful God that the Protestant Reformation established only heightened the anxiety. At the same time, the division between the self and the other (God, the Divine Logos, the Universe), with all its internal ambiguities, offered the semantic ground for aesthetic exploration. The transition from a theocentric to an anthropocentric form of sensibility and mode of discourse could be elaborated into endless, fantasized (and failed) solutions to the dilemma of a discontinuous self caught between the demands of two incompatible conceptual systems.

---

radical dualistic emphasis on the unbridgeable gulf between man and the forever obscure and dark Divine Word. This dialectic, it appears, provides a crucial thematic impetus for the problematic fusion of the Calvinist logic of exclusion (the doctrine of double-predestination) and the more Bonaventurian and Dionysian metaphysics of immanence.

What I seek to explore in the following pages is the question how far such new philosophical and linguistic perspectives are recognizable in the conceptions of the hero in Marlovian drama and what particular conflicts are brought into play. The notion of conflict is fundamental in so far as the desires and ambitions expressed by both Tamburlaine and Faustus become radical challenges to convention through the very force of their presentation - the imaginative and rhetorical originality of a new style. And if this style enabled Marlowe to project poetic power as a transformative weapon, on both the conceptual and the formal level, the heroism that is presented necessarily implicates a dangerous relation to tradition, authority, the entire referential system, in other words, with which Marlowe's predecessors could confidently portray the Christian values and norms they respected and endorsed.

Tamburlaine's and Faustus' self-centred confidence in the omnipotence of their wishes is impressive and equivocal. Such heroic and romantic desires are not altogether unfamiliar to our modern sensibilities; on the contrary, the romance-of-trespass, of violating the sacred ground of authority, is a central form in modern literature, from Coleridge and Wordsworth to the present. Modernism, as a state of mind, is in fact incurable in its ambivalence about authority and identity. The *self-conscious*, inner estrangement we have learnt to live with in our post-Romantic culture bears all the marks of a psychological guilt which - in more familiar theological terms - could be explained as the effect of the "original sin" that individualism committed against authority. The extreme compulsiveness that underlies the founding gestures of the modern self, its irresistible need to refuse acknowledgement to a superior power, can be said to typify the predicament of our modern consciousness and may not have been understood that way in the Renaissance since ideas of originality and uniqueness only began to mark the conception of the self in the 19th century. But the problematic was certainly latent even in the pre-Cartesian consciousness, and we are reminded that the attempt to acknowledge authority and, simultaneously, fulfil an antithetical identity represents a humanist ideal that ought to be considered questionable at best.

In any case, there are of course immortal paradigms, too. Lucifer's attempt to rise against the Omnipotent creates the archetypal scene of transgression, and it is in Milton's extraordinary revision of Biblical tradition that we find the true voice of the self-asserting overreacher:

> Our puissance is our own, our own right hand
> Shall teach us highest deeds, by proof to try
> Who is our equal ...
> (*Paradise Lost* V.864-68)[6]

Satan's ambition shows the necessary logic of power, and his proud rhetorical justifications (in Book V) strike us as a fearfully magnificent attempt to confute the reality of failure. In the improper desire to rise, or the desire to rise however improperly, Satan - we must conclude - *chose* to fall, thus initiating evil and re-identifying himself within *it*.

Whether or not one likes the idea of Satan as hero and successful originator of evil, the imaginative passion of Satan in the early, dramatic debates and speeches (Books I, II, and IV) cannot but portray the ambivalent grandeur of a self that is conscious of its terrible predicament, and it is the same predicament Blake's Los recognizes when he declares that he must build his own "System" or be enslaved by the ready-made order of Christian morality.[7] Satan does not ultimately succeed in creating an independent, new system; he becomes a sad, tragic figure since his rise against God remains a dialectical, negative progress which is always already a fall. A recent commentator on the "war in heaven" has suggested, however, that Satan's grim belief in his

---

6 Quoted from *Milton: Paradise Lost, a New Edition. A Poem in Twelve Books*, ed. Merrit Y. Hughes (Indianapolis: Odyssey Press, 1962).

7 Los has begun to construct the imaginary city of Golgonooza when he exclaims: "I must Create a System or be enslaved by another Man's / I will not Reason or Compare; my business is to Create" (*Jerusalem* I.10.20-21). Quoted from *William Blake:*

own triumph constitutes a *necessary* fiction, a fiction, after all, which is pervasive and final. Satan's "master plot," Stella Purce Revard writes, "laid down in Heaven, is archetype not only for the future plot in Eden, but for all plots."[8]

Less than a century before Milton published his unsurpassed poetic meditations upon Satanic plots, Divine providence, and human nature, English audiences had already witnessed the re-creation of heroic and tragic archetypes in drama. Heroic claims and ambitious enterprises turn into "desperate enterprises" when their disruptive mobility is, quite necessarily, opposed by the regulatory forces of a social, political, or natural order. Tragedy, it has been claimed, is a kind of "ordering machine,"[9] an instructive model for attaching the right and true meaning to the activities of man in society and of man in nature, and even if this description can by no means be generally applied to Elizabethan tragedy, it points exactly to the *ethical* dimension of the particular form of re-presentation ascribed to tragedy ("the goodliest Argument of all")[10] by Renaissance critical theory.

Assimilating structural devices from the Greek model (partly directly, partly through a reading of Seneca) and relying heavily on the moral coordinates of the native tradition,[11] Elizabethan

---

    Jerusalem, Selected Poems and Prose, ed. Hazard Adams (New York: Holt, Rinehart & Winston, 1970).
8 Stella Purce Revard, *The War in Heaven:* Paradise Lost *and the Tradition of Satan's Rebellion* (Ithaca: Cornell Univ. Press, 1980), pp. 86f.
9 Timothy J. Reiss, *Tragedy and Truth: Studies in the Development of a Renaissance and Neoclassical Discourse* (New Haven: Yale Univ. Press, 1980), p. 9.
10 It is interesting that Roger Ascham seems to make a conscious distinction between the fundamental "matter" of a play, namely the formal ordering of action and discourse, and the more negligible stylistic ornamentation. As a proper procedure he recommends the imitation of the Greeks:"In Tragedies, (the goodliest Argument of all, and for the vse, either of a learned preacher, or a Ciuill Ientleman, more profitable than *Homer, Pindar, Virgill,* and *Horace*: yea comparable in myne opinion, with the doctrine of *Aristotle, Plato,* and *Xenophon,*) the *Grecians, Sophocles,* and *Euripides* far ouer match our *Seneca,* in *Latin,* namely in οἰκονομια et Decoro...." (*The Scholemaster,* in *The English Works,* ed. William Aldis Wright [Cambridge:

tragedy gradually had to find its own techniques and styles, its
own forms of "dramatism" (to use Kenneth Burke's expression), and
its own ways of plotting a fateful theme - one in which the central character breaks a divine moral law and brings about his
downfall. Even those tragedies that push furthest into the secular realms of human experience remain in the grip of some sustaining "order" which can stabilize the audience's response to the
mysteries of the tragic. And even at a point when our understanding of the hero's excesses may falter, we will still be able, I
submit, to apprehend the tensions and the suffering by taking recourse to the readily available language of religion, as Rymer
so eloquently did:

> Something must stick [to the spectator, for his
> instruction] by observing that constant order,
> that harmony and beauty of Providence, that necessary relation and chain, whereby the cause
> and effects, the virtues and rewards, the vices
> and their punishments are proportion'd and link'd
> together; how deep and dark soever are laid the
> springs, and however intricate and involv'd are
> their operations.[12]

The "order" of the rise-and-fall pattern, for example, had had a
long-standing tradition, and the late medieval morality play and
the *Mirror for Magistrates* are clearly paradigms for general
cultural assumptions about principles of order, limit, hierarchy,
and divinely-ordered balance. In speaking about homiletic tradition and admonitory drama, we implicitly touch upon the problem
of our perception of "nature" in a given cultural system of meanings in which fictions and artistic representations correlate to

---

Cambridge Univ. Press, 1904], p. 276).
11 See, for example, Willard Farnham's discussion of Elizabethan dramatic judgments of and attitudes toward tragic action in *The Medieval Heritage of Elizabethan Tragedy* (Berkeley: Univ. of California Press, 1936), pp. 340-420.
12 Thomas Rymer, *The Tragedies of the Last Age Consider'd and Examin'd by the Practice of the Ancients, and by the Common Sense of All Ages, in a Letter to Fleetwood Shepheard, Esq.,* in *The Critical Works,* ed. Curt A. Zimansky (New Haven: Yale Univ. Press, 1956), p. 75. Rymer's comment serves well to

the interpretive constructions the audience (as members of the
society, or "interpretive community," as Stanley Fish calls it)
impose upon their experiences. In view of the pervasively Christian, though conflict-ridden post-Reformational culture of Marlowe's and Shakespeare's England, it would make little sense not
to expect a close relationship between the subject-matter and
style of the drama and the political and cultural events of the
age. I am most interested here in the forms in which Elizabethan
drama can be seen to embody, explore, or subvert the values and
assumptions that must have been regarded as central by the audiences that came to see the performances. The dialectic of the
rise-and-fall pattern, for example, and especially the moral view
of overreaching ambition that is implied by the pattern, seems to
correspond basically with the Christian, indeed even the pre-
Christian ethical paradox that appertains to the theodicy problem
and to the general mythical structure of man's "fallibility":
video meliora proboque, detiora sequor. [13]

This ethical paradox became a rather complicated commonplace in
the Paulinian-Augustinian revisionism of English Protestant teaching. In the words of a Calvinist poet, there

> ... remains such naturall corruption
> In all our powers, even from our parents seed,

---

illustrate a trust in tragedy's corrective evocation of an
underlying order, which is inevitably linked with a moral
reading of the primary function of mimetic action (the emphasis on the importance of human action represented within a
thoroughly ordered plot of course echoes Aristotle's ideas
about *muthos* and *praxis* in tragedy). Such an ethical perspective had been inscribed in humanist-inspired rhetorical and
poetic theory throughout the Renaissance, and I merely quote
Rymer to sum up what Puttenham, Sidney, or Jonson would have
professed too.

13 Ovid, *Metamorphoses* VII.20-21. In Golding's translation, which
was certainly the text for Marlowe's generation, the line
reads:"The best I see and like: the worst I follow headlong
still" (*Ovid's Metamorphoses: The Arthur Golding Translation,
1567*, ed. John Frederick Nims [New York: MacMillan, 1965], VII.
25). The Ovidian text is quoted from the Loeb Classical Library edition of the *Metamorphoses*, ed. & trans. Frank Justus
Miller (1916; rpt. Cambridge,Mass.: Harvard Univ. Press, 1977).

> As to the good gives native interruption;
> Sense staines affection;that, will; and will, deed:
> So as what's good in us, and others too
> We praise; but what is evill, that we do.[14]

One must understand the trope "naturall corruption" in its full and far-reaching significance. It invokes the awesome bridge between the *then* and the *now*, the myth of the Fall and its diversification of symbols (the symbolization of original sin, fault, guilt, confession, finitude, etc.)[15] which constitutes an ever-present history of ambiguity: the freedom *and* the guilt of man are inextricably mingled. In the wake of the pervasive mythologization of the Adamic Fall, mankind had to learn to bear the burden of its inherited "nature." In the Protestant redefinitions, "nature" consequently becomes determinable in a twofold paradoxical sense: man's nature (fallen nature) in its postlapsarian state makes him desire not the good, or the reasonable, but rather its opposite. His actual or corrupt nature can only be transformed into his potential or good nature by the gift of God's grace. Secondly, the larger "nature" (fallen world) of which man is a part, the physical macrocosmos, is essentially good since created by God; but it too has been corrupted by original sin and become a scene of actual misery, trial, and temptation which perpetuates itself and in which the forces of

---

14 Fulke Greville, "A Treatise of Religion," in *The Remains*, ed. G.A. Wilkes (London: Oxford Univ. Press, 1965), st. 13. The Ovidian phrase as it here reappears in Greville was undoubtedly very well known in the Renaissance. Humanist syncretism furthermore helped to link the classics with Christian teaching;Ovid's line appears quite frequently in devotional writing and in Protestant teaching. Cf. John Calvin, *Institutes of the Christian Religion*, ed. John T. McNeill, trans. Ford L. Battles (Philadelphia: Westminster Press, 1960), II.2.23.

15 Paul Ricoeur calls man's experience of sin the "crucial experience" which can in fact be traced back to a pre-Judeo-Christian language of symbols that prefigures the mythologization of the concept of evil. For an excellent analysis of the symbol systems that are connected with the concept of evil, see Ricoeur's *The Symbolism of Evil* (1967; rpt. Boston: Beacon Press, 1969), esp. pp. 6-19, and chaps. 1 and 2 of Part I.

evil are allowed to campaign for men's souls. If we accept this
as a rationalization of the cycle of living experience, namely
the Christian experience of sin, we can go so far as to assume
the notion of a universal dialectic in terms of the antithesis
between "natural order" and man's "natural" predisposition, in
its opposite moral sense, to violate this order.

According to this interpretation of human existence, man's nature becomes the terrible mirror of his loss; the dichotomy of
good and evil - always linked to what tradition has called the
"fall" - solidifies the fundamental symbolic structure of sin
and guilt and magnifies the problematic of *choice* because the act
of choosing, as self-expression of the independent and individual
will, seems always to point toward the dark threshold experience,
the "knowledge of good and evil," which lies at the centre of the
Christian theology of fault. It is hardly surprising to find the
pre-Christian vision of man's fatedness thoroughly assimilated by
the Biblical eschatologizing of the whole history of mankind,
which is in fact nothing but a transposition of the older tragic
vision - the vision of the "creation drama of evil," as Ricoeur
calls it[16] - to the position of a kind of cosmological backdrop
for the new Christologically centred drama played in the foreground.

If the beginning of the *Heilsgeschichte* brought about a grand
reversal of perspectives, revealing - in the figure of the suffering Christ - a new meaning of salvation and a new promise of justification, it can hardly be said to have abolished the dialectic
of judgment and mercy that had governed the representations of
extreme threats and extreme promises in the Old Testament. At the
level of human experience, the ethical structure of such a world
of extremes can become a perennial temptation to despair. Belief
in the justification that is promised by the Christian Kerygma
seems so indissolubly bound up with all prior experience of the
dialectic of sin and the law that it is hard to imagine how the

---

16 Ricoeur, pp. 171-74, et passim.

consciousness of guilt and the existential experience of impotence could be suppressed. The vicious circularity of Law and Sin ("Moreover the law entered, that the offence might abound ..." Rom. v.20), which has been so profoundly analysed by St. Paul, Augustine, and Luther, inevitably leads to the uncomfortable conclusion that man's "freedom" always already accuses him, a conclusion which seems built into a moral vision of the world according to which History is a tribunal, pleasures and pains are retribution, and God himself a supreme judge.

In this sense, man's freedom is of course a very finite freedom, circumscribed by the authority of values which are always limitations that invite transgression ("And the commandment, which was ordained to life, I found to be unto death. For sin, taking occasion by the commandment, deceived me, and by it slew me" Rom. vii.10-11). It is a freedom, furthermore, which is always measured against the immutable law of man's mortality; the haunting shadow of mortality and finitude at the same time reinforces the essentially tragic aspects of a theology which is founded upon an iron law of retribution and a wrathful God. The circle of condemnation is broken at the moment in which man can accept the Christological and eschatological significance of the "event," Christ's redemptive sacrifice, and believe in the gospel of deliverance and hope. The biggest problem that we encounter in the New Testament is centred upon the idea of freedom once again.

The Pauline interpretation (and, of course, the Augustinian and Protestant re-interpretations) of the paradox of grace and freedom cannot in fact dispel the shadow of the tragic theology that lies behind all human attempts to understand the justice of God. St. Paul's attempt to solve the problem indeed forces him to relinquish all those human qualities that may confuse the meaning of Christ's death. Only by a complete inversion of the concept of freedom is it possible to arrive at Paul's conclusion that "justice" is not a category of the individual's being but - contrary to man's understanding of his knowledge, will, and power - is merely conferrable. Justification is something "that comes to a man - from the future to the present, from the outward to the in-

ward, from the transcendent to the immanent."[17] If to be "just"
means to be justified by an Other, however, the whole idea of
Christian "liberty" implies a radical transvaluation: liberty
ceases to be the power of hesitating and choosing between con-
traries. It is not in the least contingent upon effort, good
will, responsibility, or self-respect. The individual, therefore,
is always dependent on the Other, the Divine decision which is
beyond his choice and which overdetermines his own acts.

The gulf between the emotional and volitional life of man and
the ineluctable justice of God widens even further as the representations of the self, in the Protestant imagination, become
somber parodies of the ideal of Christian martyrdom which Cathol-
icism had expounded over the centuries. The doctrine of predestination raised the spirits that lay dormant. As a religious experience, the extremely anti-voluntaristic idea of submission to
God's irresistible will (presiding over salvation or damnation)
comes as close to the Greek sense of uncertain fate (στυγνὲ
δαῖμον) as it can possibly come. The unbearable tension between
hope and fear is Protestantism's own enigma; the idea of predestination itself points back to the stigma of ineluctable guilt
which must confuse all human action as long as it can symbolize
the "fatality" of "freedom."

But it is this confusion of possibility and limitation which ani-
mates the internal tensions in tragic drama. The hero's freedom
of self-interpretation evolves from the "inside" of the play, and
he must always delay and resist the implication that he is, after
all, only re-enacting and fulfilling a tragic paradox. The Player
King in *Hamlet*, acting in a play-within-a-play, summarizes both
the dramatistic and the theological perspectives for us:

> Our wills and fates do so contrary run
> That our devices still are overthrown;
> Our thoughts are ours, their ends none of our own.
>   (III.ii.206-08)

---

17 Ricoeur, p. 147.

What must be, will be. The metaphor of the theatre can illuminate the disjunction between "thoughts" and "ends"; the existential and theatrical predicaments seem to reflect upon each other and to heighten the ambiguity in the art of playing. And yet, do we not speak of ambiguity only with regard to a metaphysics and theology which we assume to be unambiguous?

The fact that there is such a thing as a "theological stage" cannot be debated. Jacques Derrida, in discussing Antonin Artaud's radical proposals for a "theatre of cruelty," goes so far as to claim that the stage, enslaved by the concepts of an Aristotelian aesthetic which, in turn, has influenced the entire metaphysics of Western art, has always been a merely "spectacular intermediary with no significance of its own," a pale reflection of a primary logos which governs the theatre from a distance.[18] This critique is justified only to a certain extent; Artaud, not unlike Brecht, was of course thinking of a certain type of representational theatre. In the "Aristotelian theatre," as he called it, the implications of the theological stage are borne out in the representation of an individual (or individuals) whose struggle is taken as representing a permanent human condition and a conflictual situation the parameters of which are known unambiguously. Exposition, crisis, and resolution form a neat circle. This "order" of representation, the clear-cut relation between form and content, as well as the function of the narrative, could indeed be taken as a reflection upon or reproduction of an unquestioned authority, the authority of a primarily discursive order.

The tragedies of Marlowe or Shakespeare hardly allow such comfortable descriptions. I suggest, then, that we ask how far the representational and presentational modes in Marlowe's plays can be said to have a significance of their own by setting up the

---

18 Jacques Derrida, "The Theater of Cruelty and the Closure of Representation," in *Writing and Difference*, trans. Alan Bass (Chicago: Univ. of Chicago Press, 1978), pp. 235-38.

freedom of the hero in opposition to an inescapable "order," and how far they merely reflect the predictable devices of the theatre's "theological machinery."[19] In concluding my introductory remarks about the self-performing hero and the dialectics of fate and freedom which I regard as essential to the structure of tragic drama, I want to argue that our experience of Marlowe's plays will depend on our understanding of Tamburlaine's and Faustus' relationships with the "theological machinery," with the "God of a stage subjugated to the power of speech and text."[20]

What power? What text? These questions would perhaps appear less ambiguous if one compared Derrida's view of the stage with that of a German theologian who has recently advanced a rather different theory of the relation between drama and theology:

> ... Dramatik ist Agogik, Vorgangslehre, und wie im Verhältnis zwischen Leben und Bühne die Grenzen zwischen beiden verwischt sind, so ist im Handeln Gottes mit der Menschheit die Grenze zwischen dem Handelnden und dem 'Zuschauerraum' aufgehoben, der Mensch ist nicht Zuschauer, sondern Mitspieler im Drama Gottes, oder Zuschauer nur sofern er auch Mitspieler ist, sich nicht nur auf der Bühne erblickt, sondern wirklich auf ihr agiert. Freilich wird diese in der Theodramatik die Bühne Gottes sein; was Er tut, bleibt der entscheidende Inhalt der Handlung, niemals werden Gott und Mensch als gleichgeordnete Partner neben- und gegeneinanderstehen.[21]

Hans Urs von Balthasar intends to draw attention, above all, to important existential questions all of which he believes to have been already answered by the central "event": Christ's redemptive sacrifice (*Heilsereignis*). The theatrical metaphor of the great-stage-of-the-world is then used to relate the existential "drama" of human life to the transcendent and yet immanent supreme

---

19 Derrida, p. 243.
20 Ibid., p. 239.
21 Hans Urs von Balthasar, *Theo-Dramatik* (Einsiedeln: Johannesverlag, 1973), p. 18.

"act", "das Heilshandeln Gottes",[22] which has determined all
human action once and for all. Everything becomes a *representation* of the absolute Logos, the living present of God: "Es ist
Spiel im Spiel: unser Spiel spielt in seinem Spiel."[23] Man is
requested, von Balthasar argues, to confront the unambiguous
truth and glory of the Christian Kerygma and its eschatological
vision; he must be ready to play his "part." The analogy between
the existential and the dramatic is the basis for von Balthasar's
conception of "Theo-Dramatik"; for him, man's existential
struggle is always a struggle for meaning and truth, and this
struggle is necessarily reflected by the forms of "re-enactment"
in Christian drama. "Theo-Dramatik" is therefore defined as

> das innerweltliche Handeln der Menschen; im
> Theater versuchen sie eine Art Transzendenz,
> in der sie ihre eigene Wahrheit zugleich anschauen und richten möchten, Kraft einer Verwandlung - der Dialektik der Maske als Verhüllung and Enthüllung - durch die sie mit sich
> ins Reine kommen möchten.[24]

Entering the interpretive scene from a theological stage-door, von
Balthasar's conception of a universal dialectic which envelops all
forms of action and thought by which man understands himself in
his world may indeed bring us closer to the emergence of an interpenetration of the human and the dramatic. His bold attempt to
make aesthetics and theology join hands in order to let them show
a certain meaning or truth is especially interesting in so far as
it rests on the assumption that understanding and thought are also
modes of action, dramatic acts, which must reveal how far one has

---

22 *Theo-Dramatik*, p. 19.
23 Ibid., p. 20.
24 Ibid., pp. 11f. Dramatic "re-enactment", from this perspective,
    is understood as a kind of search for the "right" thinking and
    acting. The realization of the search comprises a threefold
    process: (1) the revelatory, aesthetic encounter with Christ's
    "act" (cf. 2 Cor.v.14f.); (2) the enactment ("action") of the
    theological drama of the revelation; (3) the understanding of
    it through action. Von Balthasar sees this process as an integration of "Theo-phanie" (aesthetics), "Theo-praxie" (drama),
    and "Theo-logie" (logic) [p.16]. The most valuable suggestion
    in this model is the rather problematic idea that understanding

become a "Mitspieler" in the master play.

Yet it is precisely the uneasy relations between the realm of theology and the mode of action in drama that I am interested in. These relations, I submit, could very well be considered as power-relationships; what is theologically meaningful may come across totally differently in a performance in which the theological frame of reference is one among others. The theological *theatrum mundi* metaphor has in fact found a radically different interpretation by Kenneth Burke who also sought for a master frame within which forms of experiencing reality and "truth" could be identified. Burke's analyses of language and thought as, primarily, modes of action made him shift his discussion of motivation completely into the realm of what he calls "dramatism." Dramatism, for Burke, must be seen exclusively as a problem of act or *form*, and this implies that the primary focus of interpretation moves from content, or such absolutizing concepts as "truth" or "knowledge," to rhetoric and style. Burke indeed suggests that "the ultimate metaphor for discussing the universe and man's relations to it must be the poetic or dramatic metaphor."[25]

It can only help us to keep Burke's notion of "dramatism"[26] in mind whenever we turn to a discussion of the stylistic and rhetorical forms in an Elizabethan play. At the same time, a language-oriented approach to a play-in-performance will not be comprehensive enough to help us understand how "poetry in the mode of action"[27] functions within a play's overall theatrical style

---

arises from and is a mode of *action*.
25 Kenneth Burke, *Permanence and Change*, 2nd. ed. rev. (Los Altos: Hermes Publications, 1954), p.263.
26 The concept of "dramatism" (Burke's coinage) and its place in Burke's philosophy of language can be studied in a number of books he published over the past decades. The role of verbal action as a manipulation of innate guilt (through multiple disguisings, metaphoric substitutions, repressions, sublimations, etc.) is brilliantly exposed in *The Rhetoric of Religion: Studies in Logology* (1961; rpt. Berkeley: Univ. of California Press, 1970), esp. pp. 17-41, et passim.
27 This expression is taken from Susanne K. Langer, *Feeling and Form: A Theory of Art* (New York: Scribner's, 1953), p. 322.

and how the play's performance dynamics alert the audience to the precise nature of its thematic significance. It is necessary, therefore, to let our literary concerns be guided by a theatrical perspective from which we can recreate the play - its peculiar interests, characteristics, and working logic - as a performance. To consider dramatic texts as scripts for the stage and to examine their cues to costuming, staging, gestures, and visual imagery is an approach no longer revolutionary, considering the recent explosion of "Shakespeare in performance" criticism. And yet, we are only at the beginning of a process of discovery; we still have to learn how to perceive a play in all its auditory, scenic, choreographic, and semantic dimensions and how to discuss these perceptions critically.

My own study, then, is meant to be an experiment in so far as it proposes to test a critical vocabulary for a reading of Marlowe's drama, which could help us to visualize the text as a theatrical experience and to examine it in the light of the questions I outlined above. That I locate the dramatic event in the centre of interest is not to be seen as a concession to von Balthasar's model at all; when he speaks about the experience and enactment of the human condition in the theatre he is always thinking of this enactment in terms of a foreground action. Behind it, he would claim, there is always a larger background, an absolute eschatological horizon.[28] It is probably true to say that a tragic artist may be concerned to trace and develop a moral question that can be expressed by the protagonist and, implicitly, flung against this horizon. But if the hero really seeks "eine Art Transzendenz," the transcending questions that we hear in Marlowe's drama hardly ever fit into the pious model of question and answer that von Balthasar has devised (in reminiscence, I surmise, of the dialogical situation between Job and his God whose thunder-

---

28 "Und dies als ein selbst dramatischer, und zwar endgültig, eschatologisch dramatischer Horizont ... Der Horizont antwortet als Ereignis. Transzendent gegenüber der transzendierenden Frage, aber Antwort gebend auf das Stichwort Tod... - [eine] einmalige Antwort auf alle Male des Fragens" (*Theo-Dramatik*, pp. 20-21).

ing counter-questions demolish all human reasoning).

The spectacles on the Elizabethan stage, almost always ambivalent and almost always violent, speak their own language, and we often experience a frightening sense of the collapse of divine mystery into the chaos of human arbitrariness or into the equally bewildering machinations of an ineluctable fate. In Thomas Kyd's *The Spanish Tragedy*, a play that appeared either shortly before or shortly after *1 Tamburlaine* and is now generally considered to be the first significant tragedy of the great era of Elizabethan drama, the hero staggers across the stage, outraged and half insane, shouting "*Vindicta mihi!*" while Don Andrea's ghost and Revenge are seated in the back as passive observers of the bizarre and bloody path "justice" is cutting across the dramatic world. Fundamental issues - the relation of revenge to justice, the conflict of the individual with the laws of God and the state, the question of freedom and fate - take shape and are eventually resolved in a heap of dead bodies. The grim irony in Hieronimo's words

> ... now behold Hieronimo,
> Author and actor in this tragedy,
> Bearing his latest fortune in his fist:
> And will as resolute conclude his part
> As any of the actors gone before.
> (IV.iv.146-50)[29]

echoes through the several theatrical frames Kyd has constructed for a play that works relentlessly towards its predestined conclusion and offers a rather perverse view of eternal justice.

George Hunter has called the plot a "justice machine," and he also observes that "the characters of the play, scheming, complaining, and hoping, are not to be taken ... as the independent and self-willed individuals they suppose themselves to be, but in fact only as the puppets of a predetermined and omnicompetent justice that they ... cannot see and never really understand."[30]

---

[29] Quoted from the New Mermaids edition of *The Spanish Tragedy*, ed. J.R. Mulryne (London: Ernest Benn, 1970).
[30] George K. Hunter, "Ironies of Justice in *The Spanish Tragedy*," *RenD*, 8 (1965), 100.

The tragedy of Hieronimo's misconceived view of himself as "author and actor" in a bad play-within-the-play that he has not even written finds its most gruesome climax in the image of his self-mutilation. Is Hieronimo's silence the seal of meaninglessness? Does it suggest a grotesque parody of the blind and silent "order"? The last words of the play, Revenge's promise of an "endless tragedy" (IV.v.48), may in fact reflect back upon Hieronimo's experience of his divided consciousness, a consciousness that seems frustratingly caught up with its own helplessness and inconclusiveness. Hieronimo's madness can be seen as an appropriate image of a turbulent world full of sound and fury; when he becomes entangled in its Babel-like confusion of tongues and mistaken purposes (and here he of course anticipates Hamlet), the effects of his own guilty trespasses work against him until they finally break him.

The pressures that work on Hieronimo's consciousness assume a concentrated immediacy which makes their more personal, psychological and their more general, religious aspects appear as one and the same thing. It is this intersection between the psychological and the religious that is one of my major concerns; the theatrical approach which I have suggested will undoubtedly help us to see more clearly what structural designs and rhetorical devices the dramatist can employ to create such effects as the ones Kyd uses in his *Spanish Tragedy*.

I include an essay on *Macbeth* in the following chapter, not in order to confuse the reader even more, but to help her or him to see the distinct ways in which Shakespeare and Marlowe work with their medium and to put Marlowe's singular achievement into a better perspective. The essay on *Macbeth*, as well as those on *Dr Faustus* and *1 Tamburlaine*, were intended to be a kind of foray into the exposition scenes of these plays, and they helped me to sort out certain problems I had encountered beforehand. When I first turned to *Macbeth* and *Dr Faustus*, I thought of them as plays that both incorporate representations of what we would call archetypal trespasses. Macbeth and Faustus, in their individual ways, overstep the boundaries and do more than "may become

a man." Both trespassers experience the terrible consequences of
their ambitious acts, and their (self-)destruction is dramatized
within the terms and forms and the structure of relations in
their particular worlds. After having started out from the premise that there is a religious consciousness or moral order that
dramatist, dramatis personae, and audience must have shared and
that the content of the plays could be clarified from a correct
theological perspective, I began to feel that it would be too
reductive to see the plays exclusively as "tragedies of damnation."
I became much more interested in exploring the heroes' trespasses
at a metaphorical and symbolic level; my reading of *Tamburlaine*,
furthermore, opened up a different way of understanding the idea
of transgression.

The phenomenon "Tamburlaine," in any case, cannot be grasped on
theological terms alone; it leads us into new and fascinating
speculations about the nature of "transgressing." The *Tamburlaine*
plays insist on a radical, even hostile transcendence, a touching of creative limits, which cannot be defined very easily. I
suggest, therefore, that we primarily respond to the intrinsic
and controlling effects of the theatrical performance as we recreate it.

My second chapter deals with such dramaturgic effects (in the
opening scenes of *Macbeth*, *Dr Faustus*, and 1 *Tamburlaine*), while
in the third chapter I try to show how they are related to the
ethic of "endless strife" which underlies Tamburlaine's desires
and actions in both parts of the play. A similar concern with
theatrical and theological perspectives dominates the following
six chapters in which I offer a close reading of the A-text of
Dr Faustus. I begin at a point where Faustus' initial self-reprobation is borne out by the events that lead up to his damnation.
I will let the scene of Faustus' "predestined" end speak for itself before I begin to retrace the circular path of Faustus'
magical enterprise - from the beginning of a dream to the limits
of possibility. The freedom of the damned hero and the astonishing theatricality of the play provoke uncomfortable questions
that I seek to address in the concluding chapter of this study.

2. A NOTE ON THE TEXTS

The gaps in our knowledge of Marlowe's life and death can hardly be more frustrating than our general confusion about what to make of the canon and the evidence that has survived. We do not know the order of composition or production of his works, nor can we be quite certain in many instances what part or parts of the received text is authentically his own. As so often happens with Elizabethan plays, critical issues are of course complicated by textual problems, and in spite of the ever-increasing knowledge we enjoy of the context, the Tudor stage, the professional companies, the performance conditions, or the printing of the texts, we are often left to the perils of educated guess-work.

Such guess-work can be rather interesting in some cases, although not many critics and editors seem to have found the textual condition of *The Massacre at Paris* particularly inspiring; C.F. Tucker Brooke confesses that he considers that text to be quite "shockingly garbled." The same cannot be said about *Dr Faustus*, although we are in the privileged position of having *two* received texts, which seems to make things even worse. It probably cannot be shown that either of the versions is wholly Marlowe's, and most editors continue the highly doubtful practice of constructing a conflation of the two. In spite of W.W. Greg's monumental parallel-texts edition of 1950, which has laid open the vast discrepancies that exist between the A-text of 1604 and the B-text of 1616, most recent editors have piously followed Greg's own predilection for the 1616 version and insisted on B as copytext.

Greg's eclecticism has had a fatal influence on our diligent editors' ceaseless attempts to uncover the play in its full, original form, and instead of facing the fact that the original has probably been lost or perhaps never existed as an entity, they confound their own efforts to interpret the texts themselves with their claims to offer us an authoritative composite version of what Marlowe "must" have written. The long-established preference for the B-text has recently come under attack by Fredson Bowers (who nevertheless adopts B as copy-text for his own old-spelling edition)[1] and Constance Brown Kuriyama[2] who both argue convincingly for a revaluation of A based on textual evidence and stylistic and aesthetic arguments. Bowers and Kuriyama primarily challenge Greg's view that none of the passages peculiar to B represent the "adicyones in doctor fostes" by William Birde and Samuel Rowley (as it is recorded by Henslowe in November 1602) and that the play is divided into separable strands as "Marlowe seems to have been responsible for the tragic action, and another hand to have contributed the comic."[3]

Kuriyama's detailed demonstration that the Birde and Rowley additions indeed belong to B and that A (especially its comic scenes) must have been extant before 1591 not only demolishes Greg's elaborate hypothesis that A is a memorial reconstruction of the collaborative original he perceived behind B, it above all demolishes an argument that had always been resting on a personal opinion about what "Marlowe" ought to have written.

I do not understand in the least what Greg had in mind when he thought that a writer of powerful tragic blank verse would not turn to writing knockabout comedy in prose for his actors. It hardly needs to be pointed out that Marlowe's *The Jew of Malta* is the best example of his astonishing capability to switch genres and create different styles. Greg's preference for the "earnest intensity" of the tragic action in *Dr Faustus* is revealing because it seems to have led him to consider the comic scenes as "merely theatrical."[4] I would argue instead that it was precisely the immense theatricality of *Dr Faustus*, in both the comic

---

1 Fredson Bowers, "Marlowe's *Doctor Faustus:* The 1602 Additions," *SB*, 26 (1973), 1-18. For his edition of the play, see *The Complete Works of Christopher Marlowe* (Cambridge: Cambridge Univ. Press, 1973), II, 123-271.
2 Constance B. Kuriyama, "Dr Greg and *Doctor Faustus:* The Supposed Originality of the 1616 Text," *ELR*, 5 (1975), 171-97.
3 *Marlowe's Doctor Faustus: 1604-1616* (Oxford: Clarendon, 1950), p. 19.
4 Ibid., pp. 97f.

and the tragic scenes, which made this play such a popular success. And the radical and sensational nature of this success, I submit, cannot even be perceived anymore in a B-text in which all blasphemous elements have been either removed or muted and in which A's vigorous and intellectually arresting drama of Faustus' self-reprobation has been partly replaced by the superstitious machinery of a clownish diabolism which nearly always turns everything into a cynical parody of Faustus' sentiments.

Of course, I am now advancing my own reading and my own preference for the A-text; yet I do so not under the false premise that one can establish a single authoritative text by defining the problems as merely bibliographical, but under the assumption that textual arguments cannot be kept independent of critical interpretation in the first place. Moreover, the two texts as they are give us sufficient evidence that the B-text implies different standards of structure and performance. Dramaturgically, B depends quite obviously on the sensationalism of special stage-effects (the "Dragon," the Devils "above," the extended, often gratuitous elaboration of comic scenes, the "discovery" of hell, the throne, etc.); and this, incidentally, confirms Glynne Wickham's assumption (*contra* Greg) that the staging of B can hardly have historical priority over A.[5]

There is considerable doubt, then, as to what we can actually claim for a text which was published twenty-three years after Marlowe's death and represents a version of *Dr Faustus* that involves different methods of staging and, consequently, a different approach to the drama as a whole. We can assume that the distinct dramaturgy of the B-text reflects the theatrical circumstances of later performances, but a close analysis of the textual changes (missing passages, censored lines, dislocated scenes, dysfunctional comic episodes, additional scenarios, etc.) and

---

5 Wickham's investigation of the London theatres arrives at the conclusion that no playhouse of 1593 could have had the means to stage the effects required by the B-text. Cf. Wickham, "'Exeunt to the Cave': Notes on the Staging of Marlowe's Plays," *TDR*, 8 (1964), 184-94.

the effects they have on the structure and significance of the play make it even more likely to think of B as an applied theatrical interpretation of the original which, I submit, systematically distorts and reworks the focus on Faustus' damnation with its own emphasis on more superficial and spectacular effects. We do not know how close the A version (1517 lines), which is considerably shorter than B (2121 lines), comes to the original and to what extent theatrical elaborations of the original playscript could have been conceivable. The difficulty with *Dr Faustus* compared, for example, with *Tamburlaine* is that the play as it has survived suggests composition in the theatre, probably in close conjunction with the company, with a view to the special conditions of performance.

The distinct nature of the scenes in A as well as the dramaturgical, aesthetic, and intellectual integrity of the 1604 version as a whole suggest, however, that we ought to make a critical decision with regard to the text we want to discuss as *Dr Faustus*. As soon as we recognize that the two primary editions of the drama record the performances of two closely-related but distinct plays, we should no longer try to interpret "the passages and meanings which the two extant versions share,"[6] as Kuriyama argues, but concentrate on their often radical dissimilarity. My own preference for the A-text may reflect my belief that A is closer to its original performances and free from obviously distorting additions, but it is, above all, meant to prove that interpretive confusion can be avoided by discriminating between two versions which share certain passages but not their *meanings*, either at the local level or in the performance as a whole.

It is indeed essential to remember "that both the A- and B-texts were published as works having their own validity," as Michael J. Warren just recently contended, and that "we must presume before reading the texts *not* their possible mutual relations but

---

6   Kuriyama, 197.

their independent integrity, their capacity individually to witness to what at a particular moment was conceived as the play *Doctor Faustus*."[7] All further speculation about the original of *Dr Faustus* will have to confront this proposition, and I do not doubt that future editions and critical studies will pay close attention to the problem of the text. It will be even more interesting to see what choices are going to be made by modern producers and directors who recreate the play in the theatre.

In the following, all quotations from *Dr Faustus* are taken from Greg's Parallel-Texts edition; I have checked the texts against the original quartos, and have myself done the minimal editing required by the passages quoted. I have also consulted Tucker Brooke's old-spelling edition of *The Works of Christopher Marlowe* (Oxford: Clarendon, 1910), which is extremely useful for its compactness and efficiency. But for the convenience of the reader, I have decided to use J.S. Cunningham's modernized edition of *Tamburlaine the Great* (Baltimore: Johns Hopkins Univ. Press, 1981), which was only recently added to the excellent Revels Plays series. All other quotations from Marlowe's works are also taken from this edition.

Quotations of other plays and poems under special consideration are taken from easily accessible modern editions whenever this was possible. All citations of Shakespeare are from *The Com-*

---

[7] Michael J. Warren, "*Doctor Faustus:* The Old Man and the Text," *ELR*, 11, no.2 (1981), 116-17. Warren's article reached me at a point when it was too late to incorporate his arguments in my main discussion of the play. His brilliant critique of the B-text's status and the editorial confusion that has beleaguered the interpretation of *Dr Faustus* over the past decades supports my own views on the distinct recognition we owe to the 1604 version. In the second part of the article, Warren discusses the function of the Old Man in both A and B, and here I must part company with his assumption that A's dramaturgy and theological subtext leave the possibility of salvation open to Faustus to the very end (cf. Warren, 138-39).

plete Works, ed. Peter Alexander (1951; rpt. London: Collins, 1953). All Biblical refernces in this study are to the Authorized Version (1611) or to the 1560 Geneva edition.[8]

---

8 The immensely popular and widespread Geneva version first appeared in 1560 but gained such a pre-eminent position as the household Bible of the English-speaking nations that it was reprinted in at least 140 editions between 1560 and 1644. The original text is also available in a facsimile edition (*The Geneva Bible: A Facsimile of the 1560 Edition*, introd. Lloyd E. Berry [Madison: Univ. of Wisconsin Press, 1969]), but I have used one of the early editions (1611) of which I own a copy. The 1611 text and the original text are substantially the same.

Chapter Two

1. MACBETH AND "HORRIBLE IMAGININGS"

> Evil into the mind of God or Man
> May come and go, so unapprov'd, and leave
> No spot or blame behind:which gives me hope
> That what in sleep thou didst abhor to dream,
> Waking thou never wilt consent to do.
> *(P.L.*V.117-21)

Adam, who does not like Eve's "uncouth dream," nevertheless comforts her by means of a little lecture on Renaissance faculty psychology, explaining the distortive power of "Fancy" which produces her "wild work" in the absence of Reason. It is significant that the fantasy-making power of the mind is here related to dreams, sleep, "irksome night"(V.35), and imagination. The scenario which Adam apparently sees behind Eve's experiences (her narcissistic turning towards her own self in IV.450 ff.; her dream of temptation in V.28 ff.)[1] and which he consequently dismisses, is the realm of the fantastic, the twilight zone of man's subconscious dreams and their more "real" forces of temptation.

Milton's unforgettable epic account of archetypal temptations - the hubris and presumption in the act of Satan's rebellion and in Adam's and Eve's transgression - is particularly fascinating because it touches upon the fundamentally or, one might say, potentially tragic nature of human freedom and choice and, quite dramatically, exposes the psychological effects of error and false judgment:

---

1 The tempter, "one shap'd and wing'd like one of those from Heav'n," promises her: "... Fair angelic Eve, / Partake thou also, happy though thou art, / Happier thou may'st be ... and be henceforth amongst the Gods / Thyself a Goddess" *(P.L.*V.74-78).

> The mind is its own place, and in itself
> Can make a Heav'n of Hell, a Hell of Heav'n.
> (*P.L.*I.254)

This is another one of Satan's self-delusions; the heroic boast tries to ward off the ironic implications. The tragic nature of this dialectic is fully realized in Shakespeare's approach to the mystery of evil. Lady Macbeth, too, prefers to ward off the implications of the deed:

> These deeds must not be thought
> After these ways:so, it will make us mad.
> (*Macbeth* II.ii.33-4)

Yet it is exactly this agonizing and maddening "torture of the mind"(III.ii.21) that is so powerfully dramatized in *Macbeth*, and the haunting "instruments of darkness" - within and without Macbeth's grasp of reality - pervade the texture of the play and create a strange atmosphere of lurking danger, ambiguity, and mystery. "'Tis strange," Banquo says to his confused partner,

> And oftentimes to win us to our harm,
> The instruments of darkness tell us truths,
> Win us with honest trifles, to betray's
> In deepest consequence.
> (I.iii.123-26)

This is a complex theatrical moment; Banquo's attempt to restrain the imagination of his impetuous comrade is rendered as an aside that may or may not reach Macbeth who seems already to have "eaten on the insane root"(I.iii.84). Yet it does reach an audience which has a superior vantage-point and knows more than both Banquo and Macbeth. We have already gained a sense of the "strangeness" in the world of *Macbeth*, and this strangeness will dominate our uneasy relation to the emotive rhetorical and visual appeals of the play-in-performance.

In concentrating mainly on the first act, I am here interested in discussing a few aspects of Shakespeare's dramatic technique which I think operate on our horrified fascination in the tragic change in the character of Macbeth as he begins to struggle with his self-created nightmare. Shakespeare approaches the mystery of Macbeth's temptation by means of a complicated and complex technique of quick, successive scenes, actions, intimations, hints, and images. We could call this method implicit and indirect; in a manner of swift movements (like those of a camera) we are slowly and gradually brought closer to an emotional apprehension of the hero's reactions - a hero who is only reluctantly drawn into the role of an *active* protagonist.

Although Shakespeare's exposition focusses on a variety of individually realized situations, on a swiftly changing orchestration of mood and tone, and on familiar, universal themes (battle, kingship, betrayal), we notice that all these sequential impressions (of characters, of Scotland) remain remarkably vague, discrete, inconclusive.

> [*Thunder and lightning. Enter three Witches*]
> When shall we three meet again?
> In thunder, lightning, or in rain?
> When the hurlyburly's done,
> When the battle's lost and won ...
> Fair is foul, and foul is fair:
> Hover through the fog and filthy air.
> (I.i.1-4;10-11)

The Witches form our first impression of inscrutable surroundings which seem mysteriously confused and equivocal (the lost *and* won battle; foul/fair). The fog, the filthy air, and the strange doubleness and paradoxical self-cancellation create an atmosphere that foreshadows confusion and double-values. Yet this first scene lasts only for a fleeting moment; as with a jumpcut, it changes, and we are brought to a panning perspective of the royal camp. The King receives tidings from the battle; which battle it is we do not learn, the only hint we get refers to a "revolt." The bleeding, fainting Captain renders a horrid picture of the martial cruelties and describes Macbeth's "bravery":

> For brave Macbeth - well he deserves that name -
> Disdaining Fortune, with his brandish'd steel
> Which smok'd with bloody execution,
> Like valour's minion, carv'd out his passage ...
> Till he unseam'd him from the nave to th'chaps,
> And fix'd his head upon our battlements.
> (I.ii.16-9;22-3)

Even if we concede that martial values have their own laws, it is rather an astonishing continuation of the mood of paradox to hear Duncan's cheerful comments ("O valiant cousin! worthy gentleman!" I.ii.24) upon the report of Macbeth's repelling "bloody execution" (the "eagle" and "lion" Macbeth would cause his opponents to "bathe in reeking wounds, / Or memorize another Golgotha" I.ii.35;39-40).

This reported scene gives us a first fragment of a characterization of Macbeth; the images and similes he is linked with are striking indeed ("lion"; "bloody executioner"; "Golgotha"). After the next report about the "disloyal traitor" Cawdor, we directly hear about Macbeth's promotion. The dramatic action continues on a linear plane, and although inside and outside worlds, shadow and reality, gradually begin to merge, there is a logic at work which retains sequence and chronology in spite of the dissolving contours of our sense of "reality" in the play.

As predicted, the Witches meet on their "blasted heath" and begin the incantation of their gruesome charm. What this theatrical presentation suggests is a mysterious realm of dark powers outside the human rationale. Macbeth "involuntarily" runs into the infected air; the encounter is a symbolic key-moment, yet most of its implications will only become understandable in the course of the play. It is only much later that we begin fully to grasp the very subtle interplay between external forces and the individual human being, between the past, the present, and the future, and we might wonder at Shakespeare's ingenious creation of bearded, sexless phantoms that possess the faculty of vanishing into thin air or that can reappear as the "juggling fiends" of man's own distorted imagination - mockingly revealing themselves as exteriorized portions of the self.

The Witches' strange incantation and the swift passage of the scene on stage leave the audience no time, however, to register all symbolic nuances, or even any sense at all in the form of an extractable meaning. I think that the power of the scene, and of many of Macbeth's subsequent soliloquies, lies not so much in their "sense" but in their "magic," in the obscurity of word and action. What we may glimpse through the quick intimations we receive is a sense of fatality "hovering" in the air.

> So fould and fair a day I have not seen.
> (I.iii.38)

Macbeth, with unwitting irony, repeats the Witches' initial oxymoron. When the Witches all-hail Macbeth and prophesy his future, the audience undergoes a split, amplified response: from their privileged position they can feel with the direct dramatic experience (Macbeth's) on the one hand, while - simultaneously - they can oversee the situation in its full impact, they can see "round" Macbeth and qualify his reactions and misconceptions.

> Banquo. Good sir, why do you start, and seem to fear
> Things that do sound so fair? I' th' name of truth,
> Are ye fantastical, or that indeed
> Which outwardly ye show? My noble partner
> You greet with present grace and great prediction
> Of noble having and of royal hope,
> That he seems rapt withal.
> (I.iii.51-7)

We are equally surprised, however, to hear the Witches predict Macbeth's kingship; the notion of "rapture" on the hero's part thus assumes a complex nature. It begins to dawn on us that a fatal confusion might arise as soon as Macbeth learns of his actual promotion. What we foresee is theatrically visualized in Macbeth's *asides* after the presentation of the title of Cawdor. It is most important to look at the staging of this crucial scene: Macbeth is not in the dramatic *centre*; he does not act, he re-acts. Spatially, he will remain on the side of the stage (the Witches presumably having occupied the centre). The "cinematographic" technique Shakespeare employs resembles a sort of "snapshot-cutting," both in terms of the quick time-sequence (Witches/Ross/Macbeth-Banquo) and the fracturing of the spatial picture (*Figurenpositionen* on stage from left to right).

The blurring effect that is achieved by this technique is reinforced by the indirect, mirrored commenting on Macbeth's gestures and reactions by Banquo. It is in fact through Banquo that our attention is drawn to Macbeth's "ravishment":

> That he seems rapt withal ...
>
> ... That, trusted home,
> Might yet enkindle you unto the crown ...
>
> Look how our partner's rapt.
> (I.iii.57;120-21;142)

Through this complicated and indistinct frame breaks the first longer *aside* that reveals the growing confusion of Macbeth (who is still at the periphery):

> This supernatural soliciting
> Cannot be ill; cannot be good. If ill,
> Why hath it given me earnest of success,
> Commencing in a truth? I am the Thane of Cawdor.
> If good, why do I yield to that *suggestion*
> Whose *horrid image* doth unfix my hair
> And make my seated heart knock at my ribs
> Against the use of nature? *Present fears*
> Are less than *horrible imaginings*.
> My thought, whose murder yet is but fantastical,
> Shakes so my single state of man
> That function is smother'd in surmise,
> And nothing is but what is not.
> (I.iii.130-41;my emphasis)

Temptation (outside/inside) is groping forward, infecting Macbeth's heart and mind; time (the here-and-now/the future-in-the-present) splits apart in his confused state of compulsion and repulsion. Marjorie Garber correctly observes that "the witches are apparitions shared by Banquo and by the audience; like the ghost of old Hamlet, they have a dramaturgical existence which purposely straddles the line between the real and the imagined."[2] Yet even more seems to happen at this moment; Macbeth introjects the spells of the Weird Sisters: the hallucinatory forces of repressed desires, of a present whisper, and of unformulated "horrible imaginings" make Macbeth create, not a necessary or real future,

---

2 Marjorie B. Garber, *Dream in Shakespeare: From Metaphor to Metamorphosis* (1974; rpt. New Haven: Yale Univ. Press, 1975), p. 110.

but a counterfeit drawn from within himself, which he then superimposes upon reality. The external cloudiness and ominous atmosphere in the dramatic world collide through Macbeth's faint fantasies and the muttered figuration of his repulsion ("horrid image doth unfix my hair") into a resulting sense of unreality ("nothing is but what is not") which compunds the unnaturalness of the threatening evil - glimpsed through the filter of various perspectives.

The play-in-performance quickly (and again logically) moves into its next stage of a further darkening of its ironic undertones. We have a very short reported scene (King/Malcolm) which almost accidentally introduces a pattern of linking analogues (backward to the executed traitor who threw "away the dearest thing he ow'd / As 'twere a careless trifle"[I.iv.10-11], and forward to a vaguely conceivable traitor-to-be):

>   *Duncan.*   There's no art
>   To find the mind's construction in the face,
>   He was a gentleman on whom I built
>   An absolute trust.
>   [*Enter Macbeth*]
>   (I.iv.11-14)

Macbeth, the "worthy gentleman" of the victorious battle, enters and is honoured.

>   I have begun to plant thee, and will labour
>   To make thee full of growing.
>   (I.iv.28-29)

The King is on *centre-stage*, and in a ceremonial act he declares his eldest son his successor - while Macbeth (at the periphery) exits, vaguely intimating the "growing" of his "black and deep desires"(I.iv.51).[3]

---

3   Milton, in Book V (600-15) of *Paradise Lost*, uses almost the same dramatistic pattern; God's exaltation of the Son ("... your Head I him appoint; / And by my Self have sworn to him shall bow / All knees in Heav'n") is conceived of as the origin for Satan's rebellion and subsequent exodus to the North.

Equally important, we hear that the King will visit Inverness. The action is propelled forward, step by step, and the bits and pieces of information somehow seem to connect and spiral upward in what rings in our ears as faint allusions to the journey to "Golgotha": "bloody execution" ... "false face"(Judas) ..."banquet" ... "the serpent under't."

The imagistic and emotional density of the dramatic spiral becomes heightened in the following moment when Lady Macbeth enters reading the letter:

> '*They met me* in the day of success ...'
> (I.v.1-2;my emphasis)

Macbeth, now calling his wife "dearest partner in greatness" (I.v.10), seems cautiously to avoid mentioning his inner confusion and refers literally to the Witches' prophecy. Yet we also hear that he "burn'd in desire" and was "rapt in the wonder of it"(I.v.3;5), and what he had admitted earlier, "the greatest is behind"(I.iii.117), is immediately picked up by Lady Macbeth.

Her soliloquy and Macbeth's soliloquy in I.vii undoubtedly form the climax of the first act. In juxtaposing the two soliloquies, Shakespeare achieves a remarkable effect: the fantastic manoeuvres of their respective flights of the imagination escalate the tension, particularly since they focus on moral decisions, and at the same time contrast the individual ways in which the two protagonists poetically and rhetorically shape, metaphorize, repress, or distance their own susceptibilities to their desires, dreams, fears - their "daggers of the mind."

The trope "dagger of the mind" is a masterful paradigm not only of Macbeth's confused and fatal visions which pull him deeper and deeper into his evil thoughts and deeds; it is also an image for the violence with which both Macbeth's and Lady Macbeth's subjective imaginations transform the natural into the unnatural, the supernatural into the natural, the horrible into the familiar. Figurative language and its fantasy-making power play an important role in this psychological landscape of temptation, delusion, and self-delusion. Lady Macbeth, after having

commented upon Macbeth's ambition and the virtues that stand in
the way, quite significantly conflates the notions of "magic"
and "words":

> Hie thee hither,
> That I may *pour my spirits in thine ear*,
> And chastise with the valour of *my tongue*
> All that impedes thee from the golden round
> Which fate and metaphysical aid doth seem
> To have thee crown'd withal.
> (I.v.22-7;my emphasis)

Lady Macbeth's "horrible imaginings" totally displace any sense
of moral responsibility:

> Come, you spirits
> That tend on mortal thoughts, unsex me here;
> And fill me, from the crown to the toe, top-full
> Of direst cruelty. Make thick my blood,
> Stop up th'access and passage to remorse ...
> (I.v.37-41)

and her perverse determination reflects back upon the progress
during which Macbeth becomes a victim of his fantasy and her rhetoric. The last glimpse we get of scene v is Macbeth's subdued
arrival and his wife's advice to "look like th'innocent flower,/
But be the serpent under't"(62-3).

The integrative presentation of verbal and visual analogues is
continued in the short scene of Duncan's "fatal entrance": the
King ("guest of summer") finds the air "sweet." The "noble hos-
tess" is dissembling in front of the entire train of the King;
the stage is filled with actors and musicians, the banquet is
prepared. From this wide-angle presentation the ensuing scene
collapses into the intensely emotional close-up of Macbeth's
first soliloquy: the Thane of Cawdor, for the first time, is in
the *centre* of the stage. Parallel to the intensification of
Macbeth's "imaginings," a gradual, interrupted, awkward yet somehow irresistible movement has taken place - a symbolic and
literal displacement.

What had been vaguely hinted at by the interrelated dramatic
imagery and the asides has resulted in a thickening of the evil

tension,[4] instigated by the Witches in the very beginning. The collage of images and allusions is now complemented by the visualized movement of Macbeth's enacted "prophecy": what he was told and what he wished has come. From the *periphery*, Macbeth steps into the *centre* of the stage.

> Thou marshall'st me the way *that I was going*.
> (II.i.42;my emphasis)

In spite of the fearful hesitation that disorders his language and pervades his hallucinations, the dramatic effect of the movement in Act I clearly emphasizes that Macbeth *was* going towards the centre, towards the "greatest." We see him become what he has conceived himself to be, yet it is of course a highly complex, ambivalent "becoming," and the full force of this ambivalence makes itself felt in the superbly dramatized dialogue which Macbeth has with himself in the long soliloquy in I.vii.

As I have tried to point out, the visual movements in Act I always have to be seen in conjunction with the verbal action; in order to appreciate the complexity of Shakespeare's stage-craft, however, we have to look more closely at the particular manner in which the physical action finds its most heightened expression in Macbeth's experience of the temptations that grow into and out of his consciousness. The transition from external movement to internal stream-of-consciousness in I.vii is a dramatic juncture that I want to examine especially in view of Faustus' opening soliloquy to which I will turn shortly.

> If it were done when 'tis done, then 'twere well
> It were done quickly. If th'assassination
> Could trammel up the consequence, and catch
> With his surcease, success; that but this blow
> Might be the be-all and the end-all here -
> But here upon this bank and shoal of time -
> We'd jump the life to come.
> (I.vii.1-7)

---

4 Cf. G. Wilson Knight, "*Macbeth* and the Metaphysic of Evil," in *The Wheel of Fire: Interpretations of Shakespearian Tragedy*, 4th ed., rev.(1949; rpt. London: Methuen, 1972), pp. 140-59.

Macbeth's soliloquy creates two effects: it disengages him - for the moment - from the external dramatic action and discloses his spiritual state. We are invited to enter his mind and to follow minutely the rhythms of his thought-processes, his pondering over the unpronouncable (the "it") construction of his own purpose. His reference to the "it" is as vague as all the other hints and allusions to his "black and deep desires." The killing of the King, the act of murder and usurpation, is always faintly implied, never clearly stated. Macbeth's unwillingness to formulate distinctly the crime ("it"; "'tis"; "this blow"; "the case"; "taking-off"; "deed"; the only clear stating of his intent comes with "th'assassination") is an expression of the way in which he shrinks back from the full consequences of his power dreams.

In the same way, the movements of his mind are recognizable only in terms of their apparently troubled and anxious inconclusiveness: the weighing of reasons for and against the act, the struggle of imagination, wishfulfilment, and reason, the whole spectrum of "free association" which is provoked by fantasies. Macbeth's associations revolve around the deed and its physical and spiritual consequences, and the powerful, emotional appeal of the situation is achieved by the experience of Macbeth's inner turmoil (the juxtaposition of "success," "risk," and the fear that it would not be the "be-all," the "end-all"). Macbeth's thought-experiments are revealed in the very process of formation; the meaning and the implications of his impulses become vivid and transparent as they unfold as an immediate *human experience* - the living-through of an experience which can be conceived yet is still ahead of us in the future.

The mode of communication between hero and audience is experiential; the expansion and unfolding of Macbeth's "deep desires" become an experience of *thinking* during which the intense subjective emotion must be shared and apprehended. If Macbeth's soliloquy is intended to evoke this co-operative experience of emotion and imagination, the response is at the same time undermined by the puzzling inner development of the soliloquy itself and by the implicit ironic qualities that relate back to the larger dramatic context and the imagistic and symbolic texture of the play as a whole.

How does Macbeth's mind work? Can we see him reach a decision? At the beginning of his soliloquy, Macbeth contemplates the assassination and its consequences in terms of their relation to the continuum of time: the wish to avoid the consequences construes what one could almost call a Faustian pact-situation. The "be-all" and the "end-all" - "here" - are Macbeth's idea of stopping the movement of time, his bargain with the devil. He would risk the "life to come." He seems to be able to rationalize the full impact of the contemplation, however; the curve of the argument bends away from the conception of the deed (the verb tenses are a curious mixture of subjunctive and conditional: "were done"; "then 'twere well it were done"; "could"; "might"; "we'd") to a number of arguments (conceived in the present tense, indicative mode: "we have"; "we teach"; "return"; "commends") that convey existential reasons for *not* committing the deed:

> But in these cases
> We still have judgment here, that we but teach
> Bloody instructions, which being taught return
> To plague th'inventor. This even-handed justice
> Commends th'ingredience of our poison'd chalice
> To our own lips.
>
> (I.vii.7-12)

Macbeth extends his calculations to a theological anticipation of man's spiritual state of damnation ("judgment here ... plague th'inventor"). In contrast to the many explicit references to theological doctrine in *Dr Faustus*, however, Macbeth's "conflict of conscience" operates on a more general ethical and metaphysical plane, and the evocation of "judgment" and "justice" conveys the more practical concept of revenge or retribution in the secular, political realm (the punishment for usurpation, as shown in the case of the former Thane of Cawdor). Yet the religious overtones are there, and Macbeth's envisaged betrayal (the King's last supper; "poson'd chalice to our own lips"; the "meek" and "virtuous" Duncan, etc.) carries a resonance of the events on the night of Gethsemane that can hardly be missed. The clearest and most powerful argument against the horrible deed follows immediately:

> He's here in double trust:
> First, as I am his kinsman and his subject -
> Strong both against the deed; then, as his host
> Who should against his murderer shut the door,
> Not bear the knife myself.
> (I.vii.12-16)

Macbeth seems to have reached a stage of self-awareness in these lines that should exclude any further progress in his evil plan. We can observe, however, that his mind is far from being rational. He has proceeded too far into the realm of vision and hallucination: the nervous rhythm of the opening lines, the syntactical complications, the subconscious misplacing of the modalities of the verbs,[5] and the overriding inversion of positive values (positive values are evoked only in the act or the prophecy of their negattion) betray his emotional imbalance.

This becomes obvious in the following juxtaposition in which Duncan's virtue and innocence are connected with the horror of his murder:

> Besides, this Duncan
> Hath borne his faculties so meek, hath been
> So clear in his great office, that his virtues
> Will plead like angels, trumpet-tongu'd, against
> The deep damnation of his taking-off;
> And pity, like a naked new-born babe,
> Striding the blast, or heaven's cherubin hors'd
> Upon the sightless couriers of the air,
> Shall blow the horrid deed in every eye,
> That tears will drown the wind.
> (I.vii.16-25)

---

5   The second part of the unit (12-16) suggests a parallel syntactical structure, which is complicated by the insertion of the relative clause "Who should ..."; the sentence remains, like the first, rather ungrammatical, and invites us to expect - after the conditional mode of "should" in the relative clause - a conclusion in the indicative mode. The stress positions in the line "Not bear the knife myself ..." accentuate "bear" (and "myself"), thus making it practically indicative and juxtaposing it to the metrically stressed "should" (conditional) in line 15.

Macbeth's argumentative tone (16-18) suddenly breaks off into a most astonishing vision of the effects of the damnable deed. Although Macbeth's images seem to be rather unusual and odd, it is true that the immediate power of emotional involvement makes the identifications (the meek Duncan's virtues suddenly become "trumpet-tongu'd angels"; "pity" becomes a "naked new-born babe" and a "hors'd cherubin") imaginable. It is a moment of great imaginative intensity, which in spite of its rhetorical quality (the underlying pathos is all the more striking since it comes as a rather abrupt change from the apparently sober and rational mood of the previous arguments) strikes us as being dead serious and right to the point.[6]

What is so astonishing about Macbeth's violent vision of Judgment (the Angels and the "last trumpet" on the Day of Judgment; cf. Rev. iv-xx) is the fact that it proves him being quite aware of the unequivocal nature of the crime. For the first time, Macbeth equates the consequences of the murder with "deep damnation"; in Macbeth's understanding this "damnation" consists of the "judgment here," the fruits of evil created in himself, in Inverness, in Scotland. His "horrid deed" would be murder as well as a pol-

---

6   The imaginative evocation of *pity* as "judgment" and the entire troping of Macbeth's anticipation of horror in the Judgment vision presents a complex and appropriately distanced, indirect configuration of the hero's multitudinous fears and superstitions which form the psychological (pre-)punishment for his crime. The internal coherence of this dramatic situation, which renders Macbeth's emotional upheaval acceptable and in line with the necessarily distanced phenomena of the mystery of evil, reflects a representational approach that is quite different from the one Marlowe uses for Tamburlaine's extravagantly hyperbolical fantasies. Compare, for example, Tamburlaine's following speech (2 *Tamb*.II.iv.96-106):
               Techelles, draw thy sword,
   And wound the earth, that it may cleave in twain,
   And we descend into th'infernal vaults,
   To hale the Fatal Sisters by the hair,
   And throw them in the triple moat of hell
   For taking hence my fair Zenocrate ...
   Raise cavalieros higher than the clouds,
   And with the cannon break the frame of heaven,
   Batter the shining palace of the sun
   And shiver all the starry firmament ...

itical crime (the usurpation of the "great office"), and it is
interesting to see how Macbeth responds to his own apprehension
of the meaning of the deed. It seems that his emotional outburst
is, above all, a kind of transference: the feeling of guilt is
manoeuvred away from a personal shock of recognition to a de-
personalized, public level. And here I begin to doubt whether the
audience is willing to go along and accept what Cleanth Brooks
has called a "magnificent" emotional struggle.[7] Do we allow him
to show us and thrill us with his interpretation of the "horrid
image" even when he is merely conceiving of the effects of a public outrage? What does he really mean by "pity"? One cannot
really know what to make of his concern about his reputation
either, because the explanation he will give to Lady Macbeth is
thoroughly half-hearted and incongruent with his behaviour:

> We will proceed no further in this business.
> He hath honour'd me of late; and I have bought
> Golden opinions from all sorts of people,
> Which would be worn now in their newest gloss,
> Not cast aside so soon.
> (I.vii.31-5)

It appears to be rather difficult to *explain* the paradox that lies
behind Macbeth's "settlement" ("I am settled, and bend up / Each
corporal agent to this terrible feat" I.vii.79-80). A serach for
motivations and stimuli might not solve the contradictions in his
soliloquy. The dramatic context and the theatrical presentation
of Macbeth's tragic entanglement alone can imply interpretations.

Macbeth's long soliloquy ends on a note of incomplete yet far-
reaching *self-defence*. First of all, it is astonishing that Macbeth seems to accept the invocation of the terrible judgment as
practically given; the image of "heaven's cherubin"("... hors'd

---

[7] The complex interrelations between the imagery and the pathos
in Macbeth's soliloquy are persuasively demonstrated by
Brooks' "The Naked Babe and the Cloak of Manliness," *The
Well Wrought Urn: Studies in the Structure of Poetry* (1947;
rpt. New York: Harcourt, Brace & World, 1975), pp. 22-49.

upon the sightless couriers of the air") is drawn over to the "I": "I have no spur to prick the sides of my intent." Macbeth metaphorically equates the consequences with the cause, and this is accurate and crucial - be the final image as feeble and helpless as it may.

> I have no spur
> To prick the sides of my intent, but only
> Vaulting ambition, which o'er-leaps itself,
> And falls on th'other.
> (I.vii.25-8)

That Macbeth has taken his decision, at least subconsciously, seems an almost unavoidable conclusion. In his most emotional and personal evocation of the "horrid deed" he uses neither subjunctive nor conditional modes for his verbs, but a precise and clear future tense ("his virtues *will* plead"; "pity ... *shall* blow"), expressing an inevitable consequence. Macbeth *has* preconceived the murder.

The anticlimactic yet honest focus in the final image of the soliloquy corroborates the present condition which is the mysterious, unfinished, unspoken impulse for the future deed: the spur of ambition has already sent him out into the night, the "dagger of the mind" has ever since begun to plague the "inventor." Macbeth's image of "ambition" breaks off; it is honest and ludicrous at the same time, an unwitting parody of the horsemanship of the cherubim. For this "horrid deed" there will be no argument.

We discover a vertical axis which resembles the one in Faustus' (or Tamburlaine's) spectrum of objectives: Macbeth's "deep desires" are directed towards "greatness" and the "ornament of life"(I.vii.42). His "vaulting ambition" offers a key-motive for these impulses that make him overreach himself - whilst at the other pole there seems to lurk an undefined vacuum of unreality ("nothing is but what is not"), disintegration, and horror. The choice between the "greatest" and "horror" pertains to a tragic catastrophe - and Macbeth's decision has be seen under this aspect of unsolvable contradictions.

What makes Macbeth's soliloquy so impressive and gripping is the way in which we are forced to participate imaginatively in his contemplation of choice - the choice that belongs to him and the terrible aspects of which he clearly perceives and understands. Following the movements of his mind, held fast, deeper and deeper in the "inside," the audience is brought closer to the secret land, the true source of tragic terror, which it can anticipate in an act of imaginative response. This imaginative appeal works on the basis of Shakespeare's extremely economic and skillful dramatic method: it is a method of indirectness, of hinting at the meaning. Throughout the first six scenes we get a series of quick impressions, moments of insight: a stage image, a reported scene, a couple of "asides," Banquo's comments, a letter, a description of scenery.

These impressions emerge as themes since the poetry - reinforced by action and symbolism - shapes them and relates them to the "inside" of Macbeth's "horrible imaginings." The audience thus receives an enhanced sense of the perturbations in Macbeth's consciousness, and I would argue that in scene vii we reach a sort of synthesis of the "outside" (dramatic context) and Macbeth's "inside" that yields a thought-provoking, unintermediate experience of the boundary-situation into which Macbeth walks of his own accord, acting out a mysterious tragic dynamic. At the same time, this synthesis does not solve the problems for us that exist in the conflict between the inside and the outside. If we say that Macbeth becomes what he has conceived himself to be, this does not clear away the inconclusiveness of the situation, namely that the temptation in Act I is dramatized as too powerful not to be inescapable.

There is something uncanny about the way in which this play works. It appears almost too fast, and too well constructed. At the end of Act I we wonder why everything appeared so inevitable. And yet, this impression is not one that could be explained very well at the conceptual level. My own reading is mainly an attempt to point out how important the relations between the play's visual and verbal rhetoric are and how suggestive the movement of the play can be. We become aware, for example, that by the end of Act I Macbeth is ready to impose his own decisions and his own power upon a situation that did not seem to be under his control. It has also become clear, however, that Macbeth's interpretation of the inconclusive situation created by the Witches' prophecy leads to an inevitable, further distortion.

What is being performed, then, is a "form" of indeterminacy of meaning that finds its most shocking expression in the paradoxical manner in which Macbeth is shown to have an intuitive knowledge of a natural and spiritual "order" which he then proceeds to destroy completely.

2. FAUSTUS' RHETORIC OF ASPIRATION

The theatrical presentations of the *Scenes* on which Faustus and Macbeth are going to act out their fatal transgressions quite distinctively create a sense of atmosphere that shapes the audience's perception of the emotions at work in the play-in-performance. Those emotions not only operate in the dramatic universe itself, but also on the spectator-as-participant. In terms of this "structure of feeling" I have said that the atmospheric effects in *Macbeth* interpenetrate the fragmentary, visual presentation of individual characters. The element of the fantastical, the insubstantial, and the unreal pervade the fabric of the play, and the nature of the human events, actions, and experiences is to be conceived in correspondence with the atmosphere of paradox and unreality.

The collage of swift changes in the presentation of the internal and external events is an important structural device; the inside of Macbeth's mind and the paradoxical quality of its "fantastical imaginings" are dramatized as a kind of nightmare scenery. The competing forces *we* have become aware of through the visual movement of the play flow through Macbeth's dream-consciousness, and the "daggers" in Macbeth's mind reflect the audience's sense of the mystery and the dark processes which so intensely express themselves in the poetic effect of the whole.

The interrelationship between the internal and the external seems far less balanced in *Dr Faustus*. Faustus confronts us directly and unmistakingly with an elaborate construction of his project and his aspirations. The nature of this construction, however, raises a number of difficult questions. The exposition of the play, first of all, introduces two Scenes, or planes of dramatic reality; we could call the Prologue's paraphrasing of Faustus' "Icarian" project the "external" Scene of Instruction. The expositor in his conventional role, reminiscent of the older morality form, sufficiently remains on the periphery of the actual theatrical event. The implicit reference to a twofold perspective - the supra-reality of a non-specific, eternal order "out of time" and Faustus' reality as a process "in time" - prefigures the dramatic clash of the external-internal and shapes our anticipation of the paradoxical simultaneity of pre-determination and assumed performatory "freedom."

> *Excelling all*, whose sweete delight disputes
> In heauenly matters of Theologie,
> Till swolne with cunning of a *selfe conceit*,
> His waxen wings did mount aboue his reach,
> And melting *heauens conspirde his ouerthrow* ...
> And glutted more with learnings golden gifts,
> *He surffets vpon cursed Negromancy* ...
>   (Prologue 19-23;25-6;my emphasis)

In a short glimpse, we perceive the contraction and the breaking apart of two planes of time, and we move from the narrative (in the past tense) directly into the theatrical "now" ("And glutted *now* ..." B 24) where Faustus settles upon his experiment and sees himself making choices. Having been told that Faustus is already fallen, we then see him self-consciously formulate his aspirations and his experiment with himself, and the psychic drama that unfolds in front of our eyes gains a different kind of effect from our ambivalent participation in his flights of imagination.

If we take the Prologue's as well as the Epilogue's assertions of "heauenly power" (Epilogue 1517) to mean that this "power" implicates Faustus' downfall in a universally recognizable "theo-drama" or "theatre of God's judgments," we are still faced with the ambiguous invitation to watch the performance of Faustus' "fortunes good or bad" (Prologue 9). How good or bad can Faustus' "fortunes" be if we are meant to trust the Prologue's censorious prediction that the outcome of the play is never really in doubt? Yet the appeal to "patient Iudgements" (Prologue 10) already allows us to ponder how successful the "forme" of Faustus' downfall may in fact be or appear to be if he - as we are to find out shortly - can manage actually to practice "more than heauenly power permits" (Epilogue 1517). The Prologue's critical outline is a tantalizing one because it ultimately introduces the very complex problem of Faustus' dream of *freedom*, and the question whether this dream collapses in or holds out against the ultimate acceptance of the limited role of the self-as-performer in God's Theatre cannot be as conveniently answered as the Prologue's paradigmatic outline suggests.

Marlowe creates considerable tension precisely by setting up the Prologue's critical summary in immediate contrast to Faustus' dramatic justification of his claims; the question whether they are good or bad is only answerable in the context in which they are now performed. Audience response begins to be manipulated in the very moment in which its involvement becomes stronger than the warning voice of the Prologue. And in view of the intensity of Faustus' soliloquizing and his absolute visual centrality on stage, the extent to which an audience becomes involved certainly depends on the effect created by Faustus' (the actor's) very immediate entry into the realm of argument, fantasy, and forbidden desire – a mixture which is explosive precisely because the moralizing Prologue has already denounced it beforehand.

Faustus' dream of freedom and transcendence is behind almost everything he says in the very beginning. "Word" and "act" articulate a sweeping revision of the prior instruction of the Prologue, and Faustus' speech of self-definition contains in itself the philosophical frame of the whole tragedy. Similar to Marlowe's other plays, reality in *Dr Faustus* is constituted and presented largely through the rhetorical *tours de force* of the protagonist (cf. Tamburlaine, Barabas, the Guise, Mortimer). Together with his astonishing stage-craft, Marlowe's control over language seems to have been magnificently conducive to the intellectual fantasies of his poetic drama.

With a swift, disruptive vigour, Faustus leaps from his implicit *appetite* ("swolne with cunning"; "glutted") through his *self-conceits* to the all-consuming project ("his chiefest blisse" Prol.28). The leap, as a means of asserting his freedom, is necessary and fundamental, and it is animated by the rhetorical style with which he voices his desires. In the centre of the Faustian ethos we therefore discover not only an intellectual concept but also a concept of the power of language, a Faustian poetics, so to speak, which corresponds to the implications of his breaking away from normative boundaries. Unlike Macbeth's half-realized, subconscious hopes and fears, Faustus' aspirations are fully and explicitly expressed; they are rendered desirable by the self-intoxicating power of the language Faustus uses.

What are the characteristics of Faustus' rhetoric of aspiration? And how are the rhetorical features related to the nature of his project? The poetic texture of Faustus' speeches exposes the precarious balance that is achieved by the heavily rhetorical quality of his "conceits." Faustus has to transform the stage into a platform for his overreaching project, and the imaginative level of his desires is transported to us by the power of *persuasion* through which Faustus can sustain the prospects for the future in the conceited space between desire and fulfilment. Rhetoric as persuasion[1] thus forms one of the central stratagems in the organization of the argument.

> Settle thy studies Faustus, and beginne
> To sound the deapth of that thou wilt professe ...
> Yet leuell at the end of euery Art,
> And liue and die ...
>   (A 1-2;4-5)

---

[1] Traditionally, persuasion has been regarded as the primary goal of rhetoric, and all rhetorical training was directed at the acquisition of oratorical skills. I am here concerned with the distinctive function of verbal organization and ornamentation in the dramatic context and in their relation to the thematic focus. Marlowe's educational background certainly exposed him to an extensive familiarity with the methods of rhetorical (oral) expression and its comprehensive applicability to all forms of writing in verse or prose. For contemporary definitions of rhetorical figures that illustrate the understanding of the "art of persuasion" in the 16th century, see Thomas Wilson, *The Arte of Rhetorique* (1553), ed. G.H. Mair (Oxford: Clarendon, 1909); Henry Peacham, *The Garden of Eloquence* (1577), ed. W.G. Crane (Gainesville,Fla.:Scholars' Facsimiles & Reprints, 1954); Abraham Fraunce, *The Arcadian Rhetorique* (1588), ed. E. Seaton (Oxford: Blackwell, 1950); George Puttenham, *The Arte of English Poesie* (1589), ed. G.D.

The ambivalence of Faustus' rhetoric, its inner- and outer-directed appeals, is further complicated by the emotiveness and intensity of the Marlovian hero's all-or-nothing attitude, which characteristically propels the language of the play into the foreground; rhetorical modes often dominate the events on stage, and it is through Faustus' language that we must try to understand what he creates about himself inside his mind. This immediately opens the question whether we see "through" Faustus' pervasive rhetoricity into his mind - as we do in Macbeth's case - or whether we in fact cannot resist complicity with the powers of poetry that kindle our own imagination.

If we take Faustus' initial remark ("be a Diuine *in shew*" A 33, my emphasis) at face value, we are advised to pay attention, first of all, to the style and the function of language in the presentation of the protagonist. The energies of Faustus' idiom are complex enough to challenge a primary, rhetorical criticism that can stay clear of the interpretive problems which are bound to arise if one approaches the play either from a "romantic" or from an orthodox-moralizing point of view.

Marlowe, well versed in the tradition of rhetoric, had already shown a particular interest in Ovid when he translated the *Elegies*. I quote from the second Book:

> Verses reduce the horned bloody moon,
> And call the sun's white horses back at noon.
> Snakes leap by verse from caves of broken mountains,
> And turned streams run backward to their fountains.
> Verses ope doors; and locks put in the post,
> Although of oak, to yield to verses boast.
> (II.i.23-28)[2]

Willcock and A. Walker (Cambridge: Cambridge Univ. Press,1936). See also Wilbur S. Howell, *Logic and Rhetoric in England 1500-1700* (Princeton: Princeton Univ. Press, 1956), and Walter J. Ong, *Ramus, Method, and the Decay of Dialogue* (1958; rpt. New York: Octagon Books, 1974).

[2] *Ovid's Elegies* presents a considerable achievement, especially if we consider that Marlowe must have been fairly young when he translated the Ovidian text. The translation gives us a good idea of the nature of his experiments with verse. Marlowe's text is particularly interesting for its divergences from Ovid and its self-conscious re-interpretations of the

The spell-binding force of rhetorical and poetical "charms" (the English word "charm," with its connotations of "magic" and "power," is derived from the Latin *carmen* – the word Marlowe correctly translates as "verse" or "song") and the momentum and violence that poetry can have (its power to "break" things apart) signal the essential function which becomes integrated in Faustus' poetic metamorphosis of his dream of freedom.

When we speak about magic or dream or power, we of course speak about a mode or style of self-expression and self-presentation which presupposes a certain attitude towards reality, "dramatic" or "real," that cannot readily be defined by the categories of the serious or "merely" rhetorical. Within the fictional worlds of poetry – and Marlowe's interest in Ovid's *Metamorphoses* and *Amores* speaks for itself – rhetorical style can very well have its own dynamic premises, and before we judge the kind of self Faustus poses in his opening soliloquy, we ought to be aware of the uneasy intersections between the contexts of rhetoric and action and the primary importance of style to which "reality" must yield.

The style of language or language-behaviour answers the questions about the dramatic *persona* who en-acts and lives his role and presents himself in some kind of dynamic relationship with those boundary conditions that normally restrict man. In Faustus' opening speech we hear a great deal about boundaries and limitations, and if we listen to the tone and the content of what he says, our first impression of Faustus' mighty line need not ground itself in any traditional ethical dimension at all. It lies in the very nature of the kind of drama Marlowe wrote that we understand the rhetorical impetus of Faustus' speech as, first of all, a dynamic assertion of his will and his individual voice.

This sense of confidence and upward-moving desire is again quite

---

original. For a more detailed discussion of Marlowe's experiments in translation, see Roma Gill, "'Snakes Leape by Verse,'" in *Christopher Marlowe*, ed. Brian Morris (London: Benn, 1968), pp. 133-50.

beautifully expressed in another boisterous revision of Ovid's elegy on poetry:

> [*vivam, pasque mei multa superstes erit*]
> I'll live, and as he pulls me down mount higher.
> (I.xv.42)[3]

It is this "leaping in poetry" that we encounter in the Faustian rhetoric. In the line from the *Elegies*, Marlowe deliberately employs the language of paradox, and the second part of the line, with its striking antithesis and its spirited assertion of immortality (we should also note the "overflow" in the extrametrical line), alerts us to the range of possibilities in the complex interplay of rhetorical figures and tonal qualities, and to the vigour and ease of the metrics and the many effects of ambiguity, irony, and paradox that can be evoked by poetic images.

We see, for example, how in the "snakes leap by verse" passage the central metaphor (the "transcending," breaking power of verse) is expanded into separate metaphors (*distributio*), variation on the theme, repetition (*anaphora; epizeuxis*), and then elaborated by the joining of tropes which tilt the meaning towards paradox and its often grotesque meanings ("horned bloody moon"; "the sun's white horses"; "leaping snakes"; "broken mountains";"turned streams"; "verse" opening "doors"; etc.).

The expression "verses boast" hints at another major rhetorical figure which Marlowe uses throughout: amplification. It is clear from the conception of his overreaching hero that *hyperbole*, the trope of excess or of the "over-throw,"[4] forms an essential, ne-

---

3 The Revels Plays editor of *The Poems* claims that Ben Jonson's version of the line is the better one: "My name shall live, and my best part aspire" (Jonson's version is incorporated in *The Poetaster*, I.i.43-84). I should think, however, that the rival version shows how accuracy becomes pale next to the Marlovian vigour and inventiveness.
4 Hyperbole as a single trope is in itself the exaggerated form of many different tropes. Puttenham describes it as the "heaping figure," and later renames it "the Ouer reacher, otherwise called the loud lyer ... by incredible comparison giuing credit" (*The Arte of English Poesie*, pp. 236f.). Peacham de-

cessary precondition for a project like Faustus', because it is a mode of speech *and* thought, relating language to ethos, which sublimates the self's exultation in its own operations. From the very beginning, Faustus' speech shows a state of mind to which the desire to transcend appears as an imperative: limitations exist to be overcome. This insatiability had already been imaged by the Prologue's allusions to Faustus' "appetite," and those images were of course entirely negative. When Faustus begins to "professe" himself, the images of hunger and gluttony become much more ambivalent and puzzling (natural appetite/metaphysical longing; fullness/emptiness; learning/cunning; beginning/end).[5]

Again, like the Ovidian "verses boast," the coupling of positive and negative connotations or ironic qualifications ("profites in Diuinitie"; "fruitfull plot"; "diuelish exercise";"sweete magicke" "chiefest blisse") creates a sense of disparity which progresses into the central Faustian rhetoric of paradox on which many of the play's symbolic disjunctions rest (external/internal; Heaven/Hell; reality/magic; infinity/human contingency). Faustus himself rushes out to confirm his paradoxical satiety, his longing, and his lack:

> How am I *glutted* with *conceit* of *this*?
> Shall I make spirits fetch me what I please,
> Resolue me of all ambiguities,
> Performe what desperate enterprise I will?
> (A 110-13;my emphasis)

---

fines hyperbole as "a sentence or saying surmounting the truth onely for the cause of increasing or diminishing ... with desire to amplifie the greatnesse or smalnesse of things by the exceeding similitude" (*The Garden of Eloquence*, p.31). John Hoskins differentiates the modes of amplification into "Comparison, Division, Accumillation, Intimation & Progression" (cf. "Directions for Speech and Style," in *The Life, Letters, and Writings of John Hoskins*, ed. L.B. Osborn [New Haven: Yale Univ. Press, 1937], pp. 103ff.).

5 The oral character of Faustus' desire and the narcissistic and erotic ramifications in the play's overall imagistic design have found illuminating interpretations by C.L. Barber, "'The Form of Faustus' Fortunes Good or Bad,'" *TDR*, 8 (1964), 92-119, and Edward A. Snow, "Marlowe's *Doctor Faustus* and the Ends of Desire," in *Two Renaissance Mythmakers: Marlowe and Jonson*, ed. A. Kernan (Baltimore:Johns Hopkins Univ. Press, 1977), pp. 70-110.

What is his "conceit"? If we look at the soliloquy as a whole and examine its rhetorical divisions, we recognize the density of its verbal composition and the interrelationship of its individual figures and metaphors. In fact, the entire staging of Faustus' opening soliloquy - in the visual and verbal enactment of his own conception of himself - could be called hyperbolical. He ventures to break down all limits, all conventions, all restrictions. After the initial *apostrophe* ("Settle thy studies Faustus, and beginne / To sound the deapth of that thou wilt professe"), the soliloquy falls structurally into two parts (the review of the human sciences; the exposition of his magical enterprise); yet rhetorically one can see a rising curve of amplication. He is "heaping up" his unconscious desires before he leaps into the unrestricted realm of imagination and the Sublime.

The explosive energy of the strain of paradox is contained in various phases of distribution, division, accumulation, and progression, and culminates in the last lines of the soliloquy:

> O what a world of profit and delight,
> Of power, of honor, of omnipotence
> Is promised to the studious Artizan?
> All things that mooue betweene the quiet poles
> Shalbe at my commaund, Emperours and Kings,
> Are but obeyd in their seuerall prouinces:
> Nor can they raise the winde, or rend the cloudes:
> But his dominion that exceedes in this,
> Stretcheth as farre as doth the minde of man.
> A sound Magician is a mighty god:
> Heere Faustus trie thy braines to gaine a deitie.
> (A 83-93)

This is the powerful climax of a puzzling stage performance. Before he actually reaches this point, he seems to be involved in what one might want to call a piece of histrionic "extravaganza." With a lot of cunning and nerve, he energetically and impatiently hurries through his review of the human sciences, or at least those that he chooses to attack. His discourse shows a good sense of timing, and his argumentation, his overtly ingenious glossing and qualifying, his multilingual disputation and his impressive verbal and theatrical performance (his browsing through the books is accompanied by a great number of short exclamations, gestures, rhetorical questions, aphorisms, clever puns, witty sneers, and self-conscious assertions) make his lecture seem highly coherent and compelling. Commentators usually tend to overemphasize the ironic undertones and the hidden contradictions in the speech; in its theatrical immediacy, I should think, the Faustian rhetoric can quite successfully mobilize our imaginations and shelter the process of mystification that goes into his "role-taking."

The heroic promise in the hero's conceit and his emphatic visual centrality (he dominates centre-stage throughout the first 160 lines) help to magnify the attraction and curiosity that pull us toward him. Two further presentational devices seem noteworthy; first, Faustus intensively turns to the *objects* of his concern and his ravishment: his books. The references to certain passages and texts are theatrically underlined by his treatment of the prop. Surveying his books, Faustus will pick them up, open them, express dissatisfaction, and finally displace them by his quest for the non-referential, abstract, and transcending "end" of desire. "Levelling at the end," striving for a goal and generating a final purpose, indicates a leitmotif that attains crucial significance in view of his "finalizing" act of trespassing (the pact with Lucifer).

Secondly, we should stress the visual immediacy of Faustus' self-presentation and his relentless enactment of what he creates as his identity. There is no gradual integration into the plot, as in *Macbeth*, but an emphatic eagerness and disposition to plunge right into the centre. The movement and urgency in his acting style create the impression of an onward surge, and this effect is reinforced and sustained by the poetry he speaks, by the progressive intensity of expression within the line or the verse paragraph. The association of technique with meaning becomes obvious in the very manner in which the speech builds up rhythmically towards the point when Faustus discloses his true objective and exclaims:
>   These Mataphysickes of Magicians,
>   And Negromantike books are heauenly.
>   (A 79-80)

Our perception of the protagonist's character is indeed formed by his use of language. His rhetoric conveys an impressive ability to originate and conclude ("settle"; "beginne"; "end"), and it seems as if he is drawing the border lines of human knowledge ("euery art"; "chiefest end"; *Summum bonum*). His discourse is permeated by figures of amplification (superlatives, comparatives), by exclamation and rhetorical questions. There is a constant interplay of antithetical positions and an emphasis on the repetition of key-words ("end"; "nothing"; "but"; "all"; "every"), and the dominant pattern in the progression of the speech is the symmetry of question and answer, thesis and antithesis. It is quite possible that this accent on dichotomies and the rhetorical bent of this kind of dialectic are based on the teaching of Petrus Ramus who had devised new methods for the construction of arguments and formulated a number of highly interesting *axiomata* for the art of discourse.[6]

Furthermore, Faustus often begins a section with a series of rhetorical questions *(pysma)* which he answers himself *(subiectio)*, falling into his typical, provocative over-statements that implicitly intensify the underlying tenor of paradox.

> Affoords this Art no greater myracle?
> Then reade no more, thou hast attaind the end ...
> Are not thy billes hung vp as monuments,
> Whereby whole Citties haue escapt the plague,
> And thousand desprate maladies beene easde?
> Yet art thou still but Faustus, and a man....
> (A 39-40;50-3)

Faustus confronts himself with the problem of mortality and finitude; the rhetorical progression moves from the external objects

---

[6] For a discussion of these *axiomata*, see Walter Ong's comprehensive study. Ramus, on the whole, is less interested in the functioning of persuasion in poetry, but at one point he argues that "this is what the poet does as a major part of his tactics, when he sets out to sway the people, the many-headed monster. He deceives in all sorts of ways. He starts in the middle, often proceeding thence to the beginning, and getting on to the end by some equivocal and unexpected dodge" (cf. Ong, *Ramus*, p. 253). I will discuss the implications of Marlowe's use of the Ramist method in my sixth chapter.

(the books from which he quotes) to the particular and defined worlds or orders they represent. Paraphrasing their individual idioms, Faustus concocts a discourse that translates and assimilates all other languages (Greek, Latin, Italian, English, and the jargons of the individual fields) into itself. His scornful review of the limited and limiting fields makes him arrive at "end-points," he moves from the outside to the inside, questioning his own status and capabilities. The terminations he arrives at paradoxically confirm his will to go forward, to transcend the limits. Of course he does not see the curious illogicality in some of his propositions. In his conscious rhetorical self-hood he seems simply to negate the limits of the generally accepted normative order which defines his human nature (his mortal body, his thinking), and he proceeds to re-define his own *summum bonum*.

His dream of freedom from limits explodes in his fantasies, and the speech in which he anticipates his magic power ("O what a world of profit and delight ...") is certainly the hyperbolical speech *par excellence*. As soon as Faustus steps outside the orthodox realm of normative tradition, outside his social and intellectual environment, his explicit formulations of his ambitions indeed convey an aura of "opening up." The speech becomes expansive, grandiose, soaring; its imaginative force opens upon abstract horizons. It is here that one feels Faustus' vision unfolding free from limits; it stretches itself and has that upward thrust ("mooue"; "raise"; "exceed"; "stretcheth as farre ...") which is so significant for the whole idea of leaping.

On the one hand, the rhetoric of paradox seems to enforce this poetic *fusion* of his self with his fiction. The paradoxical interplay ("Metaphisickes of Magicians"; "heauenly Negromantike books"; "Magician-god") transports the Faustian vision onto another level; the contradictions overlap, burst, and set free. Faustus uses the language of paradox and daringly treats magic as if it was freedom, a means of transcendence, a private eschatology.

On the other hand, one can at least anticipate the tragic ironies within the act of liberation. The burst of freedom in its paradoxical nature contains an immanent fission at the same time. The disparate elements in the rhetoric can fall apart, regressively destroy the leap and restrict again. This is most likely to become visible in the relation between the vocabulary itself and Faustus' claim to freedom. His rhetoric frees him and restricts him at the same time. Throughout the play we become increasingly aware of this double effect of liberation and restriction. During his first assertion of his dream of power (A 79-93) it already becomes obvious that he is searching for "new" words, a "new" language; yet the "Negromantike bookes" he refers to will in turn establish their own limiting system of "Lines, circles, sceanes, letters and characters"(A 81).

The language of magic that is supposed to set him free in fact merely constitutes another form of imprisonment and, ironically enough, borrows extensively from the idiom of Christianity. The greatest problem for Faustus is that he has yet to find out what his *summum bonum* really is or might be. In the "sage conference" (A 131) with his friends Valdes and Cornelius he is still trying to re-define his "ends" (cf. A 110-29). We already gain a feeling that Faustus' rhetoric of paradox cannot veil the discrepancy between his subjective "leaps" on the one hand, and his incapability of recurring to another code of language, on the other hand, which might indeed correspond to his dream of freedom.

This predicament, of course, lies at the heart of his tragic downfall. As I will try to show later on, the complicated relationship between Faustus' rhetoric of paradox and the dramatic conventions of self-condemnation which Marlowe enforces throughout is introduced and sustained in a manner which draws attention to the *style* of Faustus' transgression and not, as it is often argued, to the traditional, ethical context against which he defines his role. Christian metaphysics and ethics are referred to as an anti-background, so to speak; and this anti-background is brought into play by the energies Faustus sets free rhetorically. Whereas Macbeth recognizes his transgression - even before he has actually done the deed - as "horrible imaginings," as a bottomless dream which enmeshes him in the catastrophic consequences of an almost involuntary compulsion, Faustus celebrates his rebellious dreams of power and "heauenly" magic.

Faustus possesses the symbolic force of the will which can render him an archetype of a whole culture, or a spiritual attitude, and this force largely rests on the pervasive theme of man's desire to mount beyond natural limitation. As I suggested, Faustus' flights of imagination present a self that trusts its own power over language and, instead of allowing us to understand the precarious working of the mind, bedazzles itself and the audience with its hyperbolic mannerisms. Yet this mode of self-presentation is important for our perception of the play; unlike Tamburlaine, Faustus has no direct opponents and followers who would listen to him. He is alone with himself, and the battle is waged with the verbal, metaphysical, and psychological limitations which his very rhetoric purports to deny.

I wish to add two qualifications to which I will return during my later discussions of the plays. First, even though my ideas about the presentations of Macbeth, Faustus, and Tamburlaine may not contribute to the theory of dramatic exposition, they at least suggest ways of looking at expository technique, which can help us to see the protagonist's predicament through the affective elements of the play-in-performance. Verbal, visual, and conceptual stimuli, and the relationships among them, can have very different effects on audience receptiveness and perception, even if one central character's aspirations and transgressions are comparable to another's. Shakespeare's and Marlowe's plays are distinguishable primarily by means of their individual orchestration of stimuli, and it is only through such specific configurations of impressions that we perceive what it means to speak of a battle that is "lost and won." In *Macbeth*, as well as in *Dr Faustus* and the *Tamburlaine* plays, such battles and their contradictory appeals bring the protagonist's consciousness into prominence and influence our experience of the universe of "tragical discourse" in the theatre. In the case of Macbeth, dramatic tension is built up throughout a series of scenes up to the protagonist's soliloquy in I.vii which allows him to transcend the low and high intensity action with which Shakespeare had tied him up beforehand. By the time he faces the audience directly, we have experienced various images of meaning, and the discrepancy of awareness between actor and spectator enlarges and complicates the effect of Macbeth's discourse.

My emphasis on language and consciousness is intentional. It seems to me that it is in this relation between "tragical discourse" and the mind that one ought to search for the specific dynamics of a protagonist's style and its appeal. To examine the form of Faustus' opening speech is less interesting as an exercise in determining its tone, its figures and tropes, or its metrical patterns, than it is as an approach to the style and poetic design of a mode which is in itself a mode of action and imaginative purpose. The dramatic form and style of a monologue can thus alert us to the specific role Marlowe's application of rhetoric plays in the self-realization of the overreaching hero.

As Faustus' deconstruction of traditional learning intimates, and as Tamburlaine's violent verbal and martial imperialism will amply demonstrate, rhetoric in Marlowe's plays seems to be that part of poetic design, characterization, and dramatic tension which marks a new self-conscious mode of struggle and will-to-conflict that cannot easily be accommodated with a traditional system of philosophical and moral coordinates. Faustus' persuading himself into the power dream of magic's endless possibilities is the dominant feature of the exposition scene in *Dr Faustus*; moreover, his rhetorical self-consciousness initiates a performative stance ("be a Diuine in shew") which reflects his confidence in the power of rhetoric.

Turning to *1 Tamburlaine*, I propose to concentrate on Marlowe's manipulation of rhetoric as a means to enter this ferocious spectacle of human performance which so drastically provokes the question whether Tamburlaine's romantic heroism can be reconciled at all with those values that we normally associate with Elizabethan drama.

3. EXTRAVAGANT HEROISM: THE ADVENT OF TAMBURLAINE

Marlowe's career as a professional playwright could hardly have had a better start; *Tamburlaine the Great*, his first play written for the popular London stage, was such a commercial success that he went on to compose a sequel (Part 2) while other London dramatists were busy trying to imitate the new Marlovian style as cunningly as they could. When *Tamburlaine* was published in 1590, the octavo edition of both parts announced a text "Deuided into two Tragicall Discourses, as they were sundrie times shewed vpon stages in the Citie of London."[1] We do not know the dates of composition and first performance of Marlowe's early plays, but it is generally assumed that *Dido Queen of Carthage*, not published until 1594, preceded the *Tamburlaine* plays and dates from the last years of Marlowe's stay at Cambridge University.

In any case, *Dido* presents an early experiment in blank verse which was designed for private productions by child actors, "Played by the Children of her Maiesties Chappell," as the title-page tells us.[2] This statement separates *Dido* from Marlowe's other plays which were certainly produced in the public theatres. Early responses to the plays have helped us, among other things, to conjecture that the first Part of *Tamburlaine* may well have been performed by the Lord Admiral's Men around 1587, the year in which Marlowe, M.A., left Cambridge for a few turbulent years in the City of London. By the time he was arrested (for the first time) for involvement in a street murder (1589), Marlowe

---

1 *Tamburlaine the Great*, title-page. Quoted from C.F. Tucker Brooke's old-spelling edition of the *Works*.
2 Quoted from the Revels Plays edition of *Dido Queen of Carthage and The Massacre at Paris*, ed. H.J. Oliver (Manchester: Manchester Univ. Press, 1968). For a discussion of the bibliographical problems, see Oliver, pp. xx-xxxix.

had already shocked and startled his theatre audiences and fellow writers alike, and the popular acclaim of *1 Tamburlaine* and its sequel needs careful attention with regard to the innovative and thoroughly iconoclastic appeal which Marlowe's art arguably brought to bear upon a contemporary stage that had not witnessed such daring "entertainments" before.

A play which is so obviously full of tumultous energies and problematic issues cannot be expected to fare too well with critical readings that try to cope with its overdetermination of meaning. Modern critical perspectives have helped to illuminate the contradictions and irreducibly complicated ideas which characterize Marlowe's creation of a heroic figure whose stance commonly evokes vehement disagreement over how one is meant to react to it. Symptomatic of the development of Marlowe scholarship is the fact that we can trace back most of the critical disharmonies to two mutually exclusive points of view which hold true for practically everything Marlowe ever wrote.

On the one hand, the long silence that had befallen Marlowe's drama after the Restoration, in the theatre and in criticism alike, was lifted when the Romantic image of Marlowe began to emerge in the 19th century. Marlowe's Faustian heroes suddenly became interesting and attractive to a sensibility which, in William Hazlitt's words, found their rebellious nature and "pride of will" quite congenial. "There is a lust of power in his writings," Hazlitt observes, "a hunger and thirst after unrighteousness, a glow of the imagination, unhallowed by any thing but its own energies. His thoughts burn with him like a furnace with bickering flames ..."[3]

The idea of a rebellious, unorthodox Marlowe, enlarged by the later Victorian critics, descended from Symonds, Swinburne, and

---

3   William Hazlitt, "Lectures Chiefly on the Dramatic Literature of the Age of Elizabeth" (1831), quoted from *Marlowe: The Critical Heritage 1588-1896*, ed. Millar Maclure (London: Routledge & Kegan Paul, 1979), p. 78.

Santayana down to the first half of this century. Already in 1941, however, appeared Roy Battenhouse's *Marlowe's* Tamburlaine: *A Study in Renaissance Moral Philosophy*, a book which set the tone for all subsequent Christian interpretations. Necessarily postulating that the two parts of *Tamburlaine* are in fact one, Battenhouse confidently declared Marlowe's play to be one of the most grandly moral spectacles in the whole realm of English drama. Moral interpretations of this kind are particularly significant in terms of the efforts that have been made to grasp the ethos or philosophical concepts which the play - very much like *Dr Faustus* - represents and with which, I fear, it will continue to puzzle its commentators.

In the course of my discussion, I will try to demonstrate that there are several theological concepts articulated in the two plays which ought to trouble orthodox readings more than they apparently do, and that these concepts are only interesting and intrinsically important when seen in connection with the shaping of a complex heroic figure on which Marlowe lavished precisely that innovative, extravagant theatrical style and energy which guaranteed his demonstrably sensational impact upon London's stages.

It is appropriate, first of all, to return to the reactions of the Elizabethans for a moment, for it will help us to recognize how far apart Battenhouse stands from all those contemporary commentators who either confess to be totally repelled by the intolerable, blasphemous nature of the plays or refer to the rapture and intoxication into which their hero thrust the audience. Both responses testify to the immediate success of Marlowe's play-in-performance. Very little needs to be said about the myth of Marlowe-the-atheist in this respect. Marlowe's reputation, his "monstrous opinions" (to which Baines and Kyd have testified), and his success as playwright are certainly interrelated, yet the status of Marlowe's "atheism" is less important in itself if we only recall that the allusions to his radicalism by such fellow intellectuals as Greene, Nashe, or Harvey in fact concern themselves with Marlowe's *art*. This is the only legitim-

ate way, I think, to read Robert Greene's weary self-defence
against the "Gentlemen Poets" who obviously achieved something
he did not, namely

> ... that I could not make my verses iet vpon the
> stage in tragicall buskins ... daring God out of
> heauen with that Atheist *Tamburlan*, or blasphem-
> ing with the mad preest of the sonne: but let me
> rather openly pocket vp the Asse at *Diogenes* hand:
> then wantonlye set out such impious instances of
> intollerable poetrie: such mad and scoffing poets,
> that haue propheticall spirits, as bred of *Merlins*
> race.[4]

Greene is clearly scornful of the new tragic style, and if we
take his paradoxical complaint about "the end of scollarisme in
an English blanck verse" as a curious reference to Marlowe's
poetry, we can deduce from the date of the *Perimedes* (29 March
1588) that Greene may have witnessed the "beginning" of Marlowe's
new blank verse drama in the previous winter (1587/88). Other
references, such as Thomas Nashe's complaint about those "ideot
Art-Masters that intrude themselues to our eares as the Alcumists
of eloquence who (mounted on the stage of arrogance) thinke to
out-braue better pennes with the swelling bumbast of bragging
blanke verse,"[5] either betray perplexity about the new and
morally ambiguous dramatic writings or present themselves as oblique, almost involuntary compliments, such as the following
verses by Gabriel Harvey:

> Magnifique Mindes, bred of Gargantuas race ...
> The hawty man extolles his hideous thoughts,
> And gloriously insultes vpon poore soules ...
> The graund Dissease disdain'd his toade Conceit,
> And smiling at his tamburlaine contempt,
> Sternely struck-home the peremptory stroke.
> He that nor feared God, nor dreaded Diu'll,
> Nor ought admired, but his wondrous selfe.[6]

---

4 *Perimedes the Blacke-Smith* (1588), "To the Gentlemen readers, Health*,*" reprinted in Maclure, pp. 29-30.
5 "To the Gentlemen Stvdents of Both Vniversities" [Preface to Greene's *Menaphon*](1588), *The Works of Thomas Nashe*, ed. R.B. McKerrow (1904-10; rpt. Oxford: Clarendon, 1958), III, 311.
6 Quoted from "A Letter of Notable Contents" (1593), sigs.D 3v-D 4, reprinted in Maclure, pp. 39-40.

Harvey's "Letter" was published after Marlowe had been stabbed to death at Deptford on 30 May 1593, and his reference to the "peremptory stroke" is somewhat in line with later legends that grew up around Marlowe's violent death. Yet even the Puritan Thomas Beard, in his notorious "The Theatre of Gods Iudgements," refers not only to Marlowe the atheist, but also to Marlowe the "playmaker" and "Poet of scurrilitie."[7]

"Magnifique Mindes," "wondrous selfe," and "gloriously insulting Conceit": extracted from Harvey's oblique poem, these may indeed serve as epithets that convey something of the impression, both intellectual and sensual, that Marlowe's innovative dramatic style must have made - from the very moment when his Prologue self-consciously announced that something new was happening. Before alluding to the hero's "selfe conceit," which is, incidentally, a rather unusual way of referring to a central character, the Prologue to *Dr Faustus* draws attention, first of all, to what this play will *not* show:

> Not marching now in fields of Thracimene,
> Where Mars did mate the Carthaginians,
> Nor sporting in the dalliance of loue,
> In courts of Kings where state is ouerturnd,
> *Nor in the pompe of prowd audacious deedes,*
> Intends our Muse to *vaunt his heauenly verse:*
> Onely this (Gentlemen) we must performe ...
> (Prologue 2-8, my emphasis)

The rather important relationship between "prowd audacious deedes" and "heauenly verse" is only intimated here before the Chorus, with a rather cunning understatement, disclaims it and relegates the *Tamburlaine* world to the past, announcing "onely" the private "fortunes" of the scholar and would-be magus. As I suggested earlier, the Prologue's posture and equivocal commentary on Dr Faustus' pride and intellectual heresy can be seen as an extradramatic device which immediately creates tension between the announcement and what we experience afterwards. A conflictual

---

7 *The Theatre of Gods Iudgements* (1597), ch.xxv, reprinted in Maclure, p. 41.

context is created for the "high astounding terms" which we hear during Faustus' radical critique of human learning.

An altogether different conflictual environment is constituted by the Prologue to *1 Tamburlaine*; the Chorus' lines not only stand in integral relation to the play but have been generally regarded as Marlowe's revolutionary "manifesto":

> From jigging veins of rhyming mother-wits
> And such conceits as clownage keeps in pay,
> We'll lead you to the stately tent of War,
> Where you shall hear the Scythian Tamburlaine
> Threat'ning the world with high astounding terms
> And scourging kingdoms with his conquering sword.
> View but his picture in this tragic glass
> And then applaud his fortunes as you please.
> (Prologue 1-8)

We have of course learnt to measure the stiff, archaic, and stylistically impersonal examples of pre-Marlovian versification - Surrey's translations of Virgil; the rhymed "fourteeners" in *Cambyses*; the Senecan orations in *Gorboduc*; the Latinate declamations in *The Arraignment of Paris*, etc. - by the unprecedented vigour and expressiveness of Marlowe's dramatic blank verse, and when the Prologue to *Tamburlaine* reminds the audience that this new poetry is a corrective to the earlier "jigging veins of rhyming mother-wits," he assumes a self-consciously pompous stance which seems fully aware of the momentous change in style and absolutely certain of its popular success.

We should perhaps say that in spite of the Prologue's seeming indifference ("then applaud ... as you please") and arrogance, Marlowe's challenge to the public's theatrical taste must have been partly grounded in the assumption that his audience was ready for a positive response. I would agree with scholars such as M.C. Bradbrook, Glynne Wickham, Andrew Gurr, and J.L. Styan when they claim that one cannot expect Marlowe's new rhetorical ideal and heroic drama to have exploded into a vacuum, given the social and historical context of dramatic entertainment and the inevitable interdependence between the professional playwright's compositions and the competing demands of the public and his acting company alike.[8]

It is all the more interesting, however, to observe how Prologue and play create their own environment, so to speak, by encouraging the audience to expect an extraordinary version of a kind of heroism or fantasy of power which may or may not have been rooted or growing within the popular feelings of Marlowe's particular place and time.[9] However unambiguously the Prologue announces the "stately" action of heroic drama, the visual spectacle of warfare and conquest, and the "picture" of the hero's conduct in a "tragic glass," it is most remarkable that the crucial word is "hear": the awestruck audience will *hear* Tamburlaine's "threat'ning" and "high astounding terms," they will *hear* him carry out his quest for dominance and power over the world.[10]

This annunciation of a ruthlessly ambitious principle of Word and Sword, and especially the exulting manner in which it is expressed tentatively incorporates an image of presumptious ambition and of a universe of tragic "fortunes" which, in extension, implicate ethical evaluations of the very acts of overturning states and scourging kingdoms. This is to say that if we turn to the first

---

[8] For illuminating studies on the complex history of Elizabethan performance conditions and dramatic conventions, see M.C.Bradbrook, *Themes and Conventions of Elizabethan Tragedy* (1935; rpt. Cambridge: Cambridge Univ. Press, 1979): Glynne Wickham, *Shakespeare's Dramatic Heritage* (New York: Barnes & Noble, 1969); Andrew Gurr, *The Shakespearean Stage 1574-1642*, 2nd rev.ed. (Cambridge: Cambridge Univ. Press, 1980); and J.L. Styan, *Drama, Stage and Audience* (1961;rpt.Cambridge: Cambridge Univ. Press, 1975). The most significant study on Marlowe which deals with these questions is Thomas P. Cartelli, "Marlowe's Theater: The Limits of Possibility," Diss., University of California, Santa Cruz, 1979.

[9] Following R.Southern's assertion that theatre is essentially a *reactive* art, Styan suggests that "since the activity of the theatre is designed expressly to touch and involve an audience, a segment of society, that audience and that society must in part control the kind of activity found in the theatre"(*Drama, Stage and Audience*, p.109). If "society gets the theatre it deserves," it is still not clear to me why Marlowe's play was so widely misunderstood.

[10] For similar views on the purpose of the Prologue, see Robert Kimbrough, "1 *Tamburlaine*: A Speaking Picture in a Tragic Glass," *RenD*, 7 (1964), 20-34, and Richard A. Martin, "Mar-

two scenes which introduce us into the play's heroic and chivalric world of kings and courts, we must bear in mind that the promised speaking pictures of the "Scythian Tamburlaine's" awesome career touch upon widely popularized accretions of the historical and *un*historical images with which the Humanist chroniclers had tried to capture the miraculous rise of Timur Khan.

The primary and secondary materials out of which Marlowe created his heroic drama are important at least in so far as the main features of the Scythian's life, his campaigns and victories, and the relentless and cruel expansion of his power provided the substance for mythographic transmutation into a legend of magnitude and terror which, for an Elizabethan audience accustomed to the conventional, didactic structures of *de casibus* morality, entailed clear implications about the nature of both heroic and tragically misguided aspiration.[11] As a source of expectations, the mythical image of Tamburlaine's lifelong career of conquest was inextricably bound up with the Christian, Humanist ethos which ruled historiographical and literary depictions of princes and conquerors and provided the values that we find reflected in the didactic tradition of Boccaccio's *De casibus virorum illustrium* and the English "mirror" literature (*The Steel Glass, The English Mirror, A Mirror for Magistrates*, etc.). The concepts of Fortune and retributive justice granted readily available models of explanation with which even a fascinating and awe-inspiring career such as Timur's could be curtailed and subjected to etho-political judgments.

---

lowe's *Tamburlaine* and the Language of Romance," *PMLA*, 93 (1978), 248-64.

11 Marlowe's primary sources are Pedro Mexia, *Silva de varia lección* (1542) and Petrus Perondinus, *Magni Tamerlanis Scytharum Imperatoris Vita* (1553). Numerous variants of the *Vita* preoccupied Italian historiography before Timur's career was made available to the Elizabethan by Thomas Fortescue's (*The Foreste*, 1571) and George Whetstone's (*The English Myrror*, 1586) translations of Mexia and by Pierre de la Primaudaye's version in his *The French Academy* (1586). For discussions of the Humanist redaction of the "myth" of Timur, see Eric Voegelin, "Das Timurbild der Humanisten," *Zeitschrift für Öffentliches Recht*, 17 (1937), 545-82, and Cunningham, ed., *Tamburlaine the Great*, pp. 9-20. See also Ethel Seaton, "Fresh

The question is, therefore, how Marlowe would respond to the unmistakable, ethically inspired ambivalence that was built into the received portrait of a heroic figure of both princely ambition and barbaric cruelty, and what form of theatrical presentation of dramatic conflict he would choose in order to approach the antithesis between worldly ambition (value; virtue; virtù) and divine sanction (Fate; Fortune; Providence) in a "tragic glass." Does the play, following the Prologue's intimation, invite us to apprehend the scene of political crisis between Mycetes, King of Persia, and the acquisitively rebellious Cosroe (and the following events of Tamburlaine's ascendancy and rebellious overthrow of a rebel) as structural signifiers of a conditional world of *de casibus* morality?

What kind of "stately" gestures do we see, and how are they articulated by the play's language and theatrical mode?

> Brother Cosroe, I find myself aggrieved
> Yet insufficient to express the same,
> For it requires a great and thund'ring speech:
> Good brother, tell the cause unto my lords;
> I know you have a better wit than I.
> (1 *Tamb*.I.i.1-5)

Significant contrasts and stimuli are generated from the very beginning. As one of the primary sensory effects the scene introduces emblems and "stately" images which pretend to emphasize the allegorical forms of hierarchical order and princely authority. Mycetes, King of Persia, appears on centre-stage, presumably wearing royal costume and crown, surrounded by his noblemen and councillors. The tableau, as an explicit theatrical mode, has all the aspects of ceremony, stylized spectacle, and symbolic acting which can create a visual representation of authority in the tradition of civic pageantry or regal procession. The effect is immediately undercut, however, by the inadequacy of Mycetes' opening speech. The relationship between the regal trappings and the implications

---

Sources for Marlowe," *RES*, 5 (1925), 385-401, and Hugh G.Dick, "*Tamburlaine* Sources Once More," *SP*, 46 (1949), 154-66.

of Mycetes' speech is all the more important because Marlowe instantly activates our sense of ambivalence through dramatic opposition, which will become a crucial pattern for the already imminent crisis of power.

Even more surprisingly, the play which had announced itself in the heroic mode, claiming a complete departure from "such conceits as clownage keeps in pay," mockingly presents clownage in the figure of the effete and incapable Persian King. Mycetes' address to his brother is an unwitting confession of his inability to live up to the style required for heroic attitudes. He cannot "express" his grievances because he lacks the "wit," or imagination, to make himself heard with a "great and thundering speech." Most fatally for someone who occupies "the seat of mighty conquerors"(I.i.7), he resigns his *voice*, thereby giving up the means to initiate and control action and becoming the victim of Cosroe's wisecracks.

During the ensuing dialogue, his inadequacy with words appears like a farcical degradation of royalty, and his implicit belief in the hereditary right and divine sanction of his kingship is of course exposed as meaningless by almost every "witty" remark he makes. Tamburlaine, during their encounter in the second Act, thoroughly exploits Mycetes' attempt to hide his crown in a hole and exposes him completely:

> *Myc.* Away, I am the king, go, touch me not.
> Thou breakest the law of arms unless thou kneel
> And cry me 'mercy, noble king!'
> *Tamb.* Are you the witty king of Persia?
> *Myc.* Ay, marry, am I; have you any suit to me?
> *Tamb.* I would entreat you to speak but three wise words.
> (II.iv.20-6)

In a world of armed conflicts, which is early on evoked by Cosroe's and Meander's speeches (and the latter's first reference to the "sturdy Scythian thief" and his "incivil outrages" I.i. 36;40), Mycetes' failure to use language actively and convincingly is fatal:

> *Myc.* ... I might command you to be slain for this,
> Meander, might I not?

>   *Mea.* Not for so small a fault, my sovereign lord.
>   *Myc.* I mean it not, but yet I know I might.
>   Yet live, yea, live, Mycetes wills it so.
>   (I.i.23-7)

Nobody takes him seriously; his uncertainty about what he "might" or "might not" command reveals his lack of authority as well as his fundamental inability to see the role of imagination and "invention" (expressing itself, rhetorically, as eloquence) in determining dramatic events. Ironically, it is Mycetes himself who propounds the central rhetorical and theatrical aesthetic for the heroic action to come:

>   Go, stout Theridamas, thy words are swords,
>   And with thy looks thou conquerest all thy foes.
>   I long to see thee back return from thence,
>   That I may view these milk-white steeds of mine
>   All loaden with the heads of killed men,
>   And from their knees even to their hoofs below
>   Besmeared with blood, that makes a dainty show.
>   (I.i.74-80)

The identity of *words* and *swords*, the conquering power of language (and looks, as Tamburlaine is to prove shortly), is the principle underlying all claims to heroic and chivalric achievement, and Mycetes has hardly uttered his ominous injunction when he misapprehends the role of imaginative creation (the envisioned blood-ritual) by deflating it into a "dainty show." Even more misplaced is his curious attempt to translate Theridamas' projected capturing of Tamburlaine into a mythopoeic simile:

>   Go frowning forth, but come thou smiling home,
>   As did Sir Paris with the Grecian dame.
>   (I.i.65-6)

Richard A. Martin has drawn attention to the play's pervasive use of mythic metaphors which are almost always important means of characterizing the user of figurative language, and it is of course vital to see the contrast between Tamburlaine's use of poetry and myth and his antagonists' insufficient control over their rhetorical strategies. Although Martin stresses the truly important function of metaphorical language in building up the play's richly evocative mood of romance and myth,[12] he does not refer to the theatrical implications of Marlowe's almost ritualistic insistence on punctuating the battle of "wit" and "words" with presentational devices which escalate the tensions between weak and strong, effeminate and masculine voices - preparing for the advent of Tamburlaine's supreme, *self*-conscious exploitation of the language of power.

When Mycetes, who has made a complete clown of himself, leaves the stage muttering his hilarious rhymed couplet (I.i.104-5), Cosroe replaces him in the centre-stage position and voices his calculating plans to usurp the throne. Without his own influence, however, the ritual procession of lords carrying a crown ("*Enter ORTYGIUS and CENEUS, bearing a crown, with others*" s.d.,I.i.135) practically interrupts his plotting and presents him with a *fait accompli*: "fortune" (as Menaphon states the case) is giving him opportunity to be the new emperor, and the visual play of giving and taking the crown is a conspicuous ritual foreshadowing of events to come. The "imperial crown"(I.i.157), the central emblem of the play's structure of emblems, is presented, accepted, and passed on to a usurper who is crowned while his followers paradoxically sum up the rebellion with their pious exclamations: "God save the King"(I.i.188).

At the end of the first scene we are left with the impression of an unresolved political crisis; although Marlowe presents us with

---

[12] Cf. Martin, "Marlowe's *Tamburlaine* and the Language of Romance," 251-54. It is interesting to compare Mycetes' sexual confusion of the metaphor (making Tamburlaine Helen to Theridamas' Paris) to the other notable Marlovian use of the Paris simile in Faustus' apostrophe to Helen:

> I wil be Paris, and for loue of thee,
> Insteede of Troy shal Wertenberge be sackt ...
> Brighter art thou than flaming Iupiter,
> When he appeard to haplesse Semele.
> (A 1364-5;1372-3)

The vision of rape and consummation undergoes perplexing transformations in this case, because the Faustus-Paris relation is shifted to Semele-Jupiter, with Faustus identifying himself with both Semele *and* Jupiter.

a spectacle of dynastic supplementation, the rhetorical and material value of the title "king" is inconclusive since neither the clownish Mycetes, who listens to others make "kingly resolutions" on behalf of himself, nor the rebellious Cosroe seem to understand the problems that lie at the source of power and authority. The act of coronation itself, intended as "assurance of desired success" (Ortygius' proclamation in I.i.160), appears to be an insubstantial expression of purposefulness and definition in so far as Cosroe, too, is not seen to act on his own behalf but is elevated into the role of emperor by other men's favour.

Cosroe is competent enough to outwit Mycetes and point out to us the important relation of language to power, but we do not hear *him* conceive of a strategy to consolidate his estate and to "triumph over many provinces"(I.i.173). It is indicative of his unself-conscious ambition that the actual projections of future imperial politics (I.i.160-69) and martial exploits (I.i.140-54) are rendered by Ortygius and Ceneus. Dramatic and rhetorical details in this opening scene thus constitute contrasts and parallels between Mycetes and Cosroe which are preparatory for but hardly comprehensive of the absolute heroic ideal that the "Scythian shepherd" is going to bring into the play during his first appearance on stage.

The scene shifts to the purportedly pastoral realm of Scythian shepherds and "country swains"(I.ii.47), but our first impression is another stunning, colourful entry, continuing the bold visual symbolism of the play: [*Enter*] *"TAMBURLAINE leading ZENOCRATE; TECHELLES, USUMCASANE, other Lords [among them MAGNETES and AGYDAS] and Soldiers loaden with treasure"*(s.d.,I.ii). Like so many of the stage effects, this carefully orchestrated ritual of entry and the focal visual display of the captured Zenocrate and her treasure of gold and jewels immediately expands the imaginative scale of all those speaking pictures of the dramatic action that are framed and foregrounded by such elaborate gestures (e.g. grouping, dress, accoutrements, colour-codes, effects of ritual and emblematic suggestion [gold], etc.).

Marlowe's dramaturgy is undoubtedly a challenge to any director's interpretation of the text's theatrical notation, and the contrasts or symmetries of acting style, ritual, visual effect, sound effect, grouping, function of properties, etc., require a lot of attention to the rich diversity of engagement between the choreography of action and that of the dramatic poetry itself. *Tamburlaine the Great* has rarely been mounted on the modern stage, however. Those few productions that we know of indeed encountered considerable problems in dealing with the play's epic proportions and difficult stylistic features.[13] All of them nevertheless exacted all the resources of modern stage-craft to enlarge those images which, according to Tyrone Guthrie's and Donald Wolfit's production-formula, proved most symptomatic of the play's flamboyant visual and verbal rhetoric: "pageant effect," "ritual dance," "savage oratorio."[14]

While Guthrie's production often lapsed into merely spectacular and fantastic effects of scene design and excessive histrionics, Peter Hall's widely celebrated production for the National Theatre in London (1976) translated stage- and text-directions into a comprehensive and subtle scheme of developing sights and sounds, effectively extending the symbolic use of costumes and

---

13 Cf. Nancy T. Leslie, "*Tamburlaine* in the Theater: Tartar, Grand Guignol, or Janus?", *RenD*, 4 (1971), 105-20. Leslie's brilliant survey focusses on those three major *Tamburlaine* revivals which have earned much critical acclaim yet must still be regarded as highly controversial experiments in proving the two plays' theatrical viability (presented as a 10-act tragedy by all three productions). I rely on Leslie's reviews of the 1919 Yale production, directed by Stephen Vincent Benét and Edgar Woolley; the highly controversial Guthrie-Wolfit production at the Old Vic (1951; reproduced at the Stratford-Ontario Shakespearean Festival in 1956); and the 1964 Tavistock Repertory Company production at London's Tower Theatre, directed by Robert Pennant Jones, whereas I will add my own impressions of Peter Hall's superb adoption of Marlowe's first major play for the opening of the Olivier Stage in 1976, a project which strained the National Theatre Company during six months of rehearsals and finally surpassed even the wildest expectations.
14 Donald Wolfit and Tyrone Guthrie, "Introduction," *Tamburlaine the Great: An Acting Version* (London:Heinemann,1951), pp.x-xi.

properties suggested by Marlowe's playscript itself. For the
first two scenes, Hall had the entire colour scheme of the stage
change three times: pink for the court of the effete Mycetes,
blue for the crowning of Cosroe, and gold for the arrival of Tamburlaine and Zenocrate. This interpretation convincingly demonstrated how bold colour changes and transitions reflect and support changes of situation, and the progressive pattern of course
prepares for the most conspicuous Marlovian colour symbolism: the
white, red, and black tents and costumes which mark the siege of
Damascus near the end of Part 1.

Emblematic meanings of visual appearance, chivalric and mythic
images, tableau-effects, and the influence of repeated visual
motifs each contribute to the tone and atmosphere which Marlowe's
play projects, but one always has to see these stimuli in conjunction with or juxtaposition to the language and the staging of
the play as a whole. In his very influential study on the development of dramatic speech in Elizabethan drama, Wolfgang Clemen
emphasizes this relation and asserts that "Marlowe created a
highly individual dramatic style in which stage-tableau and stagebusiness combined with the long speeches to produce a new kind of
unity."[15] Recognition of structural unity alone cannot really
explain, however, to what effects the combination of speech and
spectacle is used, especially in these early exposition scenes
where the tension and disparity of styles provoke many questions
about the world of kings and rebels that is presented to us.

---

15 Wolfgang Clemen, *English Tragedy before Shakespeare*, trans.
T.S. Dorsch (London: Methuen, 1961), p. 125. Clemen identifies the various influences operating on Marlowe's theatrical
style as "those of the pageants, of the spectacular elements
in the masques, and of the Italian 'trionfi'" (p. 129). Ethel
Seaton finds that Marlowe's colour symbolism comes directly
out of the world of medieval romances, such as *Richard Coeur
de Lyon* or *Morte d'Arthur*. The conflict pattern of tournaments, however, is transformed into Tamburlaine's principle
of strife which has little resemblance to the civalric code.
For the role of medieval romance, see Seaton, "Marlowe's
Light Reading," in *Elizabethan and Jacobean Studies Presented
to Frank Percy Wilson*, ed. Herbert David and Helen Gardner
(Oxford: Clarendon, 1959), pp. 17-25.

If we say that tension is built up through the crisis of power in the first scene, the second scene, then, is crucial for the definition of power which the drama must find in and through the qualities of the hero. Tamburlaine has already been present throughout the first scene - not physically but in the rumour of the Persian court ("that sturdy Scythian thief"; "wicked Tamburlaine") - and when he enters, still "disguised" in his shepherd's weeds, he is addressed by Zenocrate along the same lines:

> Ah shepherd, pity my distressed plight
> (If, as thou seemest, thou art so mean a man)
> And seek not to enrich thy followers
> By lawless rapine ...
> (I.ii.7-10)

Zenocrate's plea for pity (which is an important motif in the play, distinguishing her from Tamburlaine and leading to the severe conflict in Act V) and her allusion to Tamburlaine's "mean" estate (his identity; his appearance) already signal crucial questions of definition. What image of the hero is presented? How can the putative hero, as a "lawless" and "base" shepherd, legitimize himself, and in what generic context will his role as protagonist be recognized? Since there are at least three perspectives from which Tamburlaine's self-discovery and transgression of convention and "lawfulness" are represented or mirrored (his own, that of his followers, and that of his antagonists), this scene is a revelation in terms of its expository technique - pointing toward the entire problem of how to grasp Marlowe's new conception of a theatrical mode suitable for his purposes.

Although the vertical thrust of Tamburlaine's aspirations is established within less than 200 lines (from "lord" to "mighty emperor" to "May we become immortal like the gods"), this imaginative thrust is dramatically realized by carefully graded contrasts and a gradual evolving of Tamburlaine's *style*. Already after his second speech we notice that Zenocrate does not address him as "shepherd" any longer but as "my lord"(I.ii.33). Tamburlaine immediately takes up the cue:

> I am a lord, for so my deeds shall prove,
> And yet a shepherd by my parentage.
> (I.ii.34-5)

He enters into the role he will "prove" with zest and self-confidence, and it is of course quite ironic that he should mention the gap between his low parentage and his claims to lordship. But he has already discarded the relevance of conventional generic attributes with regard to the "deeds" that will prove his authority:

> But now you see these letters and commands
> Are countermanded by a greater man,
> And through my provinces you must expect
> Letters of conduct from my mightiness ...
> (I.ii.21-4)

At this point, Tamburlaine's "countermanding" of all established authority is of course purely rhetorical; the antithetical thrust of his rhetoric is an expression of his effective "command" of *language* as a mode of personal and political mastery. The "mightiness" of Tamburlaine's eloquence manifests itself through the enormous verbal and stylistic self-assertiveness which, simultaneously, works as an active seduction and imaginative appeal upon those who listen. In the context of the scene, his eloquence draws attention to itself as an active self-revelation, building up momentum (in passages of six, twelve, and eighteen lines, I.ii. 1-6;21-32;34-51) and achieving an astonishing admixture of military discourse and poetic hyperbole:

> But lady, this fair face and heavenly hue
> Must grace his bed that conquers Asia
> And means to be a terror to the world,
> Measuring the limits of his empery
> By east and west as Phoebus doth his course.
> (I.ii.36-40)

This is the first climactic moment in the play; Tamburlaine's first and very spectacular act of self-realization is expressed by a symbolic change of costume:

> Lie here, ye weeds that I disdain to wear!
> This complete armour and this curtle-axe

> Are adjuncts more beseeming Tamburlaine.
> (I.ii.41-3)

At a stroke, Tamburlaine *becomes* the chivalric leader he has projected; he transforms himself into the new role, exchanging his weeds for the proper "adjuncts." As Joel Altman remarks, "the logical-rhetorical term is especially fitting, for Tamburlaine seems intent upon fashioning a personage for himself by literally annexing the 'accidents' appropriate to his inward vision."[16]

There is a sense of wonder which accompanies Tamburlaine's daring conviction; his self-confidence is of course an expression of his power of speech, and this power of speech, in turn, substantiates his conceits and imagined ideal of manly power and sovereignty. In this perspective, Tamburlaine's self and his image exactly reflect each other, and this is immediately underlined by a mirror-passage which Marlowe gives to the admiring Techelles:

> As princely lions when they rouse themselves,
> Stretching their paws and threat'ning herds of beasts,
> So in his armour looketh Tamburlaine ...
> (I.ii.52-4)

Having established his hero's presence for us through Tamburlaine's initial performative speech-acts, Marlowe elaborates the image of the warrior-rhetor by placing him in the dramatic context of two important battles of persuasion. The first is a "passionate" wooing speech addressed to Zenocrate ("Disdains Zenocrate to live with me ..." I.ii.82-105), during which Tamburlaine's poetic imagination for the first time takes off into a flight of extensive romantic hyperbole. His visions and heightened comparisons are fantastic creations of the mind which even carry the persuasive rhythms of loving praise, yet the upward movement of Tamburlaine's speech is more a sign of his own verbal power than of a sensitive regard toward the woman he seems to be talking to.

---

16 Joel B. Altman, *The Tudor Play of Mind: Rhetorical Inquiry and the Development of Elizabethan Drama* (Berkeley: Univ. of California Press, 1978), p. 324.

Zenocrate, "fairer than whitest snow on Scythian hills," is to be drawn "with milk-white harts upon an ivory sled" amidst "the frozen pools" and on the "icy mountains' lofty tops" – an unusually abstract and cold conceit which conveys less a feeling of love than of extravagant, self-gratulatory adolation. Zenocrate, elevated into the furthest regions of the imagination, in fact becomes another outward symbol (like the gold and the jewels) of Tamburlaine's triumphant status as conqueror. Most astonishingly, the speech works in the theatre, and the Olivier production, for example, profited from the light, exuberant, almost humorous mood that characterized Tamburlaine's early encounters. Techelles' perplexed question, "What now? In love?", and Tamburlaine's joking aside, "Techelles, women must be flattered," brought the house down, but Peter Hall was sensitive to the very quick transitions required by the text, and the joke was used to stress the contrasted conviction of Tamburlaine's next line: "But this is she with whom I am in love" (I.ii.106-08).[17]

Such contrasts, which the staging of the play can effectively transmit, are not always so obvious on the page, and it is especially the range of comic tones in this scene which contributes to the diversity of impressions we gain of Tamburlaine's performance and character. The visible delight he takes in evolving his style; his honesty and respectfulness towards Zenocrate and his followers; his baffling self-confidence and the ease with which he seems able to make the best of all situations: these various aspects are important dramaturgic strategies which combine to draw Tamburlaine's audience, onstage and offstage, into a delighted and admiring partisanship with his rise to power. The presentation of heroic character, then, is primarily conceived of as an outer-directed theatrical realization of an extravagant energy and mental vitality. And this vitality is pro-

---

17   For critical evaluations of these aspects of the Peter Hall production, see J.S. Cunningham and Roger Warren, "*Tamburlaine the Great* Re-discovered," *ShS*, 31 (1978), 155-62, and Sibyl Truchet, "*Tamburlaine* on the Modern Stage," *CahiersE*, 13 (1978), 53-59.

gressively revealed not simply as rhetorical competence; rather, we are meant to perceive Tamburlaine's immediate success by virtue of an eloquence which is essentially a will-to-persuasion and conquest.[18]

That Tamburlainean heroism emerges as a test and contest of will (*pathos*) becomes nowhere clearer than in the persistent transfiguration of the traditionally distinct images of the warrior and the poet-rhetor into the provocative, composite image of the *rhetorical conqueror*.

> Then shall we fight courageously with them,
> Or look you I should play the orator?
> (I.ii.128-29)

The news that Theridamas' thousand horsemen are about to attack is readily picked up by Tamburlaine and transformed into an occasion to prove his heroic vaunts "substantial" (I.ii.212). The preparation for the encounter with Theridamas and the encounter itself conclude the expository scenes in a manner which is truly paradigmatic of the conquests to follow and, indeed, of the logic of the whole play. The question whether Tamburlaine "should play the orator", in spite of its humorous tone and its overt theatrical allusion to role-playing, is a crucial one and invites a more complex response than that of his immediate stage-audience. Tamburlaine's aspirations distinguish him from the conventional ambitions of his peers:

---

18 Marlowe scholarship has by and large failed to see *Tamburlaine*'s use of theatrical and rhetorical hyperbole (which identify the hero's conquering ambition) in a context of philosophical and linguistic interests other than that determined by formal Tudor teaching of rhetoric and dialectic. Even a very competent study such as Altman's *The Tudor Play of Mind* recognizes the practical importance of rhetoric to Marlowe's drama mainly in terms of the familiar idealistic and ethical notions underlying Renaissance humanism and its revival of Ciceronian perspectives on oratory. The radical poetic that makes itself felt in *Tamburlaine*, however, seems conceptually closer to the non-ethical, agonistic modes of discourse which are fundamental to the rhetorical theories of, for example, Gorgias and Longinus. I owe some of these

> *Tech.* No: cowards and faint-hearted runaways
> Look for orations when the foe is near.
> Our swords shall play the orators for us.
> (I.ii.130-32)

and seem to work at one remove from the non-aesthetic level of martial confrontation implied by Usumcasane's tactic of a "sudden and an hot alarm"(I.ii.134).

Tamburlaine's authoritative command, "Stay, Techelles, ask a parley first"(I.ii.137), and his preparatory, choreographic directives for the scene of persuasion ("Lay out our golden wedges to the view, / That their reflections may amaze the Persians. / And look we friendly on them ... Keep all your standings, and not stir a foot" I.ii.139-41;150) heighten the suspenseful effect of this situation which is of course unmistakably dangerous. But Tamburlaine's oratorical power transforms the encounter with Theridamas into a complete triumph - a triumph of vision and persuasion, moreover, which prefigures the grandiose mythopoeic fantasies that will characterize Tamburlaine's style of self-fashioning throughout the rest of the play.

The persuasion of Theridamas is Tamburlaine's first major "substantial" *tour de force*, and the functional architecture of this very long speech (45 lines) tells us a lot about the profound connection in Marlowe's verse between metrical instrumentation, rhythm, movement, intensity of expression and their imaginative purpose.

Tamburlaine's basic method of persuading Theridamas is to stress his own invincibility and impending world conquest and to invite Theridamas, whom he always respectfully addresses as a "mighty man-at-arms," to share his future glory. The crucial mythic conceit which dominates and links both arguments is the figurative

---

insights to Kimberly W. Benston's provocative forays into the speculative and linguistic foundation of Marlowe's poetry. Benston's study is particularly interesting in its approach to the possible connections between Marlowe's rhetorical ideal and the philosophical concepts of Renaissance Hermeticism. See his "The Shaping of the Marlovian Sublime," Diss., Yale University, 1980.

allusion to "Jove himself"(I.ii.179) as the powerful, divine protector of Tamburlaine's triumph. The speech as a whole is no "sure and grounded argument"(I.ii.183) in the sense that it develops a carefully reasoned topos; on the contrary, it has a counterlogical momentum which nevertheless works on its own terms as a heaping up of juxtaposed thought-patterns or sections that give it a feeling of ever-increasing expansion. There are ten of these sections, each consisting of an unbroken series of run-on lines which effect rhythmical movement and produce what we could call the characteristic onward and upward surge of Marlowe's "mighty lines."

There are other devices which help to create progressive intensity of expression: phonetic correspondences, assonance, varied pace and rhythm within the firm metrical context of the blank verse, and - above all - repetition of words in stressed positions. I think it is especially these pronounced internal echoes and the structure of the verse sections which highlight Tamburlaine's new style. The rhetorical aim of persuasion which is so crucial to Tamburlaine's speech is in fact reflected by those leaps and transitions, from one section to the next, which reveal Tamburlaine's necessary performative acts of bridging the "real" and the "ideal."

> Join with me now in this my mean estate
> . . .
> And when my name and honour shall be spread
> . . .
> Then shalt thou be competitor with me
> And sit with Tamburlaine in all his majesty.
> (I.ii.201;204;207-8)

Structurally, the leaps connect the individual sections that are clearly dominated by the echoes of the "I" ("me","my"), the "thou" and the "we" (e.g. "Forsake *thy* king and do but join with *me*, / And *we* will triumph over all the world"[171-72]; "That *I* shall be the monarch of the East ... If *thou* wilt stay with *me* ... Both *we* will walk upon the lofty clifts"[184;187;192; my emphases]). Most important, however, is the fact that this alternating sequence of referents is interrupted three times by Tamburlaine's sublime self-assertions through mythic images of cosmic power (God/Jove):

> Draw forth thy sword, thou mighty man-at-arms,
> Intending but to raze my charmed skin,
> And Jove himself will stretch his hand from heaven
> To ward the blow and shield me safe from harm.
> See how he rains down heaps of gold in showers
> As if he meant to give my soldiers pay;
> And as a sure and grounded argument
> That I shall be the monarch of the East,
> He sends this Soldan's daughter rich and brave
> To be my queen and portly emperess.
> (I.ii.177-86)

It is in such passages that the iconoclastic character of Tamburlaine's and his author's stance before "received ideas" and traditional notions of authority (worldly and divine) becomes most visible. Overtly, Tamburlaine uses the first image of Jove as a triumphant declaration of the god's protective patronage of his own heroic career.[19] At the same time, it is placed in the dramatic context of a developing battle for *voice* and *authority* during which Tamburlaine, and he alone among all the other stage characters, will use a rhetoric of naming and unnaming that will produce contradictory relationships with Jove or the Gods.

In his earlier, aggressive self-annunciation as the Apollonian hero, "measuring the limits ... as Phoebus doth his course," who will be a "terror to the world," Tamburlaine had already prefigured a restlessly soaring desire to transcend correspondences such as the one evoked by his allusion to Jove's protective father-role. In his address to Theridamas, his deific aspiration already becomes more intensive in his oblique allusion to the myth of Danae according to which Jove had metamorphosed himself into a shower of gold and come down through the roof of Danae's prison to conceive a son, Perseus. Mythic metaphor and dramatic

---

19 In this connection, see my commentary (Chapter VIII) on Dr Faustus' similar but inverted trust in the devil's protective power *against* God: "When Mephastophilis shal stand by me, / What God can hurt thee ..." (A 464-65).

representation are effectively fused in this spectacular moment: although there are no stage-directions, the text clearly suggests ("see", "this Soldan's daughter") that Tamburlaine points to the gold that his soldiers had laid out and to Zenocrate who is of course onstage, standing behind him among his followers.

The National Theatre production reinforced these gestures by drawing audience attention to the magnificent golden carpet laden with blindingly glaring jewels and to Zenocrate who was wearing a dazzling, golden costume. Such effects of spectacle are certainly intended by Marlowe, and we should remember that Tamburlaine himself also wears a "sun-bright armour"(cf.II.iii.22), which renders the visual symbolism complete. Such emblematic effects may have implications, however, which collide with the actual thrust of Tamburlaine's progressive verbal usurpation of all cosmic and solar images. It may be true that Tamburlaine's lines "romanticize the action by viewing the gold as a real extension of a poetic world and not merely as an analogue to it."[20] Martin correctly points out too that Tamburlaine's figures and mythic metaphors "work" (cf. "You see, my lord, what *working words* he hath" II.iii.25, emphasis mine), that his imaginative language (as opposed to Mycetes') *can* control his world. But I hesitate to follow Martin's assertion that Tamburlaine successfully "remade" the myth of Danae by suppressing the metaphoric equation with Danae's role (receiving the shower of gold) and fusing part of the Danae myth to the "material world of earthly riches to fashion his own reality."[21]

Surely Tamburlaine is twisting, turning, and remaking the language of myth, and he is persuading us to accept his perspective as our critical origin. But he is, I believe, fashioning a myth of epic success in his own image, usurping the divine attributes of all those prior figures such as Jove, Apollo, Hercules, Alexander, Achilles, etc., with whom he is compared in the play, and

---

20 Martin, "Marlowe's *Tamburlaine* and the Language of Romance," 252
21 Ibid., 252.

then displacing them with tropes of transcendence, not comparison. The allusion to Danae may very well be less interesting than the implicit reference to the underlying Perseus myth. In Ovid's *Metamorphoses* we read that Perseus, victorious hero and conqueror, "flew over the whole earth ... towards the east, and often toward the west," carrying the horrid head of Medusa. When he encounters the beautiful, captive Andromeda, he begins to woo her by revealing his identity: "My name is Perseus, son of Jupiter and of Danae, *whom Jupiter made pregnant with his fertile gold*...."[22] Perseus eventually subdues her resistance after having proved his love in a heroic battle.

I would argue that Tamburlaine's allusion to the myth above all intimates the idea of his divine conception and sonship; the gold on stage has no function as a concrete embodiment of the "material world" but is at best a symbolic representation of Tamburlaine's *meta-physical* claims. And these claims are complicated by the referential ambiguities in the projected conflation of Jove-Danae-Andromeda-Perseus; these complications are of course built into most of the claims that are made in the play. No fixed position can be assigned to Tamburlaine in these associations of the hero with mythical figures such as Perseus or Hercules,[23]

---

22 *Metamorphoses*, IV.626-27; 698ff. The emphasis in the latter quotation is mine. The translation that comes closest to the original passages is provided by the Penguin Classics edition, trans. Mary M. Innes (1955; rpt.Harmondsworth: Penguin Books, 1979), from which I cite in this case.
23 Theridamas is the first to connect Tamburlaine with the Herculean image of heroic anger ("His looks do menace heaven and dare the gods;/His fiery eyes are fixed upon the earth ..." I.ii.156-57). As a symbolic description of Tamburlaine's appearance, Theridamas' "aside" forms an important link in the dramatic exposition between the protagonists's hyperbolic self-revelation and complementary mirror-passages provided by Tamburlaine's audience *onstage*. Dramatic and verbal signs and counterpoints, such as the reactions of the "passionately" impressed Theridamas or the shocked, confused Zenocrate (who remains shocked even when she turns to admiring Tamburlaine), subject our response and judgment to divergent pressures that are, in themselves, a reflection of the violent antithetical nature of Tamburlaine himself:
    Zen. The Gods, defenders of the innocent,

especially since his extravagant vaunts and his already enacted self-transformation (from nameless shepherd into Apollo-like warrior and demi-god) promise continually to strive against and reverse images of limitation (Jove's divine authority; the law; Fate; cosmic and external influence).

To reverse images of limitation means to invent representations of aboriginal power; this, I suspect, is the idea that lies behind Tamburlaine's extraordinary vision of ascent and transcendence:

> I hold the Fates bound fast in iron chains,
> And with my hand turn Fortune's wheel about,
> And sooner shall the sun fall from his sphere
> Than Tamburlaine be slain or overcome.
>   . . .
> Both we will walk upon the lofty clifts,
> And Christian merchants that with Russian stems
> Plough up huge furrows in the Caspian Sea
> Shall vail to us as lords of all the lake.
> Both we will reign as consuls of the earth,
> And mighty kings shall be our senators.
> Jove sometimes masked in a shepherd's weed,
> *And by those steps that he hath scaled the heavens*
> *May we become immortal like the gods.*
>   (I.ii.173-6;192-200;my emphasis)

> Will never prosper your intended drifts.
>   . . .
> *Ther.[Aside]* Tamburlaine?
>   A Scythian shepherd, so embellished
>   With nature's pride and richest furniture?
>   (I.ii.68-9;154-55)

Theridamas' verbal mirror fuses the reference to Tamburlaine's rhetorical posture with a more fearful interpretation of his "piercing" eyes ("As if he ... meant to pierce Avernus' darksome vaults/And pull the triple-headed dog from hell" 158-60). This Herculean image (cf. Hercules' descent into Hades in Ovid, *Metamorphoses*, VII.409ff. or IV.450-51) suggests a Tamburlainean conquest of hell, and hell can of course be seen as one of the poles of the play's bold imaginative geography. The other pole is imaged in Tamburlaine's projected attack on Jove's sky and the Sun itself, archsymbol of that priority which he seeks to displace ("For *I, the chiefest lamp of all the earth* ..." IV.ii.36ff., my emphasis).

One has to *hear* such lines and see them uttered in order to grasp the meaning of Nashe's reference to the new drama and its protagonists "that intrude themselues to our eares as the Alcumists of eloquence ... mounted on the stage of arrogance."[24] *Arrogance* and *presumption* are perhaps perfect descriptions of the extravagant heroism which Marlowe's drama projects. Tamburlaine's agonistic imagination, exalting the *idea* of ambition as such, leads the audience into a dramatic world in which representations of the transgressive power of will (and will to power) seem intended to break down all conventional "reality."

Such transgressions are of course not re-presentable except by supermimetic flights of rhetoric, operating in an exotic world in which all secure ethical and metaphysical assumptions are undermined. Tamburlaine's quest thus turns into a form of "theatre which is not confined by the conventional notions of tragedy, heroism, divine justice, authority, order, etc. that are usually applied to the drama of the period.

1 Tamburlaine, from the start, plays with these conventional expectations and indulges in the inadequacy of the established order (represented in the dramatic world) in coping with the threats and "high astounding terms" of the "Scythian thief." It is helpful to recall, as Stephen Greenblatt points out, that certain aspects of Tamburlaine's ambition could surely find their objective correlatives in Marlowe's historical and political context, and that Tamburlaine's relentless "thirst of reign"(II.vii. 12) was probably not more "heterodox" and subversive than the "relentless power-hunger of Tudor absolutism ... [or]the acquisitive energies of English merchants, entrepreneurs, and adventurers."[25] But Greenblatt's merchants and adventurers, whom he

---

24 Another contemporary testimony is supplied by Joseph Hall who is describing a performance of *Tamburlaine* when he claims that the dramatist "can with words Italinate,/Big-sounding sentences, and words of state,/Faire patch me up his pure Iambick verse" and, consequently, he "ravishes the gazing scaffolders" (*Virgidemiarum*[1597],I.iii). See Maclure, p.41.
25 Stephen J. Greenblatt, *Renaissance Self-Fashioning: From More to Shakespeare* (Chicago: Univ.of Chicago Press, 1980),p.194.

depicts cruising around the South Sea and committing senseless crimes against the native Indians, seem to have little to do with the creation of a sublime landscape of imaginative aspirations which Tamburlaine, provoking the audience into apprehending the unlimited possibilities of his performance, brings to fruition in his *rhetorical* self-conception.

If the representability of power fantasies is at stake, and this is the most crucial problem that Greenblatt encounters in his inquiry into Renaissance modes of "self-fashioning," then one can certainly regard the *Tamburlaine* plays as being little concerned about any limits of theatrical and practical possibility. For Marlowe, dramatic development in his hero and dramatic conflict in the world presented on the stage are poised well above the question of dramatic *mimesis*. From its very conception, *Tamburlaine* is directed towards the theatrical embodiment of energies and states of mind that make themselves felt through distinct modes of vision, poetic textures, emblematic images, and through contrasts in rhetorical efficacy.

In *Macbeth* as well as in *Dr Faustus* we are able to see, from the very beginning, that the heroes discover themselves placed into a context which makes them aware of the immanently tragic delimitation of consciousness. Macbeth's feverish vision of the consequences of his transgression and Faustus' defensive self-persuasions prefigure their failures to overpower the disenchanting apprehension of the conditional nature of freedom. Faustus keeps telling us that he is trying to extend this limited freedom even though he knows the (self-)destructive consequences of his wilful act.

It seems to me that the fundamental difference in the disclosure of Tamburlaine's will to "live at liberty"(I.ii.26) rests in the fact that his wilful ambition *can* extend itself and demonstrate its power because within and through its rhetorical expression there arise no ethical and ontological problems for Tamburlaine. This is to say that the opening Act of *Tamburlaine* develops the greatness of its hero's character and will through a first, prototypical verbal conquest during which Tamburlaine's apparently unlimited rhetorical strength substantiates his heroic claims. The persuasion of Theridamas, completely successful in both its rhetorical display and military consequence, suggests that if the verbal representation of power is itself power,[26] if cause and effect are identical or, in fact, reversible, then Tamburlaine can be said to operate in a world which is potentially limitless and in which success or failure can be measured by rhetorical efficacy and poetic superiority, and not by assumptions about natural or moral order.

Actions and re-actions among the characters in the dramatic world are therefore placed under the fundamental verbal premise already acknowledged by Mycetes, namely that a "great and thund'ring speech" will be the mirror in which heroic stature and achievement are to be perceived. The inadequacies of Mycetes' clownish conceits and Cosroe's unself-conscious rhetoric are highlighted in contrast with the ease with which Tamburlaine's verbal power, bearing, and temerity transform themselves into an effective mode of action:

> *Ther.* What strong enchantments tice my yielding soul?
> . . .
> Won with thy words and conquered with thy looks,
> I yield myself, my men and horses to thee:
> As long as life maintains Theridamas.
> (I.ii.223;227-29)

As Theridamas "yields," he tells us that he yields to a god-like figure: "Not Hermes, prolocutor to the gods, / Could use persuasions more pathetical"(I.ii.209-10). The mythical precepts that flow into the portrayal of Tamburlaine's superhuman quali-

---

[26] In discussing characteristic rhetorical stances and modes of vision in "strong poetry," Harold Bloom contends that poetry always is a question of power and that eloquence is thus always "self-preservation through persuasion, and the imagination can do anything because self-preservation makes us giants and heroes and magical, primitive formalists again" (*A Map of Misreading*, pp. 67-68).

ties - Jove, Apollo, Hercules, Perseus, Hermes (the god of eloquence) - are indicative of the extraordinary admixture of seemingly contradictory potentialities which Marlowe depicts in the central figure of the play and which become the fundamental expression of his theme. Eugene Waith's splendid study of the "Herculean" prototype in the heroic background of Marlowe's drama has helped us to understand the complementary parts of the compound, idealized model of the Herculean demi-god which the Renaissance had received from the Classics.[27] Marlowe makes a deliberate effort to draw together the ambivalent aspects of the hubristic figure (valour, pride, ambition, egotism, cruelty, physical and intellectual vigour)and, disregarding the historical portrait of the lame Timur Khan, presents his protagonist as a beautiful, fiery-eyed shepherd.

In the second scene we witness how the shepherd transforms himself into an irresistibly eloquent and pitiless warrior who wills to conquer everything conquerable. The play has opened on a low key (scene i) and then immediately set up the high mark of Tamburlaine's "threatening terms" against which all characters and actions will be measured. The seduction and subjugation of Zenocrate and Theridamas are expository demonstrations of his potential for "pathetical persuasion" and poetic self-conception, which initiate a long procession of battles in which Tamburlaine will triumph over increasingly formidable antagonists and increasingly challenging conflicts (the most crucial of which, significantly, is resolved in his grand soliloquy on "beauty" in Act V).

It can be said, then, that Marlowe's dramaturgy devises a context of conflicts in which Tamburlaine's dynamic subjectivity can evolve and pursue excessive goals of a kind that had not been represented or even thought conceivable on an English stage prior to Tamburlaine's arrival. The originality of Marlowe's dramaturgy lies in the form and structure of the play which are made to re-

---

27   Cf. Eugene M. Waith, *The Herculean Hero in Marlowe, Chapman, Shakespeare and Dryden* (London: Chatto & Windus, 1962), esp. chaps.1 and 2.

flect the *successful* hyperbolical revelation of heroic potentialities. As Tamburlaine's claims grow more outrageous and his poetic sublimations more daring, his self-mythologization still works almost exclusively in terms of its aggressive rhetoric. As the later Scenes of Triumph become more and more inhuman and fantastic, the question whether the play advertises Tamburlaine's ritualized glorification as a spectacle of possibilities utterly beyond orthodox judgment seems unavoidable and has been asked by practically all commentators.[28]

With this question in mind, Martin's contention that both *Tamburlaine* plays assert the supremacy of the hero's poetic "word" of limitless creativity against the Word of the Christian faith[29] is all the more interesting since it draws attention to Marlowe's original and thoroughly vexing propositions about the conception of tragic drama. The new idea in Marlowe's drama is the centrality of Tamburlaine's word-as-action, presented in a daringly new style of theatrical hyperbole which indeed suggests that heroism is correlated to aggressive, wilful eloquence. For Tamburlaine, "battles" such as the one against Theridamas must be won at the level of words, and the style he evolves is all the more astonishing since he is absolutely convinced of its *prophetic* efficacy, too:

> Nor are Apollo's oracles more true
> Than thou shalt find my vaunts substantial.
> (I.ii.211-12)

---

28 Nancy Leslie stresses the conflict of opposed feelings about what the play-in-performance offers us and sums up: "At issue, of course, is whether *Tamburlaine* glorifies Machiavellian virtù, denigrates it, or asks us to suspend moral judgment; is the play immoral, moral, or amoral? No two *Tamburlaine* productions have posited the question in the same way"(p.119). It is certainly not incidental that the Guthrie-Wolfit production (1951) chose to present Tamburlaine as a megalomaniacal, half-insane Hitler-type, and that practically all modern productions preferred to transform the two plays into a tenact tragedy. Following Battenhouse's Christian interpretation (and his "two-parts-into-one" theory), almost all critics except Kocher, Waith, Kimbrough, and Martin ultimately subject *Tamburlaine* to a moralizing conclusion.
29 Cf. Martin, 262.

Chapter Three

ENDLESS STRIFE: PERFORMANCES OF POWER

In his *The Tudor Play of Mind*, Joel Altman advances the interesting theory that the explorative character of *Tamburlaine* removes the plays so much from the notion of tragedy which the Elizabethan stage had yet entertained that we "are to take Marlowe's tragic intention more seriously and try to find dramatic and psychological meaning in the paradox that the play represents not the tragic fall but the tragic *rise* of a great man."[1] Equally troubled by the "puzzling relationship" of Tamburlaine's word-magic to stable values of history and continuity, another recent critic seeks to approach Marlowe's "tragic riddle" by pointing out that since the plays' metaphysical frame or landscape "constantly reminds us of limits, we are apt to grow sceptical of Tamburlaine's romantic trust that all the barriers in his world are permeable."[2] Both critics, although they do not exactly know what to make of Marlowe's "tragic glass," seem to agree that judgment has to be found not only through the protagonist but through his victims as well and, more importantly, that the tragic elements of the play are reflected in the consequences of human imagining.

Clearly, interpretation of the plays in this light will yield new perspectives on Tamburlaine's style, his rhetorical power, and his singular heroic conceit as well as on the placing of Tamburlaine himself in relation to a given range of values. It

---

1 Altman, p. 323. Harry Levin, in *Christopher Marlowe: The Overreacher* (1961; rpt.London: Faber & Faber, 1973), was probably the first to comment on the formal and generic implications of Marlowe's new "tragedy of ambition" (pp. 75 ff.).
2 Judith Weil, *Christopher Marlowe: Merlin's Prophet* (Cambridge: Cambridge Univ. Press, 1977), pp. 106-07. For a contrasting view on the "language of romance" in drama, see Martin, 248ff.

may prove difficult, however, to find a consensus of opinion about these values, and we will probably continue to struggle with two plays that to many of us appear confusing, contradictory and unwieldy.

Battenhouse's special pleading that the two plays are in fact one does not help much either; his defence of Marlowe's orthodoxy is a typical instance of the debates that can arise from the ambivalent religious and doctrinal positions in *Tamburlaine* and, by implication, from the dramatist's "failure" to express clearly his moral stance and his attitude towards his hero. Did Marlowe want his audience to admire Tamburlaine as a virtuous, though pitiless, man of action, fulfilling his prophecies and achieving a god-like stature in the process? Or did Marlowe wish to "teach and delight"[3] his audience by using Tamburlaine as the perfect example of a proud atheist whose disrespect for fortune and the gods eventually turns in on him?

Battenhouse, in pursuit of his Christian interpretation, welcomes Tamburlaine's fatal illness towards the end of Part 2 as a clear sign of divine retribution. In this episode, Tamburlaine extends the destruction of Babylon to the burning of "the heaps of superstitious books / Found in the temple of that Mahomet" (2 *Tamb*.V.i.173-74) and phrases his challenging speech in a deliberately blasphemous manner:

> In vain, I see, men worship Mahomet ...
> Now, Mahomet, if thou have any power,
> Come down thyself and work a miracle ...

---

3 However uneasy the intersections between drama and formal rhetoric may have been, there is ample evidence of a sense of decorum among Tudor writers which adhered to an ethically inspired conception of the purpose of poetry. The Horatian formula, *aut prodesse aut delectare*, was of course a commonplace. I quote from Sidney's Aristotelian description: "poesy therefore is an art of imitation ... that is to say representing, counterfeiting, or figuring forth ... a speaking picture - with this end, to teach and delight" (*An Apology for Poetry*, ed. Geoffrey Shephard [1965; rpt. Manchester: Manchester Univ.Press, 1973], p. 101).

> Why sendest thou not a furious whirlwind down
> To blow thy Alcaron up to thy throne
> Where men report thou sittest by God himself,
> Or vengeance on the head of Tamburlaine
> That shakes his sword against thy majesty
> And spurns the abstracts of thy foolish laws?
> (V.i.178;186-7;191-6)

Tamburlaine's outrageous act of defiance against one of the prevailing deities of the play not only includes an explicit allusion to the Jews' challenge to the crucifield Christ; it also presents a violent travesty of the similar scene in Act II, in which the betrayed Orcanes had torn the articles of peace and solicited revenge from Christ ("Behold and venge this traitor's perjury. / Thou Christ that art esteemed omnipotent, / If thou wilt prove thyself a perfect God ... Be now revenged" II.ii.54-56;58), which was promptly granted.

In performance, the visual hyperboles and stage effects of the scene reinforce the powerful impact of Tamburlaine's speech. Tamburlaine himself, all in black, is mounted high on his chariot, drawn by the bridled kings; in the background we can envisage the Governor of Babylon, suspended in mid-air and transfixed by arrows.[4] And downstage we must imagine the flames rising from the pit indicating the burning of the "superstitious books."

Peter Hall's Olivier production vividly underscored these bold images and placed great emphasis on Tamburlaine's grim challenge; after he had spoken the lines I quoted above, there followed a long pause as Tamburlaine and his followers looked up to heaven, waiting. No whirlwind. No sign. Tamburlaine calmly concluded his speech:

> Well, soldiers, Mahomet remains in hell;
> He cannot hear the voice of Tamburlaine.
> (V.i.197-98)

---

[4] The shooting of the Governor, incidentally, caused a sensation in London when a serious accident interrupted a performance of *2 Tamburlaine* on November 16, 1587. If we can trust the witnesses' report, a child and a pregnant woman were killed and a man severely injured by the actors' wild shots. Cf. E.K. Chambers, *The Elizabethan Stage* (Oxford: Oxford Univ. Press, 1923), II, 135.

Several speeches were made before Tamburlaine turned his chariot to drive off; only then did he say he was "distempered suddenly"(V.i.217). This at least raised the possibility of Mahomet's revenge, and the immediately following scene of Callapine's military preparations enforced the impression of an impending catastrophe. But Tamburlaine's triumphant victory over Calapine's army completely destroyed that possibility and restored the ambivalent impact of this scene. Cunningham and Warren, when reviewing the production, found the staging convincing: "*Maybe* Mahomet could hear, maybe not - this exactly catches Marlowe's equivocal tone."[5]

Marlowe's "equivocal tone" has become the subject of unending debate. Ellis-Fermor, Kocher, Cole, and Steane, among other critics, refer to the complete absence of any explicit moralizing in the play itself that would justify Battenhouse's contention that divine retribution strikes down the defiant blasphemer.[6] Gardner and Ribner maintain that Tamburlaine is simply overcome by his mortality.[7] Eugene Waith does not see any divine retribution in Tamburlaine's death, but an occasion for apotheosis.[8] Robert Kimbrough, finally, contends that all explicit interpretation is avoided on Marlowe's part. He thinks instead that Marlowe simply presented the "viewers with a pict-

---

5 "*Tamburlaine the Great* Re-discovered," 158.
6 Cf. Una Ellis-Fermor, *Christopher Marlowe* (London: Methuen, 1927), pp. 24-60; Paul H. Kocher, *Christopher Marlowe: A Study of His Thought, Learning, and Character* (1946; rpt. New York: Russell & Russell, 1962), pp. 90-91; Douglas Cole, *Suffering and Evil in the Plays of Christopher Marlowe* (1962; rpt. New York: Gordian Press, 1972), pp. 115-16; and J.B. Steane, *Marlowe: A Critical Study* (Cambridge: Cambridge Univ. Press, 1964), p. 101. For Battenhouse's view, see *Marlowe's Tamburlaine: A Study in Renaissance Moral Philosophy* (1941; rpt. Nashville: Vanderbilt Univ. Press, 1964), pp. 256-58. Martin (pp.262-63) thinks that the Koran-burning scene contains nothing offensive to the religious feelings of a *Christian* audience.
7 Cf. Helen Gardner, "The Second Part of *Tamburlaine the Great*," *MLR*, 37 (1942), 18-24, and Irving Ribner, "The Idea of History in Marlowe's *Tamburlaine*," *ELH*, 20 (1953), 251-66.
8 Cf. *The Herculean Hero*, p. 85.

ure of ambition that was perfectly in keeping with sixteenth century moral thought" and allowed them "to draw their own conclusions."[9] Kimbrough is perhaps thinking of those conventional ideas about heroism which Eugene Waith has so impressively examined. Or he may refer to the fact that Marlowe was undoubtedly influenced by his religious background. But he does not explain in his article why some of Marlowe's contemporaries, such as Greene, Nashe, or Harvey, *did* "draw their own conclusions" and complained about "the end of scollerisme" and Marlowe's "daring God out of heauen with that Atheist Tamburlan." And if Greene found Marlowe's ideas "intollerable," is this not squarely at odds with the assumption that *Tamburlaine* was in perfect line with conventional moral thought?

Although I cannot explore the *Tamburlaine* plays as extensively as they deserve, I wish at least to suggest a few ideas in the following pages which might help to illuminate the problems I have addressed above. I start from the assumption that it is not enough to demonstrate that a play reflects the literary or religious conventions of its time without also showing how the dramatist manipulates those conventions, how he develops his own theatrical mode in order to project the ideas and dramatic interests he entertains.

The theatrical realization of the episode at the end of Part 2 in which Tamburlaine performs his daring, blasphemous challenge to Mahomet, falls ill and defeats Callapine's army may be a good example to start with. What I want to draw attention to in the following are exactly those dramatic collisions and transitions (often realized as collisions of speech and action) which emphasize Tamburlaine's rhetorical flights and heighten their problematic relationships to the immediate or wider dramatic context. As the tonal irregularities and polarizations of theatrical effect are intrinsically connected with the tension between aesthetic and moral significance, we ought to be concerned about

---

9 "*1 Tamburlaine:* A Speaking Picture in a Tragic Glass," 31.

placing these expressions of significance in relation to one another in order to find a unifying perspective from which we can infer the play's central dynamic. Since the Koran episode, for example, clearly shows how Tamburlaine's heroic self-glorification and contempt for the gods can affect our sense of moral and tragic pathos (regardless of the allegorization that his sudden death may invite), I wish to concentrate, first of all, on Tamburlaine's relation to the symbolic and theological concepts of godhead in order to approach the aesthetic and ethical principle underlying his disruptive hunger for power.

Let us go backward from the scene of Tamburlaine's penultimate defiance (his last one is of Death himself, whom he addresses as "my slave, the ugly monster" V.iii.67) to its beginnings. When Tamburlaine orders the burning of the "abstracts" of Mahomet's "foolish laws," he re-enacts the characteristic posture with which we have learnt to identify him from the very first moment of his transformation - the moment when he begins to challenge established authority and law (divine and human), shaking his "sword against thy majesty" and asserting the "*voice* of Tamburlaine." Sword and voice, swords and words; acts of self-naming commingle with word-wounds perpetrated against the authority of prior signification: Tamburlaine's violent rhetoric is always at once onomatopoeic (name-making) and onomatoclastic (name-breaking), constantly symbolizing his subversive power to create (prophesy *and* actualize) his forward march toward the heights of imagined glory.[10]

Already during Tamburlaine's second appearance onstage (1 *Tamb.* II.iii), Marlowe intensifies the impression that his hero's poetic Word of limitless creativity is more than human and capable of imagining a world more wonderful - in terror or beauty - than the one we know. Cosroe, the new Mycetes, "re-

---

10 In his vow of friendship to Theridamas, Tamburlaine already hints at the ultimate destination and purpose of aspiration: "Until our bodies turn to elements / And both our souls *aspire celestial thrones*" (I.ii.235-36, my emphasis).

poses" in Tamburlaine's "approved fortunes"(II.iii.1-2) and, accepting Tamburlaine's predictions of victory as "assured oracle"(II.iii.4), blindly delegates all control to his eventual successor. Cosroe's trust in Tamburlaine's "oracles" ironically heigtens the impact of the latter's clear and unambiguous self-assertion:

> For fates and oracles of heaven have sworn
> To royalise the deeds of Tamburlaine
> And make them blest that share in his attempts ...
> The world will strive with hosts of men at arms
> To swarm unto the ensign I support.
> (II.iii.7-9;13-4)

Then his battle-field forecast suddenly breaks off into a dazzling, inspired vision:

> Our quivering lances shaking in the air
> And bullets like Jove's dreadful thunderbolts
> Enrolled in flames and fiery smouldering mists
> Shall threat the gods more than Cyclopian wars;
> And with our sun-bright armour as we march
> We'll chase the stars from heaven and dim their eyes
> That stand and muse at our admired arms.
> (II.iii.18-24)

At this point in the play, Tamburlaine is already redefining the image he has created of himself and which has been complemented by his friends' and antagonists' references to his "smiling stars" and special Fortune ("... a wondrous man: / Nature doth strive with Fortune and his stars / To make him famous ..." II.i.32-4). In a very peculiar way, Tamburlaine seems to acknowledge his relation to astral influence ("For fates and oracles of heaven have sworn"), which would render his outstanding destiny at least explicable in terms of a system the ultimate cause of which is some larger supra-natural power (Fortune, God/Jove, Mahomet). But Tamburlaine immediately goes beyond Cosroe's and Menaphon's traditional conception of influence and cosmological order and projects ("Shall"; "We'll") his future transcendence of such barriers to his deific aspiration.

Tamburlaine's vision of his army's forward/upward march ("threatening the gods") is the first explicit reference to his *rivalry* with the gods. It is an imaginative leap which actually makes no sense as a prediction for Cosroe's benefit and appears all the more disproportionate in its context since the battle, after all, is against the weak and clownish Mycetes. But his rhetoric leaves a very strong impression on his auditors ("You see, my lord, what *working words* he hath" II.iii.25, emphasis mine), and even if there is only a thin line between the serious and the comic (a line that will of course be crossed during the thoroughly mirthful encounter between Tamburlaine and Mycetes in II.iv), it would be a mistake not to see that behind the "jest" ("'Twill prove a pretty jest ..." II.v.90) and the "sport" (the declaration of war on Cosroe whom Tamburlaine "only made ... king to make us sport" II.v.101) lurks a dead-serious determination.

This sense of self-determination can be seen in Tamburlaine's increasingly hyperbolical self-portrayals which either foreshadow or run parallel to his enacted rise in power and specifically illuminate his "thirsting with sovereignty" in its relation to transcendent Power. At first sight, the concepts of godhead that dominate the play seem confused and contradictory. Tamburlaine's initial affirmation of Jove's protective patronage

> And Jove himself will stretch his hand from heaven
> To ward the blow and shield me safe from harm.
> (I.ii.179-80)

is quickly replaced by the concept of the gods as examples to be emulated:

> And by those steps that he hath scaled the heavens
> May we become immortal like the gods.
> (I.ii.199-200)

The third concept which evolves already in the second Act reflects a shift in emphasis that is crucial for the entire drama. As his oblique reference to the "Cyclopian wars" indicates, Tamburlaine's deposition of Mycetes (foreshadowing that of Cosroe) is now imaginatively correlated to the wars in heaven - to the idea of imitation as imitation of "heavenly" *revolt*.[11] The relationship between the views of the gods as examples and rivals remains complicated, however, since there are references in the text to both the successful revolt of Jupiter and to the unsuccessful revolt of the Titans. When Marlowe refocusses attention on the developing dramatic conflict between the newly established Persian King (Cosroe) and Tamburlaine's growing will-to-usurpation, the conflict is carefully prepared by the contrasting perspectives on "kingship" that we gain from Tamburlaine's camp

> *Tamb.* Is it not passing brave to be a king
> And ride in triumph through Persepolis?
> *Tech.* O my lord, 'tis sweet and full of pomp.
> *Usum.* To be a king is half to be a god.
> *Ther.* A god is not so glorious as a king.

and then from the Persian court. The blasphemous hyperbolical comparisons voiced by Tamburlaine's followers ought to be seen in full contrast to Cosroe's remarkable defence of the "powers that govern Persia":

> What means this devilish shepherd, to aspire
> With such a giantly presumption,
> To cast up hills against the face of heaven,
> And dare the force of angry Jupiter?
> But as he thrust them underneath the hills
> And pressed out fire from their burning jaws,
> So will I send this monstrous slave to hell
> Where flames shall ever feed upon his soul.
> . . .
> And since we all have sucked one wholesome air,
> And with the same proportion of elements
> Resolve, I hope we are resembled,
> Vowing our loves to equal death and life.
> Let's cheer our soldiers to encounter him,
> That grievous image of ingratitude,
> That fiery thirster after sovereignty ...
> That thus opposeth him against the gods
> And scorns the powers that govern Persia.
> (II.vi.1-8;25-31;39-40)

---

11 The Cyclops, freed from captivity by Zeus, in fact manufactured Zeus' thunder and lightning as a sign of their gratitude. Tamburlaine merges the "Cyclopian thunderbolts" into an oblique allusion to the revolt of the Titans.

The moral outrage that looms large in the reactions of the Persians reminds us of Mycetes' earlier complaints about the "lawless Scythian thief"; but in a more striking reversal of earlier praises of their ally, Cosroe and his followers now completely disqualify Tamburlaine's "presumption" as "monstrous," unnatural ("For he was never sprung of human race" II.vi.11), and "devilish" ("... such a devilish thief" II.vi.20). Cosroe's condemnation of Tamburlaine's "giantly presumption" and, especially, his description of Tamburlaine's *unnatural* ambition initiate a long series of loud protestations (the Persians, Bajazeth, Zabina, the Soldan, Arabia, Zenocrate) which the play invites us to compare with Tamburlaine's own interpretation of his quest, with his own understanding of Nature, rebellion and the will-to-power.

The play's dramatic structure, its developmental presentation of conflicts (offstage battles, onstage rhetorical confrontation), and its repetition of ritualized theatrical effects and stage images increasingly force the audience to dwell on Tamburlaine's relation to the moral censures expressed by those who suffer from the tragic reality of loss and defeat.

The way in which Cosroe's defeat is dramatized in fact highlights the clash of perspectives and values and points directly to the centre of Marlowe's conception of *1 Tamburlaine*. It is important to visualize the two crucial speeches of II.vii in their theatrical context. After the lost battle, the dying Cosroe is literally a "fallen prince"; Cosroe is "down" - at Tamburlaine's feet - whereas the victorious and upward striving Tamburlaine is "up" visually and symbolically. This central stage-tableau underscores the pathetically conventional moralization with which Cosroe responds to his own fall:

> Barbarous and bloody Tamburlaine,
> Thus to deprive me of my crown and life!
> Treacherous and false Theridamas,
> Even at the morning of my happy state,
> Scarce being seated in my royal throne,
> To work my downfall and untimely end!
> . . .
> Bloody and insatiate Tamburlaine!
>   (II.vii.1-6;11)

Cosroe's complaints, on the one hand, reinforce his earlier attack on Tamburlaine's blasphemous defiance of degree and order and continue to place Tamburlaine's "bloody" and unnatural presumption in a moral and theological context which provides stable assumptions about the sin of pride (cf. Meander's verdict: "Since with the spirit of his fearful pride / He dares so doubtlessly resolve of rule / And by profession be ambitious" II.vi.12-14), the violation of order, and the unnatural origin of power (cf. Ortygius' claim: "What god or fiend or spirit of the earth, / Or monster turned to manly shape ..." II.vi.15-16).

Furthermore, Cosroe's reference to the medieval Wheel of Fortune enlarges these moral assumptions and securely defines Cosroe's own ambition *within* a universe that is ordered and contained and explicabale. Cosroe, quite logically, finds himself betrayed by a rival who has demonstrated to him the evil and bloodshed manifest in a dramatic world of tragic limitations. Cosroe's tragic sense of the universe, heightened by his slow and agonizing death in front of his successor, places a heavy burden on Tamburlaine's defence of *his* view of the world. Needless to say, Tamburlaine's striking transumption of Cosroe's etho-political schemata has come to be seen as the most significant passage in the entire Marlowe canon.

> The thirst of reign and sweetness of a crown,
> That caused the eldest son of heavenly Ops
> To thrust his doting father from his chair
> And place himself in th'empyreal heaven,
> Moved me to manage arms against thy state.
> What better precedent than mighty Jove?
>   (II.vii.12-7)

The primary dramatic impact of Tamburlaine's entire speech is of course its overwhelming poetic superiority. Significantly, his imagination seems to become fully inspired only through fundamental comparisons with the gods and their symbolic representation of original power and authority. Tamburlaine turns Cosroe's moral argument completely upside down by first of all defining his victory as a *successful* usurpation of the royal seat (modelled after Jove and not after the unsuccessful Titanic revolt). In fact, he is not even interested in commenting upon Cosroe's downfall because he is instantly pursuing a symbolization of his aspirations on a more comprehensive level.

> Nature, that framed us of four elements
> Warring within our breasts for regiment,
> Doth teach us all to have aspiring minds:
> Our souls, whose faculties can comprehend
> The wondrous architecture of the world
> And measure every wand'ring planet's course,
> Still climbing after knowledge infinite
> And always moving as the restless spheres,
> Wills us to wear ourselves and never rest
> Until we reach the ripest fruit of all,
> That perfect bliss and sole felicity,
> The sweet fruition of an earthly crown.
> (II.vii.18-29)

Tamburlaine is translating the immediate theatrical reality (Cosroe's dying complaint) into another realm of significance entirely, and the upward reaching thrust of the poetry is perfectly expressive of the "restless" movement and surging ambition he is talking about. His sublime flight is in itself a kind of overmastering of Cosroe's static vision of fixed principles; Cosroe's insistence on stable systems of authority (natural and cosmic order; *de casibus* morality; divine retribution) that are basically derived from a common theocentric perspective is almost effortlessly swept aside by Tamburlaine's un-limiting metaphors.

There are two related aspects in this speech which I want to emphasize in particular. First, it seems important to approach Tamburlaine's view of Nature through his provocative use of mythical precepts. Contrary to his antagonists' subservience to a transcendent, divine Power, Tamburlaine not only claims "mighty Jove" as a suitable "precedent" for his own *god-like* aspiration but indeed seeks to introject the very power with which he can displace prior models and assert himself totally – subsuming all values into himself or, rather, creating them for himself and for others.

This is the hubristic tenor of Tamburlaine's metaphors of boundless "moving," "aspiring," and "climbing after knowledge infinite," which one must surely interpret as tropes for the basically non-specific will-to-power in order to avoid making nonsense of the metaphorical conception that lies behind Tamburlaine's new ethos of "restless" strife. Those values - and they are human values after all - which Tamburlaine seeks to "perfect" are values derived from both a divine and natural "order" which, paradoxically, is neither "ordered," nor constant, hierarchical and definite. In fact, Tamburlaine argues, it is precisely because the whole state of Nature is one of perpetual strife that our "souls" make us strive towards perfect fulfilment of that restless energy, insatiability, and contention which must be regarded as reflections of the universal principle.

What emerges here is a complicated and, in its consequences for the play's later orgies of violence and bloodshed, thoroughly shocking and unnerving doctrine.[12] It is complicated because its rhetorical celebration of limitless energy is apparently incongruous with its postulating of a definite, limited goal.[13] It becomes even more complicated, of course, if one tries to connect its basic thrust with the Neo-Platonic overtones which seem to promise the soul's upward striving from one level of beauty to another, to the final union with God ("that perfect bliss"). Yet Tamburlaine describes a limitless, restless strife or striving of a different kind, which he has already referred to as a god-like activity, and the culminating line that has

---

12 A.D. Hope, probably one of the few critics who is sensitive to Tamburlaine's provocative stance, offers an interesting reading of what he calls Tamburlaine's "humanism of war" (p. 119). From the classical texts accessible to Marlowe Hope infers that the dramatist may have borrowed the concept of "eternal strife" from Heraclitus. See "The Argument of Arms," *The Cave and the Spring* (Sidney: Rigby Ltd., 1965), pp. 117-128.
13 The view that the last line ("earthly crown") undermines the speech's metaphorical consistency and breaks its nobly aspiring movement has haunted Marlowe critics ever since John Addington Symonds called the line "Scythian bathos." As long as the speech will be quoted out of context and in conjunction with pious Neo-Platonic models of explanation, this view will most likely perpetuate itself.

upset so many critics could only be called anticlimactic and "bathetic"[14] if it pronounced its highest human ambition ("an earthly crown") in a naive or literal sense. But the jarring effect, if one wants to call it that, is too deliberate not to be regarded as an attempt to relate, however insufficiently, the sublime infinite quest through some kind of metonymic representation (*a* crown) which is - appropriately enough for Tamburlaine's stance - in itself a staggering rhetorical blasphemy.

But whereas Harry Levin, for example, declares the whole speech blasphemous because he starts out from the last line and contends that the "earthly crown is the notorious emblem of worldliness, heterodoxy, and pride of life,"[15] it seems more important, I believe, to recognize the tension between the aesthetic and moral content of the speech. And this tension can be resolved if we assume that the underlying logic of the speech works towards a complete transvaluation of the moral argument put forth by Cosroe.

As opposed to Cosroe's notion of a harmonious natural balance of energies, Tamburlaine enunciates his ethos of "restless" and "insatiate" movement, conceived for a world of complete *natural discord*. In contrast to the Renaissance belief in *discordia concors*, Tamburlaine's vision of the "warring" elements' permanent imbalance creates and determines a value-system, in accordance with the principle of strife and disorder, within which success is only measurable in terms of power and violence. From Cosroe's "fallen" perspective, such a morality and aesthetic of power must appear incomprehensible and terrible:

> The strangest men that ever Nature made!
> I know not how to take their tyrannies.
> (II.vii.40-41)

But in the very moment when Cosroe utters his dying words, Mar-

---

14 Cf. Levin, *The Overreacher*, p. 57.
15 Ibid.

lowe's dramaturgy enforces the vital reality of Tamburlaine's view of life with an expressive stage-tableau - a gesture frozen into significance: "*He* [Tamburlaine] *takes the crown and puts it on*" (s.d.II.vii.52). Tamburlaine takes possession of "an earthly crown," he performs the act of crowning *himself*, thus carrying out the very idea of "placing himself"(II.vii.15) in the foremost position, which he had preconceived in the image of the usurping Jove. At the same time, his "climbing up" becomes an image of the "restless" movement and struggle he had glorified in his speech, and while he is acting out his own self-image, Tamburlaine valorizes his concept of "endless strife" through a very important turn:

> *Though Mars himself, the angry god of arms,*
> *And all the earthly potentates conspire*
> *To dispossess me of this diadem,*
> *Yet will I wear it in despite of them.*
>   (II.vii.58-61;my emphasis)

He can no longer be satisfied with emulating divine "precedents": he has to assert himself against their power and make his own "will" absolute.

This self-assertion, which is fundamental to Tamburlaine's understanding of his quest for authority, becomes the central notion in a problematic series of escalating conflicts which I would again prefer to look at from the perspective of Tamburlaine's developing relation to the gods. It is in fact vital for our perception of the play to see Tamburlaine's encounter with his most formidable enemy in the light of the ever-increasing hubristic pride with which he *interprets* his relentless pursuit of earthly glory. When Bajazeth and his immense Turkish army rise as a challenge to Tamburlaine's power, Marlowe restricts the actual representation of the battle to a bare minimum (two trumpet signals; Bajazeth's fleeing across the stage, III.iii) and focusses instead on the elaborate dramatization of Tamburlaine's by now firmly ritualized strategy of verbal warfare.

It is his progressively agonistic confrontation with the gods, however, which establishes a pattern of verbal presumption that is directly relevant to his rhetorical outmanoeuvring of all human rivals. After having claimed Jove's special protection in the beginning, Tamburlaine gradually grows more determined and passionate in his wish to emulate his divine "precedents" for the sole purpose of challenging them, of becoming a rival or even superior "god of war"(cf.V.i.451). The sense of prophetic power that he claims to have ("I speak it, and my words are oracles" III.iii.102) is part of this comprehensive wish or will to subdue all external authority as well as all familiar metaphysical ideas of justice and order.

> For Will and Shall best fitteth Tamburlaine,
> Whose smiling stars give him assured hope
> Of martial triumph ere he meet his foes.
> I that am termed the scourge and wrath of God,
> The only fear and terror of the world,
> Will first subdue the Turk, and then ...
> (III.iii.41-6)

The "Will" and "Shall" of Tamburlaine's self-assured rhetoric reaches a peak of intensity during his encounter with Bajazeth. Acting out his threat to terrorize the world, Tamburlaine's treatment of his opponent becomes an almost unbearably brutal and shocking spectacle. It is certainly difficult to avoid the impression that the manner in which he humiliates his defeated rival - especially in the scenes in which he uses Bajazeth as a footstool or tortures him in a cage - seems to demonstrate, above all, the perverse wilfulness with which Tamburlaine carries his verbal and martial triumphs to the limit of possibility.

At the same time, his aggressiveness can appear so gratuitous and reckless that it becomes even more troublesome to hear him claim the consent of the Christian God. Even before the actual battle, Tamburlaine calls himself the "Scourge of God," a title awarded the historical Timur *after* he had raised the Turkish siege of Christian Constantinople in 1402. While Marlowe in fact presents Tamburlaine as a liberator of enslaved Christians from Islamic oppression, he does so only in order to manipulate the concept of vengeance which can be expected to underlie Tamburlaine's role as scourge. As so often in the play, Tamburlaine seems to echo the apocalyptic language of the Old Testament books where these portray the punishment God inflicted upon the sinful. The divinely appointed scourge of Isaiah x, for example, gives us the biblical paradigm for the workings of God's wrathful vengeance: after having been first used by God to castigate the wicked, he is destroyed in turn when he finally begins to mistake God's plan and accomplishments for his own.

The scourge thus stands in a highly ambiguous relationship to the god whose agent he is, and the conception of such a god itself can only be one that emphasizes ideas of divine wrath, revenge, and punishment. These ideas may point to a new representation of godhead that again conflicts with all the other images of deity that are expressed throughout the *Tamburlaine* plays.[16] But it is precisely this sense of inconsistency in Tamburlaine's views of the gods as protectors, examples, rivals, and punishers which ultimately helps us to understand the progressive pattern from which Tamburlaine's ethos of rebellion and struggle evolves.

The crescendo of Tamburlaine's glorification of his ethos of conflict culminates in his appropriation of the most frightening aspects of God's retributive justice. That his self-representation as "Scourge of God" appears blasphemous and perverse from the start is a measure of his tendency to keep the metaphysical and theological implications of such a representation at a distance and to see the God of vengeance - regardless of whether it is the Old Testament God or some other god - in his own image.

He constantly creates and recreates metaphors for those extreme spiritual states in which he experiences his own pervasive,

---

16 In her new book, *Hammer or Anvil: Psychological Patterns in Christopher Marlowe's Plays* (New Brunswick,N.J.: Rutgers Univ. Press, 1980), Constance Brown Kuriyama offers a perceptive analysis of the confusing picture established by the hero's contradictory attitudes toward religious concepts (pp. 9-14). However, she does not explore the conceptual contradictions in their relationship to the new ethos and form of the drama because she is mainly interested in psychobiographical aspects of Marlowe's work.

wrathful power as conqueror supreme. Life and death, heaven and hell, destruction and mercy seem to become aspects of the symbolic force with which Tamburlaine controls the action and ceaselessly strengthens the myth of his own divinity. Biblical images of divine wrath assume new emblematic meanings in the name of that "honour"(IV.ii.21)[17] which he defines for himself as heroic expression of an inflexible will to conquer and destroy.

Just before he initiates his new ritual order of colours - white, red, and black - Tamburlaine announces the end of an older authority represented by the outraged Turkish empress:

> ... her time is past:
> The pillars that have bolstered up those terms
> Are fall'n in clusters at my conquering feet.
> (III.iii.228-30)

A few moments later, he wears the white costume which is to symbolize his mercy; in this same costume, however, he literally mounts over a brutally degraded human footstool to his throne:

> Stoop, villain, stoop, stoop, for so he bids
> That may command thee piecemeal to be torn,
> Or scattered like the lofty cedar trees
> Struck with the voice of thund'ring Jupiter.
> (IV.ii.22-25)

As Tamburlaine mounts the throne, his use of Bajazeth as a foot-

---

[17] The most remarkable reversal of meaning in connection with the play on the word "honour" occurs in Act V, when the Virgins' address

> Most happy king and emperor of the earth,
> Image of *honour* and nobility,
> For whom the powers divine have made the world,
> And on whose throne the holy Graces sit ...

is first answered by Tamburlaine's merciless decision to have them slaughtered and, later on, cynically reinterpreted from his own perspective:

> *All sights of power to grace my victory;*
> And such are objects fit for Tamburlaine,
> Wherein as in a mirror may be seen
> *His honour, that consists in shedding blood.*
> (V.i.74-7;475-78,my emphasis)

stool provides not only a graphic visual representation of his
ascent to power, but also reflects and reinforces the aggressiveness of the imagery with which he projects the apocalyptic aura
of his competition with the gods. Just which god Tamburlaine has
in mind ("The chiefest God, first mover of that sphere ..." IV.
ii.8) is left in doubt, but the footstool motif could very well
imply the daring use of Psalm 110: "The Lord said unto my Lord:
'Sit thou at my right hand, until I make thine enemies thy footstool.'"[18]

It is obvious, however, that the play does not offer a familiar
Christian god; the symbolic footstool episode presents Tamburlaine's ideal of divine *furor* in such a shocking way that it becomes troubling to see it in connection with those images, drawn
from Christian as well as classical eschatology, which constantly
invoke the terror and chaos of the ultimate wrath and judgment.
By setting himself up in God's name as a "scourge and terror"
(IV.ii.32), Tamburlaine in fact begins to equate his fiery aspiration with the destructive fire of divine vengeance.[19] What is
so remarkable and disturbing about *Tamburlaine* is the fact that
the image of the fire of vengeance collects around itself most
of the others already mentioned; it heightens the impression
that divine power, however variously represented, is essentially
a paradoxically one-sided power. Within the orthodox Judeo-Christian tradition, God's anger has always been seen as a measure of

---

18 See also Cunningham, "Introduction," p. 46.
19 It has often been observed that fire and air are Tamburlaine's
    proper elements and that his imagery is full of cosmic figures
    of solar and meteoric energy. Cf. F.P. Wilson, *Marlowe and
    the Early Shakespeare* (Oxford: Clarendon, 1953), p. 31. It is
    interesting to see Tamburlaine's "fiery" rhetoric in relation
    to the Prophetic descriptions of the wrath of God. Jehovah's
    anger is generally conceived of in images of fire: "Behold,
    the name of the Lord cometh from far, burning with his anger,
    and the burden thereof is heavy: his lips are full of indignation, and his tongue is as a devouring fire ... And the
    Lord shall cause his glorious voice to be heard, and shall
    show the lighting down of his arm, with the indignation of
    his anger, and with the flame of a devouring fire, with scattering, and tempest, and hailstones" (Isa.xxx.27;30). See
    also Num.xi.1, and Rom.xiii.1-4.

his mercy and love;[20] for Tamburlaine, the God whose image he compares to his own, is always a God of War - a God whose punishing, rejecting left hand wields a tyrannous and bloody power that concedes no redemption.[21]

The effects of this idea of divine retribution on the two *Tamburlaine* plays are of considerable interest, and the questions of ethics and belief that are generated by Tamburlaine's self-styled role as scourge complicate our understanding of Marlowe's drama in a way that prefigures the difficulties we encounter in *Doctor Faustus*. One major effect is clearly noticeable in the new dramaturgical emphasis which Marlowe gives to the suffering of Tamburlaine's victims. Joel Altman argues that the Bajazeth-episode is the beginning of a development which places Tamburlaine's actions "in a recognizably 'tragical' context."[22] Altman's claim that Tamburlaine's infliction of humiliating punishments on Bajazeth and Zabina *magnifies* the two victims' physical pain and mental deterioration and thus exposes Tamburlaine as a cruel, barbarous, and bloody tyrant is clearly addressed to Marlowe's technique of manipulating audience sympathy. While it is certainly true that Tamburlaine's tyranny excites revulsion, it is also correct to say that the play asks its audience to admire his awesome integrity and view his actions under the imperatives of heroic conquest.

It is perhaps best to speak of a doubleness of effect; the audience's sympathy for the unusual boldness of Tamburlaine's success-

---

20 Although the ideas of the wrath of God have a distinctly emphatic presence in the Old Testament and the New, the fundamental concept of God's justice entails a generally balanced view of divine mercy and righteous anger. Accordingly, this concept is aligned with simple ethical principles: good is rewarded, evil retributively punished. For the Biblical texts that link these ideas of God's justice with the concept of the "Scourge," see Isa. x.24-27, and 1 Chron. xxi.15.
21 Cf. Susan Snyder, "The Left Hand of God: Despair in Medieval and Renaissance Tradition," *Studies in the Renaissance*, 12 (1965), 58-59, et passim.
22 *The Tudor Play of Mind*, p. 334.

ful rise is stressed against its growing awareness of the actual monstrosity of his claims and deeds. This monstrosity, vastly amplified and complicated in the second part of *Tamburlaine*, has generally been thought to clarify the ethical purport of the drama. Nothing becomes clearer, however, when we hear Tamburlaine proclaim:

> Now clear the triple region of the air
> And let the majesty of heaven behold
> Their scourge and terror tread on emperors ...
> For I, the chiefest lamp of all the earth,
> First rising in the east with mild aspect
> But fixed now in the meridian line,
> Will send up fire to your turning spheres
> And cause the sun to borrow light of you.
> (IV.ii.30-2;36-40)

It is almost as if Tamburlaine's disturbing self-conception as the "Scourge of God," which is here connected with the daring image of his ascent to godliness ("the chiefest lamp"), is to test the rigour and consistency of conventional values and sensibilities. If we say that Tamburlaine breaks every rule; that he humiliates his capitive enemies by forcing them to suffer their total degradation; that he demolishes a code of war which others take for granted and defines his own moral code; that he extends his pride and insatiable ambition into a mania for destruction and defiance of gods and men, ordering massacres, devastating whole cities, and even killing his own son (in Part 2), then we are describing one aspect of Marlowe's manipulation of audience response. Then we are talking about the audience's outraged sense of justice and what Altman called a "recognizably 'tragical' context."

Tamburlaine, to be sure, possesses "to an unsurpassable degree those traits which, in tragedy, traditionally provoke retribution from fate and are meant to be regarded as tragic sins."[23] It may be indicative of the manner in which Marlowe's strategy works, therefore, to find a critic such as Altman duped into sympathy

---

23 Timothy G.A. Nelson, "Marlowe and his Audience: A Study of *Tamburlaine*," *SoR*, 3 (1969), 249.

with Tamburlaine's enemies[24] and into protest against the hero's brutal treatment of them without noticing that the dramatist is quite deliberately and provocatively arousing in his audience a confident expectation that Tamburlaine's hubristic bravura will be punished with an unusually terrible fall.

Practically all of Tamburlaine's enemies - Mycetes, Cosroe, Agydas, Bajazeth, Zabina, the Soldan, Arabia, the Governor of Damascus (in Part 1), and Orcanes, Callapine, Olympia, Jerusalem, the Governor of Babylon, Amasia (in Part 2) - express their views on what is happening to them in conventional moral terms. They persistently prophesy Tamburlaine's fall, pray for superior powers to stop and punish him, or throw the most horrible curses at him. Bajazeth's ominous prediction

> Great Tamburlaine, great in my overthrow,
> Ambitious pride shall make thee fall as low
> For treading on the back of Bajazeth.
> (IV.ii.75-7)

can be said to concur as poignantly with the audience's normal preconceptions about the nature of tragedy and of life as Zenocrate's anxious moralizing hymn over the dead bodies of Bajazeth and Zabina:

> Those that are proud of fickle empery
> And place their chiefest good in earthly pomp-
> Behold the Turk and his great emperess!
> Ah Tamburlaine my love, sweet Tamburlaine,
> That fightest for sceptres and for slippery crowns,
> Behold the Turk and his great emperess!
> (V.i.353-58)

A few lines later, Zenocrate's warning against transitory pomp and vain pride and her vision of justice and forgiveness are directed immediately at Tamburlaine:

> Ah mighty Jove and holy Mahomet,
> Pardon my love, O pardon his contempt
> Of earthly fortune and respect of pity,

---

24 See his claim, for example, that Bajazeth and Zabina, as well as Zenocrate, can be regarded as the "moral touchstones" of the play (*The Tudor Play of Mind*, p. 335).

>   And let not conquest ruthlessly pursued
>   Be equally against his life incensed
>   In this great Turk and hapless emperess!
>   (V.i.364-69)

Nearly all commentators quote Zenocrate's lament and point out that it is Tamburlaine's own mistress whose verbalization of fear and indignation provides the true ethical tenor, the true "thesis,"[25] underlying the spectacle of Tamburlaine's titanic insolence. Taking up Zenocrate's judgment about "slippery crowns" and the "wavering turns of war," the Reverend Moelwyn Merchant believes that the play "insistently" asserts "the older moral order by which the private virtues of pity and humulity are relevant in statecraft" and uses this order for the "fullest criticism" of the "mere" amoral force of virtù backed by Fortune, "the ideal of the Machiavellian powerful ruler."[26] He concludes that nearly all the concepts Marlowe presents in his drama are commonplaces and prove him "almost oppressively orthodox."[27]

We could have agreed with the Reverend M. Merchant, had he only noticed that Marlowe indeed exploits his audience's orthodox expectations and reactions by systematically enhancing the *de casibus* pattern in his play and letting it escalate toward Tamburlaine's anticipated overthrow, only to swerve sharply away from all assumptions about tragic "rightness" and inevitability at the critical points.

It has been largely overlooked that Marlowe augments the movement of potentially tragic significance almost exclusively by having Tamburlaine's victims enact a series of *de casibus* moralities, while the play's actual dramatic logic works towards and

---

25 The term is Altman's (p. 335), but the idea is basically identical with all those interpretations that have followed Battenhouse's and Cole's moral reading of the two plays as one ten-act tragedy.
26 "Marlowe the Orthodox," in *Christopher Marlowe*, ed. Brian Morris (London: Benn, 1968), pp. 189f. This collection of essays from the York Symposium on Marlowe (1968) will be quoted as *Morris* from now on.
27 Ibid., p. 182.

demands acceptance of a new ethos, a new logic of power which is interpreted as a permanent crisis that produces and, in turn, is subsumed by Tamburlaine's individual acts of *will*. It is of course interesting to know that there has been a traditional scourge concept which "serves to explain historical calamities by showing that they are chastisements of sin ... and it assures tyrants that God is not helpless before their power but that He will, when He has used them, destroy them utterly."[28] But even after we have heard the Soldan of Egypt's terrified condemnation,

> A monster of five hundred thousand heads,
> Compact of rapine, piracy, and spoil,
> The scum of men, the hate and scourge of God,
> Raves in Egyptia ...
>   (IV.iii.7-10)

we cannot but admit that the Soldan, too, has misunderstood Tamburlaine's self-styled role as "scourge and terror" and the force of his will and imagination which triumphs over all supposedly ruinous attributes of his aspiration.

Tamburlaine is *not* "utterly" destroyed. Imposing *his* will on all others, he continues to enact, with relentless violence, his own principle of endless strife - defying all traditional assumptions with his successful, unpunished hubris. After his victory over the Turkish Emperor, and after he has made good his claim to be a "Scourge of God," Tamburlaine is not onstage anymore when Bajazeth and Zabina (and Zenocrate later on) voice their complaints. He has already marched off to fight and win another battle, and his absolutely triumphant will-to-power remains a persistent challenge to the belief that, in a world of divine justice, he is as vulnerable to retribution as Bajazeth is.

Tamburlaine enjoys the brutal punishment of the vainglorious Bajazeth and proceeds to the sadistic slaughter of the Damascus Virgins in a manner which stands out as a shocking defiance against the very order of retributive justice whose "instrument"

---

28 Battenhouse, p. 113. See also Fredson Bowers, "Hamlet as Minister and Scourge," *PMLA*, 70 (1955), 740-49.

he claims to be. The failure of Zenocrate's sentimental preconceptions about the tragic nature of pride and ambition becomes obvious; her moral pieties come to appear totally inadequate in comparison with Tamburlaine's absolute morality of power. Zenocrate's assumptions about a higher Law are countered by Tamburlaine's progressive realization of his own prophecies: he indeed becomes god-like in achieving the highest felicity of all, the supremacy of power which makes him conquer Fate and "countermand the gods."

At the end of Part 1, Marlowe's triumphantly victorious hero has displaced all tragic implications of his "conquest ruthlessly pursued," and Zenocrate herself, emblem of beauty and pity, is symbolically overcome by Tamburlaine's decision to crown her as his Juno-like queen:

> As Juno, when the giants were suppressed
> That darted mountains at her brother Jove,
> So looks my love, shadowing in her brows
> Triumphs and trophies for my victories.
> (V.i.511-14)

Silently, Zenocrate yields to Tamburlaine's self-assertion and her becoming an icon of his power. Even before the play celebrates the hero's unimpeded pursuit of power in this final stage tableau, there are at least two moments in which Marlowe draws attention to the Tamburlainean ethic of conflict and provokes his audience to compare it with the moral ideals voiced by Zenocrate. It is hardly surprising that these passages have been overlooked by those commentators who wish to see Zenocrate as the moral touchstone in the play. And both moments, I believe, are crucial to the conception of Tamburlaine's heroism in Part 1 as in Part 2.

In the first incident, it is Bajazeth himself who, after all his railing, finally reaches an unexpected insight into the true nature of Tamburlaine, which of course leaves him no further hope and brings about his suicide:

> Ah fair Zabina, we may curse his power,
> The heavens may frown, the earth for anger quake,

> But such a star hath influence in his sword
> As rules the skies, and countermands the gods.
> (V.i.230-33)

Zabina immediately adds:

> Then is there left no Mahomet, no God,
> No fiend, no Fortune, nor no hope of end
> To our infamous, monstrous slaveries?
> (V.i.239-41)

Tamburlaine's unambiguously cruel yet absolutely triumphant power is seen here as exploding all preconceptions about divine or infernal control of human affairs. One cannot say, however, that the world Tamburlaine dominates is best mirrored in madness and suicide, with Bajazeth and Zabina. Bajazeth in fact accepts the inevitable truth that a defeat in the struggle for absolute, unlimited power must involve the loss of everything. Defeat, like victory, is total, absolute. Whether or not this view of life is strange and repugnant to most of us, it must be taken seriously since the whole poetic thrust and the language of action in the *Tamburlaine* plays are based on it.

The "virtue" of "true nobility" which Tamburlaine celebrates in his long soliloquy on "beauty" can only be understood in terms of the morality of power and the logic of power that Tamburlaine conceives of as intrinsic to human aspiration: only the "highest reaches"(V.i.168) of human desire can achieve the transcendence of all conventions and norms which seek its containment. Only the capability of striving for the perfection of the human in terms of power can have meaning and value,[29] and Tamburlaine demonstrates that it is only through his heretical rebellion

---

[29] As Hope puts it, "Tamburlaine's passion for sovereignty has the same ultimate source as the insatiable scientific impulse and the quest for beauty." It is one passion that makes Tamburlaine ceaselessly strive for the perfection of his nature, and only "if it is taken as one argument has the play meaning and coherence." Hope adds that it is the power of Tamburlaine's *poetry* which shares the supremacy of his nature and makes us apprehend his real genius. See "The Argument of Arms," pp. 119;127f.

against and overmastering of other systems of authority that he can *create meaning*, "confute those blind geographers"(IV.iv.77) and moralizers, and make "sights of power" in his own name.

Zenocrate is quite right in assuming that such power is perpetually endangered ("the wavering turns of war") because it is determined by a measurement of competing forces. But her fear and moral sensibilities are challenged by an important judgment that Anippe provides for us:

> Madam, content yourself and be resolved
> Your love hath Fortune so at his command
> That she shall stay, and turn her wheel no more
> As long as life maintains his mighty arm
> That fights for honour to adorn your head.
> (V.i.373-77)

The image of limitation (a transcendent *Fortune*) is transformed here into an image of Tamburlaine's superior power; yet, more importantly, Anippe's assertion recalls for us Tamburlaine's vision of unending strife and confrontation which is amplified during the coronation scene at the end of Part 1.

> The god of war resigns his room to me,
> Meaning to make me general of the world:
> Jove, viewing me in arms, looks pale and wan,
> Fearing my power should pull him from his throne.
> (V.i.451-54)

As Tamburlaine makes abundantly clear, especially in the continuous references to his competition with the gods, the end of his pursuit of power is *not* achievment of "an earthly crown" nor truce-taking "with all the world"(V.i.530) but *endless strife*. He has hardly announced his marriage to Zenocrate when he reaffirms his unquenchable "thirst" for expanded conquest and projects new objectives for his unfulfilled desire. If Part One ends with a daring invitation to admire a shockingly capacious heroic image, Part Two - despite its internal complications - logically follows and re-affirms Tamburlaine's conception of strife as a norm of human living and pursues its ambitious theme as well as its theatrical style in a sustained, deliberate response to the original play.

Immediately after his entry to I.iii (*"with drums and trumpets"* s.d.), Tamburlaine sets the tone for the play by returning to the soaring idiom of those visions of unending conquest which inspired his career at its inception. Zenocrate still fails to understand his "argument of arms":

> *Zen.* Sweet Tamburlaine, when wilt thou leave these arms
> And save thy sacred person free from scathe
> And dangerous chances of the wrathful war?
> *Tam.* When heaven shall cease to move on both the poles,
> And when the ground whereon my soldiers march
> Shall rise aloft and touch the horned moon,
> And not before, my sweet Zenocrate.
> (*2 Tamb*.I.iii.9-15)

Tamburlaine's answer points to the fundamental, abstract principle that had governed the huge fantasy of power and conquest in Part 1 and enabled him to rise to a sublime flight beyond all conceivable tragic limitations. Having defined his own ethos of power, Tamburlaine succeeded in deflating and subduing cosmic as well as merely human adversaries and in suspending any doubts about the context of limitless performance which his iconoclastic imagination has created.

I would argue that the revolutionary meaning of *1 Tamburlaine* resides to a large extent in the theatrical power and imaginative appeal with which Marlowe sustains this heroic idealism and brings it to a triumphant "conclusion," a conclusion which, in fact, symbolically suggests that Tamburlaine's vital force is in a perpetual state of *potentiality*.

We can say, then, that Tamburlaine's answer to Zenocrate also points to the severe problem Marlowe faced in having to dramatize his hero's continued quest for omnipotence in a sequel that was not planned and therefore apt to foster repetition and exhaustion of the original style and substance. In view of the marked sensationalism and dramaturgical extravagance of Part 2, it is quite important to recognize Marlowe's changed attitude towards the theatrical resources of his stage, which in turn affects the imaginative orientation of the "phenomenon" Tamburlaine the Great and, on the whole, intimates new dramatic interests and concerns. If we speak of a change in theatrical perspective, it is necessary to keep the original conception of *Tamburlaine the Great* in mind.

Ellis-Fermor suggests that the hero of Part 2 "is marked by a savageness, an ever-increasing extravagance, a lack at once of inspiration and balance" which have "little or nothing to do with the glittering figure of the earlier part ... These later qualities are the logical outcome of the situation that Marlowe created when he set out to write a 'second part' to the study of a character who can, by the very nature of his being, only have a first part."[30]

I have tried to suggest that the sensational success of Marlowe's "glittering figure" upon the London stages must have been due to the extraordinary vision of greatness which the play's enormous rhetorical and metaphorical power inspires. It is this power of Tamburlaine's heroic rhetoric which largely represents those qualities in Marlowe's overreaching hero which must have puzzled the contemporary audiences because they provocatively called into question both the ethics and the structure of earlier plays. I have tried to show how Tamburlaine's audacious proclamation of imaginative freedom works in terms of the play's underlying logic which is clearly at odds with comfortable preconceptions about the workings of divine providence and will in drama and, therefore, is essentially engaged in subverting theatrical orthodoxy.

The singular aesthetic force of Tamburlaine's imaginative overreaching is successfully sustained mainly because the hero's new ethos of power can rule in an unconditioned dramatic world in which his transfigurative speech-acts create forms of symbolic significance that outpace the requirements of *concrete representation* (including our modern notion of "naturalistic" acting). I want to ask in the remaining pages what problems

---

30 Ellis-Fermor, *Christopher Marlowe*, p. 39.

Marlowe obviously encountered when facing the full, logical consequences of his hero's position in the second play which he apparently wrote to exploit the general success of the original appeal. How could he uphold the original's purity of conception - the vision of unending strife and conquest - and at the same time place Tamburlaine in a dramatic context in which possibilities are limited and "the ugly monster Death" will end his career: "For Tamburlaine, the scourge of God, must die"(V.iii. 248)? And if we think of the symbolic dimension of Tamburlaine's heroic conceits in Part 1, how do we interpret Marlowe's increased indulgence in the sensationalism of violence and cruelty and , at times, rather furious iconoclasm, which often tends to reduce Tamburlaine's ambitions to mindless rage and aggression?

One could of course argue that Marlowe is capitalizing on the sensational theatrical effects precisely because they grant him a provocative and mischivious exploration of the nightmare world that Tamburlaine creates with an endless *repetition* of the very conquests which Zenocrate has become so weary of. It is also interesting to consider the fact that the death scene at the end of Part 2 could be interpreted as another surprising *coup* - a kind of crowning panegyric on the departing and still triumphant conqueror.[31] I want to restrict myself here to a comparison between two images which have a crucial status both in Part 1 and Part 2 and convey the distinct theatrical modes in which Marlowe realizes Tamburlaine's affirmation of his hubris. Moreover, the images in question have a larger significance for the entire Marlowe canon.

Right after his victory over Bajazeth, Tamburlaine not only compares himself to a greater sun than any ruled by Jove ("For I, the chiefest lamp of all the earth ...") but goes on to surprise us with an even more audacious vision:

---

31 Cf. Nelson, "Marlowe and his Audience," 251. Waith speaks of the "infinite pathos" of the final scene whose "dominant appeal is to the wonder aroused by vast heroic potential" (*The Herculean Hero*, pp. 86-87).

> *As was the fame of Clymen's brain-sick son*
> *That almost brent the axletree of heaven,*
> So shall our swords, our lances and our shot
> Fill all the air with fiery meteors;
> *Then, when the sky shall wax as red as blood,*
> *It shall be said I made it red myself,*
> To make me think of nought but blood and war.
>
> (1 Tamb.IV.ii.49-55, my emphasis)

This is a typical but especially powerful instance of the manner in which Tamburlaine's poetry, in Part 1, rises with astonishing visionary faith above the immediate dramatic context and interprets the emblematic meaning of his appearance and his deeds. "Interpreting," for Tamburlaine, usually means *transforming* disturbing circumstances into positive symbolic significance. This is particularly true for the scene I refer to; after all, he had just brutally degraded his victim and proclaimed his tyrannous and bloody rule as "scourge and terror" of the world.

Against this background of the spectacular fall of an emperor, Tamburlaine begins a long oration during which he projects his meteoric rise as a terrifying cosmic element that threatens both heaven and earth with its consuming fire. At the pivotal point of this vision, he proceeds to a further hyperbolical turn - conjuring up the violent image of Phaeton's catastrophic ride on the Sun's chariot.

This is not a struggle between Tamburlaine and Bajazeth any more; it is a struggle of comparison, fought with poetic images. Tamburlaine seeks confrontation with the "chiefest god"; he will himself attempt to burn Jove's sky and outdo the "fame" of Apollo's son. Comparing his march against Damascus to the havoc Phaeton wrought when he tried to control the chariot of the sun, Tamburlaine appropriates the myth of Phaeton's fate[32] and pro-

---

[32] The Phaeton myth, like that of Icarus, has a prominent place among the reiterated images which carry the peculiar impetus of heroic desire with which we identify Marlowe's overreaching heroes. See, for example, *Dido Queen of Carthage* (V.i. 243-45); *Dr Faustus* (Prologue 21-23); *The Massacre at Paris* (I.ii.99-104), and *Edward II* (V.i.11-22). For a discussion of Marlowe's "obsession" with the archetype, see Levin, *The Overreacher*, pp. 182-85.

jects his heroic desire in figures of a *successful* cosmic disaster, inviting us to admire his daring ambition to set fire to heaven itself.

The classical myth must have been thoroughly familiar to Marlowe's audience; Ovid's *Metamorphoses* supplied the Elizabethans with their favourite handbook of mythology. Ovid's depiction of the rebellious son's failure to displace the sun-father is translated into an unmistakably moralized version by Arthur Golding, however, and this moralized account of the myth inevitably links Phaeton with Lucifer's revolt against God and thus transforms the tale into a topos of blasphemous ambition with tragic consequences.[33]

It seems as if Tamburlaine rejoices in the most awesome aspects of this emblem of tragic pride: he emphasizes the very qualities of reckless disruption and turns a myth of tragic failure into a myth of glorious success, completely transfiguring the traditional ethical tropes into an autistic fantasy ("It shall be said I made it red myself, / To make me think of naught but blood and war"). As so often in the play, Tamburlaine's hubris defies tragedy, and it is an almost obsessive fascination that speaks through the rhetorical blasphemies of Marlowe's hero. The stress pattern in the passage I quoted is particularly interesting as the "mighty lines" are here full of important key-words and internal echoes ("fame"; "brain-sick"; "son"; "air"; "fiery";"red", etc.). Tamburlaine exalts the very *madness* or damnable ambition which has always been outlawed by tradition and the dominant culture. In order to do so he must violently reshape the language of myth in his own creative and destructive images of "fiery" passion.[34]

---

33 Phaeton's audacity becomes an expression of "ambition blynd ... the end whereof is miserie." For Golding's portrayal of the "rechelesse sonne," see *The xv Bookes of P.Ovidius Naso...*, Bk.II, 1-415 (Nims, pp. 31-42).
34 For a similar though more detailed and provocative interpretation of this important passage, see Benston, "The Shaping of the Marlovian Sublime," chap. 3.

Consuming fire and passion are a norm of feeling in this unusual play, and words and actions reflect Tamburlaine's wish to court disaster and think "of naught but blood and war" with shocking insistence. In Part 1, the iconoclastic character of Tamburlaine's stance makes itself felt especially through those images of disaster which Marlowe deliberately exploits for his own purpose. The emblem of "Clymen's brain-sick son," like the concept of the Scourge of God, is daringly relativized: it ceases to be simply a homiletic commonplace whose function is to warn against rebellion and to reinforce authority.[35] *1 Tamburlaine*, to a large extent, creates a successful fantasy of epic glory, valorizing Tamburlaine's heroic "madness" in its own context. As he demonstrates in his extraordinary soliloquy on Zenocrate's idealized beauty, the Tamburlaine of Part 1 is not obsessed by the kind of frantic "madness" that overshadows Part 2 and that makes him indeed think *exclusively* of "blood and war."

The change in tone and physical impact becomes immediately recognizable after Zenocrate's death in Part 2. The cohesion between metaphorical claim and dramatic realization, word and deed, emblem and significance, which characterized the structure and theatrical orientation of *1 Tamburlaine*, begins to break apart when Tamburlaine's "impassionate fury" (title-page to Part 2) over the death he cannot prevent dissipates the symbolic power his former rhetorical flights possessed. His desperate lament and impotent rage sound merely unnerving

> *Ther.* Ah, good my lord, be patient, she is dead,
> And all this raging cannot make her live.
> If words might serve, our voice hath rent the air...
> Nothing prevails, for she is dead, my lord.
>   (II.iv.119-21;124)

and finally culminate not in hyperboles of grief, but in the gruesome spectacle of a burning town (Larissa) with the flames of which Tamburlaine wants to make the sky literally red.

---

35 Cf. Greenblatt's view of *Tamburlaine* as a playfully "admonitory" fiction which teases its audience with the "form" of the cautionary tale, "only to violate the convention"(p.202).

Tamburlaine's continuing pursuit of power and conquest is more and more placed inside a visible context which is less inspiring than simply horrific. The glamour and mystery of the earlier conquests are largely dissipated by the orgy of atrocities that are showered upon the stage by the forced literalization of gestures and claims which could, otherwise, be expressed in terms of symbolic action had the sequel not dictated their continued "performance."

I am interested here in the most famous literalization of all, one that needs careful attention because it involves an irreconcilable ambivalence which, ultimately, reflects back upon the whole problem of the play's ethical position.

Near the end of Act IV, Tamburlaine makes good one of his earlier "dreaming prophecies" from Part 1 ("Is it not passing brave to be a king, / And ride in triumph through Persepolis?") and comes on stage literally drawn in his chariot by the captive Turkish kings, "*with bits in their mouths*," as the stage-direction informs us; we can envisage Tamburlaine himself standing upright, "*reins in his left hand, in his right hand a whip, with which he scourgeth them*" (s.d.IV.iii). Exulting in his triumphant power, he baits his captives and shouts his famous lines:

> Holla, ye pampered jades of Asia!
> What, can ye draw but twenty miles a day,
> And have so proud a chariot at your heels,
> And such a coachman as great Tamburlaine?
> . . .
> The horse that guide the golden eye of heaven
> And blow the morning from their nostrils,
> Making their fiery gait above the clouds,
> Are not so honoured in their governor
> As you, ye slaves, in mighty Tamburlaine.
> (IV.iii.1-4;7-11)

The response to such a performance can only be divided, contradictory, uncertain. Eugene Waith, for example, calls it "a theatrical image of unforgettable brilliance, presenting eye and ear with this conqueror of conquerors who calls himself 'the scourge of God,'" but admits that it is also coloured with a savage humour that "invites comic treatment, and thus, momentarily at least, undercuts Herculean nobility."[36] Cunningham thinks it is awkward and ponders: "Boötes drives oxen through the sky; Phaethon the sun's chariot; Tamburlaine his captive kings, scourging them with a metaphor turned all too literal, on the brink of absurdity."[37] In whatever way we react, the stage image surely remains one of the most powerful in Elizabethan drama, and part of that power must lie in the paradoxical ease with which it combines its magnificent and grotesque aspects. The emblem and its connotations - triumph, glory, cruelty, pride, excess - seem clear enough. And yet, moral interpretations will not work in the unequivocal fashion in which they were prescribed by Gascoigne's *Jocasta*, where we encounter the allegorical pantomime of a king sitting in a chariot "drawne in by foure Kinges ... Representing unto us Ambition,"[38] or by Heywood's *The Hierarchie of the Blessed Angells* which links together Tamburlaine's precursor-figures as examples of futile, blasphemous pretentiousness:

>   What madnesse is it for an heauy load
>   Of putred Flesh, that onely hath aboad
>   Here in the lower world ...
>   Either like bold aspiring *Phaeton*,
>   To aime at the bright Chariot of the Sun?
>   Or with his waxen wings, as *Icarus* did,
>   Attempt what God and Nature haue forbid?
>   What is this lesse, than when the Gyants stroue
>   To mutiny and menace war 'gainst *Ioue*?[39]

---

36 Eugene M. Waith, "Marlowe and the Jades of Asia," *SEL*, 5 (1965), 231-32.

37 "Introduction" to *Tamburlaine the Great*, pp. 69-70. See also J.R. Mulryne and Stephen Fender, "Marlowe and the 'Comic Distance,'" in *Morris*, pp. 51-58; Robert Cockcroft, "Emblematic Irony: Some Possible Significances of Tamburlaine's Chariot," *RMS*, 12 (1968), 33-55, and Aden Ross, "Tragedy of the Absurd: Marlowe's *Tamburlaine* and Camus's *Caligula*," *Thoth*, 13, no.2 (1973), 3-9.

38 *Jocasta*, first dumb show, in *The Complete Works of George Gascoigne*, ed. John W. Cunliffe (1907; rpt. New York: Greenwood Press, 1969), I, 246. The last dumb show in this play presents another elaborate stage picture: the personification of Fortune enters riding in a chariot. The stage-business is meant to reflect the fickleness of Fortune in her dealings with proud and mighty men. The stage-directions conclude: "This done, she was drawen eftsones about the stage in this

The dramatic action in the chariot scene, on the other hand, confuses the issue even more; while Tamburlaine is claiming that the strength with which he can drive the chariot *well* (unlike poor Phaeton) proves his "valour more divine"(IV.iii.15), his followers have already begun to mock and brutalize the other captive kings, and shortly afterwards there is another shift in tone when the savageness of the stage violence gives way to farce as the soldiers begin to chase the Turkish concubines around the stage.

Eugene Waith thinks that this incident, seen as a "burlesque rape of the Sabine women,"[40] must have been theatrically successful precisely because of its frivolity. And Harry Levin admires the whole scene because it audaciously takes a metaphor and acts it out, "turning a manner of speaking into a mode of action ... concretely realizing what had theretofore subsisted on the plane of precept and fantasy."[41] Yet the question remains the same: just how literal can one get in depicting Tamburlaine's "lust" for power? Is Marlowe playing a trick on his audience? Is he pushing the representation of his hero's ambition to the brink of anarchic playfulness, of murderous practical jokes?

The strained conjunction of metaphor and fact may point to a more serious problem, however, that is intrinsically connected with the second play's emphasis on the sadistic excess and night-

---

order, and then departed, leaving unto us a plaine Type or figure of unstable fortune, who dothe oftentimes raise to heighte of dignitie ... and in like manner throweth downe from the place of promotion ..." (*The Complete Works*,I,308). Huston Diehl, in "The Iconography of Violence in English Renaissance Tragedy," *RenD*, 11 (1980), 27-44, mentions this dumb-show (*Jocasta*) in connection with *Tamburlaine* and comes to the conclusion that a great number of stage images in Elizabethan drama have a clear significance as symbolic icons and, necessarily, develop and advance widely understood moral and ethical concepts.

39 Thomas Heywood, *The Hierarchie of the Blessed Angells.Their Names, Orders and Offices. The Fall of Lucifer with his Angells* (London: Adam Islip, 1635), Bk.III, p. 147.
40 "Marlowe and the Jades of Asia," 232.
41 *The Overreacher*, p. 67.

marish compulsiveness of Tamburlaine's never-ending obsession with conquest. Such an obsession, simply by the logic of Tamburlaine's pursuit of an elusive absolute, almost inevitably leads to theatrical improvisations, to collisions that reveal the terrible limitations looming behind a life doomed to endless repetition.

The conditionality of a world in which the literal aspects of conquest increasingly show their ugly faces[42] proves hostile to Tamburlaine's immortal longings. The material immediacy of his chariot, drawn by exhausted captives, indeed indicates that the fantasy life of the Scythian "Scourge of God" has lost much of its imaginative and prophetic dimensions - especially if we compare the "pampered jades of Asia" to Tamburlaine's earlier self-projection as a successful Phaeton. The Tamburlaine who actually sits on a chariot and prepares himself for his march against Babylon wields a literal scourge and merely looks like a self-obsessed tyrant:

> Thus am I right the scourge of highest Jove,
> And see the figure of my dignity
> By which I hold my name and majesty.
> (IV.iii.24-26)

But near the end of this scene, when the idea and impact of Tamburlaine's "figure" (literally: the whip and the chariot onstage) seem very nearly exhausted, something very astonishing happens. Leaving the exasperating context of gratuitous stage-business behind, Tamburlaine bursts into a tremendous paean to his unstilled heroic desire. Outlining further conquests and projecting his triumphal return to "my native city Samarcanda"(107),

---

42 See, for example, Techelles' morbid depiction of the sack of Babylon (V.i.203-208):

> Thousands of men, drowned in Asphaltis' lake,
> Have made the water swell above the banks,
> And fishes fed by human carcasses,
> Amazed, swim up and down upon the waves
> As when they swallow asafoetida,
> Which makes them fleet aloft and gasp for air.

Tamburlaine's breathtaking fantasies rise to new, ecstatic heights:

> Thorough the streets with troops of conquered kings
> I'll ride in golden armour like the sun,
> And in my helm a triple plume shall spring,
> Spangled with diamonds dancing in the air,
> To note me emperor of the threefold world:
> Like to an almond tree ymounted high
> Upon the lofty and celestial mount
> Of ever-green Selinus, quaintly decked
> With blooms more white than Herycina's brows,
> Whose tender blossoms tremble every one
> At every little breath that thorough heaven is blown.
> Then in my coach like Saturn's royal son,
> Mounted his shining chariot, gilt with fire,
> And drawn with princely eagles through the path
> Paved with bright crystal and enchased with stars,
> When all the gods stand gazing at his pomp:
> So will I ride through Samarcanda streets
> Until my soul, dissevered from this flesh,
> Shall mount the milk-white way and meet him there.
> To Babylon, my lords, to Babylon!
> (IV.iii.114-33)

Reclaiming his former sublime rhetoric, Tamburlaine's speech transports him back to the realm of metaphorical conquest and *poetic* competition with the gods. He not only compares himself in his chariot first to Apollo and then to Jove, but also projects his ultimate elevation to a higher throne. In this grandiose fantasy of his final march, the proud charioteer becomes a god whose image of himself again reinforces the ethos of power that he had pronounced all along: Tamburlaine, like "Saturn's royal son," has taken part in the archetypal ritual of rebellion, the perpetual struggle against authority, which alone could afford him to rise above the limits of his condition.

In the original play, Tamburlaine's heroic fantasy was as unlimited as his conquests were effortless. In this scene, however, the great effort of will is obvious, and the significance of his speech is a different one. The breathless hyperboles of his poetic flight amount to a series of extreme gestures - as if to counteract and exorcise threatening limitations and to hold on to his grand illusion of divine omnipotence. And these gestures cannot be seen or heard without the theatrical image with which they are juxtaposed.

At the beginning of his long speech, we find an implicit stage-direction in the text; answering Techelles' proposal to start with the attack on Babylon, Tamburlaine shouts: "We will, Techelles - forward then, ye jades!"(IV.iii.97). The chariot cannot be swung round and moved off since Tamburlaine here begins his long triumphant speech (36 lines) for which he will need at least two or three minutes. The staging, therefore, becomes problematic because the chariot ought to keep moving according to the text-direction. Most likely, the performance will provide us with a most significant "speaking picture" at this point: the chariot will move in a *circle*, and it will probably have to stop several times in order to allow Tamburlaine to speak head on to the audience. We can also expect a number of physical gestures - Tamburlaine's handling of the reins and the whip - that will increase the disjunction between the poetry's imaginative appeal and the physically oversubstantiated chariot.

Peter Hall's Olivier production superbly rendered the ambivalent effect of the spectacle, and the visual impact of the chariot's circling movement was enforced by the stage design. The enormous golden circular lighting grid, which was suspended over the whole stage of the Olivier Theatre, poured down light onto another matching circle painted on the floor and, with full intensity, highlit Tamburlaine at one of the crucial moments of his speech: "I'll ride in golden armour like the sun." This dazzling effect was matched, however, by the more ominous, symbolic significance of the stage circle which had turned blood-red at each horrific moment of conquest in the play, suggesting Tamburlaine's violent destruction and re-mapping of the known world.

In spite of Tamburlaine's heroic fantasy of rising to the lofty heavens, the staging suggests that his very physical chariot keeps moving round and round, along the blood-stained ground of "this disdainful earth"(V.iii.122) which is not yet complete-

ly conquered, not yet completely consumed and ransacked (cf.IV.
i.192-206). The circling movement of Tamburlaine's earth-bound
chariot conveys a sense of the maddening futility that is the reverse side of the triumph and glory of his exulting pride. This
sense of futility grows stronger in proportion to the increasingly hyperbolical efforts Tamburlaine must make in order to defy
the limitations that have become visible and transform them into
imagined success.

The unconquered hero, inspired and trapped by the god-like hunger
of his imagination, continues his restless striving, and the
movement imparted to the play by Tamburlaine's ceaseless marches
and countermarches reflects the unending rotation of the universe itself - thus raising his final collapse into a larger perspective ("For earth hath spent the pride of all her fruit, / And
heaven consumed his choicest living fire" V.iii.250-51). Even if
Tamburlaine's final gestures appear utterly futile

> Come let us march against the powers of heaven
> And set black streamers in the firmament
> To signify the slaughter of the gods.
> Ah friends, what shall I do? I cannot stand.
> Come, carry me to war against the gods,
> That thus envy the health of Tamburlaine.
> (V.iii.48-53)

his unbroken defiance of the gods is a true sign of the intense
pathos which we have come to recognize as the essential language
of this first Marlovian hero. In the end, when his servant Death
turns on his master, the chariot stops and he has to be lifted
out of it.

There is a shocking, almost grotesque consistency in his rhetorical demand to be *carried* "to war against the gods," and
Marlowe follows the pathos of this posture through to the ambivalent tragic-heroic ending of the play. Up to his last breath,
Marlowe subjects the "figure" of Tamburlaine's heroic dignity
to intense dramatic pressure and, with his hero's compensatory
efforts to aestheticize death itself, increases the audience's
need to make sense of this extravagant tyrant's unpunished

hubris. The play's ending still "performs" a denial of all those moral convictions which normally attend to one's sense of poetic justice.

Tamburlaine remains frustratingly defiant; realizing that he cannot control death, he revisits the map that bespeaks his conquest in this world and, once again, idealizes his own "brainsick" pride (cf. V.iii.228-44) with which he had ruled his "proud rebelling" antagonists. His all too human efforts at aesthetic compensation are perhaps significant, especially since the play as a whole, unlike Part 1, shows that Marlowe had begun to integrate the problems of tragic necessity and mortality into a dramatic world that seemed infinitely malleable by the wilful imagination of the overreaching hero.

Chapter Four

FAUSTUS' UPWARD FALL:

THEOLOGY IN MARLOWE'S DRAMA

In trying to determine the nature of Faustus' ambition and flights of imagination in their specific poetic and rhetorical configuration, we have already touched upon some of the central energies within the play's intellectual and thematic structure. Faustus' search for self-transcendence, conceived in his extravagant vision of "magical" dominion (scene i), initiates in its own heroic and tragic terms a theatrical experience which, in spite of complicated and sometimes contradictory fusions of artistic parts, achieves a successful and coherent psychological unity. The defining unity rests upon the course of events during which Faustus' dream of power becomes transformed into a nightmare of impotence and failure, and upon the wider moral and theological implications which underlies the psychological drama and give it a substance and form that elevate *Dr Faustus* to the status of a great and controversial religious tragedy.

On formal as well as on thematic grounds, Faustus' rebellion against the Christian idea of man's fate, his progress from his rejection of humane and divine studies to his obliterating, unforgiven death, necessarily assumes an individual identity against the backdrop of a traditional morality structure. Since it is obvious that Marlowe's play employs many formal elements of the older "morality play," we should now turn to the specific textual and dramaturgical construction of *Dr Faustus* in order to clarify whether and to what extent Marlowe modifies existing conventions and transforms the motifs and ritualistic patterns of religious drama.

In using the expression "controversial religious tragedy," I am referring to the play's inherent tensions and ambiguities, those tensions that exist in the text itself and that are borne out in the theatrical event, building a new experience in language, characterization, and intellectual argument on top of still existing formulae and mechanisms of an older dramatic tradition. Granting the multiplicity of dramatic levels, of tone, and of style in *Dr Faustus*, one is hardly surprised to find Marlowe's critics widely disagreeing about the emphasis they want to bestow upon the different levels of the play as morality play, homiletic tragedy, heroic and romantic tragedy, or psychic drama. Over the last five decades, this disagreement has resulted in radically opposed evaluations of the play, and both the romantic idealizations of Marlowe's defiances in the name of his rebel-hero and the so-called "objective" critique of Marlowe's drama which stresses the solid, orthodox lines on which the hero's actions are judged and put into a moralizing perspective, seem as yet to oversimplify the play that Marlowe actually wrote.

It seems to me that Marlovian drama in general is distinguished by an overlap and conjunction of structures and attitudes, by discontinuities and disruption, and by inescapable ambivalences arising from the plays' direct focus on the intense single-mindedness of the protagonsits. If we grant the curious immorality which for many of us marks Marlowe's plays, and if we also grant the multiple ironies that so often counterpoint the overt glorificattion of the hero, we should have a better sense of the difficult interplay between the author's detachment from and his deep involvement in his heroes, and this should make us avoid reductive either/or interpretations.

Recent criticism has paid much more attention to this ambiguity and has examined the mixed response evoked by the flexibility of tone and the complexity of the dramatic ironies in the plays. It is not enough, however, to assert the ambivalence in the experience of a play in the theatre or to attribute all effects to the irony at work in Marlowe's texts. In the case of *Dr Faustus*, Marlowe's hero has been hailed as a true Renaissance superman, waging a desperate, noble battle for intellectual freedom and power against medieval pieties and divinely-ordained limitations; on the other hand, orthodox critics have challenged the notion of Faustus as heroic rebel by arguing that the homiletic structure of the play and its proper moral condemnation of the hero's perverse will thoroughly unmask his foolishness and depravity. Beyond the one-sided readings, one seems to face the difficult task of defining exactly what the conflicts and ambiguities in the play consist of. Roma Gill, for example, suggests that

> Marlowe's play demonstrates the fearful consequences of violating the Christian ethic, and for this it may be called a Christian document. But Marlowe's sympathies (if the energy of the verse means anything at all) are for the rebel, the man who is ... frustrated in his efforts to assert his individuality.[1]

Again, this view does not entirely avoid the temptation to romanticize Marlowe's "atheism." Following the course of Faustus' frustrated rebellion , one perhaps ought to focus, first of all, on the form in which the "Christian ethic" is implicated in the play's dramatic structure, the energies of the poetry, and the staging of the scenes in order to determine the character of the dominant motifs.

In other words, the following chapters are devoted to a critical investigation into the terms in which Faustus' tragic fall as a human experience is dramatized according to Christian theology and belief. The play is to be seen as a thoroughly theological play in so far as it fundamentally deals with religious concepts and doctrines and gains its dramatic force by the continual parallelism between the impact of Faustus' tragic fall and clearly visible theological structures and implications. It will not ne enough, however, to point out the dominant theological themes and the background of English Reformation theology which infuses the texture of the play. It is my concern to delineate Marlowe's technique of transforming these themes into direct theatrical

---

1 Roma Gill, ed., *Doctor Faustus*, The New Mermaids (1965;rpt. London: Benn, 1967), p. xxvii.

experiences: inquiries into Marlowe's background and subtexts will only prove worthwhile if we can determine their immediacy in the play-in-performance.

As I have indicated earlier, the plays that were performed in the late 1580s and the early 1590s were the primary targets of the criticism that was launched against Marlowe, and the contemporary reactions that I mentioned in connection with *Tamburlaine* are equally relevant with respect to the controversial success Marlowe had with *Dr Faustus* and Edward Alleyn, who once again took over the starring role (he also starred in the *Tamburlaine* plays and in *The Jew of Malta*). It is not difficult to see why the protagonist of this later play in particular has been linked with the picture of the author's personality, career, and melodramatic death which we have to piece together from a number of scattered hints and allusions. It remains unclear what sort of affinity one would want to posit between Faustus' apostasy and Marlowe's alleged "atheism"; the image of a radical Marlowe, which Thomas Kyd's and Richard Baines' charges have helped to sustain, is interesting in so far, however, as it points to the controversial elements of his drama that are at issue here.

In the preface to the only work published in Marlowe's lifetime, the "Two Tragicall Discourses" of *Tamburlaine* (1590), the printer Richard Jones explains that he has purposely "omitted and left out some fond and friuolous Iestures, digressing (and in my poore opinion) far vnmeet for the matter," which had been used for the stage, "of some vaine conceited fondlings greatly gaped at ... shewed vpon the stage in their graced deformities," yet were not fitting, so Jones, for "the eloquence of the Authour."[2] We will probably never know what he left out, yet it is significant that Jones praises Marlowe's eloquence while he obviously shrinks away from the playwright's more blatantly provocative and frivolous spectacles ("Iestures"?). It seems that Jones'

---

[2] "To the Gentlemen Readers: and others that take pleasure in reading Histories," quoted from Tucker Brooke's edition of *The Works*.

rather obscure reference intimates something of the dangerousness of the blasphemous or irreverent subject-matter which, to a similar extent, was to be expurgated and tampered with in the 1616 text of *Dr Faustus*. Again, the actual status of Marlowe's "atheism," or the myth of his "atheist lecture,"[3] for that matter, are not of primary interest, and in any case, "atheist" should not be seen as a technical term, but as a word of abuse for iconoclasts, unorthodox thinkers, and generally irreverent or dangerous men. George Hunter is perhaps right in saying that the Baines Note rather suggests a "God-haunted atheist, involved simultaneously in revolt and the sense of necessity for punishment against such a revolt."[4]

If we examine Marlowe's dramatic style and stress the supreme eloquence with which Faustus, Tamburlaine, or Barabas sustain the aggressive and iconoclastic fervour which is so characteristic of their performances, we will touch upon the same, more exposed and more sensational, elements of the total composition, which were highlit by such contemporary responses as Greene's or Nashe's laments over the popular success of Marlowe's verse. I have already quoted Gabriel Harvey's oblique reference to Marlowe's "tamburlaine contempt," but there are two other comments that are worth mentioning. First, Harvey thinks that the dramatist's work shows "no Religion, but precise Marlowisme," and in another place he calls the plays "Marlowes brauadôs."[5] This judgment may come closer to the nature of Marlowe's innovative style, to the momentum that was caused by his "high astounding terms" and his provocative stage-craft. If we connect further

---

3   See Kocher's attempt at reconstructing the outlines of an "atheist lecture" in his *Christopher Marlowe*, pp. 33-68, and in two articles: "Marlowe's Atheist Lecture," *JEGP*, 39(1940), 98-106; and "Backgrounds on Marlowe's Atheist Lecture." *PQ*, 20 (1941), 112-32.
4   George K. Hunter, "The Theology of Marlowe's *The Jew of Malta*," *JWCI*, 27 (1964), 240.
5   Gabriel Harvey, "A Letter of Notable Contents," and "Marginalia," in *The Works of Gabriel Harvey*, ed. Alexander B. Grosart (London: Huth Library, 1884), I, 297; II, 234.

threads of the Marlowe-reception, from Thomas Beard's moral condemnation of the Cambridge "scholler," "by practice a play maker, and a Poet of scurrilitie, who by giuing too large a swinge to his own wit, and suffering his lust to haue full raines, fell to that outrage and extremitie, that hee denied God and his sonne Christ,"[6] to Michael Drayton's more enthusiastic appraisal of the "fine madness" in Marlowe's "raptures" ("those brave translunary things, / That the first Poets had ...")[7] - then we gain a sense, after all, of the tremendous impact Marlowe's new style must have had.

The contemporary allusions attest Marlowe's uniquely controversial stature as a radical literary provocateur and intellectual; my previous discussion of Marlowe's conception of rhetoric and his deliberate displacements of traditional humanist principles in *Tamburlaine* has prepared us to distrust a "straight" morality structure in *Dr Faustus*, and we should therefore try to determine how Marlowe "places" his subject-matter in relation to his dramaturgy. I find my interest in Marlowe's rhetoric and stage-craft confirmed in the warning voice of another playwright whose sincere humanism speaks for itself:

> The true Artificer will not run away from nature,
> as he were afraid of her; or depart from life, and
> the likeness of Truth; but speak to the capacity
> of his hearers, and though his language differ
> from the vulgar somewhat, it shall not fly from
> all humanity, with the *Tamerlanes*, and *Tamerchams*
> of the late age, which had nothing in them but
> the scenical strutting, and furious vociferation,
> to warrant them to the ignorant gapers.[8]

How "far away from nature" and from the "likeness of Truth" are we taken by the rhetoric of Faustus' flights of imagination? Or rather, how is Faustus' "fleeing" from all humanity performed?

---

6   *The Theatre of Gods Iudgements*, chap. XXV.
7   "To my Most Dearely-Loved Friend Henry Reynolds, Esquire, of Poets and Poesie," in *The Works of Michael Drayton*, ed. J. William Hebel (Oxford: Oxford Univ. Press, 1931), III,228-29.
8   Ben Jonson, *Timber: or Discoveries*, in *The Complete Poems*, ed. G. Parfitt (Harmondsworth: Penguin Books, 1975), pp. 397f.

In the truly climactic Helen of Troy Scene, which is full of complicated stage business, we obtain a full picture of the complex operations of Marlowe's dramatic style. The scene orchestrates the central tensions and paradoxes of Faustus' *flight* and its consequences in such a unique manner that I will use it as a starting-point for answering our questions.

>   [*(Faustus and Helen)Exeunt*]
> O.Man. Accursed Faustus, miserable man,
>   That from thy soule excludst the *grace of heauen*,
>   And *fliest* the throne of his *tribunall seate*.
>   [*Enter the Diuelles*]
>   Sathan begins to sift me with his *pride*,
>   As in this furnace God shal try *my faith*,
>   *My faith*, vile hel, shal triumph ouer thee,
>   *Ambitious fiends*, see how the *heauens* smiles
>   At your repulse, and laughs your state to scorne,
>   Hence hel, for hence *I flie vnto my God*.
>   (A 1377-86; not in B; my emphasis)

The reader will have noticed that I propose to take the image of Faustus' *flight* as a key-concept of the idea and structure of the play. Not only does the Prologue introduce the Icarus emblem in the very beginning, the Faustian rhetoric of transcendence subsequently establishes the complicated nature of his project in terms of hyperbolic images of *flight* (soaring ambition; "fleeing" of reality), and this basic dualistic concept is genuinely fused with the entire theological symbolism which dominates Faustus' psychomachia: the paradoxes of life and death, sin and forgiveness, grace and damnation, hope and despair, free will and necessity.

The paradoxical quality adhering to the entire Faustian "enterprise" indeed becomes reinforced by the religious vocabulary of contemporary Protestant theology - faithfully echoed by the Old Man in the text quoted above - and those doctrines in particular which in one way or another touch upon the *mysterium iniquitatis*[9]

---

9 Anybody who is familiar with the writings of Luther, Calvin, Colet, and the English Reformers will not only recognize the specific emphasis that was placed upon the theological content

and the Protestant key-concept of justification by faith alone.

"To fly away from God" or "to fly unto God": the antithesis which underlies the dilemma of Protestant views on man's relation to God and on his fallen nature is taken up quite directly by Marlowe's dramaturgical juxtaposing of the Old Man and Faustus at a moment of especially heightened tension. This long scene opens with Wagner announcing Faustus' last supper. Faustus' meandering journey through the middle sections of the play has come to an end; he is back in Wittenberg. Upon the request of his scholar-friends, Faustus once again displays what he is "able to performe" by "art and power of [his] spirit"(A 1078-79). In the course of the play, the performances of his "art and power" have never come anywhere near his initial visions of *power* and *omnipotence*; his dreams have never become "substantial," and Faustus' imagination resembles the "prison" Hamlet describes so aptly:

> *Ham.* O God, I could be bounded in a nutshell and
> count myself a king of infinite space, were
> it not that I have bad dreams.
> *Guil.* Which dreams indeed are ambition; for the
> very substance of the ambitious is merely
> the shadow of a dream.
> *Ham.* A dream itself is but a shadow.
> (*Hamlet* II.ii.253-59)

---

of Pauline teaching, but also a characteristic rhetoric that distinguishes most radical Reformers and their emerging doctrinal concern with the *mysterium iniquitatis* (cf. 2 Thess. ii.3-14), the problem of man's depravity and its consequences for his relation to God, and all the interrelated concepts of justification, predestination, imputation, etc.. Looking at *Dr Faustus* from the perspective of the theological structure of its sources, the German *Faustbuch* (*Historia von D. Johann Fausten*, 1587) and its English translation (*The Historie of the Damnable Life ...*, 1592), one must stress the absolutely unambiguous and genuinely Lutheran conception of a didactic tale which focusses *not* on Faustus as "vnsatiable speculator" but on the phenomenon of man's sinfulness. The admonitory exploration into the paradox of sin (apostasy/self-assertion/daemonization), a phenomenon which the FB describes as "kein Menschliche Schwachheit, Thorheit und unvergeßlichkeit, oder, wie es S.Paulus nennet, ein Menschliche Versuchung, Sondern ein recht Teuffelische Boßheit, ein muthwillige Unsinnigkeit und grewliche Verstockung, die mit Gedancken nimmermehr ergründet, geschweige dann mit Worten außgesprochen werden kan" ("Vorred an den Christlichen Leser"), lies at the heart of

Faustus' ambition has become very much shadow-like; how literally "*quiet* in conceit"(A 1174, emphasis mine) he has almost become can be felt in the subdued and frustrated tone Faustus uses during the meeting with the Scholars. Almost nothing is left from the noisily hyperbolic flights of imagination of the early Faustus, when he invokes Helen of Troy for the first time and warns his fellows:

> Be silent then, for danger is in words.
> [*Musicke sounds, and Helen passeth ouer the Stage*]
> (A 1290)

I wish to draw attention to the theatrical notation of this scene; the quickly successive stage-directions, for example, are particularly significant for the counterpoint method in these crucial moments of Faustus' final "flights." While the Scholars are still dazzled by Helen's appearance and try to praise her "heauenly beauty",

> ... we haue seene the pride of natures workes,
> And onely Paragon of excellence ...
> (A 1296-97)

the Old Man, a perfectly rendered example of the morality agent of repentance and exhortation, enters:

> Ah Doctor Faustus, that I might preuaile,
> To guide thy steps vnto the way of life,
> By which sweete path thou maist attaine the gole
> That shall conduct thee to celestial rest.
> Breake heart, drop bloud, and mingle it with teares,
> Teares falling from repentant heauinesse
> Of thy most vilde and loathsome filthinesse,
> The stench whereof corrupts the inward soule
> With such flagitious crimes of hainous sinnes,
> As no commiseration may expel,
> But mercie Faustus of thy Sauiour sweete,
> Whose bloud alone must wash away thy guilt.
> (A 1302-13;not in B)

---

the early Faust-conception, and the conception of Faustus' sinfulness and damnation in Marlowe's play will involve inquiries into the same doctrinal themes.

The scene exploits the effects of the traditional, climactic morality tableau of counterpoised hope and despair, repentance and un-repentance, and this is again emphasized in the Old Man's and Faustus' speeches that are full of antithetical images.

> Ah stay good Faustus, stay thy desperate steps,
> I see an Angell houers ore thy head,
> And with a violl full of precious grace,
> Offers to poure the same into thy soule,
> Then call for mercie and auoyd dispaire.
>   (A 1319-23)

The accompanying stage-direction, *"Mepha. giues him a dagger"*, completes the picture of a perfectly classic, and decidedly old-fashioned, theatrical moment. The protagonist is poised between the Old Man's promise and Mephostophilis' dagger, the latter being a traditional stage emblem of despair.[10] Marlowe over-emphasizes Faustus' despair, however, and the dramatized psychic struggle shows Faustus wavering back and forth, to the very end, between an imaginative conception of himself, which seems to allow him the freedom to repent, and the opposite, more urgent and pressing conception of himself whereby he cannot repent. Very abruptly, Faustus answers the Old Man's good council with obvious resignation and grasps for the dagger:

> Where art thou Faustus? wretch what hast thou done?
> Damnd art thou Faustus, damnd, dispaire and die,
> Hell calls for right, and with a roaring voyce
> Sayes, Faustus come, thine houre is come,
> And Faustus will come to do thee right.
>   (A 1314-18)

Since I see a strictly coherent and logical development of the play's theological themes up to this point, and since in conjunction with all the major religious motifs the question of the possibility of Faustus' repentance emerges as the central theological problem, I wish to pause for a moment and consider this

---

10 Cf. T.W. Craik, *The Tudor Interlude* (Leicester: Leicester Univ. Press, 1962), pp. 52f.;65. See, especially, Susan Snyder's brilliant inquiries into the literary and iconographic background of the topos in her "The Left Hand of

issue, which has caused so much critical misreading, from a fresh perspective. It will prove valuable, too, to clarify Faustus' unrepentance first before trying to determine the nature of his initial trespass or of his "filthinesse" and corrupted soul, as the Old Man calls it.

Paul Kocher and many other critics maintain that "in a theological sense, the basic doctrine of the play is that Faustus is at all times free to resist the temptation to evil and to repent after he has fallen."[11] The form in which Marlowe dramatizes his hero's psychic struggle forbids such speculation, however, and we ought to look at the theology of Marlowe's period in order to find the correct implications. Keeping the Helen/ Old Man scene in mind, and especially the morality tableau which one can assume to have conditioned certain responses and expectations, how would the theologically aware in Marlowe's audience have seen Faustus - as one having free will, able to repent if he wished to, or as a reprobate and, therefore, unable to repent?

According to Reformation theology, repentance is a gift of the all-powerful God and, consequently, not something which man could attain to by himself.[12] William Perkins calls it a Popish fallacy "that a sinner hath in him a naturall disposition, which being stirred vp by Gods preuenting grace, he may and can work together with gods spirit in his owne repentance: But indeede all our repentance is to be ascribed to Gods grace wholly, Eph. ii.4. The soule of man is not weake, but starke deade in sinne, and therefore it can no more prepare it selfe to repentance, then the body beeing dead in the graue can dispose it selfe to the last resurrection."[13] If this is the case, then it is quite

---

God: Despair in Medieval and Renaissance Tradition," 18-59.
11 Paul H. Kocher, ed., *The Tragical History of Doctor Faustus*, The Crofts Classics edition (New York: Harlan Davidson, 1950), p. xi. See also Michael Poirier, *Christopher Marlowe* (1951; rpt. London: Chatto & Windus, 1968), p. 141; Lily B. Campbell, "*Doctor Faustus:* A Case of Conscience," *PMLA*, 67 (1952), 238, and Levin, *The Overreacher*, p. 156.
12 Cf. *The Early Works of Thomas Becon*, ed. John Ayre, The Parker Society (Cambridge: Cambridge Univ.Press, 1843), p. 93.
13 Thomas Perkins, *Workes* (London, 1612-13), I, 468.

erroneous to hold that man can repent when he wishes to.[14] Perkins goes on to explain this position by examining the stages of repentance. First, one must have knowledge of four things: the law of God, sin against the law, the guilt of sin, and God's judgment against sin. Second, one must apply this knowledge to oneself. Third, one must experience fear and sorrow. At this point, if one is in danger of falling into despair, one must go on to four more steps. First, one must possess knowledge of the Gospel (the truth) and God's mercy. Second, one must apply this knowledge to oneself. Third, one must experience joy and sorrow: joy that man's sins are pardoned in Christ and sorrow that man's sins displease such a loving and merciful God. Finally, one must decide never to sin again, but "to live in newness of life."[15]

In accordance with the doctrine of justification - man's passive role as the receiver of God's free gift of justifying faith - none of these steps can be taken unless God gives grace. Perkins asserts that "No man can repent, vnlesse hee first hate sinne, & love righteousness; and none can hate sinne, vnlesse he be sanctified ... He that turnes to God, must first of all be turned of God, and after that wee are turned, then we repent."[16] Calvin makes exactly the same point: "But we mean to show that a man cannot apply himself seriously to repentance without knowing himself to belong to God. But no one is truly persuaded that he belongs to God unless he has first recognized God's grace."[17]

Now this seems to be the problem in Faustus' reaction to the Old Man; the Old Man's speech makes it clear, in a Calvinist sense, that God's "mercie" alone can "wash away" the guilt. The Old Man's sermon, at the same time, opens up further questions of a particular, doctrinal nature. The Protestant system of doctrines

---

14 Perkins, *Workes*, II, 422. See also Peter Martyr, *The Common Places* (London, 1583), p. 123.
15 Perkins, *Workes*, I, 457.
16 Ibid., 455.
17 *Institutes*, III.3.2. For a detailed examination of these issues, see Raymond H. Reno, "The Theological Background of Christopher Marlowe's *The Tragical History of Doctor Faustus*," Diss., George Washington University, 1958.

(the doctrine of human depravity, of the helplessness of man; the doctrine of justification; the doctrine of sin, repentance, and regeneration; and, ultimately, the doctrine of double-predestination) finds its most complicated and problematic expression in the radical Calvinist insistence on the twofold predestination of election and reprobation. That this issue is always treated very cautiously by theologians should make it even less likely that a dramatist would explicitly use the doctrine, especially since Royal Proclamations and censorship prohibited a too obvious treatment of controversial theological issues on the stage.

With regard to the problem of repentance, a reprobate was conceived of as incapable of true repentance, even if he thought he was repenting. To the reprobate, God gives "first, a signe of sinne: secondly, a kind of sorrow for it: thirdly, a confession of it: fourthly, a resolution for a time to sinne no more. But that part of repentance, which hath the promise of mercie annexed, that is, a conversion of the whole man to God, he neuer giveth it."[18] This surely is the picture of Faustus that FB and EFB draw: "In this perplexitie lay this miserable Doctor Faustus, having quite forgot his faith in Christ, neuer falling to repentance truly ... he might haue remembered through true repentance sinners come againe into the fauour of God ... but he was so in all his opinions doubtful, without faith or hope, and so he continued."[19]

In spite of all poetic and dramatic metamorphoses in Marlowe's Faustus-conception, the theological execution of the theme retains the same indices of a lack of faith and hope:

>   Accursed Faustus, where is mercie now?
>   I do repent, and yet I do dispaire ...
>   (A 1329-30)

---

18 Perkins, *Workes*, I, 416-17.
19 *The Historie of the Damnable Life, and Deserued Death of Doctor Iohn Faustus*, by P.F., Gent. (1592), ed. P.M.Palmer and R.P. More (1936; rpt. New York: Haskell House, 1965), pp. 151-52.

Since the reprobate does not rely on the power of God's mercy, but only on his own strength, he is helpless before the power of the devil. As Luther claims: "You have no comfort or refuge against the devil, for he always has the advantage of driving you back upon your own conscience and the testimony of your own efforts ... In short, you are overcome by yourself and are convicted by the sentence: The good must be done."[20] The elect, on the other hand, cannot be defeated by the arguments of the devil that "Thou hast sinned against God; therefore thou must die," for the elect knows that "In myself I am a sinner, but in Christ, my righteous-maker, I am righteous. For he hath forgiven me all my sins, and hath taken me into his grace, favour and tuition."[21]

This is the kind of faith which is not represented in Faustus' actions, and - as Luther described it - the devil has little trouble in turning his mind away from "repentance." Mephostophilis' tactics of threatening Faustus back into submission become a repeated experience in the play:

> Thou traitor Faustus, I arrest thy soule
> For disobedience to my soueraigne Lord,
> Reuolt, or Ile in peece-meale teare thy flesh.
>   (A 1333-35)

Faustus' inability to proceed towards repentance, to see God as a God of mercy, clearly indicates the typical blindness and insecurity of a reprobate. There are a number of very successfully staged juxtapositions within the quadrangle of the four main characters in this scene: Faustus-Old Man; Faustus-Mephostophilis; Faustus-Helen; Helen-Old Man; Old Man-Faustus; Old Man-Mephostophilis. The crucial theological meaning lies in the exactly opposed behaviour of the desperate, unrepenting Faustus and the faithful, persevering Old Man. Combined with Faustus' inability to see God as a God of mercy is what one would theologically call

---

20 *The Precious and Sacred Writings of Martin Luther*, ed. John N. Lenker (Minneapolis: The Luther Press, 1903-10), XII, 56.
21 Thomas Becon, *The Catechism, with Other Pieces*, ed. John Ayre, The Parker Society (Cambridge: Cambridge Univ. Press, 1844), p. 630.

"hardness of heart," preventing the sinner from feeling sorrow over his sinfulness or, perhaps more precisely, from experiencing true contrition for sin. This hardness of heart is, according to the Reformed theology of the period, another characteristic of the reprobate. The origin of the condition, however, is not quite clear. Sometimes it is spoken of as merely the result of the habit of sin ("If sin by custome grow not into nature ..."B 1819) - thus psychological in origin; and at other times as if it resulted from a particular act of God. Perkins, for instance, accounts for four degrees of sin - temptation, conception, birth, and perfection - in the last degree of which (Perkins here echoes Augustine's notion of "perfect perversity") "men are growne to a custome and habit in sinne, vpon long practice. For the often committing of one and the same sinne, leaves an euill impression in the heart, that is, a strong or violent inclination, to that or any other euill. And sinne thus made perfect, brings forth death: for custome in sinning brings hardness of heart; hardnesse of heart impenitencie; and impenitencie, condemnation."[22] Such a heart, so Thomas Wright, "may resist the sweete calling of God."[23]

Calvin, on the other hand, thinks that "whatever we conceive of in our minds is directed to his own end by God's secret inspiration." The blindness and infatuation of the reprobate "are inflicted by God's just judgment ... It is said that he hardened Pharaoh's heart (Ex.9.12), also that he made it heavy (10.1) and stiffened it (10.20,27; 11.10; 14.8)." Nor will Calvin allow a merely *permissive* action on God's part. "Scripture cuts off any occasion for such cavils. 'I will restrain,' says God, 'his heart'(Ex.4.21)." And Calvin concludes: "Since God's will is said to be the cause of all things, I have made his providence the determinative principle for all human plans and works, not only in order to display its force in the elect, who are

---

22 Perkins, *Workes*, II, 10.
23 Thomas Wright, *The Passions of the Minde* (London, 1601), p. 331.

ruled by the Holy Spirit, but also to compel the reprobate to obedience."[24]

Calvin's rhetoric is extreme, and his rigorous position seems to be implied in Faustus' blunt, determinist formula "Che sera, sera" with which he rejects exactly that system of thought that lies behind Calvin's doctrine of an all-powerful God. At the same time, Calvin's position is the logical continuation of one very widely held, namely that - as the Homilies put it - it depends on God whether "we repent, which reacheth forth his merciful hand to raise us up. If any will we have to rise, it is he that preventeth [influences our will ahead of time] our will, and disposeth us thereto."[25] As another sermon in the same collection says, "Must we beware and take heed, that we do in no wise think in our hearts, imagine, or believe, that we are able to repent aright, or to turn effectually unto the Lord by our own might, and strength."[26] Repentance, and the necessary sorrow for sin, is a free gift of God; therefore, he who cannot repent has not been given the gift; whose heart is hard, God has not softened it. In any case, God's *influence* is posited as the only effectual power.

If we sum up the picture of the reprobate as presented by Reformed theologians, and especially by Perkins,[27] we can say that he is someone who has a knowledge of God and of good and evil and who - if called by God - might even be offered salvation, "yet this calling is not so effectuall in them as it is in the elect."[28] The reprobate prefers his own blindness,

---

24 *Institutes*, I.18.2. Along with other theologians of the day, Henry Bullinger also discusses Pharaoh. Whereas the general tenor of the passage in *The Decades* is that God's action is a permissive one, Bullinger seems uncertain at some points. He prefers to conclude, however, that from the various statements with regard to the hardening of Pharaoh's heart "must be gathered a godly sense; such a sense, I mean, as maketh not God the author of evil." Cf. *The Decades*, ed. Thomas Harding, The Parker Society (Cambridge: Cambridge Univ. Press, 1849-52), II, 381-82.
25 *Certain Sermons or Homilies* (1547; rpt. Oxford: Oxford Univ. Press, 1840), p. 432.
26 Ibid., p. 476.

but even if he wanted to respond to God's call, "yet could he not answer, and be obedient to the calling of God."[29] Quite significantly, the reprobate does experience remorse and sorrow for sin; this sorrow is not, however, true contrition, but merely the result of his fear, and its consequence is nothing more than a further hardening of the heart. The reprobate, "when he repenteth, he can not come vnto God, and seeke vnto him: he hath no power, no not so much as once to desire to giue one little sobbe for the remission of his sins: if hee could giue all the worlde hee cannot so much as giue one rappe at Gods mercie gate, that he may open to him."[30] The reprobate may confess his transgressions, but this occurs only when his soul is tormented by its fears of God's anger.

At this point it is important to see the logical consequence of the psychology of reprobation; the dilemma of the reprobate ultimately makes God appear as a God of wrath. He cannot appeal to his "father" as the elect does; to the reprobate God is "a terrible Iudge."[31] Perkins goes on to assert that

> Reprobates haue some prerogatiues of God: as that he is patient towards them: that before he will destroy them, he vseth many meanes to win them ... But after a certaine time God in his iust iudgment hardeneth their hearts, blindeth the eies of their minds, he maketh their heads giddie with a spiritual drunkenness, and by the strength of their inward lusts, as also by the effectuall operation of Sathan, they fall to open infidelitie, and contempt of Gods word, and so runne headlong to their own damnation, and perish finally.[32]

This may stand as a fairly accurate "theological description" of

---

27 See, especially, Perkins' elaborate *Treatise Tending unto a Declaration Whether a Man Be in the Estate of Damnation or in the Estate of Grace* (London, 1598).
28 Ibid., p. 4.
29 Ibid.
30 Ibid., p. 8.
31 Ibid., p. 64.
32 Ibid., p. 22.

what we in fact see on stage in our scene; the juxtaposition of
an elect (Old Man), whose "faith is great" and whose soul Mephostophilis "cannot touch" (A 1345), and Faustus-as-reprobate is
comprehensively worked out. Faustus is "called" upon by a messenger of God, whose patience and mercy are emphasized; his response is doubt, despair, and an imperfect contrition:

> Ah my sweete friend, I feele thy words
> To comfort my distressed soule,
> Leaue me a while to ponder on my sinnes.
> (A 1324-26)

This is a moment of high theatrical suspense. Faustus may be seen
as choosing the traditional path to repentance, and his acknowledgement of sin would be the first vital step in the process.
The B-text, in this respect, seems to suggest that the operations
of the devil are quite "effectuall," however, since it continues
to stress Mephostophilis' function as seducer and manipulator.
Faustus' hardened heart not only drives him to despise the Old
Man, whose torment he orders ("greatest torments that *our* hel
affoords" A 1344/B 1859, my emphasis), but also activates the
"headlong" flight into "inward lust" and "spiritual drunkenness"
which Perkins describes. He wants to "glut the longing of [his]
hearts desire" (A 1349) by the erotic embrace of Helen, and
Mephostophilis can sardonically summarize the Faustian escapism
(in the quite obviously deflationary phraseology of the B-text):

> How should he, but in desperate lunacie.
> Fond worldling, now his heart bloud dries with griefe;
> His conscience kils it, and his labouring braine,
> Begets a world of idle fantasies,
> To ouer-reach the Diuell; but all in vaine ...
> (B 1906-10;not in A)

Before we enter a discussion of the problems involved in the
fusion of a recognizable morality pattern, containing a controversial theology in itself, and Marlowe's particularly intense
poetic thrust in the Helen scene, we should stress the traditional significance of moral drama with regard to its conception
and its effects on audience expectations. If our scene, as I

have described it so far, indeed points to Faustus' tragic fall
conceived in terms of the concept of reprobation, we are left
with further problems; the controversial issues of free will
and predestination disclose ambiguities that lie at the heart of
Reformation theology, and these issues are of course related to
the play's dramatic effectiveness. If we look at earlier morality plays such as *The Castle of Perseverance*, *Mankind*, *Everyman*, *Hickscorner*, *The World and the Child*, *Calisto and Malibaea*, *Wyt and Science*, or *Nature*, the stage-convention which
concludes these plays with the representation of repentance and
salvation certainly gains dramatic power from their unstaged
alternative - the understanding that a "tragic" end always
threatens.

Yet the medieval morality play does not like ambiguities; it will
always conclude with a reassertion of divine order, acknowledging and praising the old rhythm of forgiveness. The English morality or homiletic tragedy of the Reformation period, however,
places a decidedly new emphasis on *faith*, on the faith that one
has been forgiven and is saved. Despair - closely related to
the doctrine of faith and predestination - becomes a problem of
great concern, and particular tragic actions move to the foreground of the stage while the older ritualistic pattern of Innocence/Fall/Redemption recedes into the background.

This development, which is noticeable in plays such as John
Bale's *God's Promises*, Richard Wever's *Lusty Iuventus*, Thomas
Ingerland's *Nice Wanton*, *Misogonus* (anon.), *New Custom* (anon.),
William Wager's *Enough is as Good as a Feast*, George Wapull's
The Tide Tarrieth no Man, can be best illustrated in Nathaniel
Woodes' *The Conflict of Conscience* (1572), which I want to
choose because of its relevance to *Dr Faustus*. Woodes' play
picks up the notorious case of Francesco Spiera[33] and presents

---

33 Cf. Celesta Wine, "Nathaniel Wood's *Conflict of Conscience*," *PMLA*, 50 (1935), 663-70, and Lily B. Campbell, "*Doctor Faustus*: A Case of Conscience," 219-39. For contemporary theologians that referred to Spiera's case, see Peter Martyr, *The Common Places*, pp. 23-24; Perkins, *A Treatise*, p. 105;

the fullest dramatic portrait of a reprobate in the literature of the period.

Philologus' (Spiera) dilemma is announced by the Prologue:

> A cruell Conflict certainely, where Conscience
>   takes the foyls,
> And is constrained by flesh, to yeld to deadly
>   sinne,
> Wherby the grace and loue of God, from him sinne
>   reaues and spoyls,
> Then (wretch accurst) no power hath, repentance
>   to beginne,
> Farre happier, if that vnborne and lyfelesse he
>   had bene.   (57-61)[34]

After Philologus' apostasy, having surrendered to the demands of the legate and the promptings of Sensuall Suggestion, he is told by the Spirit that it is still possible for him to be saved, if he will renounce his sin and ask God for grace.

> Renownce thy crime, and sue for grace, and
>   do not captiuate
> Thy Conscience vnto mortall sinne, the yoke
>   of Christ doo beare,
> Shut vp these wordes within thy breast, which
>   sound so in thine eare ...
>   (1701-03)

Philologus, however, rejects the Spirit's exhortation and, continuing in his apostasy, is eventually assailed by another allegorical figure, Horror. Interestingly, Horror does not try to frighten him or to make him change his mind; he appears merely as an agent of God's vengeance to torment Philologus. He tells him that he has come because Philologus despised God's mercy and grace and therefore cannot expect any consolation in Christ's death.

> The peace of Conscience faded is, in stead whereof
>   I bring

---

    and Hugh Latimer, *Sermons*, ed. G.E. Corrie, The Parker Society (Cambridge: Cambridge Univ. Press, 1845), I, 425.
34 Nathaniel Woodes, *The Conflict of Conscience* (1581; rpt. Oxford: Malone Society, 1952).

> The spirit of Sathan, blasphemy, confusion and
> cursing.   (1982-83)

After giving Philologus the "Glasse of deadly desperation," Horror explains:

> Thus haue I caught thee in thy pride, and brought
> thee to damnatiõ:
> So that thou art a pattern true, of Gods iust
> indignation.   (1987-88)

Philologus falls into despair, and Woodes lingers on the dramatization of the reprobate's agony. In his anguish, Philologus calls himself a "childe of condempnation" and cries out to Christ: "Thou art no Lambe to mee, but Lion fearce and boulde" (1999). He believes that God is determined to punish him; and he is unable to appeal for mercy since "Christs death doth me no good / Neither for my behoofe, did Christ shed his most precious bloud" (2007-08). To his friends, who tell him to trust in God, he declares that this would be of no help anyhow: "My name within the Booke of Lyfe, had neuer residence" (2033). This clearly indicates his belief in having been a reprobate from the very beginning. His friend, Theologus, maintains that he should not despair, that God is merciful to the repentant, and that Christ's death has compensated for his sins; he cites the examples of Peter and the Good Thief, who received forgiveness for their sins, and advises Philologus to be comforted by the words of the Scriptures. Philologus, however, insists that he cannot repent in spite of his desire to do so.

> ... for I woulde faine attaine
> The mercie, and the loue of God, but he doth
> me disdaine.   (2108-09)

He asserts that "I alas, am reprobate, God doth my soule reproue" (2117), and while his lips speak words of prayer, his heart remains filled with blasphemy and cursing (2118-19). As Theologus and Eusebius continue to urge him to repent, Philologus argues that he is excluded from grace because his heart is hardened and does not possess *true faith*:

> But whence do this true fayth proceede to vs, I do you pray,
> It is the only gift of God, from him it comes alway.
> (2163-64)

Philologus' basic assumption is that God has not given him such a "true fayth." His friends cannot understand this, but in spite of all their arguments Philologus remains unable to overcome his despair and his belief that he will be "destroyed" by God's judgment (cf.2248-49). Up to the very end, he lives and suffers under the burden of this knowledge.

> God hath condemned my Conscience, to perpetuall greife and feare.
> I would most gladly chuse to lyue, a thousand, thousand yeare.
> So that at length I might haue ease ...
> But I alas, shall in this lyfe, in torments still remaine,
> While Gods iust anger, vpon mee, shall be reuealed plaine,
> And I example made to all, of Gods iust indignation,
> Oh that my body were at rest, and soule in condemnation.
> (2321-29)

This strange and awkward play comes to an end when the (historically correct) outcome of Philologus' struggle is announced by a messenger; the protagonist's suicide appears a logical, tragic conclusion to the plot - the moment of tragic finality is moved offstage, however. This leaves us with two questions. It seems as if the rigid Calvinist doctrine of reprobation can only be dramatized by having the protagonist die impenitent. Toward such a conclusion, the dramatization of the psychomachia will always be ambiguous; one cannot tell whether the hero is a reprobate until after he has died, and we see that both in *The Conflict of Conscience* and in *Dr Faustus* the scholar-friends try until the very last minute to convince the hero that he may be pardoned.

If final impenitence is the only clear-cut mark of reprobation, the doctrine of predestination, which was meant to provide assurance, in fact works towards its opposite effect. Although it took salvation out of man's hands and made it rest entirely upon God, it developed no certain sign that God's will towards one is good, and that one is chosen as a member of the elect. Therefore, every man's lot is thoroughly ambiguous, and assurance can only come as a result of convulsive acts of will-power which appear to be so notable an aspect of both Reformation theology and the drama written in the wake of that theology.

If one is incapable of performing that act of *believing* in one's justification, one is obviously lost. Can we assume that the sternness and ambiguity of this concept was too troubling? The general unease with Calvinist rigidity, which we detect among theologians in Elizabethan England, is probably reflected in Woodes' intriguing revision of his play's ending. In a second version of his *Conflict of Conscience*, edited in the same year, Philologus "that would haue hangde himselfe with coard, / Is nowe conuerted vnto God, with manie bitter teares."

It takes Woodes only two lines to turn his damned hero into a saved hero - thus making nonsense of the Calvinist rhetoric he used throughout his play. Can we go further and assume that he hesitated, after all, to break down more traditional moral expectations of an audience that anticipated the old sequence of repentance and forgiveness? And if the representation of "perfection" (the history of salvation, or its negative opposite, damnation) has become problematic, what does a change in cultural paradigms suggest for the applied logic and aesthetics of Christian belief in the theatre? Or, in other words, how far does it grant the imagination a new, unexpected freedom while emptying "reality" and "history" of that secure theological meaning which had seemed consubstantial with them?

The effects that lie in breaking down assumptions and expectations in my opinion offer the key to Marlowe's art; in the light of Calvinist theology and the obvious case-study of Philologus-Spiera, it should now become clear where and in what manner Marlowe's poetic and dramaturgical skill disrupts or intensifies

certain aspects of his theological subtext. From the moment of
Faustus' initial fantasies, and more clearly from the moment he
makes his contract with Lucifer, his psychological experience is
bound to be reductive. He has proceeded to reduce his many alternatives (intellectual pursuits) to two: negromancy[35] and, implicitly, divinity. This is to say that once he has chosen his
daemonization, he has only two alternatives left: be resolute
or repent. According to the picture that I have drawn of the
Protestant doctrine of reprobation, no such alternatives in fact
exist for Faustus. The logic of the system forbids the possibility that the reprobate is able to repent.

What is dramatized in Marlowe's play, then, is the peculiar and
terrible effect of Faustus' misconceived *flight* upward which we,
in a theological sense, are bound to see as a prolonged fall
downward. Faustus' "fleeing" of reality predestines the narrowing down of his alternatives, and both forward and backward
flights invoke terrible fears: fear of God's retribution and
fear of the devil. This is in fact a clever dramatic stroke:
God's and the devil's faces become one.

Looking again at this predicament, one will have to reject
Kocher's and Campbell's assertions that "viewing Faustus not as
one whose fate was determined by his initial sin [of abjuring
God] but rather as one who until the fatal hour might have been
redeemed, we can account for the suspense which the play
creates"[36] and that the presence of the Old Man is direct evidence that Faustus' will is free, making "untenable any theory
that Faustus' fall is predetermined in a Calvinist sense."[37]
On the contrary, the Old Man is no evidence at all that Faustus
was not a reprobate. From a Calvinist perspective, both the Good
Angel and the Old Man can be seen as messengers sent from God to

---

35 I follow George Hunter's suggestion to maintain the older spelling of the word since the original connotations of *black* magic are too important in this context to be sacrificed to modern spelling conventions.
36 Campbell, "A Case of Conscience," 239.
37 Kocher, *Christopher Marlowe*, p. 108.

deprive the reprobate of all possible excuse for his sin, to entangle him even more in his own despair, and thus lead him safely to damnation. Calvin explicitly states that "the Lord sends his Word to many whose blindness he intends to increase" and "transmits his doctrine wrapped in enigmas in order that they may not profit by it except to be cast into greater stupidity."[38] Surely, Calvin's position is extreme and quite unpleasant; but so is Marlowe's play in its implication of a tragic theology, and Faustus' dilemma is precisely that he cannot resolve the "enigma" he has created for himself.

What turns the Helen/Old Man scene into a true Marlovian "bravado," therefore, is the way in which Marlowe can be seen to exploit theatrically this dilemma of the reprobate and to overextend the conventional morality set-up. Faustus is seen repenting yet despairing, hell striving with grace for conquest in his breast. What *appears* to be a moment of crucial suspense, is demolished immediately; any hopeful expectations of a morality ending invoked by Faustus' pondering on his sins are shattered completely.

> *Meph.* Thou traitor Faustus, I arrest thy soule
> For disobedience to my soueraigne Lord,
> Reuolt, or Ile in peece-meale teare thy flesh.
> *Faus.* Sweete Mephastophilis, intreate thy Lord
> To pardon my vniust presumption,
> And with my blood againe I wil confirme
> My former vow I made to Lucifer.
> (A 1333-39)

The devil's threat is effective; the audience may be rightly shocked by the diabolical reversal Marlowe imposes upon the ritual of exhortation and repentance. Faustus' counter-repentance is another strong moment of a typically Marlovian mockery; an Elizabethan audience would not have missed the parody of Christian repentance:

> Now there be four parts of repentance ... The first is the contrition of the heart: for we must be earn-

---

38 *Institutes*, III.24.13.

estly sorry for our sins, and unfeignedly lament and
bewail that we have by them so grievously offended
our most bounteous and merciful God ...
The second is, an unfeigned confession and acknowledging of our sins unto God, whom by them we have so
grievously offended, that, if he should deal with us
according to his justice, we do deserve a thousand
hells, if there could be so many ...
The third part of repentance is faith ... It is evident and plain then, that although we be never so
earnestly sorry for our sins, acknowledge and confess
them; yet all these things shall be but means to bring
us to utter desperation except we do steadfastly believe that God our heavenly father will, for his son
Jesus Christ's sake, pardon and forgive us our offenses
and trespasses, and utterly put them out of remembrance
in his sight ...
The fourth is, an amendment of life, or a new life, in
bringing forth fruits worthy of repentance.[39]

Faustus' speech contains all four parts: the contrition that moves him, the confession, the appeal for and belief in mercy, and the resolution to amend. Turning Mephostophilis (Lucifer) into a Christ, a Messiah, is another one of Faustus' incredible blasphemies. True to his disposition, Faustus at once begins to bring forth "fruits worthy of repentance." He renews his vow in blood (the second renewal), begs Mephostophilis to torture "that base and crooked age" (A 1342), and, finally, asks for the intoxicating embraces of Helen in order to avoid "temptation" - the unpleasant and harsh face of reality.

>   That I might haue vnto my paramour,
>   That heauenly Helen which I saw of late,
>   Whose sweete imbracings may extinguish cleane
>   These thoughts that do disswade me from my vow
>   And keepe mine oath I made to Lucifer.
>   (A 1350-54)

If we keep the morality pattern in mind, the introjection of the Helen-apostrophe certainly signals a complete reversal of values. In a way, however, Faustus' heightened, Dionysian moment of

---

[39] "The Second Part of the Sermon of Repentance," in *Certain Sermons or Homilies, Appointed to be read in Churches in the time of Queen Elizabeth* (1562), ed. J. Griffiths (Oxford: Clarendon, 1840), pp. 477-82.

ravishment is just another desperate flight, here rendered in the play's finest poetry, and as such it is merely another manifestation of his predicament - his reprobation if we want to use the theological term - and of his "extinguishing cleane" the truth. There is no reason to invent a "sin of demoniality" or to assume that this act upsets "the nice balance between possible salvation and imminent damnation."[40] What the staging of the Helen apostrophe achieves, however, is a uniquely theatrical moment, fusing inspirited poetry, "heauenly beauty," magic, trance, and irony into a captivating, exhilarating experience.

Looking at the play as a whole, Faustus could be said to place at the end of all his flights of imagination the immortal Helen of Troy as the supreme emblem of "perfection." Her dazzling appearance (if it is staged as such), then, marks the climax of all the former visions of transcendence:

> Was this the face that launcht a thousand shippes?
> And burnt the toplesse Towres of Ilium?
> Sweete Helen, make me immortall with a kisse:
> Her lips sucke forth my soule, see where it flies:
> Come Helen, come giue mee my soule againe.
> Here wil I dwel, for heauen be in these lips,
> And all is drosse that is not Helena ... [*Enter Old Man*]
> O thou art fairer then the euening aire,
> Clad in the beauty of a thousand starres,
> Brighter art thou then flaming Iupiter,
> When he appeard to haplesse Semele,
> More louely then the monarke of the skie
> In wanton Arethusaes azurde armes,
> And none but thou shalt be my paramour. [*Exeunt*]
> (A 1357-63;1370-76)

But Faustus' ecstatic apostrophe, at the same time, reflects quite magnificently the opposed extremes of absolute beauty and absolute destruction (Troy; Jupiter-Semele; Faustus-as-Paris) that lie behind his self-consuming project. The extreme vigour of Faustus' fantastic flight washes away the feeble voice of the Old Man who enters (does the audience notice his entrance at all?) while Faustus is still soaring high and whose complaints are pale

---

40 W.W. Greg, "The Damnation of Faustus," *MLR*, 41 (1946),105-06.

and awkward in contrast to the splendid delights of imagination
with which Faustus manages to replace reality and hang on to his
insubstantial dreams. The Old Man's condemnatory speech ("Accursed
Faustus ...") of course brings the *theological* meaning back to
our memory, and one would have to argue that there is no doubt
about the extreme despair that qualifies Faustus as reprobate. In
his over-intensification of the harsh Calvinist concept of reprobation, Marlowe only heightens Faustus' tragic predicament, even
though the deliberate thrust of the immortalizing encounter with
Helen at least potentially undermines the presence of a thoroughly negative theology.

The stage-direction places the Old Man's entrance into the middle
of Faustus' invocation of Helen with which he gluts "the longing"
of his heart's "desire." Again, we could say that Helen becomes
the pervertedly transcendentalized version of Faustus' "chiefest
bliss," his *summum bonum*, and this echo of Faustus' early projects is compounded by the Old Man's unwittingly ironic use of
the word "fly" ("fliest the throne of his tribunall seate ...
hence I flie vnto my God"). The Old Man's exclamation becomes
a kind of *Mene Tekel*,[41] and his use of the word's semantic ambi-
buities ("flight"; "flying through the air"; "soaring"; "rising";
"fancy"; "fleeing"; "running away"; "escape", etc.) reflects
back upon the motif of *flight* that I regard as symbolic for
Faustus' upward fall. In the earlier pact-scene, Faustus had
been confronted with a most explicit *Mene Tekel*:

> But what is this inscription on mine arme?
> *Homo fuge*, whither should I flie?
> If vnto God hee'le throwe thee downe to hell,
> My sences are deciu'd, here's nothing writ,
> I see it plaine, here in this place is writ,
> *Homo fuge*, yet shall not Faustus flye.
> (A 517-22)

Faustus' hallucinations and his interpretation of them are as
significant as his determination *not* to go backward: "yet shall

---

41 Cf. the writing on the wall in Daniel v. 24-30.

not Faustus flye." If the Old Man episode suggests and clarifies the Calvinist context for the play, can the drama be seen, then, to imply that inside a Calvinist system of thought *only a reprobate* is able to act as a separate individual - and so as a *hero?* The Old Man sees a "violl full of precious grace"; the Scholars will urge Faustus to repent; and even Mephostophilis tells the truth most of the time - but Faustus as a protagonist has to reject all these invitations to stop being separate, different, individual. If his consciousness is to remain the arbiter which allows him to feel and speak as if in control, choosing this and rejecting that, then he must remain reprobate and cling to his own visions of "immortality."

It is quite ironic that Faustus' question "whither should I flie" echoes the very cry of the psalmist:

> Whither shal I go from thy Spirit?
> or whither shal I flee from thy presence?
> If I ascend up into heaven thou art there;
> if I lie downe in hel, thou art there.
> Let me take the wings of the morning,
> and dwell in the uttermost partes of the sea,
> Yet thether shal thine hand lead me,
> and thy right hand hold me.
> (Ps.139.7-10)

From the outset, Faustus has refused to see the meaning involved in these words; he never saw God's "right hand" but preferred to conceive of himself as being under the sway of God's retributive "left hand." The question of the psalmist implies the answer that there is no place where God's love and help will be denied him; Faustus' question implies that he has found such a place. He is "resolute" in his belief that wherever he might flee, condemnation is certain. This clearly indicates Faustus' conception of himself as reprobate. Such use of biblical allusion by Faustus, at the same time, intensifies the tragedy of his end, since we must assume that Faustus as theologian can only blaspheme and reverse the meaning of the Word deliberately - defining his individuality and his desire for power in opposition to the power of the Word. The 1616 text, incidentally, makes nonsense of this conception; B's dramaturgy and theological perspective shifts the emphasis to a different level altogether, making Faustus appear as a hopelessly pathetic victim. In B, his blindness and *mis*conception was "sent" him, effected in him by a twist of divine intention. This is a problem which would have to be examined in the light of the passage which we only find in the B version and in which Mephostophilis gleefully admits that it was he who "damb'd vp" Faustus' "passage," turning the leaves of the Bible and "leading" Faustus' eyes (cf. B 1988-92).

In the A version, however, it is Faustus who takes all the decisions, and it is his own apostasy - in the logic of its psychology - which forces (allows) him to consider himself damned. The tragedy of Faustus, in this perspective, is the tragedy of a man who deliberately and perversely *asserts* his own conception of himself - no matter how he reached this conception. His daemonic, self-imposed and self-prolonged reprobation thus initiates his heroic and pathetic fall.

Considering the difficulty of the theological assumptions sustained in a structure which so strongly builds up the catastrophic termination of Faustus' career and his portrayal as an unrepenting, unforgiven, and thus reprobate sinner, it appears helpful to have started our exploration of the theological themes with the Helen-Old Man episode which occurs near the tragic climax of Faustus' "upward fall" and assumes a particular significance in its strongly symbolic, contrapuntal orchestration. The scene is a considerable artistic achievement. First of all, it generates a strong suspense through its ominous juxtaposition of a double-edged seduction (the Old Man's invitation to repent; the erotic lure of Helen), which projects Faustus' internal conflicts into not altogether unambiguous dramatic emblems (Old Man as the apparent figure of Hope and Comfort in accordance with traditional morality symbolism/Helen of Troy as the emblem of perfection and beauty, concomitant with the image of her inexpressible excellence and her dangerous destructiveness). The emblematic situation, furthermore, is hardly comparable to anything we would find in popular legends or conventional moral drama. The despair-hope tableau, ostensibly presenting Faustus' wavering between good and evil, damnation and salvation, exploits the tension between the Old Man's exhortation and promise and the dagger of despair, silently handed over to Faustus by Mephostophilis who does not even bother to employ any insinuating rhetoric that is to be expected in a moment when he could capitalize on Faustus' de-moralization.[42] The latter's soul is so "distressed" that the Old Man's vision of an angel hovering over Faustus' head becomes a rather complicated issue.

Visual and verbal imagery - the Old Man's allegorical representation of Faith and Hope and his use of metaphor ("sweete path"; "teares, / Teares falling from repentant heauinesse"; Christ's "bloud alone must wash away thy guilt") - is employed to stress the developing significance of the dramatic action, and the suggestive, emotional directness of the emblematic juxtaposition serves to intensify the idea of a psychological struggle in Faustus' consciousness. Yet the dramatic spectacle does not simply provide a direct realization of the words; the stage picture could be seen as counterpointing the implied meaning of the situation, of the words, and thus the visual imagery becomes ironic rather than complementary. This effect is elaborated by the complex ambiguity that lies in the division between the emotional impact of the imagery and the overall psychological and theological continuity that I have tried to explain by the rigorous Calvinist premises which inform the language and structure of the play.

---

42 That so much space is allowed to the Old Man's attempt to "influence" Faustus is significant in itself. Silent Mephostophilis, obviously certain of his eventual victory, seems to become one of a line of figures of Despair, tempters with ropes and daggers, persuading men to the sin of Judas, who betrayed Christ and went ou to hang himself. The temptation to despair was a familiar topos and could be found everywhere in religious and literary texts. Parallel cases can be examined in *Nice Wanton, The Conflict of Conscience, A Looking-Glass for Lodnon, The Fairie Queene* (Book I), even in Sordido's farcical attempt to put an end to himself in *Everyman out of his Humour*, to quote just a few examples.

In terms of the concepts with which Marlowe's Christian theology in the play is concerned and which give clear implications of a Faustus-conception that questions the hero's self-assumed reprobation against the background of a Reformed religious philosophy (the doctrines of predestination, grace, and fiduciary faith), the Old Man's promise of God's grace would, on the one hand, abstractly signify the existence of this possibility. On the other hand, remembering Calvin's and Perkins' explanation that reprobates may be admonished by the word of God yet cannot answer the calling because God has "hardened" their hearts in the first place, the Old Man's lecture could be seen as paradoxically enforcing Faustus' utter demoralization and thus remaining a mere taunt - a splendid mockery handed down by an all-powerful system. The Old Man's farewell

> I goe sweete Faustus, but with heauy cheare,
> Fearing the ruine of thy hopelesse soule.
> (A 1327-28)

enforces the impression that there is indeed no help for Faustus' "hopelesse soule" (the B-text uses the much weaker "haplesse" [B 1842], in the sense of "unfortunate") and that the Old Man's stage appearance is almost comically subverting the power of an old, conventional emblem (I am here thinking of the Old Man's timid entries and exits, his pathetic sermonizing, his ineffectiveness, and Marlowe's placing of his re-entrance right in the middle of the Helen apostrophe).

Could we go so far as to say that Marlowe's "naturalistic" devices oftentimes de-conventionalize the traditional significance of moral and spiritual references?[43] One can easily demonstrate this with the spectacle of the Seven Deadly Sins, for example; in the Helen/Old Man episode the manipulation of language and

---

43 The case for Marlowe's tendency to translate metaphor into literal fact or to invert spiritual and physical realities and deprive conventional symbols of their moral imperatives can be made with regard to a number of scenes in Marlowe's works that have justifiably provoked the notion of his iconoclasm (cf. the amoral "thirst of reign" in *Tamburlaine* and,

visual imagery is more complicated, however. The second point I want to make about this episode will not only refer to these manipulations, but also help us to see how the relationship between imagery and theatrical juxtaposition complements the theological ideas in the play's total structure and intensifies the problematic theological *agon* which seems to qualify Faustus' attitude from the very first scene.

In spite of the ambivalent nature of the Old Man's role, his appearance and his exhortation fulfil an important function with regard to Marlowe's dramatic method of confronting two contradictory points of view with each other. Whatever theological rigour one might apply in view of the play's demonstrative intensification of the Calvinist system of predestination and reprobation, it is clear from the outset that the Faustian flights of imagination and his apostasy stress a principle of heroic self-assertion that necessarily pits this aesthetic of individualism and self-determinacy against the normative tradition of a system which blocks the individual's striving for freedom.

The drama of Faustus' *flight* enacts precisely this double-aesthetic and brings to collision the conception Faustus has of himself and of his culture's cherished orthodoxies and those orthodoxies themselves which are mainly externalized and brought forward in the spectacle of the doctrinal world crushing the voice of the monopolist hero who chose to stand apart, separate and uncompromising. The "ouerthrow" that the Prologue predicts terminates the hero's flight in the final scene of retributive justice; the question of the inevitability of Faustus' fall has to be seen in conjunction with all the other dramatic and theological antitheses or contrarieties that energize the Faustian movements "upwards" and "downwards." I think one can say that there is

---

especially, the hero's sadistic jests in the "footstool"-, "cage"- and "chariot"-scenes, or the unusual treatment of emblems in *The Jew of Malta* and *Edward II*). For a discussion of Marlowe's ironic method, see D.J. Palmer's essay "Marlowe's Naturalism," in *Morris*, pp. 153-75.

a particularly interesting division between the plot structure, which seems to constitute a rigid, linear progress towards the tragic climax, and the poetry of *Dr Faustus*, which in a dialectical movement qualifies and undermines the orthodox, homiletic plot and creates the central *agon* - the psychic convulsions of the protagonist whose progressive poetic struggle to stand up for his expression of who he is (or wants to be) isolates him further and further in his resistance to the structure of the doctrinal world and finally destroys him.[44]

Faustus' dream of power, which is first of all a dream to be able to carry out one's choices, is theatrically presented in the typical manner of Marlowe's strongest poetic energy. Faustus' poetry of aspiration communicates the lively picture of a man whose soaring imagination necessarily claims the freedom to make choices; these choices, however, place him into opposition to a system, represented by the sciences and the theology he rejects, which possesses the only models of explanation and, of course, disapproval for Faustus' negative act of disassociating himself from the shared consciousness. It is very significant that Faustus' own consciousness is overridden by a strange mixture of repulsion at the determinism of the Calvinist system he so fervently attacks, and an obviously unavoidable adherence to the psychology which informs the formulae and principles of this system and as such defines the materialistic and metaphysical

---

44 This isolating movement, which is recognizable in the clearly defined stages of the play's act-structure, has traditionally been described as a "downward" fall, a social and intellectual descent, which consequently invites firm, moral judgment. See, for example, George K. Hunter, "Five-Act Structure in *Doctor Faustus*," *TDR*, 8 (1964), 77-91. However, the poetic power of Faustus' fruitless rebellion and the uncomfortable rigidity of the theological system that does not resolve (explain) its reprehensible doctrinal ambiguities, may very well point to a different conception on Marlowe's part of the Faustian desire to "trie the vttermost," a desire that has a claim to greatness regardless of all the pressures in favour of conformity. That the *plot* finally confirms orthodox values does not mean too much in the light of Marlowe's poetic iconoclasm; compared to *Tamburlaine*, however, it shows a rather different attitude toward what is possible.

implications of his negative posture.

Faustus' belief in his role as decision-maker, a role which would allow him to speak and feel as if in control, forces him to go through the turmoils resulting from his singular commitment to a conception of himself which locks him up in a stalemate. The play thus dramatizes the problem of a paradox which reverberates through the major theological doctrines of predestination and grace themselves. Faustus' choice indicates the potential of movement, of change, of alteration through conflict - and we surely have to assume that a mental state of *stasis* is alien to upward-moving *flights* as it is alien to the fundamental Christian belief in man's perfectibility through insight, repentance, and self-amendment. On the surface, however, the stalemate I mentioned seems to preclude any redemptive process since Faustus' own self-determination, his belief that he is reprobate, is counterpoised with the necessitarianism from which Faustus' inference is drawn and which lies at the centre of the play's tragic theology.

Since I now wish to explore the crucial terms of the theological *agon*, I will turn to the contests of theological repartee and to the rhetorical flights that distinguish Faustus' attitude and his relationship with the doctrinal world. Maximum suspense is created by the theatrical expression of the inward, spiritual struggle in Faustus' mind, and whether or not the outcome of this struggle is predictable, the agony of doubt becomes the crucial experience, both theatrically and theologically, within the Faustian dilemma. Mephostophilis' dagger is a most telling dramatic symbol for the almost suicidal frustration that aggravates Faustus

> But fearefull echoes thunders in mine eares,
> Faustus, thou art damn'd, then swordes and kniues,
> Poyson, gunnes, halters, and invenomed steele
> Are layde before me to dispatch my selfe,
> And long ere this I should haue slaine my selfe,
> Had not sweete pleasure conquerd deepe dispaire.
> (A 649-54)

and he has to answer the insinuations of the more Macbethian

"dagger of the mind" (the temptation to do "the deed," as the
B-text reads, B 593) with ever-renewed efforts to "resolve" himself. The Faustian ordeal seems to reflect a striking insight
on Marlowe's part into the Protestant religious temper, and it is
not difficult - on account of the Reformation maxim of *fiducia*
which could so readily subject the embattled Christian conscience
to the perennial question of possible or impossible assurance of
faith and salvation - to see how Marlowe used the polarity of his
double-aesthetic in order to move his hero's flight into the
dramatic foreground of the Faust material he borrowed from the
Lutheran Faust Book, which by itself afforded enough space for
the construction of an unrelieved tragedy. The tragic conception
of the Faustian ordeal, understood in this context of fideistic
doctrines, can be further illuminated by contrasting Marlowe's
dramatization of the theological *agon* with similar literary treat-
ments of the problem.

First of all, it is interesting to recall the older Catholic
tradition and its representations of a compact with the Devil,
which had had deep roots in religious belief and popular fancy
alike and, in the form of the Theophilus-legend, merged into the
16th century Lutheran creation of the Faust-myth and the Faust-
Book material. That material, of course, had undergone a further
metamorphosis (P.F.'s translation) by the time it reached Marlowe. There is a marked contrast between the former, merciful
tradition and the Protestant Faust-Book which lays so much
emphasis on the gloomy working out of retributive justice. In
those miracle plays that to my knowledge most significantly
hold on to the pre-Reformation conception of a sinner who is
saved by the intervention of the Virgin Mary, *Le Miracle de
Théophile* and *Mariken van Nieumeghen*,[45] the devil-compact and

---

45   *Le Miracle de Théophile* (c.1261), ed. Grace Frank, Classiques
     Français du Moyen Age (Paris: Librairie Ancienne Honoré Cham-
     pion, 1949). Translation provided by J. Stevens and R. Axton,
     eds., *French Medieval Drama* (Cambridge: Cambridge Univ.Press,
     1974). The Dutch legend of *Mary of Nemegen* (ed. H.Morgan and
     A.J. Barnouw, facsimile rpt. [Cambridge,Mass.: Harvard Univ.
     Press, 1934]) first appeared in an English translation(1518)

the battle over the sinner's soul stand in the centre of the dramatic interest. The Catholic logic focussed on the belief in an ultimate reconciliation and the mediating influence of the Blessed Virgin who would plead for mercy and help the seduced sinners to escape the punishment for dealing with the Devil. This implies that the protagonists of the older morality or miracle plays were to be shown as retaining their hope and trust in God and Mary, in spite of their sinfulness and in spite of the satanic spell.

In the crucial scene of the Dutch drama, Mariken, who had been portrayed sympathetically despite her sinful compact with Satan, almost despairs after the seven years of her contract have run out. In the inset play of Masscheron, the devil's procurator, the pageant of the traditional mercy-justice theme allegorizes the devil's plea for justice and his demand of God that the sinfulness of Mankind be judged by the same measure as that of the fallen angels. The devil's advocate has such a strong case that God regards it as necessary to have recourse to punishment - yet at this point the Virgin averts the disaster by her compassionate intervention. To Mariken, the pageant is an effective exemplum; her tears begin to flow and her repentance breaks the satanic spell. The devil's insistence on the validity of the pact is made ineffective by the Virgin's plea, and the play ends with the happy idealism expressed through God's ultimate benevolence and mercy.

In the French play, Théophile's contract with Satan also runs out after seven years, and he finds himself "trapped" in his agony:

> Pathetic wretch! What will become of me?
> How can the earth support my sinful weight,
> When I've renounced my God and venerate
> A fiend as lord, who causes sin and misery?

---

and, in the same year, in a Dutch dramatic version as *Mariken van Nieumeghen* (Antwerpen: Willem Vorsterman, 1518).

> God I denied - the secret can't be kept.
> I've lost the balm of life; I'm caught
> Upon the Judas tree. The devil bought
> My title deeds: my soul must pay the debt.
>
> What will you do with this unhappy fool,
> O God, whose spirit will go to the boiling heat
> Of hell, there to be trampled by devils' feet?
> Break open, earth, and swallow up my soul!
>
> Lord God, what will this desperate outcast do?
> Despised by God, exposed to ridicule
> By men, betrayed and trapped by fiends in hell ...
>   (*Théophile* 384-97)

Yet he finds the way to the Virgin's Chapel and to repentance, and after his address to Mary, the Virgin snatches the covenant from the claws of Satan and returns it to Théophile. It is a far cry from these pact-makers' miraculous resurrection to the harsh Protestant climate in the Faust story. The advice, for example, of Mary of Nemegen's uncle, "say nat so good cosen for there is nobody loste without the fall in despayer,"[46] is almost immediately represented by Mary's own trust and hope in forgiveness. Mary, although she confesses to have been "the dyuels paramoure by the space of vij yere,"[47] recaptures her hope for salvation.

The Protestant conception of Faustus' deterioration and fiendish disposition (in the legend) renders him a prey to his own egocentric passions, his despair, and his fear of the consequences. The Protestant doctrines and their pessimistic view of the world influence the Faust-conception in Marlowe's source to such an extent that the traditional balance between mercy and justice, between salvation and damnation, is obviously upset. This leads to a change in the direction which homiletic structure and plot take in the Faust story and, consequently, it affects the protagonist's image of God too. I should think that the pessimistic and deterministic philosophy underlying the story of Faust's fall leaves very little room open for any expectations of miraculous

---

46 *Mary of Nemegen*, sig.C lv.
47 Ibid., sig.B 2.

epiphanies and surprise reversals. The way to despair and to the prospect of just and eternal damnation had been mapped out too well.

The awesome stress in the picture of Faustus' career seems to rest on the impending catastrophe, on the psychological impossibility of forgiveness. The emphasis on punishment for man's sins becomes a new admonitory strategy. In the source as well as in Marlowe's drama, doubt and despair become dreadful states, for they are qualified by the enveloping, formal theology of the Reformation and have to be set against the backdrop of election and reprobation. The syndrome of hopelessness is already outlined quite distinctly in the Faust-Book and its English translation. We read how Faustus was "neuer falling to repentance truly" but "in all his opinions doubtfull, without faith or hope."[48] To Faustus, knowledge of sin, without fiduciary faith, becomes sheer agony:

> What meane I then to complaine where no helpe is? No, I know no hope resteth in my gronings. I haue desired that it should be so, and God hath sayd Amen to my misdoings.

There is no merciful God, nor an intervening intermediary for Faustus, and he ends in utter resignation:

> Ah wo is me, for there is no help for me, no shield, no defence no comfort. Where is my hold? knowledge dare I not trust: and for a soule to God wards that haue I not, for I shame to speake vnto him.[49]

In Marlowe's play, the condemnatory diagnosis of Faustus' motives and the homecoming of hell to a depraved creature are replaced by a dramatic intensification of those symptoms that make the hero's upward flight of imagination and his downward lapse into doubt and despair a radical and disturbing experience because it casts a long shadow on the soteriological terms by which the Lutheran-Calvinist system is construed. From Faustus' opening

---

48 *The Historie of the Damnable Life*, chap. XIII (Palmer and More, p. 151).
49 Ibid., chap. LXI (Palmer and More, p. 225).

interpretation of the Pauline and Johannine texts and throughout his ensuing struggle to retain his self-chosen pose, there is a clear and logical pattern of Faustian despair mingled with presumption which implicates the ominous consequence that he has not and will not pass the test of "election." Even if the play in its double-aesthetic insists on the *potential* existence of hope, the hero's introspection serves to prolong the deadlock. Reformed theology modelled the notion of assurance, or absolute reliability, on one of the favourite proof texts, the Pauline injunction to "Prove your selves whether ye are in the faith: examine your selves: know ye not your own selves, how that Jesus Christ, is in you, except ye be reprobates?" (2 Cor.xiii.5).

This makes it clear, I think, that the outside world (the Old Man's vision of the "violl"; the Scholars' assumptions), and what we may perceive of it, is not entirely relevant to the individual's inner state of introspective knowledge - the burden lies exclusively on the individual's *self*-examination. Translated into theatrical terms, this seems to be the compulsive idea behind the play of mind in the play: if Faustus thinks he is in pain, he is; if he thinks he is determined to die a sinner, he is. If Faustus cannot find fiduciary faith in himself, he has none.

This is an urgent problem, because it reflects back upon Faustus' confrontation with the concept of predestination and free will. For Luther as for the Reformation generally, predestination is a grim and terrifying doctrine. "When a man begins to discuss predestination," Luther says, "the temptation is like an inextinguishable fire; the more he disputes, the more he despairs. ... I forget all that Christ and God are, when I get to thinking about this matter, and come to believe that God must be a villain."[50] Faustus' contempt for law, logic, medicine, and theology touches the heart of "this matter":

---

50 *A Compend to Luther's Theology*, ed. Hugh Thomson Kerr (Philadelphia: Westminster Press, 1943), p. 36.

> Diuinitie is basest of the three,
> Vnpleasant, harsh, contemptible and vilde.
> (A 141-42, not in B)

For the true believer, there can be no scandal in stating the doctrine of predestination in its most rigid terms, which Luther and Calvin do. It is, Luther asserts, "essentially necessary and wholesome for Christians to know: that God foreknows nothing by contingency, but that he foresees, purposes, and does all things according to his immutable, eternal, and infallible will." And, he adds at once, "by this thunderbolt, Free-will is thrown prostrate, and utterly dashed to pieces."[51] Both the cause of salvation and the cause of damnation therefore are thought to rest in God's inscrutable will.

The scandal that is cautiously hinted at by Faustus' theological *agon* is exactly this inscrutability; it conveys a sense of "almightie doome" which Faustus nervously brushes aside. Recrosse, in the Cave of Despair episode of Spenser's *Fairie Queene, Book I*, has a similarly depressing encounter with the highly rhetorical voice of despair:

> Is not his deed, what euer thing is donne,
> In heauen and earth? did not he all create
> To die againe? all ends that was begonne.
> Their times in his eternall booke of fate
> Are written sure, and haue their certaine date.
> Who then can striue with strong necessitie,
> That holds the world in his still chaunging state,
> Or shunne the death ordaynd by destinie?
> When houre of death is come, let none aske whence,nor why.
> (*F.Q.* 9.42)[52]

"What euer thing is donne" is, if not a divine deed, still the necessary effect of the divine cause. The argument that God's providence is all-pervading is not necessarily new; yet the crucial Reformation doctrine of justification by faith alone extends the medieval tradition (Boethius, Aquinas, Ockham, etc.)

---

51 Martin Luther, *On the Bondage of Will*, trans. Henry Cole (London: T. Bensley, 1823), p. 26.
52 *The Poetical Works of Edmund Spenser*, ed. J.C. Smith and E. de Selincourt (1912; rpt.London: Oxford Univ. Press, 1969).

considerably and places everything in the hands of the Creator, to whose omnipotence all things yield. Redcrosse is reminded that there are people who, no matter what they *do* or *feel*, are damned - and were so, indeed, "before the foundations of the world were laid."[53] If Faustus understands the implication that *what is by free will is in fact from predestination*, then his total rejection of the system and his dream of "power, of honour, of omnipotence" become a poignantly clear presumption. Faustus' intention to countermine the limits that the system imposes on him goes further; he seems to *embrace* the idea that there can be no assurance of salvation for him, because this is the only way of asserting his will-power, as he makes clear in his exegesis of the Gospel.

Spenser's "Booke of Holinesse," while it correctly states the doctrine of imputation and God's grace, at the same time intensifies the problematic of fiduciary faith and appears to call rather systematically Redcrosse's former assurance in question, which is most intensely felt in Despayre's rhetorical attack on Redcrosse's "guilt":

> What man is he, that boasts of fleshly might,
> And vaine assurance of mortality ...
> Ne let the man ascribe it to his skill,
> That thorough grace hath gained victory.
> If any strength we haue, it is to ill,
> But all the good is Gods, both power and eke will.
> (*F.Q.*10.1)

The categorical determinism in this comment by the narrator is unmistakable; God, we are told, provides not only the power to will the good, but the act of will itself. If everything is written in God's "eternall booke of fate," and if one can establish an orthodox necessitarianism from the working out of God's decree, then one can sympathize with Faustus' sophisticated sophistry: "we must sinne, and so consequently die" (A 74-5). Behind these lines, one can feel the lingering problem of theo-

---

53 Quoted from Article 17 of the Thirty-Nine Articles.

dicy, a problem even Milton could barely solve in his providential scheme of *Paradise Lost*.

There are two ways out of the impasse for Faustus: either he draws the heterodox inference that, regarding the inevitability of fall, God is the direct cause of or an accomplice in human sin; or he can believe that the only way of actually asserting his *free will* is acting contrary to God's will. Faustus performs this act of will; his dismissal of the doctrinal world is an effective theatrical demonstration of what he means by separating himself from the system of predestination and grace. If man cannot be made capable of his own salvation, then he may be free to will his own daemonization.

> A sound magician is a mightie god:
> Heere Faustus trie thy braines to gaine a deitie.

Faustus' hubris and presumption are part of the sophistication with which he pushes aside all disturbing perceptions; in other words, his presumption and extravagant imagination serve as logical counterparts to what one would theologically describe as despair. "Vaine assurance" or "presumption" is itself a form of despair, the form incarnated by Orgoglio in Spenser's Canto 7.

Is the Faustian voice a voice out of a bottomless cave? Could we see his flight of imagination as suicide, as a synecdoche for the *deliberate rejection* of Christian hope? I think that what may be an adequate theological description would nevertheless make complete nonsense of Faustus' poetic voice. Marlowe's total emphasis is without doubt placed upon the hero's poetry of individual aspiration; as opposed to Shakespeare's more elegiac mode in the soliloquies of his great tragic heroes, Marlowe's Faustus presses forward with the relentless energy of a total, undetached involvement. The fact that he is caught in his emotional pursuit which makes his lines so powerful, increases the distance between him and the ironic undertones provided by the plot-construction (the parodic scenes) and the play's theological structure. What Marlowe's drama achieves through this technique is a tragic polarization of the double-aesthetic I mentioned before: Faustus' self-willed performance asserts his independence, while this assertion at the same time implies a self-destructive mechanism.

In looking again at the Helen/Old Man episode, one can see that the spiritual agony of doubt, or the "return of the repressed" as one might call it, has caught up with Faustus' overactive and impatient imagination. The struggle over mercy and justice, despair and damnation seems perfectly conventional in its dramatic presentation; yet contrary to the treatment in earlier morality plays, it hinges clearly on Protestant solifidianism. The A-text is again more to the point in explicitly stressing the crucial issue of God's mercy:

> Accursed Faustus, where is mercie now?
> (A 1329)
> Accursed Faustus, wretch what hast thou done?
> (B 1843)

Faustus' question has the form of an apostrophe: God, where are you now? What could mercy possibly do for *me*? That Faustus calls on God in this scene is not quite consistent with his former rejection of the very same Saviour-God whom he now recognizes as the only possible source of salvation (cf. "See see where Christs blood streames in the firmament" A 1463). It is consistent, however, that the A-text emphasizes the personalized conflict between Faustus and God, between Faustus' apostasy and hubris and the image of the God he rejects and who almost exclusively possesses the face of a stern, relentless judge. This personalized conflict is only carried out in the A version,[54]

---

[54] The absence of this personalization, effected by editorial changes in the B-text, is also consonant with a wholly different tone in B. Compare, for example, the following passages: "What God can hurt thee Faustus? thou art safe" (A 465) / "What power can hurt me? Faustus thou art safe" (B 413); "If vnto God hee'le throwe thee downe to hell" (A 519) / "If vnto heauen, hee'le throwe thee downe to hell"(B 466); "And Faustus vowes ... Neuer to name God,or to pray to him" (A 725-26; missing in B).

and it is again only the A-text which constructs the symbolic double-temptation (Faustus' despair and embrace of Helen/the Old Man's trial by the devils) which one could almost appreciate as parodic if the context was not so serious. Faustus' wavering doubt is terminated by the devil's threat (which results in Faustus' mock-repentance), whereas the Old Man's faith is put to the test:

> Sathan begins to sift me with his pride,
> As in this furnace God shal try my faith,
> My faith, vile hel, shal triumph ouer thee ...
> (A 1381-83)

The Old Man's martyrdom and faith become an impressive, contrasting allegory of *fiducia* - and since it only underlines Faustus' own failure and impotence (looked at from the point of view of the doctrinal world), it turns into a spectacle of mockery.

Marlowe seems to enjoy playing with these theatrical effects; he uses at least three other traditional devices which rather ironically comment upon themselves and upon the tragic predicament of Faustus himself. Firstly, the grandfatherly Old Man suggests "teares, / Teares falling from repentant heauinesse" (A 1306-07, in a speech which drastically differs from B 1813-29). We remember that for Mary of Nemegen the tears of repentance signified the breaking of the satanic spell, the nullification of the pact. For Faustus, the devil's insistence on the pact is too powerful and threatening, especially since it converges on his own understanding of the situation. This effective consolidation of the compact indicates how far removed Marlowe's tragic conception is from the Catholic tradition. Faustus himself repeats the allusion to the allegory of the tears:

> ... ah my God, I woulde weepe, but the diuel drawes
> in my teares, gush forth bloud, insteade of teares,
> yea life and soule, Oh he stayes my tong ...
> (A 1416-18)

The most remarkable reversal, however, is launched through the staging of Helen's "second Coming." This is a great theatrical moment which practically topples the entire allegorical Old Man

episode. Faustus has just been overawed by Mephostophilis'
threats - it is a moment when in the older Virgin Mary plays
the Virgin would have entered to intervene and to help the poor
sinner. Marlowe, however, uses the apparition of Helen as a
spectacular vehicle for poetic sublimation, grim ironic comment,
and blasphemous parody. The "heauenly Helen" is conjured up to
help Faustus keeping his daemonic oath; if Helen could be seen
as a parody of divine intervention, the blasphemous contrast
between Helen as the personification of destructive and volupt-
uous beauty and the Blessed Virgin could not be greater. I am
inclined to establish this connection, since Marlowe does not
hesitate, in *The Jew of Malta*, to give a thoroughly profane,
literal meaning to the image of "infinite riches in a little
room" (I.i.37), which, as George Hunter has demonstrated,[55]
was a conceit traditionally applied to the Virgin Mary who bore
the Son of God in her womb.

Faustus' apostrophe is certainly the poetic climax of the hero's
many flights of imagination, and the verses that glitter and
shine so much transport Faustus into another intense self-realization, which makes it possible for him to look at Helen and
declare: "heauen be in these lips." At the same time, the
tragic meaning makes itself felt through the extreme pathos of
Faustus' self-bedazzlement; again, the poetry is emotional and
involved, and Faustus does not realize that he is worshipping a
gigantic illusion. The ironic undertones seem accidental;
Faustus is unaware of them, while the audience perceives the
enticing destructiveness of Faustus' "paramour."

The images used for Helen include "burnt", "suckes forth",
"sackt", "combate", "wound", "flaming", "wanton", and "haplesse." Helen's "intervention" cannot save Faustus - she does
not even speak to him but silently passes over the stage. His
despair remains unaltered, and his immortalization is nothing

---

55 See "The Theology of Marlowe's *The Jew of Malta*, 221-25.

but a beautiful dream.

Theologically, Helen of Troy represents little harm except that she serves as a further intoxication for Faustus' agonized consciousness, a further denial to see the truth and to recognize that his self-determined "pursuit of aloneness" and individualism has been self-destructive.

Chapter Five

CHOREOGRAPHY IN THE DAMNATION SCENE

In an interesting attempt to elicit a new immediacy of audience participation in the experience of Faustus' tragic fall, the Polish director Jerzy Grotowski rearranged the script in order to focus on the staging of the hero's "last supper" and final damnation.[1] Using the entire auditorium as playing area, Grotowski's production begins with Faustus inviting his friends (the Scholars) and guests (the audience) to join his last banquet and take part in a feast which is gradually transformed, however, into a spectacle of confession and re-enactment of the Faustian quest, ending in the violent victimization scene during which Faustus tastes the martyrdom of his hell and eternal damnation.

Grotowski takes considerable freedom in re-constructing the plot along the lines of a confession, retrospectively offering the episodes of Faustus' "upward fall" - yet I think there is some justification in the special emphasis that is laid upon the underlying archetypal form of the hero's career or autobiography. If we look at the original text of the scene, we can certainly notice how the play reaches a special tone or level of suspense at this moment of Faustus' career (his last conversation with the Scholars), a mood of pending finality which already expresses Faustus' awareness and acceptance that his 24 years of "liberty", "pleasure", and "daliance"(B 862-63) have come full circle.

---

[1] Cf. Eugenio Barba's report on Grotowski's production-approach, "Dr. Faustus: Textual Montage," which is included in Jerzy Grotowski's *Towards a Poor Theatre* (New York: Simon & Schuster, 1968), pp. 79-98. Grotowski's version of the play was originally produced by the Theatre Laboratory in Opole, Poland, in 1963. Barba's notes were first published as *"Doctor Faustus in Poland,"* TDR, 8 (1964), 120-33.

```
Fau.     Ah Gentlemen!
1.Sch.   What ailes Faustus?
Fau.     Ah my sweete chamber-fellow! had I liued with
         thee, then had I liued stil, but now I die
         eternally.                  (A 1388-91)
```

The astonishing, elegiac mode of Faustus' encounter with his friends is contained in a prose passage of considerable complexity. In terms of Marlowe's orchestration of dramatic events, the swift contrapuntal shift from the extraordinary poetic rapture of the Helen apostrophe to the somber, earnest leave-taking scene tells us a lot about the techniques Marlowe uses in order to engage our imaginative participation in the creation of an intricate theatrical experience. Precisely because so little is left of Faustus' earlier flamboyant flights of imagination, the prose scene with its remarkable plainness of tone and diction and almost complete lack of ornament and metaphor gains an emotional intensity which significantly underlines the hero's precarious self-revelation, the recognition and acceptance of his transgressions.

Faustus' rise in tragic stature is correlated to the psychological and ethical paradox behind this recognition: the man who has attained it cannot be saved by it. Whatever degree of fascination or exasperation we might have reached in our response to Faustus' performance, his despairing confession of failure has an emotional impact which surpasses much of what was before. In a way, his self-accusations are more powerfully moving than his poetic visions were enticing. Faustus' "desperate enterprise" becomes truly desperate in the moment when he moves towards a grasping of his responsibility for his own destruction, and the theological perspective in the play becomes most crucially enforced at a point where Faustus reaches a kind of genuine, emotional despair which cannot be relieved any more.

While Faustus' enormous "self-conceit" finally breaks down in the face of what now announces itself as an objective, unavoidable reality, Marlowe very effectively directs our response towards sympathy and pity. The farewell scene exhibits the great affection which the Scholars feel for the doctor and their concern for his fate; the sad, moving expressiveness of Faustus' prose has been observed by many critics, yet the most poignantly emotional response on which I wish to comment seems to originate from the quivering fear and terror that is built into Faustus' discourse and raises it above mere lament - thus connecting this scene directly with the following damnation scene.

At a closer look, the speeches reveal emblematic and symbolic dimensions which far transcend the immediate narrative and point to the play's iterative imagistic patterns, while at the same time a number of text directions supply cues for visual and verbal enactment which link the scene stylistically with the final damnation scene and prepare us for the amplification of Faustus' psychic agony.

> ... looke, comes he not? comes he not?
> . . .
> O would I had neuer seene Wertenberge, neuer read booke ...
> Faustus hath lost both Germany, and the world, yea heauen it selfe, heauen the seate of God, the throne of the blessed, the kingdome of ioy, and must remaine in hel for euer, hel, ah hel for euer, sweete friends, what shall become of Faustus, being in hel for euer?   (A 1392;1407;1410-14)

There is more than desperation in this language. Caught up by the pressures of association, which are now embodied with a content that is *not* negated, blasphemed, or ridiculed any more ("hel"; "God"; "heauen", etc.), Faustus' mind yields to its projections of terror and fear, choked with the sudden panic of impotence. The most characteristic stylistic element of the speeches is the staccato-like rhythm of the exclamations (self-fragmenting references to his past or to the imminent threat of everlasting death) which adequately transpose the quivering heart into verbal (and visual) action.

These jerking motions are intensified by a syntax broken into many antithetical components, parallelisms, and negative conjunctions ("liue...die"; "on God...on God"; "in hel for euer,

ah hel for euer"; "Eue may be sau'd, but not Faustus"; "neuer
seene...neuer read"; "I would weepe, but..."; "I would lift...
but..."), the word "but" most clearly signalling the struggle
in Faustus' mind. The figure of *epizeuxis*

> I would lift vp my hands, but see, they hold them,
> they hold them ...
> I pray for me, pray for me ...
> (A 1419-20;1442)

not only expresses the hero's impotence and fear verbally, it is
here also meant to extend the verbal action into a visual image
(Faustus' attempt to lift up his hands, to pray). The linguistic
structure and emotional content of the speeches achieve a concentrated theatrical fusion with the gestic effects: the symbolic significance of Faustus' inability to "lift himself up"
lies in the powerfully suggestive form in which internal conflicts are projected into theatrical images. The visual details
contract the symbolic levels for the entire scene, turning action
and language into a single emblem of failure - an emblem of
Faustus' loss of his former, self-confident bravura.

The image of the Faustian failure *and* of his un-repentance
furthermore relates to the hero's poetic "flights" and the
play's inherent dialectic between aspiration and limit. The
limits had always been there, yet Faustus had flung his self-
assertions against them, and the vertical patterning of his
rhetoric of transcendence represented a successful force through
which Faustus tried to "live" his self-projections and self-
images. The dramatic tensions and ironies in the play draw their
special significance from the fact that Marlowe directs the
energy of Faustus' individualistic assertion against the most
severely limiting norms of a rigid Calvinist determinism. The
farewell scene, then, discloses the tortuous transformation of
a rebellious upward thrust into a tragically impotent attempt
at abandoning the *consequences* of the confrontational pursuit.
The vertical pattern is echoed with heightened passion, but the
earlier "I will ... I will ... I shall" has changed into "I

would":

> I woulde weepe ...
> I would lift vp my hands ...

This image of Faustus' languishing weakness and constriction ("they hold them, they hold them") anticipates the most striking re-enactment of his upward leap in the last scene, where his imagination can create innumerable fantasies of refuge but still no break with his conception that places salvation tantalizingly beyond his upward reaching:

> O Ile leape vp to my God: who pulles me downe?
> See see where Christs blood streames in the firmament,
> One drop would saue my soule, halfe a drop, ah my Christ.
> (A 1462-64)

In many ways, the spectacular scene of Faustus' death is bound to rouse a considerable emotional response, especially since Marlowe's shifts in tone and presentation, as I mentioned earlier, indicate his dramaturgical concerns about how to involve the audience in an experience of extreme terror and suffering and make it so immediate and painful that one may feel compelled to shake off any prevailing sense of moral justice and, on the contrary, ponder the suggestion that the hero is more sinned against than sinning. (This, incidentally, was the main idea behind Grotowski's production.)

Regardless of interpretive disagreements, we should be primarily interested in responding to what the dramatist offers to his theatre audience, to the features of his dramaturgy which control our involvement in the rhythm of the ending. I am here concerned with the specific dynamics in Faustus' final soliloquy or, in other words, with the orchestration of stage speech and presentational devices as it is implied by Marlowe's text. The terms "orchestration" and "choreography" as I use them are meant to refer to the dramatist's control of stage action - in all its aural, verbal, visual, and kinetic dimensions - and to his basic efforts to structure and maintain the live pressures of his poetry in performance conditions (as "lived" by the Faustus-

actor). Such efforts obviously have to be met by the director
and the actors. The reason why I mentioned Grotowski's *Faustus*
production in the beginning was not so much my interest in his
textual montage or his quite eccentric mythical interpretation,
as rather my fascination with his attitude towards theatre, namely his effort to strip the play-in-performance of all sophisticated and unnecessary technological effects and to strive for a
pure, "poor," and confrontational creation.

Grotowski's concentration on the "orchestration of voices" and
the "controlled use of gesture"[2] as well as his suggestions for
specific spectator-actor relationships (Faustus' "last supper"
in a monastery refectory, enacted among the audience) seem to
bring his theatre closer to what we have learnt to understand as
the peculiar felicities of the Elizabethan theatre: its bare
stage, its acting conventions, its spatial, emblematic design,
and the poetic immediacy through which its dramaturgy could make
ideas and images collide through words, creating magic-like
visions of anything the imagination could body forth - "The
cloud-capp'd towers, the gorgeous palaces, / The solemn temples,
the great globe itself ... such stuff / As dreams are made on"
(Prospero in *The Tempest* IV.i.151-53;156-57).

In a recent study on the language and theatrical mode of Marlowe's *Tamburlaine*, the valuable suggestion has been made to in-
vestigate the play's "theatre poetry," i.e. the "functional
architecture of the speeches," their "physical demands on the
actor," as well as their linguistic structures as they correspond to a kind of "emblematic presentation of character."[3] This
approach to the patterns of Marlowe's verse and their performance
function within the visual and scenic structures of the dramatic
action is an important step beyond earlier studies on the ritual-

---

2   *Towards a Poor Theatre*, p. 21.
3   Margaret Shewring and Clive Barker, "The 'Theatre-Poetry' of
    Christopher Marlowe, with specific reference to *Tamburlaine*,
    Part I and *Part II*," Unpubl. paper presented at the Shakes-
    peare Institute, 28 May, 1981 (quoted with permission of the
    authors).

istic quality of Marlowe's drama and its scenic devices by Glynne Wickham[4] and on his elaborate use of visual spectacle by Jocelyn Powell.[5] If we think of the last Act in *Dr Faustus*, and the stage-directions in the B-text in particular (e.g. the disclosure of Hell and Heaven's throne; Lucifer's ascent to the platform "above"), Marlowe's recourse to the medieval dramatic tradition and to the residual religious symbolism of the Elizabethan playhouse may appear obvious. I am not so sure whether Powell succeeds in placing Marlowe's dramatic adventures on the right spot when he talks about a transitional moment from abstract to narrative theatre. However, I agree that Marlowe was conscious of the "inherited limitations of resource similar to those that bound the morality writers. He adapted their structural solutions to the problem, and he also took over their language of spectacle ... patterning the performance of living emblems (e.g. actors) in such a way as to create dramatic images of the spiritual action they describe."[6]

One must add, nevertheless, that Marlowe's most interesting and puzzling visual effects deflect from or subvert traditional concepts; in *Tamburlaine* and *Dr Faustus* we see him emptying out old ideas and concepts, filling them with new life or with a perverted, parodic content, and thus creating his own images - giving them significance through the immense energy of the poetry and complementing or interrupting the verbal action with extravagant stage-pictures.

My concern for "theatrical perspectives" has therefore been an attempt to extend Shewring's and Barker's notion of a "choreography of speech-patterns" and to look at the choreographic and theatrical notation for the total language of action in Marlowe's play-in-performance.[7]

---

4 Glynne Wickham, "Notes on the Staging of Marlowe's Plays," in *Shakespeare's Dramatic Heritage*, pp. 121-31.
5 Jocelyn Powell, "Marlowe's Spectacle," *TDR*, 8 (1964),195-210.
6 Powell, 197.
7 The expression "theatrical notation" has more recently been used in Shakespeare criticism to define an approach which

> [*The clocke strikes eleuen*]
> Ah Faustus,
> Now hast thou but one bare hower to liue,
> And then thou must be damnd perpetually.
> (A 1449-52)

The clock strikes, and the since the eleven strokes will take some time, there is a certain momentum which creates high suspense and intensifies the resonance of Faustus' former, factual statement: "Gentlemen farewel, if I liue til morning, Ile visite you: if not, Faustus is gone to hel" (A 1446-47). The audience has time to concentrate exclusively on the man who is now alone on stage, alone with himself - as in the beginning - and with the horror of the present moment. The clock initiates the final fear and trembling.

It is the patterning of the words, images, and syntactical units through which Marlowe has to make Faustus express his suffering and his passionate breakdown; a lot will depend on stress and rhythm and the manner in which the actor can make the words, exclamations, questions, or screams *work* for him in performance terms. There is no doubt that some of the lines are extremely difficult to render, and the irregularities of the verse structure, the stoppages and shifts of intensity or emphasis make considerable physical demands on the actor's voice and body. Shewring and Barker acutely observe the relationship between speech-impulses and bodily movement in space, and their view of a "choreography of speech" implies that the actor, very much like a dancer, has to be able to control his balance or central stance alongside the constant shifts, gaps, and juxtapositions

---

sees dramatic texts as scores containing in their verbal action most of the information necessary for the organization of all gestic, mimic, and scenic forms of the play-in-performance. Studies representative of this latest trend in drama criticism are: John Russell Brown, *Shakespeare's Plays in Performance* (London: Edward Arnold, 1966); J.L. Styan, *Shakespeare's Stagecraft* (Cambridge: Cambridge Univ. Press, 1967); Rudolf Stamm, "The Theatrical Physiognomy of Shakespeare's Plays," *The Shaping Powers at Work* (Heidelberg: Winter, 1967),pp. 11-84, and Jörg Hasler, *Shakespeare's Theatrical Notation: The Comedies* (Bern: Francke, 1974).

that may affect pitch and energy control in his speech.[8] The
problem of overbalancing the stance or missing or misplacing the
drops in pitch or emphasis holds true especially for the long and
complicated set-speeches in *Tamburlaine* (cf. Tamburlaine's long
soliloquy on "beauty"), where the energy of the rhetoric often
"runs" on and on and overtaxes the actor's breath and control.
The speech-sections carrying particular modes (interrogative mode;
exclamation; persuasion; lament; outrage; accusation; logical
argument; etc.) and reflecting the intellectual or emotional
thrust of the verse can be very long in *Tamburlaine*, which gives
them a programmatic and exhortative character, constantly blown
up by abounding hyperbole.

The Faustian mode of rhetoric is much more argumentative, and the
speech-sections are much shorter, especially in the last soliloquy where the intensity of their compression can in fact convey a sense of final enclosure in Time and Space. The imminent
sense of enclosure is the dominant aspect of Faustus' last speech,
and his first lines are already filled with echoes of the determinism (damnation) which he had initially set up for himself as
the concrete boundary ("end") he meant to transcend and leave behind. But "now" he has reached another self-chosen "end" : the
"one bare hower" on a bare stage, which terminates 24 years of
"freedom" secured by his diabolic contract.

The crushing inevitability of the end ("thou must") is vividly
rendered in the hammering (and thus echoing the strokes of the
clock)[9] staccato rhythm of the 15 monosyllables (A 1451-52),
and the ultimate effect is of course achieved by having the two
lines close on the long, drawn-out sound of "perpetually." The
juxtapositions between "now" and "then" (the eternal damnation),

---

8 Cf. Shewring and Barker, "The 'Theatre-Poetry,'" 3-4.
9 Modern productions occasionally take the idea of the clock
   (the emblem of Time) quite literally and use a stage clock
   for the last scene. To have Faustus' lines spoken on top of
   (and against) the constant ticking of a clock can of course
   create strong psychological effects. The feeling of time running out is intensified in the second half of the speech
   which is far more compressed (only 17 lines).

"to liue" and "be damnd", "one hower" and "perpetually", seem like a paradigm for the patterning of the entire speech which is full of such antithetical constructions.

> Stand stil you euer moouing spheres of heauen,
> That time may cease, and midnight neuer come:
> Faire Natures eie, rise, rise againe, and make
> Perpetuall day, or let this houre be but a yeere,
> A moneth, a weeke, a naturall day,
> That Faustus may repent, and saue his soule.
> (A 1453-58)

Whereas Faustus' introductory lines sound like stoical acceptance of his end, the second section radically shifts the focus towards the more agonizing and desperate desires that flash into his mind, as he twists to evade what is going to become of him. He now jumps quickly from image to image, thought to thought, creating a chain of paradoxes ("stand stil...euer moouing"; "time... cease"; "perpetuall day...houre...yeere...moneth...", etc.). It is a significant shift, because at the same time when Faustus' tortured mind recaptures its poetic power of imagination, the swelling rhetoric extends into gestures and visual detail (he is pointing towards the "heavens" of the theatre, his hands "lifted up") that directly express his attempt to project the old trope of *flight* (Faustus' symbol for aspiration and transcendence) into a new *vision*, a new vertical aspiration for escape into salvation ("rise, rise againe ... That Faustus may repent, and saue his soule").

I emphasize the word "vision" because I want to draw attention to the fact that the dramaturgy of the A version clearly indicates that we are dealing only with Faustus' ultimate, *subjective* experience of his inescapable death and punishment or, in other words, of his incapacity or unwillingness to repent. The damned Faustus whom we see onstage, facing the hour between eleven and twelve and desperately warding off the idea of dying, is quite different from the Faustus we see in the 1616 version of the play. In B, Faustus' subjective "reality" - his desperate escapist fantasies - is most poignantly filled with referential ambiguities; his primary cosmic images can equally well refer to the immediate theatrical space - "heavens" being the conventional term for the upper reaches of the stage. What is only implicit in A, becomes a powerfully suggestive spectacle of a different kind in the B-text staging of the final Act, which greatly enlarges our sense of Faustus as a victim of external powers. Inserting the ascent of the infernal conclave (Lucifer, Belzebub, Mephostophilis),

> *Luc.* Thus from infernall Dis do we ascend
> To view the subiects of our Monarchy,
> Those soules which sinne, seales the blacke sonnes of hell,
> 'Mong which as chiefe, Faustus we come to thee,
> Bringing with vs lasting damnation,
> To wait vpon thy soule; the time is come
> Which makes it forfeit.
> (B 1895-1901)

the B-text considerably changes Faustus' status as hero and heads towards a different conclusion. What had already been suggested earlier (cf. the staging of the conjuration scene in B) is now made explicit: the drama of Faustus' self-willed reprobation turns itself into a bizarre, superstitious spectacle which somehow even manages to convey its homiletic message. Mephostophilis is extremely happy that he can finally "confess" to Faustus that he had been manipulating him all the time anyway ("'Twas I, that when thou wer't i'the way to heauen, / Damb'd vp thy passage" B 1989-90), and immediately afterwards the Good and Bad Angels enter and, in a congenial, brotherly fashion, together tell Faustus of his inevitable fate.

Their speeches are supported on the stage by an emblematic throne ("*Musicke while the Throne descends*," s.d. B 2006) and a hellmouth which represent visually the point that the unholy trinity and the Angels are making verbally: poor Faustus has indeed lost "celestiall happinesse" (B 2007). Among the grotesque panoply onstage - the throne (suspended somewhere in mid-air, one must assume), the hellmouth, the wildly gesticulating Angels, and the infernal trinity - Faustus must indeed begin to look rather miserable. The impact of the hero's individualism and self-willed damnation that was so strongly sustained by the intellectually invigorating drama in the A version is here almost completely diffused by the picture of the stage machines that surround Faustus and make him look like a fool.[10]

At the same time, both texts make it clear that "hell" has encroached upon the theatre; by contrast with B, the Old Man's experience in A is primarily related to Faustus' subjective "reality" and to his psychological dilemma:

> O.Man. Accursed Faustus, miserable man,
> That from thy soule excludst the grace of heauen,
> And fliest the *throne* of his *tribunall seate*.
> [*Enter the Diuelles*]
> . . .
> As in *this furnace* God shal try my faith ...
> Ambitious fiends, see how *the heauens smiles*
> At your repulse, and laughs *your state* to scorne,
> Hence hel, for hence I flie vnto my God.
> (A 1377-80;1382;1384-86,my emphasis)

The dramaturgy in B persuades us to read the Old Man's references as allusions to the theatrical spaces as well and as an indication for the ironic inversions that are taking place. These dramaturgical devices imply the blurring of all literal, metaphorical, and emblematic levels, and if we visualize all down- and upstage locations occupied by Hell (Lucifer, Belzebub, and Mephostophilis *above*, in "state"), all metaphorical allusions become double-edged ("the throne of his [Lucifer's?] tribunall seate"; smiling

---

10 Constance Kuriyama, in her brilliant analysis of the textual problems in A and B ("Dr. Greg and *Doctor Faustus*: The Supposed Originality of the 1616 Text") is of course right in saying that the differences between A and B are so great that "an interpretation based on one, especially if it involves much close reading, will not necessarily hold good for the other" (P. 171). Commenting on the inserted passages in the B-text, Kuriyama concludes that "the B text also, because of its author's fatal attraction to the coarser episodes of the *Faustbook*, tends to reduce Faustus' struggle to terms that I find hopelessly lurid and vulgar" (p. 177). A similarly strong case against the B version has been made by Michael Warren ("*Doctor Faustus*: The Old Man and the Text," 133-39).

"heauens"; an empty "throne" lowered by Lucifer from the upper stage?). The B-text indeed asks for a diabolonian dramaturgy; the Second Scholar's confidence: "Yet Faustus looke vp to heauen, and remember mercy is infinite" (B 1935-36) comes to sound almost unbearingly ironic, even cynical, if one envisages Lucifer enthroned "above." A clever production could multiply the visual ironies by having a beautiful, Helen-like Lucifer, dressed as a blindingly white angel, preside over the stage action on the upper throne and "smile" maliciously at the flustered Faustus downstage.[11] And, finally, this spectacle of an inverted universal order would be complete if one connected the Good Angel's reference to the descending "heavenly" throne with *Lucifer*:

> ... Faustus behold,
> In what resplendant glory thou hadst set
> In yonder throne, like those bright shining Saints.
> (B 2011-13)

At any rate, Marlowe's last Act presents a spatial spectacle (at least in the B version) which is able to employ the emblematic design of the multi-levelled Elizabethan stage and its referents for bold dramaturgical purposes. If we think of the conventional locations (hell in the cellarage; this world and its protagonists on the platform; and its secular and divine kings "above" or in "state") and their implied religious symbolism (in its sacramental, vertical axis that resembles church architecture: the tomb-the altar-the throne), the choreography of Faustus' damnation indeed suggests spectacular emblematic analogues and contrasts

---

11 This interpretation, incidentally, was put into practice very effectively by the 1979 *Dr Faustus* production for the Oregon Shakespearian Festival in Ashland. In the Grotowski production, such ironic inversions were part of a different and more complicated concept. The part of Mephostophilis was played simultaneously by a man and a woman. In Scene 7 of the montage, the first appearance of the devil was staged as a kind of "annunciation," with the male Mephostophilis singing his lines, like a soaring angel, accompanied by an angelic choir. The female Mephostophilis, representing the Pietà, promised Faustus a new life and comforted him by rocking him in her lap. This tableau was later transformed into a scene of erotic seduction during which Helen-Mephostophilis made love to Faustus and immediately gave birth to a child.

which carry significant parodic resonances.[12] Looking at the incredible stage machinery with which the B version clutters up the action, one cannot be quite certain, after all, what this diabolical spectacle is supposed to mean and how seriously one is meant to take the intellectual and aesthetic world of the B version, especially if one finds another additional scene *after* the final damnation scene in which we hear that the Scholars discover the hero's "limbs, / All torne asunder by the hand of death" (B 2099-2100).

In the 1604 version we discover no angels, no thrones, and no hellmouth. There is only Faustus, alone on an oppressively bare stage, invoking the Sun to "rise, rise againe, and make / Perpetuall day" or at least to turn the ominous night into a "naturall day" which would leave him time to think about possible ways to "saue his soule." Returning to the passage that I was discussing, I want to add that the visual image of "rising" is complemented by the rhythmic, aural emphasis on the "s" alliteration ("cease", "rise", "saue", "soule") which helps to intensify the connection between "rise" and "salvation." Ironically enough, the vertical patterning of Faustus' emotional speech-gesture (the image of the upward rising sun) is a double motion upward/downward since the outward, infinitely stretching image (and sound) of "perpetuall day" is immediately countered by the inward, shrinking image of Time ("yeere", "moneth", "weeke", "day", "houre").

By invoking these first emphatic motions towards escape, Faustus is dramatically placed against a huge cosmic background ("you euer moouing spheres of heauen ... Faire Natures eie ... The starres mooue stil ...", etc.). It is a background, however,

---

[12] The parodic inversion of ritualistic action can be extremely effective and ambivalent at the same time, if we think, for example, of the scenes of the Seven Deadly Sins or the Papal malediction in the Rome episode. The play's most shockingly blasphemous parody occurs in the contract scene, where Faustus solemnizes his diabolic pact in an elaborate pantomime imitating the drawing up of a legal deed of gift, and then proceeds to use the Saviour's momentous words, "*Consummatum est*," to sign away his soul.

which is as mute and unresponsive as the silent immediacy of the theatrival space - the physical confinement which Faustus' *words* try to contradict. While these spatial dimensions enlarge Faustus' tragic stature and intensify the audience's awareness of his agony, the theatre audience itself is elevated into a sort of cosmic audience, looking down on a despairing Faustus who is caught in his unbelieving, subjunctive stance ("That Faustus *may* repent").

His cosmic invocation under the present circumstances gains an even more striking significance since it presents a direct visual analogue to the earlier incantation scene. In that scene he was craving for the "gloomy shadow of the earth" (A 244) and using the "Figures of ... the heauens ... By which the spirits are inforst to rise" (A 254; 256) in order to conjure up the devil:

> Ist not midnight? come Mephastophilis,
> *Veni veni* Mephastophile!
> (A 468-69)

The last scene completely inverts the former poise of the proud magician, yet it is all the more compelling to watch him use these invocations which echo the imperative charms he once applied in his conjuring circle. His words ("Stand stil ... that midnight neuer come") rise in pitch and emotional intensity, and they almost sound like a desperate last effort to cast a spell:

> *O lente lente curite noctis equi.*
> (A 1459)

Faustus' irrational, haunted imagination jumps from the concern over his soul to the beautifully evocative Latin counterpoint; what in Ovid's *Amores* ("*lente currite, noctis equi!*" I.xiii.40) is a wish to extend a night of sexual pleasure becomes for him an outburst of apocalyptic dread. The extrametrical line (Marlowe spontaneously intensifies and extends the Latin original) is a singularly poetic expression of Faustus' passion, and although it is incommensurate with the context of the theological *agon*, it gives the actor a necessary emphatic pitch from

which the next two lines tumble downward, in broken rhythms and
a fragmented syntax:

> The starres mooue stil, time runs, the clocke wil strike,
> The diuel wil come, and Faustus must be damnd.
> (A 1460-61)

What makes this last soliloquy so spectacular verbally and visually, is the contrapuntal technique of having the actor employ two different "voices," so to speak; the choreography of the speech requests constant shifts or breaks through which the actor brings alive the two internal, struggling impulses. The fantasizing and "fleeing" self occupies the more spectacular, fluent and poetic lines of visionary flashes, whereas the despairing, terrified, and more "realistic" self cancels the vision ("time runs"; "wil strike"; "wil come"; "must be damnd"). The splitting of the heroic voice into antithetical components poetically and dramatically externalizes the Faustian psychomachia; the alternating verse movements (upward and downward) thus compress the play's central image of the "upward fall" in a vivid stage picture.

This becomes most clearly visible in the next section, where Faustus' language fluctuates with terrifying suddenness between hope and despair:

> O Ile leape vp to my God: who pulles me downe?
> See see where Christs blood streames in the firmament,
> One drop would saue my soule, halfe a drop, ah my Christ,
> Ah rend not my heart for naming of my Christ,
> Yet wil I call on him, oh spare me Lucifer!
> Where is it now? tis gone.
> (A 1462-67)

The hallucinatory quality of Faustus' visions and the agony of the moment (the flash of redemption in the "heavens") grow into a torrent of concentrated language which faces the audience with the difficult task of assimilating the opposing voices of the psychically and almost physically divided hero. The actor certainly has to find a way to express the tensions and rents in visual gestures (the "leaping" upwards, which could be enacted on a bare centrestage or by a leap upon a table or desk, if the set was to represent Faustus' "study"; the terrified cringing and crawling on the floor, etc.). It may also be difficult to decide upon the question whether the lines merely project the incessant torture and despair that might have blanked out any other subjective reality than *damnation* in Faustus

> One drop *would* saue my soule, halfe a drop, ah my Christ.
> (A 1464)
> One drop of bloud *will* saue me; oh my Christ.
> (B 2049, my emphases)

or whether Faustus' ultimate glimpse and recognition of "his" Christ's redemptive blood transforms the spoken lines into a prayer, an impotent yet visible gesture towards repentance. Theatrically, both interpretations have strong emotional effects; from its vantage point the audience perceives either the tragic despair of a hero who has given up yet who *sees* and *knows* what he is losing (the vision of Christ's blood forming the cosmic and spiritual background for this insight), or it might feel the pathetic outburst of *praying* (who wants to decide at this point whether Faustus has faith or not?), which could be enforced by the actor making the sign of the cross.

Yet Faustus' outcry, his leap toward a silent heaven, is ineffectual (the Grotowski production made it clear at this point that God, in his guilty indifference, had missed his last chance to show himself powerful enough to rescue a soul at the instant of its damnation) - and fear and terror are experienced as emotions too compelling to be quelled ("rend not my heart"). The pauses and shifts within the lines are ambiguous, as it has been amply demonstrated by Max Bluestone,[13] and both texts remain unclear about the emotional thrust of Faustus' addresses (who is

---

13 Cf. Max Bluestone, "*Libido Speculandi:* Doctrine and Dramaturgy in Contemporary Interpretations of Marlowe's *Doctor Faustus*," in *Reinterpretations of Elizabethan Drama*, ed. Norman Rabkin (New York: Columbia Univ. Press, 1969), esp. pp. 76-80. See also Weil, *Merlin's Prophet*, pp. 79f., and Gerald Morgan, "Harlequin Faustus: Marlowe's Comedy of Hell," *HAB*, 18 (1967), 22-34.

the addressee: Christ or Satan?):

> Yet wil I call on him, oh *spare me Lucifer!*
> (A 1466)
> Yet will I call on him: O *spare me Lucifer.*
> (B 2051,my emphases)

Is there a sudden shift in the middle of the line, a drop from determination (to call on Christ) to fear? If "Lucifer" in B's "O spare me Lucifer" is not vocative, on the other hand, it would transform the entire line into an invocation, a prayer for Christ to spare Faustus from Lucifer ("Lucifer" in the dative). If the latter is true, then one can understand why the subversively diabolic side of Marlowe's dramaturgy has been interpreted as offering a spectacular, heterodox provocation of the "tragic theology" that becomes visible in this moment: a repentant and dying Faustus is paradoxically damned by a cold and indifferent God.[14] In his Theatre Laboratory production, Jerzy Grotowski approached the play from this perspective and turned the damnation scene into a spectacle of Faustus' Passion, playing the hero's "innocence" off against the "sin of God." For Grotowski, Faustus' actions are "a grotesque paraphrase of a saint's acts; and yet, he reveals at the same time the poignant pathos of a martyr."[15]

I find the Romantic view of a "saintly" Faustus quite incongruent with the dramatic development of Faustus' self-conception as wilful reprobate; the theological and psychological consistency in the damnation scene is nevertheless subject to an enormous emotive potential which can stimulate the contradictory quality of the spectacle either way. This contrariety, in itself a reflection of the rents, the deep divisions in Faustus' self, is further

---

14 See, for example, Robert Ornstein, "Marlowe and God: The Tragic Theology of *Dr. Faustus*," *PMLA*, 83 (1968), 1378-85, and Richard Waswo, "Damnation, Protestant Style: Macbeth, Faustus, and Christian Tragedy," *JMRS*, 4 (1974), 63-99.
15 "*Doctor Faustus* in Poland," 133;123. (*Towards a Poor Theatre*, pp. 86;80f.)

complicated by the hero's alternating vision of Christ the Redeemer and God the wrathful Judge.

> And see where God stretcheth out his arme,
> And bends his irefull browes:
> Mountaines and hilles, come come, and fall on me,
> And hide me from the heauy wrath of God.
> No no, then wil I headlong runne into the earth:
> Earth gape, O no, it wil not harbour me ...
> (A 1468-73)

"Yet wil I ... No no ... then wil I ... O no ...": the shifts and juxtapositions continue to dominate Faustus' speech, and his haunted imagination conjures up the most extraordinary escapes. At the same time, it becomes apparent more and more that his "fleeing," which is here most vividly expressed in apocalyptic images ("then wil I headlong runne into the earth: / Earth gape"; "Mountaines and hilles ... fall on me"), is ultimately a fleeing away from a deeply-rooted feeling that he is fated at any rate:

> You starres that raignd at my natiuitie,
> Whose influence hath alotted death and hel,
> Now draw vp Faustus like a foggy mist ...
> (A 1474-76)

This reflects back upon the whole problem of reprobation, of course, and it should help to explain the dilemma that lies at the heart of Faustus' theological *agon*. Whereas his mind readily fluctuates between two theological conceptions (Christ the Redeemer whose "blood streames in the firmament"; God the Judge who "bends his irefull browes"), these two antithetical eschatological visions seem to be washed away by an instinctively *negative* relationship to everything outside Faustus' self-image. Faustus' inside, therefore, has no ground on which it could differentiate between a saving and a retributive God, since he has accepted a negative, determinist vision for himself in the first place. The God-images (cf. Lucifer's famous line: "*Christ cannot saue* thy soule, for he is *iust*" A 714, emphasis mine) are therefore interchangeable, and the vision of the threatening Devil is collapsed into the idea of the punishing God. This may also explain why the final images of violent self-destruction and metamorphosis appear so confused and megalomanic.

The final sections of the soliloquy, then, exhibit not so much a *Christian* martyrdom but rather a subjectified, poetic frenzy of despair and disillusionment. All the images of transmigration, metamorphosis, or dissolution of identity which Faustus takes up and then abandons only heighten his overriding desperation that ultimately expresses a deep aggressiveness against himself.

> Oh God, if thou wilt not haue mercy on my soule,
> Yet for Christs sake, whose bloud hath ransomd me,
> Impose some end to my incessant paine ...
> O no end is limited to damned soules ...
> Curst be the parents that ingendred me:
> No Faustus, curse thy selfe ...
> (A 1483-85;1488;1496-97)

Divided by the striking of the clock, the soliloquy falls structurally into two parts; interestingly, both parts end on the word "heauen" (A 1480; 1498). Faustus' frenzy and ecstasy of fear, despair, and aggression turn the speech into an acting *tour de force*; the sense-units often extend over a number of lines, and the escape images continue to work through their internal counterpoints ("God"/"earth"; "earth"/"cloud"/"air"; "hel"/"heauen"; "some end"/"no end"; "flie from me"/"dissolued in elements"; "ayre"/"Ocean"; "God"/"Lucifer"). More important still, these images will build up tension in a cumulative manner, and starting from the second striking of the clock,

> Ah, halfe the houre is past:
> Twil all be past anone.
> (A 1481-82)

which provides a point of quietness from which the last climax can rise, the verse is rendered in continuously high pitch and in a more frantic pace.

There is considerable physical action; the actor will try to transform the lines into gestures, throwing himself to the ground ("Earth gape"), rising up, kneeling down to pray, jumping up desperately, crossing the stage, jerking his head upwards to the stars, turning and twisting to avoid the threatening faces of his projected fear (God, Lucifer). There are no stage-directions, yet all these gestures and movements and the emphatic moments in the verse are implied by the text, and the actor merely has to pay attention to how his sentences are phrased.

What all these poetic images and visual gestures effect is not so much an exposure but an intensely realized expression of Faustus' fear of dying. Marlowe's choreography of the dramatic action achieves to show Faustus' "end" almost wholly internalized in its effect, and as such the scene is certainly unique in Elizabethan drama. Marlowe directs all our attention to Faustus' agony, amplifying it so much that when the hero's final and most vivid poetic fantasies are cut short and he is dragged offstage (or simply collapses onto the platform), we must recover from a dramatic experience which has been choreographed in an oppressively realistic manner. I mean to say that at the end of Faustus' last hour the audience has been drawn into the immediate fear and pain of the hero, and his desperate self-references ("Faustus, curse thy selfe"; "body turne to ayre"; "soule ... fal into the Ocean") give us a totally new sense of what it means to represent "Hell" not so much spatially (where it merely has a tinge of a parodic gambit), but first of all psychologically.

>My God, my God, looke not so fierce on me:
>Adders, and Serpents, let me breathe a while:
>Vgly hell gape not, come not Lucifer,
>Ile burne my bookes, ah Mephastophilis.
>   [*exeunt with him*]
>   (A 1505-08)

The clock strikes twelve, and thunder and lightning terminate Faustus' last "flights." By the time when the devils enter the stage to carry him away, he has himself employed a last vertical image ("fal into the Ocean") which adequately conveys the failure of ascent and transcendence. While he is still alive, uttering his ambiguous and often-quoted last lines, his voice reaches the highest peak of terror - piercing, almost inarticulate cries of the victim caught in his own trap.

There is not much left of any ironic detachment, a detachment that had been present in the opening scenes and that Marlowe manipulates throughout the play. The spectacle of Faustus' damnation, in the end, is the revelation of an immense psychic struggle, and the immediacy and emotional realism of Faustus' language and of his compelling gestures make it a most haunting experience of human suffering. The moralizing devices that the play carries around with itself (cf. the Epilogue's concluding lecture) certainly operate on a level of explanation which must appear quite inadequate in the face of the problems Faustus' beautiful dream of power and imaginative freedom has created for himself and for us.

Chapter Six

THE END OF EVERY ART:
FAUSTUS' DIALECTIC OF SELF-REPROBATION

> Man is
> the symbol-using animal
> inventor of the negative
> separated from his natural condition by
> instruments of his own making
> goaded by the spirit of hierarchy
> and rotten with perfection.
> (Burke, *Language as Symbolic Action*)

If one were to imagine, within a single work, a parody of hope and salvation set against a vision of despair and damnation, one would also discover an oscillation between the two representations that enforces the rhetorical impact of each even though the two opposites may seem to cancel one another. Within the play of thought that underlies the "dramatistic" definition of man as a "symbol-using" actor,[1] such juggling with opposite terms and negative constructs (and the principle of positive/negative or good/evil) seems absolutely fundamental to the idea of theory as well as of theatre or, in other words, to the whole playing field of debate, invention, paradox, and comedy which can open a new space of action.

The motive of play becomes a mode of negative thought which would narrow the world to a single point in order to derive, from that point, a new world, an anti-world, by negation. It is only because man lives in a world of symbols and representations that he can thus manipulate the symbols through his powers of abstraction

---

[1] I slightly extend Kenneth Burke's semiotic conception of man as a "symbol-using animal" to include the notion of play and playfulness. For Burke's definition, see *Language as Symbolic Action* (Berkeley: Univ. of California Press, 1966), pp. 9-17.

and condensation. A system of theological knowledge, for example, that includes such mutually negating opposites as election and reprobation can only exist in a realm of symbols where a dialectic of absolute freedom and total restraint, of free will and predestination, can be *thought*. And such thought is performed, as Kenneth Burke would argue, with the negations and abstractions of a common code of language which can be used to create perfection (e.g. the idea of God, of infinitue) out of imperfection (man, the finitude of human knowledge, etc.).

Without the idea of complete self-negation, of self-humiliation and abandonment, Protestant theologians would not have been able to open up the new space for a philosophy that promised a new kind of assurance in an all-powerful God which, paradoxically, was to be grounded in the unmediated, subjective experience of the individual.[2] This same philosophy, by a significant trick of the mind, at the same time recommended its godly followers not to trust paradoxes. "With regard to God," Luther maintains, "and in all that bears upon salvation or damnation, [man] has no 'free will', but is a captive, prisoner, and bondslave, either to the will of God, or to the will of Satan," and this bondage must relegate any discourse about free will to the realm of *rhetoric*, where it, as Luther suggests, may be used by "actors and confidence tricksters."[3]

When I described the convolutions of Faustus' conscience and the dilemma of his "pursuit of aloneness" in the previous chapters, I was at no point trying to suggest that Marlowe in fact "be-

---

[2] Cf. Jacques Maritain, *Three Reformers: Luther, Descartes, Rousseau* (New York: Scribner's, 1929), pp.13 ff. In his chapter on Luther, entitled "The Advent of the Self," Maritain points out that in spite of the "self-effacement," the centre of Protestant theology lies not in God but in man. He sees this principle as a kind of "metaphysical egoism" which produces a body of doctrines that transfers "that absolute assurance in the divine promise which was formerly the privilege of the Church and her missions to the human individual and his subjective state" (p. 14).

[3] *The Bondage of the Will*, ed. and trans. J.I. Packer and O.R. Johnston(1957;rpt.Cambridge:Cambridge Univ.Press,1973),pp.106f.

lieved" in Protestant theology and its doctrine of reprobation or that the play is overtly involved in any religious polemics. Rather, I think that the negative world of the reprobate offered a "perfect" playing field for Marlowe, a perfect space of abstraction in which the rigorously authoritarian philosophy of predestination, with its distinct psychological basis and its distinct, even unique purpose, could be used as a context for the dramatization of Faustus' *rhetorical* gestures and aspirations. Whatever it is that is determined in the play, it is Faustus who makes the momentum, the madness, and the magic, and the playwright must have enjoyed the possibility of focussing the psychological movement of the verse precisely on the manifest singularity of his protagonist's case - the case of a battle against incomparable odds.

I dwelled on the Reformation doctrines for a little while because a firm grasp of the theological ideas and interpretations can only help us to understand all the connotations in Faustus' discourse. Having started with the concluding scenes of Faustus' struggle, I now wish to concentrate on the opening of the play and to examine *how* Faustus manipulates the authoritarian obstacles of "his" religion in order to be able to pursue his personal "chiefest blisse."

It is perhaps not unimportant to remember that Marlowe's sources, the German *Faustbuch* and its English translation, are both completely consistent in their treatment of Faustus' specific motives and in their strict adherence to a religious attitude which is pervaded by the Lutheran theology of sin. There is never any doubt, from the first to the last chapter of the fable, that Faustus' apostasy deserves anything other than damnation:

> It is written ... thou shalt not tempt the Lord thy God: but Faustus threw all this in the winde, and made his soule of no estimation, regarding more his worldly pleasure than the ioyes to come: therefore at the day of iudgement there is no hope of his redemption.[4]

---

4   *The Historie of the Damnable Life,*   chap. I.

Whatever ideology was imposed upon the Faust myth later on, and whatever tendency one may already perceive, in P.F.'s translation, towards de-emphasizing Faustus' wickedness and towards stressing the scholar's "wonderfull Speculation," it is still indisputable that Marlowe was to draw from a source which clearly centred its moral theme on the doctor's transgression of the First Commandment. The images in the story apply this view to Faustus' self-destructive will to power:

> ... and taking to him the wings of an Eagle, [he] thought to flie ouer the whole world, and to know the secrets of heauen and earth ...
> ... [he] forgot the Lord his maker, and Christ his redeemer, became an enemy vnto all man-kinde, yea, worse than the Gyants whom the Poets fayne to climb the hilles to make warre with the Gods: not vnlike that enemy of God and his Christ, that for his pride was cast into hell: so likewise Faustus forgot that the high climbers catch the greatest falles.[5]

It seems interesting that Marlowe picks up two topoi from his source, one historical, the other tropological, and in the Prologue's introductory lines these directly converge on the central dramatic issue: the hero's pursuit of his own idea of "chiefest blisse" ("Nothing so sweete as magicke is to him / Which he preferes before his chiefest blisse" A 27-28; B 26-27). In a first, topical allusion, the Prologue introduces Faustus as a scholar from Wittenberg University, recipient of a doctor's degree in Divinity. Wittenberg, of course, was the centre of the Protestant Reformation in Germany; furthermore, the historical Faustus was an almost exact contemporary of Luther and Melanchthon. The Protestant context thus intensifies the meaning of "chiefest blisse," which in Reformation theology denoted the central concern about man's salvation.

In this connection we hear of Faustus' excellence in *disputing* ("... disputes / In heauenly matters of Theologie" A 19-20); what he disputes we are to learn from Faustus himself in the first scene. The very immediate link between the scholar's love

---

5 *The Historie of the Damnable Life*, chaps. II, V.

for disputation, his "excelling all," his "selfe conceit," and
his "chiefest blisse" is important. Marlowe here inserts the
Faustbook image of the soaring "Eagle" - an image which had a
long tradition in Christian theology, medieval literature, and
the visual arts, and which had been commonly associated with
superbia, chief sin among the seven cardinal sins.[6] The idea of
pride as the root of all sin (cf. Eccl.x.13) is implied in the
concept of "original sin," which became the cornerstone of all
Christian anthropology; in its symbolic function it extends
prior mythic constructions of tragic hubris which had in fact
concentrated more provocatively on the polarization between human
rebellion against a god on the one hand, and divine hostility or
jealousy on the other.[7]

Marlowe ingeniously conflates all those symbolic layers in his
poetic emblem of the Fall of Icarus ("His waxen wings did mount
aboue his reach, / And melting heauens conspirde his ouerthrow").
I am inclined to think that the ambiguous trope of the conspira-
torial "heauens" (when did the "conspiration" take place?) already
points forward to the problematic doctrine of predestination
which Faustus sets against himself during his first soliloquy.

The dramatic spectacle of Faustus' "decisions" in the opening
scene creates a very complex experience of the hero's personality
and is full of implications for the subsequent events on stage.
As the soliloquy unfolds, the heroic dimensions of Faustus'
scholarly enterprise, of his intellectual efforts to explain himself through a virtuoso show of his speculative, sceptical stance,
become increasingly qualified and complicated by the ambiguous
manner of his argument. The elaborate rhetorical design of his
discourse never breaks down, yet the flashes of paradox and
irony, which undermine the semantic content of his formulations
and his proposals for a "greater subiect" (A 41), express very

---

[6] Cf. Morton W. Bloomfield, *The Seven Deadly Sins: An Introduction to the History of a Religious Concept, with Special Reference to Medieval English Literature* (East Lansing: Michigan
State College Press, 1952), pp. 69-104;245.

[7] See Ricoeur, *The Symbolism of Evil*, pp. 211-31.

well how precarious Faustus' quest for power and freedom really is. This precariousness is especially felt in those moments which emphasize Faustus' self-references, his impulse towards validating his own behaviour and his inward desires. In the context which Faustus creates this impulse seems equivalent to what he regards as his *freedom* to choose by eliminating alternatives. On the one hand, then, Faustus' rhetoric of paradox provides him with the ground on which he can establish the "conceited" space for his desire; within the semantic ambiguities of the opening soliloquy, all the crucial issues of Faustus' tragic flight are mutually implicated. If we recognize how he turns "heauenly matters" and other matters upside down, as the Prologue already implies, we could, on the other hand, ask ourselves whether he uses a specific approach or method in his review of the academic disciplines which might disclose a deeper relationship between his aspirations for magical freedom and his rejection of divinity.

What the audience witnesses during the opening scene is Faustus' personal, rhetorical *defence* of what constituted the compelling temptation to break free. In the dramaturgical context it becomes clear that Faustus has already been "ravished," that he *has* embraced magic, that he is bent to explore the dreams of his imagination. He is now "professing" or justifying exactly the "deapth" of these deep desires which have lifted him up and which generate the upward leaps of his self-conceit.

> Settle thy studies Faustus, and beginne
> To sound the deapth of that thou wilt professe:
> Hauing commencde, be a Diuine in shew.
> (A 31-33)

It is difficult to avoid the impression that Faustus is far from "settling" his studies in the sense of a careful, disciplined, and dignified examination of his fields of knowledge and learning. He is rather setting himself against their claims, against the inhibitions that are contained in the orthodox traditions of learning, and the scornful and impatient tone in his voice seems to confirm my suggestion that Faustus - from the outset - puts on a "show" (in the modern sense of the word), a decorous dialogue with himself during which he re-confirms his subversive posture. Having said this, I would go on to suggest that Marlowe does not dramatize a hero whose discourse makes him the victim of numerous ironies which attend his quotations, misattributions or reductive misreadings, but rather emphasizes Faustus' radical self-confidence by having him deliberately subvert traditional authorities and institutions. It is particularly significant that Faustus asserts himself by using a dialogical style. Since his dialectic enquiry culminates in the dismissal of theology, the implications of his argumentative method are especially poignant.

>And liue and die in Aristotles workes:
>Sweete *Analitikes* tis thou hast rauisht me,
>*Bene disserere est finis logicis*,
>Is, to dispute well, Logickes chiefest end?
>Affoords this Art no greater myracle?
>   (A 35-39)

First of all, Faustus' wording makes it clear throughout his speech that his desire expresses a will to go forward, opening up new spaces and aiming at a goal or "end." "Liue and die" therefore indicates not only Faustus' confrontation with boundaries or limits, as physical or institutional resistances, but also with Time and the problem of finality. The temporal sense of "attaining ends" (cf. A 40;48) intensifies the impression we get of Faustus' projective, eschatological fixation, his vision of transcending "final ends"; yet this is curiously combined with his assumption that the mastery of a field of knowledge in no way offers creative fulfilment or the means for extension but includes in itself sets of finite, static irreducibles which confine the individual and put him into a closed world of order and hierarchy.

If we see Faustus rebelling against this reduction, it becomes clear why he so mockingly and sarcastically detaches himself from established concepts of a "*summum bonum*" (A 46). His comment on Aristotle: "liue and die in Aristotles workes: / Sweete *Analitikes* tis thou hast rauisht me" can only be meant ironically since he immediately rushes on to undermine Aristotle's *Analytics* by quoting not Aristotle himself but Petrus Ramus, the author of 20 books of *Aristotelicae Animadversiones*:

> *Bene disserere est finis logicis.*

That Faustus starts by reviewing logic first is hardly a surprise. When Ramus declares dialectic to be the centre and core of all philosophy ("It seeks to be not only an art, but the queen or indeed the goddess of the arts"),[8] he is simply extending the tradition of medieval arts scholasticism which had always recognized logic or dialectic (within the liberal arts curriculum) as its chief pedagogical concern preparing the students for the higher faculties of medicine, law, or theology. Scholastic theology stood quite apart from this arts course and was solely taught by the religious orders; it is the world of a non-epistemological, mathematical type of logic and concrete physics (containing grammar and rhetoric as propaedeutic arts) into which Ramus' formal, methodical dialectic emerged, and not the metaphysical-theological world of Thomist or Scotist scholasticism.

It is indeed precisely this Thomist-Aristotelian tradition of metaphysics which the newly defined Ramist dialectic sought to displace. The new topical dialectic, elevated into an "art" (*"summus et generalissimus finis logicae, ars bene disserendi"*)[9] and projected to assimilate *all* other "arts" (rhetoric, grammar, mathematics, ethics, religion, etc.), became a pedagogical programme which was meant to govern all life in the intelligible

---

8 Petrus Ramus, "Preface" to *Scholae metaphysicae*, in *Scholae in liberales artes* (1569), cols. 828-29. Quoted from Walter J. Ong, *Ramus, Method, and the Decay of Dialogue*, p. 182. The maxim that Faustus quotes can be found, in variant forms, throughout Ramus' works, and it may ultimately go back to Peter of Spain's similar claim that *"dialectica est ars artium, et scientia scientiarum, ad omnium methodorum principia viam habens"* (*Petri Hispani Summulae logicales* [1246], ed. I.M. Boschenski [Rom: Marietti, 1947], Tr.I,1.01. p.1).
9 This is, most likely, the phrase Faustus picks up to unravel Aristotle; it appears in Ramus' *Scholae dialecticae*, Lib.IV, in *Scholae in liberales artes* (1569), cols. 155-56. This de-

universe.[10] Since Marlowe's residence at Cambridge University coincided with the spread of Ramism in England and since recent scholarship has confirmed the curious links between Ramus' methodizing logic and radical Protestantism,[11] Marlowe's evident response to the Ramus-Aristotle controversy needs further clarification.

Within the context of the humanist re-organization of the liberal arts course and within the specific intellectual milieu of a Cambridge University saturated with disturbances by radical Calvinist teaching and preaching,[12] Marlowe's exposure to philosophical controversies assumes a wider significance. As I already indicated, dialectic was claimed as the most important subject in the students' university curriculum. At Cambridge, this new emphasis instigated John Seton to write the first Latin textbook on logic published in England (1545). Two other Cambridge students, Thomas Wilson and Ralph Lever, composed the first treatises on dialectic within the English vernacular.[13] In 1568, when Laurence Chaderton (one of the most prominent Calvinist

---

finition is also quoted and discussed in Ong, *Ramus*, pp. 43f.
10 It is interesting, in this connection, to see that Ramus regarded metaphysics to be nothing else but theology sieved through logic (cf. *Scholae in lib. art.*, cols. 828-29). In the posthumous *Commentariorum de religione christiana libri quatuor*, ed. Theophilus Banosius (Francofurti: Wechelus,1576), we discover that Ramus in fact attempts to reduce religion to nothing more than an "art" and to organize the *loci* of that art alongside those of grammar, rhetoric, dialectic, and geometry.
11 In addition to Ong, pp. 295-314, and Howell, pp. 238-41, see Perry Miller, *The New England Mind: The Seventeenth Century* (1939; rpt.Cambridge,Mass.: Harvard Univ. Press, 1954); Neil Ward Gilbert, *Renaissance Concepts of Method* (New York: Columbia Univ. Press, 1960); Lisa Jardine, *Francis Bacon: Discovery and the Art of Discourse* (Cambridge: Cambridge Univ. Press, 1974), and Barbara Kiefer Lewalski, *Protestant Poetics and the Seventeenth-Century Religious Lyric* (Princeton:Princeton Univ. Press, 1979). Only one noteworthy contribution has been made to Marlowe criticism so far; see R.W. Dent, "Ramist Faustus or Ramist Marlowe?", *NM*, 73 (1972), 63-74.
12 Cf. Harry C. Porter, *Reformation and Reaction in Tudor Cambridge* (1958; rpt.Hamden: The Shoe String Press, 1972), and Peter Milward, *Religious Controversies of the Elizabethan Age* (London: The Scholar Press, 1977).

preachers) began lecturing on Peter Ramus' *Ars logica*, the Ramist challenge to orthodox scholasticism embroiled Cambridge in a formidable battle over the reconsideration of Aristotelian method. In fact, the methods and principles to be used in differentiating between valid and invalid statements became one of the hotly disputed issues, and we hear that there was considerable interest in Ramus' *Unica Methodus*, "which in those times prevailed much."[14] Ramus' work had been known in Cambridge since the time of Roger Ascham. When Gabriel Harvey was named Professor of Rhetoric at Cambridge in 1574, the logic and rhetoric of Ramus were replacing those of Cicero and Aristotle. In the same year, Roland MacIlmaine brought out the first two London editions of the *Dialectica*, Ramus' main work, and at Cambridge William Temple published another in 1584, the year in which Marlowe took his B.A. degree.

By that time a tremendous infusion of Ramism had come to England, particularly after the Huguenot André Wéchel had put out over a hundred editions of Ramus' own works together with competing works by the German humanists (Agricola, Piscator, Roding, Beurhaus) and other controversial literature on Ramism by Everard Digby, Piscator, and Temple. The repercussions can be traced in a number of Cambridge intellectuals, Greene, Nashe, John Case and the Harveys among them, who became involved in the disputes. Dudley Fenner, a radical Calvinist, published his *The Artes of Logike and Rhetorike* in 1584. He went so far as to adapt the Ramist "method" for the Puritan cause, claiming that God prescribed "method" and "right reasoning" as an instrument in man's efforts for salvation. I find this astonishing indeed, since strict Protestant teaching, as we have seen earlier, would of course have to insist on the premise that man's reason is corrupt

---

13 Wilson's *Rule of Reason* was published in 1551 and Lever's *The Arte of Reason, Rightly Termed Witcraft* in 1573 (although probably written around 1550 while Lever was studying at St. John's). For the pedagogical controversies in Cambridge, see Lisa Jardine, "Humanism and the Sixteenth Century Cambridge Arts Course," *History of Education*, 4 (1975), 16-31.
14 John Strype, *Annals of the Reformation*.... (Oxford: Oxford Univ. Press, 1824), II, Pt.2, 405.

and, in any case, *antithetical* to faith which is only God's free gift.[15]

The attempt to place Marlowe's dramatic "method" in its intellectual context seems to have led us right into the middle of the confusing, heterogeneous world of Renaissance thought, a vast, paradoxical universe which, to use Francis Bacon's sceptical description, "to the eye of the human understanding is framed like a labyrinth."[16] Disentangling the threads of Faustus' opening disputation allows us to gaze deeply into the inventory of the Renaissance mind; a review of human learning - such as Faustus' - will always give occasion to raise fundamental questions about the meaning of terms such as reason, law, faith, free will, grace, art, nature, knowledge, ignorance, etc., and the differences in emphasis and perspective could be demonstrated by such texts as Nicholas de Cusa's *De docta ignorantia*, Marsilio Ficino's *Quaestiones quinque de mente*, Pico della Mirandola's *De hominis dignitate* and *Heptaplus*, Erasmus' *The Praise of Folly* and *On the Freedom of Will*, Thomas More's *Utopia*, Cornelius Agrippa's *De incertitudine et vanitate scientiarum*, Philip Sidney's *The Defence of Poesie*, Walter Raleigh's *History of the World*, Francis Bacon's *The Advancement of Learning*, Fulke Greville's *A Treatise of Humane Learning*, and many others.

As the evidence leading up to Marlowe suggests, practically all doctrines and philosophical systems, whether they originate in

---

15 Cf. Calvin, *Institutes*, III.21-24. The problem of reconciling God's grace with man's reason and free will was of course the basis of many controversies about predestination. Richard Hooker's attempt, in his *Of the Laws of Ecclesiastical Polity* (1593), to construct a rationalized theological compromise is by no means representative of the mainstream, more radical Calvinism that dominated the Elizabethan scene (cf. the Lambeth Articles of 1595). When William Perkins uses Ramist ideas for his true "method" of preaching, he is of course preaching the doctrine of predestination. See, for example, his *A Golden Chaine* (1591) and *De praedestinationis modo et ordine* (1598).
16 Francis Bacon, Preface to the *Instauratio Magna*, in *Works*, ed. J. Spedding, R.L. Ellis, and D.D. Heath (London: Longman, 1858-74), IV, 53.

scholastic, humanist, or Protestant conceptions of man's power or impotence, contain certain similar though perplexingly contradictory features. These features reflect a common framework of traditional beliefs based on a theocentric perspective and on the insistent assumption that the Fall of man is the dominant fact of human history. Man's earthly interests, his quest for new wisdom and the free exercise of the faculties, slowly begin to demystify and literalize the older symbolic structure. In Marlowe's age, however, intellectual pursuits still engendered biblical exegesis, faith in revelation, and self-conducted, sceptical examination of man's sin and his "Idols." In a way, almost all late Renaissance thought seems to balance the claim of "art" and freedom against compromise or even self-humiliation. Works from the period very often reflect and produce these contradictory motives which develop from the impact Protestantism and humanism had upon each other, and the paradoxical connection between Ramism and Puritanism is just another case which complicates our response to the intellectual and theological controversies that were waged during the time when Marlowe wrote his plays.

If we weave the strands together that lead us toward the opening scene of *Dr Faustus*, we may be persuaded to see the complex referentiality of Faustus' disputation in a new light. Marlowe situates us with a theatrical and rhetorical spectacle in which Faustus conflates a specific dialectical method with a purposeful exegesis directed at the central, sacred texts of his culture, and the conflation makes his disputational "show" a deliberate artifice to which orthodox criticism has by and large proved thoroughly insensitive. It simply does not do to observe that the scene becomes a "portrayal of Faustus' grandly inquiring mind,"[17] or that Marlowe demonstrates the ignoble folly of a one-time "fearless seeker after knowledge and truth."[18] Nor does it pay justice to Marlowe to claim that his hero goes out on the

---

17 Susan Snyder, "Marlowe's *Doctor Faustus* as an Inverted Saint's Life," *SP*, 63 (1966), 577.
18 Greg, "The Damnation of Faustus," 99.

stage simply to demolish himself by revealing his inability to attribute quotations correctly and to attend to the full contexts of his biblical passages.[19] On the contrary, the theatrical effect of Faustus' deconstructive tour through his library is so strong because the audience is taken aback by his rhetorical self-consciousness, never quite knowing how much of it is utterly serious and how much is flippant and cynical. The mixture of both makes for a very cunning attempt to control the terms (the language, the modes of discourse) of his rebellion, those terms which render themselves so readily yet will remain revengefully ambiguous.

The ambiguity is clearly built into Faustus' project, and since the issues at stake are of serious nature, we should note his characteristic self-defence:

> And I that haue with Consissylogismes
> Graueld the Pastors of the Germaine Church,
> And made the flowring pride of Wertenberge
> Swarme to my Problems ...
> (A 145-48)

By asserting his skill in debate and his role as a radical challenger of received ideas, Faustus may here attribute the same power to his "concise syllogisms" that Peter Ramus once demonstrated when he baffled the proud doctors of Paris with his M.A. thesis: *Quaecumque ab Aristotele dicta essent, commentitia esse?* [20] As Faustus' assertion (A 145-48) shows, and as his application of "concise syllogisms" to the biblical texts confirms, the confusion of the "art of dialectic" with its perspectives on religion is certainly intended. Most Protestant

---

19 See, for example, Kocher, *Christopher Marlowe*, pp. 104-09; Cole, pp. 197-201; H.W. Matalene, III., "Marlowe's *Faustus* and the Comforts of Academicism," *ELH*, 39 (1972), 495-501, and Edward Snow, "*Doctor Faustus* and the Ends of Desire," pp. 70-80.
20 Ramus' ferocious attack on Aristotle became a *cause célèbre*, and his early academic career evidently reflected his splendid triumph over his rivals. Cf. Banosius' biography, which appeared in 1576 and was dedicated to Sir Philip Sidney (*Petri Rami Vita*, in *Commentariorum de religione Christiana*).

"Pastors" would have been horrified by Faustus' assertion, namely that he explained theological "Problemes" with the help of "Consissylogismes"; from their Wittenberg pulpits they had thundered the condemnation of Aristotle, the "blind pagan teacher," and of all logic in general, according to Luther's ferociously polemical contention that "reason is the devil's greatest whore."[21]

Faustus, in true Ramist fashion, could have claimed, on the other hand, that logic and the syllogistic method (as the principle means by which a "Problem" may be examined, knowledge ordered, and the necessary conclusion achieved) were indeed the means to ascend to godhead, to the "divine light which feeds the universe from within."[22] Faustus' method, however, is more relentless still, for he is twisting and turning his own artistic dialectic, now condemning Aristotle, now Ramus, then again using both against each other and against other objects of his contempt. A recent critic has pointed out that Ramus' "victimization" in *The Massacre at Paris* betrays Faustus' own "shallowness" and indeed "perfectly describes" Faustus' symptomatic "failure to 'sound anything to the depth.'"[23] The parallel is of course highly interesting, but

---

21 Luther's condemnation of logic surfaces throughout his exegetic writings and his sermons. My excerpts are quoted from Maritain, *Three Reformers*, pp. 32-33, who offers a brilliant analysis of Luther's apparent anti-intellectualism. John Henry Newman harks to the same antithesis of faith to reason when he takes St. Ambrose's aphorism as his motto: "Not through dialectic has God elected to save his people" (*An Essay in Aid of a Grammar of Assent* [London: Burns, Oates & Co., 1870], title-page).
22 Ramus, *Dialecticae institutiones* (1543), fols. 38-9, quoted from Ong, *Ramus*, p. 189. This Ramist idea of the art of logic as an instrument in man's effort for salvation must have appealed to Perkins, since he is one of the first Calvinists to make extensive use of charts, diagrams, and visual aids, and his application of spatial models and logical synopses is nowhere clearer than in his *A Survey or Table declaring the Order of the Causes of Salvation and Damnation, according to God's word....*(1590). The *Table* is reprinted in Porter, ed., *Puritanism in Tudor England* (Columbia: Univ. of S.Carolina Press, 1971), pp. 295-300.
23 Snow, pp. 76f. For contrary views, see Wilbur Sanders' attack on Marlowe in *The Dramatist and the Received Idea* (Cambridge: Cambridge Univ. Press, 1968), pp. 20-37, and John Ronald

Edward Snow's commentary rests, I believe, on a misunderstanding of both the scene in *The Massacre* and the mode of Faustus' discourse.

In its dramatic context, the Ramus scene in *The Massacre* far surpasses all the other murder episodes and thus assumes a special character. In spite of its ironic design, it gives the confrontation between Ramus and the Guise a psychological and emotional depth which is unusual for the surviving text of the play, and it ultimately results in a cynical unmasking of the Guise's diabolic ambition in contrast to the positive strength with which Ramus endures his martyrdom.

> *Ram.* O good my Lord, wherein hath Ramus been so offensious?
> *Guis.* Marry, sir, in having a smack in all
> And yet didst never sound anything to the depth.
> Was it not thou that scoff'dst the *Organon*
> And said it was a heap of vanities?
> He that will be a flat dichotomist
> And seen in nothing but epitomes
> Is in your judgment thought a learned man;
> And he, forsooth, must go and preach in Germany,
> Excepting against doctors' actions
> And *ipse dixi* with this quiddity:
> *Argumentum testimonii est inartificiale.*
> To contradict which, I say, Ramus shall die.
> How answer you that? Your *nego argumentum*
> Cannot serve, sirrah.- Kill him.
> (IX.23-37)

Ramus' defence against the pure violence of a power too strong to argue with remains ineffective; yet to the end he refuses to flee ("Tell me, Taleus, wherefore should I fly" IX.6) or to ask for mercy.

The situation, in the way I tried to describe it, has an obvious bearing on the confrontational pattern in *Dr Faustus*. The power that crushes Faustus is a doctrinal world which, provoked by the Faustian challenge, asserts its overbearing authoritative validity by breaking the rejection of this validity *within* Faustus - making him the desperate victim of his own feelings of guilt and

---

Glenn's apology in "The Martyrdom of Ramus in Marlowe's *The Massacre at Paris*," *PLL*, 9 (1973), 365-79.

of the "objective" truth. When Ramus asks what his offence was, his Catholic persecutor turns on him with a shockingly sarcastic argument, judging him by enumerating his "crimes" of intellectual subversion (his eclecticism, his anti-Aristotelianism, his dichotomizing and epitomizing) and concluding with a bitter travesty of reasoning: "Ramus shall die." Although his proposition that Ramus will die is an "inartificial" argument, and thus logically invalid, the defendant cannot deny the very real and brutal force behind it. The Guise's main thrust is against Ramus' rejection of the validity of "authority" in logic: "*Argumentum testimonii est inartificiale*." The Latin quotation is taken directly from Ramus' own dialectical system which distinguishes between two classes of argument: "artificial" (using the methodical, logical process) and "inartificial" (relying on testimony from prior authorities and thus invalid).[24] Ramus' "*nego argumentum*" would not serve - the validity or existence of the irrational, the monstrous, and the external in general cannot be denied.

Whereas in *The Massacre* the confusion between valid and invalid arguments is secondary to the clear breaking of ethical norms, the juxtaposition between Faustus' logical-rhetorical self-assertion and the normative standards he breaks is much more complex because the dramatic and psychological identity of the hero in *Dr Faustus* precisely rests on and originates from the incompatibility of the normative principles that govern Faustus' world and of what he himself sees as the essence of his spiritual and intellectual freedom. In form and structure, Marlowe's drama unmistakingly upholds the identity and reality of the supra-human,

---

24 Ramus, *Dialecticae libri duo, A. Talaei Praelectionibus Illustrati* (Parisiis, 1566), sigs. B 3r; N 3r. Ramus' definitions and assortments of arguments undergo various changes throughout his career. It may suffice to add here that Ramus' "art of dialectic" consists of two parts: "invention" and "judgment," and the dialectical process works its way from the proposition through the invented arguments to its judgment (arranged and concluded in syllogistic structure). Cf. *Dialecticae institutiones* (1543), fol. 20. Excerpts are reprinted in Ong, *Ramus*, pp. 178-93.

divine Order; and Faustus' *Being* on the purely human plane, the world as the place of his actions, the here and now, is inextricably connected with the metaphysical structure of this immanent Order. How this Order functions within the dramaturgy of the play is one of the crucial questions to ask. The dramatic focus is on the lonely figure in the centre of the stage, yet Faustus' self-realization, his manipulation of space and time within the scene that he builds, is necessarily experienced through his relationship with and understanding of the external "ends" and limits he rejects. The interplay between Faustus' view of his role (himself) and the metaphysical assumptions that at the same time govern both his own and our understanding of his dilemma makes for the immense theatricality of the theology in *Dr Faustus*.

The main thrust of Faustus' arguments and his resolutions are of course inextricably entwined with the issue of salavtion, and the significance of the questions Faustus asks is therefore directly related to the manner in which Marlowe's dramaturgy translates the questions into action.

>   Is, to dispute well, Logickes chiefest end?
>   . . .
>   A greater subiect fitteth Faustus wit,
>   Bid *Oncaymaeon* farewell ...
>   (A 38;41-42)

Faustus' method of cutting the Gordian knot of authorities is significant. From his defining conjunction ("Is, to dispute well, Logickes chiefest end?") he proceeds to dismiss Aristotle, which he can do by cunningly doubling his argument with the implications of the Ramist definition: "the art of dialectic is to dispute well," namely that the "end" of dialectic should be the formal knowledge of how to resolve explicitly formulated questions. The implication thus goes further: Ramus' formal logic is meant to unravel the order of things in our mind and is not furnished to approach philosophical problems for what these problems are in themselves. Questions of truth and falsehood, for Ramus, cannot be solved by restricting them to either affirmative or negative statements, and when applied to ontological or metaphysical problems these distinctions become hopelessly confusing, as he explains in his rejection of Aristotle's *Metaphysics*.[25]

When Faustus dismisses logic *and* metaphysics, he is therefore not confusing the issues, as most commentators would have it,[26] but expressing his scorn at being unable to "resolue ... all ambiguities" (A 112) that are suggested by the locution "Being and not Being." This clearly anticipates Faustus' interpretation of theology. His dismissal of medicine and law follows the same pattern. Each discipline undergoes a quick synecdochical treatment, and from each double quotation Faustus infers the limitations that these systems impose on him and the absence of any real "*summum bonum*" which he could see fulfilling his aspirations.

> Yet art thou still but Faustus, and a man.
> Wouldst thou make men to liue eternally?
> Or being dead, raise them to life againe?
> Then this profession were to be esteemd.
> (A 53-56)

Medicine, the practical "end" of which is the "easing" of man's progress towards death, does not give him the power to make such a fundamental choice as between mortality and immortality. The "wondrous cure" that resurrected Christ and "eternizde" him is not available to Faustus, and the rebellious undertone of his scornful gestures (implicitly towards Christ, explicitly towards his own "myracles" of past medical success) modulate his actual frustration about his human predicament: "Yet art thou still but Faustus, and a man." The scorn finds its release in the almost parodic derision of the authorities which he quotes at random, calling on Gelen but quoting from Aristotle instead, deliberately distorting Aristotle's meaning and using it against

---

25 See Ramus, *Aristotelicae animadversiones libri XX* (Lutetiae, 1548), fols. 63;67;71-73. See also Ong, *Ramus*, pp. 207-10, and Jardine, *Francis Bacon*, pp. 41-48.
26 Representative of the usual misreadings are Snow, p. 76, and A.L. French, "The Philosophy of *Dr. Faustus*," *EIC*, 20 (1970), 127-28.

him, and thereby facetiously commenting on their inadequacy in
countering the fatality that looms large over human existence.[27]
His belittlement of authority is nowhere clearer than in the case
of his treatment of the "seruile and illiberall" law:

> A pretty case of paltry legacies:
> *Ex haereditari filium non potest pater nisi:*
> Such is the subiect of the institute
> And vniuersall body of the Church:
> His study fittes a mercenary drudge,
> Who aimes at nothing but externall trash.
> (A 60-65)[28]

His seemingly accidental text-selections from Justinian may not
be accidental at all; since Faustus' mind seems clearly stuck
on the problem of fatality and determinism, his free association
between Roman law and Christian doctrine (Calvin's "Institutes"?)
becomes quite poignant: "Such is the subiect of the institute /
And vniversall body of the Church." The subject of the Protestant Church's teaching, as Faustus will demonstrate instantly, is
indeed how man avoids getting cut out of the Heavenly Father's
legacy of eternal life, or - and this is the crucial Calvinist
twist - how he may never expect an eternal life in the first
place because the Father has decided to cast him away.[29]

The dramatic climax of his *anatomia scientiarum* is reached when
Faustus opens his Bible: "When all is done, Diuinitie is best"
(A 67). What he means to say is "worst" - of "best" for his
case. As the repetition of the first biblical quotation and his
careful translation suggest, Faustus has his finger virtually

---

27 "*Vbi desinit philosophus, ibi incipit medicus*" (A 43;not in
    B) and "*Summum bonum medicinae sanitas*" (A 46;B 44) are free-
    ly adapted from Aristotle's *De sensu*, 436a and *Nicomachean
    Ethics*, 1094.a.8. Cf. Dent, "Ramist Faustus or Ramist Mar-
    lowe?", 66-70.
28 The B-text reads "body of the law" (B 60) for A's "body of
    the Church." The quotations from Justinian's *Institutes* are
    not literal but derived from the sense of passages in Book
    II, title xx and title xiii.
29 How fatal the "influence" of a determinist theology can be is
    testified by the Calvinist poet William Cowper ("The Cast-
    away") who nearly went insane when he began to believe in his
    damnation.

on the spot here, and his gestures and utterances present a vital
theatrical moment. It goes without saying that Marlowe had to be
careful with this section of his play - no Elizabethan play with
explicitly perverted or scandalized Scriptural passages could have
been performed or published. Yet Faustus' exegesis fulfils its
function perfectly well; it does not need any further paraphrasing, nor any explicit mentioning of the names of God or Christ.
If the Elizabethan audience knew what texts he "omitted," as it
has been again and again stated by practically all commentators
who have consequently turned Faustus' "overlooking" of the central
tenets of the Christian dogma into a critical commonplace, then
it must have also known exactly which predestinarian crux Faustus
referred to.

As we experience Faustus' rhetoric and his self-definition within
the dramatic context, there is no point at all in speaking about
"forgetting" or "overlooking." The doctrinal world he describes
to us is a world cast in an uncompromisingly Calvinist mould. If
I am correct this implies that Faustus' sensibility does not
allow him to project the doctrinal world in other than the most
rigid and uncompromising terms. Faustus' quest for transcendence,
his escape from limitations and imposed "ends," only makes sense
if *he* can choose his own end for the sake of which he can aspire,
transgress, and overleap.

> *Stipendium peccati mors est:* ha, *Stipendium etc.*
> The reward of sinne is death: thats hard.
> *Si pecasse negamus, fallimur, et nulla est in nobis veritas.*
> If we say that we haue no sinne,
> We deceiue our selues, and theres no truth in vs.
> Why then belike we must sinne,
> And so consequently die.
> I, we must die an euerlasting death:
> What doctrine call you this?
> (A 69-77)

Faustus' method of exegesis is certainly in keeping with his
mastery of the Ramist "art of dialectic." Ramus' prescriptions
for the unweaving of texts suggest that one simply has to find
the two premises of every syllogism buried in a text and then

cut out the preliminary syllogisms in order to arrive at the final master conclusion.[30] What is Faustus' master conclusion? What conception of God or divinity does he have?

The first important point is that Faustus' rejection of divinity is not dramatized as a particular psychological crisis; at this point of his rhetorical *tour de force* he merely concludes his disputation with another logical dilemma. A momentous moment of choice is almost played down to a few gestures, pauses, and arguments rendered with mechanical indifference. The only text-directions for the actor lie in the two repetitions (A 69;75-76) and the exclamations "ha" and "thats hard." The tone of the actor's voice will carry the main burden - and the pitch in this prose section is built towards the final stress on the amplified resolution (A 76-78).

The premises Faustus uses for his resolution are taken from two New Testament texts (Romans; I John) which, quite significantly, contain practically all the essential christological, dogmatic and ethical perspectives that pertain to the theological concepts in *Dr Faustus*. The major premise of Faustus' syllogism comes right out of Paul's exposition of the doctrine of sin (Rom.v-viii) and proposes Paul's negative thesis of man's natural corruption, his natural sinfulness before the Law: *The reward of sinne is death.*[31] In the minor premise we have the assumption

---

30 "When you have cut out from the parts of the continuous discourse the many syllogisms therein, take away all the amplifications, and, after making brief headings to note the arguments used, form into one syllogism the sum total of the discourse, this sum total being ordinarily self-evident, although it may be swelled to undue proportions by accumulation of ornaments" (*Dialecticae institutiones* [1543], fol.48; translation provided by Ong, *Ramus*, p. 191).
31 "For the wages of sinne is death: but the gift of God is eternall life, through Iesus Christ our Lord" (Rom.vi.23, Geneva version). Faustus' "reward" corresponds to the translations in the Bishops' Bible and the Great Bible. He picks the line from a chapter in which Paul throughout juxtaposes negative and positive concepts. These juxtapositions seem to be resolved (Rom.vii) by Paul's affirmation that with Christ man has ceased to be under the Law. Protestant exegesis takes vi.14ff. and vii.14ff. to mean, however, that man is

> If we say that we haue no sinne,
> We deceiue our selues, and theres no truth in vs.

which is taken from John's First Epistle. The Epistle has a clear Christological centre and stresses the fundamental connection between *faith* and *love*. The tensions in John's dualisms of light (faith) and dark (sin), however, were rigorously taken over by Calvin for the purpose of underscoring his doctrine of justification by faith alone.[32]

Faustus concludes his categorical syllogism by resolving the disjunctive assumption of his minor premise in terms of the major. What was hypothetical is now rendered imperative:

> Why then belike we must sinne,
> And so consequently die.
> I, we must die an euerlasting death.

It seems odd that Faustus arrives at the necessity of *universal* damnation; he may be thinking of the universal doctrine of original sin (man's natural corruption), which would explain his generalizing conclusion. Or he may be simply repeating the plural used in John's disjunctive proposition. Yet this does not solve

---

32 *never* free from sin; man remains *simul iustus et peccator*. This significant formulation, prefiguring the dilemma of doubt about salvation, is supplied by the Geneva Glosses on the immediate context of Faustus' quotation: "He granteth, that sinne is not yet so dead in vs that it is vtterly extinct ... By nature we are slaues to sinne and free from righteousnesse, but by the Grace of God we are made seruants to righteousnes, and therefore free from sinne...."
"If we say that we haue no sinne, wee deceiue ourselves, and trueth is not in vs. If we acknowledge our sinnes, hee is faithful and iust, to forgiue vs our sinnes, or to cleanse vs from all vnrighteousnesse. If we say we haue not sinned, we make him a liar, and his word is not in vs" (I John i.8-10, Geneva version). The Geneva Gloss runs like this: "The vse of this doctrine is this that all of vs being coupled and ioyned together with Christ by faith ... for this our sanctification which walke in the light, is a testimonie of our ioyning and knitting together with Christ: but because our light is very dark, we must needes obtaine another benefit in Christ to wit, that our sinnes may be forgiven vs being sprinkled with his blood: and this in conclusion is the prop and stay of our salvation. There is none but needeth this

the problem of his obvious bypassing of the doctrine of salvation.
I take it that Faustus' scornful emphasis on the deterministic
principle which he has deduced

> What doctrine call you this, *Che sera, sera,*
> What wil be, shall be? Diuinitie, adieu.
> (A 77-78)

points beyond the doctrine of original sin to the enigma of the
Calvinist concept of double-predestination. If we remember the
context (Romans, I John) from which Faustus quotes, and the fact
that this context was vital for the 16th century Protestant polemic on *fiducia*, Faustus' aesthetic and intellectual revulsion
against the categorical determinism explicit in this polemic
proves his point sufficiently. He need not go on to quote the
other side of this doctrine because it contains the same deterministic principle or premise, spelled out in the same elusive
terms ("the gift of God is eternall life"; "hee is faithful and
iust ...") of a "universal promise"[33] that cannot resolve the
notorious dilemma: how can one distinguish between salvation
and damnation, between true knowledge and false knowledge? If
one is predestined to damnation in the first place, what can
one do to save oneself? That God is capable of forgiving does
not mean that he will or, in other words, it is one thing to say
that there are no conclusive grounds for rejecting *hope* and quite
another to find a conclusive ground for embracing it.

Faustus could construct a long chain of such questions and arguments, and he would still balk at the same obstacle: the insistence on the Pauline "full assurance of hope unto the end" (Heb.
iii.6) creates a scandal by in fact making a Christian duty out
of a psychological impossibility. It is, then, the dilemma of

---

benefite, because there is none that is not a sinner. They
doo not only deceiue themselues, but are blasphemers against
God." The Johannine text itself (esp.i.7-10 and iii.6-10) is
worth studying since it is not free from ambiguities and confusions (see, for example, the confusions between the epithets for God and Christ).

33 Cf. Rom.iii.21-28;v.5; viii.24f.;xi.26-32; II Cor.xiii.4-6.

faith, provoked by a doctrine with equivocal predestinarian premises, to which Faustus draws our attention. His response in its full implications transcends theological inhibitions as such to engage a deeper concern about problems of knowledge, power, and freedom of the self.

The soteriological terms of divinity, which Faustus unravels in his master conclusion "What wil be, shall be", imply the same basic acceptance of his unfreedom and the same imposed determinism that he has rebelled against throughout his opening soliloquy. If Faustus is therefore directing our attention to this existential dilemma between perhaps illusory hope and fatal constriction, his syllogism need not be called a "fallacy" in my opinion, since the "suppressed halves"[34] of the quotations will not render anything new to Faustus' apprehension of the fallibility of the Calvinist doctrine itself or, rather, to his sense of the complete externality of any good being offered by it. Faustus' dialectical enquiry reaches its dramatic climax when he scornfully dismisses the inevitable ("What wil be, shall be") that he sees imposed on him; his contemptuous exclamation and gesture

> What doctrine call you *this?*

indeed invites the audience in the theatre to judge the texts of his exegesis, his understanding of them *and* their own understanding. Even if a Christian audience is meant to endorse what he rejects, the sympathy that we can show for Faustus' resentment against an intrinsically scandalous doctrine renders the theatrical experience of the opening scene highly ambivalent.

The ambivalence of audience response is built into Marlowe's dramaturgy, and as the play unfolds our power of judgment and discrimination is continuously shifted back and forth between our understanding of the implied base line of orthodox theology and the admiration and fascination which Marlowe excites in us through the ironic counterpoints that his hero self-consciously

---

34 Cf. Hunter, "The Theology of Marlowe's *The Jew of Malta*," 212.

creates throughout his iconoclastic enterprise. There is one more
question to be solved, then, if we want to clarify our judgment
on Faustus' rejection of a deterministic theology. As my exposition of the Reformantion doctrine of predestination was meant to
show, the inference Faustus draws from his biblical texts states
a dilemma which neither he nor we are capable of solving. If we
have to accept the necessitarian concept that Faustus "proves" in
his syllogism as orthodox, are we then to criticize Faustus' lack
of faith or his specific *mode* of argument? I wish to emphasize
once again that Faustus' intellectual struggle ought not to be
mis-represented by claiming that there is an obvious fallacy in
his syllogism and that typical constructions of the same syllogism and its "correct" solution can be found in other contemporary works.[35]

In the First Book of Spenser's *Fairie Queene*, Despayre's indict-
ment revolves around the same issue, and the configuration of his
speech is quite Protestant in style:

> Is not he iust, that all this doth behold
>   From highest heauen, and beares an equall eye?
> Shall he thy sins vp in his knowledge fold,
> And guiltie be of thine impietie?
> Is not his law, Let euery sinner die:
> Die shall all flesh? what then must needs be donne,
> Is it not better to doe willinglie ...
>   (9.47)

My point is that Una's rhetorical refutation does *not* solve the
dilemma[36] that Despayre had so sardonically insinuated to Redcrosse:

> Come, come away, fraile, feeble, fleshly wight,
>   Ne let vaine words bewitch thy manly hart,

---

35 Kocher instances two parallels, Thomas Becon's *The Dialogue between the Christian Knight and Satan* and William Whitaker's *A Disputation on Holy Scripture*, and goes on to say that the statement of the dilemma, in the way Faustus formulates it, is almost never found without the accompanying statement of the apparent solution, namely that salvation is available to those with faith (*Christopher Marlowe*, pp. 106-09).
36 For a different view see George Hunter, "The Theology," 212.

> Ne diuelish thoughts dismay thy constant spright.
> *In heauenly mercies hast thou not a part?*
> *Why shouldst thou then despeire, that chosen art?*
> (9.53;my emphasis)

These questions, applied to Faustus, can only answer themselves by presupposing as axiomatic that Faustus may be among the elect! Within its predestinarian context, the refutation would have to appeal not only to Faustus' *theoretic faith* that some men are elected by God but also to his *fiduciary faith* - his assurance that he *is* such a person. In other words, Faustus would have to examine himself and arrive at a point of firm knowledge, embracing the Holy Spirit which is the sole counterpoise to total corruption in the righteous - or rather in those upon whom righteousness is bestowed by a fiction of divine law (cf. Rom.v.5; viii.10ff.; Eph.i.13-14; I Cor.ii.2-16).

The metaphysical intimations are undoubtedly clear to Faustus; yet he has already discarded a metaphysics which enclosed him with insoluble propositions (Aristotle), and he does exactly the same with divinity. When he uses his syllogism, he deliberately takes the metaphysical assumptions that govern the imputation of righteousness and the gift of grace under the formality of dialectic, and face to face with his "logical" enquiry the Calvinist doctrines cannot but fail to convince. Faustus' "fantasy" will receive no such "obiect" for his "head," as he later confesses (A 136-37, not in B); the obscure "obiect" of his desire is a gigantic dream-vision which he is still suppressing in the opening part of his dialectical "show." And it seems that all the arguments within his partitive schema amount to the same basic, almost phenomenological decision against restraint.

Faustus wishes to be *more* than a man; when we see him in the first scene, we witness him abstracting and rationalizing all the obstacles that are in his way. Theological doctrine is the ultimate test-case; the irrational principles on which the concepts of faith and hope are built present the greatest temptation for him. We could say that he fails to make sense out of the theological problem of faith because he is a reprobate and therefore blind to its solution. Yet this goes against the dramatic emphasis on Faustus' own will-power. The only valid suggestion that I can make is that Faustus deliberately cancels out anything that could restrict and denigrate his potential to be an "overman." His conclusion, "What wil be, shall be," summarizes his scorn for timeless necessity, for eternal predestination, which - as he has deduced - is *imposed* upon him by the soteriology and eschatology of Christian religion. His logic actually makes an astonishing leap over the "end" of "euery Art": his fatalist construction reveals a logical necessity in the *future*, fulfilling the past event of Christ's redemptive sacrifice. The problem of Time, which becomes so crucial in the play (his 24 year compact; the final hour before his damnation) is here already a central issue for Faustus. The future of the Christian dispensation will always remind him of his imprisonment in Time, in the divine scheme of promises, gifts, imputations, restrictions, threats, and hopes - and all the accompanying feelings of guilt and doubt. It will always remind him that he is only a man, a creature that is required to humiliate himself.

Christian eschatology can only speak of transcendence as something given to man, postponed to his afterlife. Faustus' daring and spectacular choice, and it is one that is probably unique in the history of English Renaissance drama, signals his rejection of this entire metaphysical structure. Projecting a transcendence, an immortality, *in Time*, in the here and now, requests therefore that Faustus self-determines his life, his time. When he starts drawing magical circles around himself, Faustus indeed swerves away from the existential, linear progression towards his natural death. Above all, the circle indicates that he is willing to create his own temporary space by *damning himself*.

When Faustus dreams of his magic, he opens up the prospect of his own "liberty" ("my four-and-twenty yeares of liberty" B 862, not in A) - his self-created end-points in the past and the future, his own history of what "has been, shall be." It is this prospect which will make him feel like being a "mighty god" who has command, power, and omnipotence. At this point in the soliloquy, Faustus' passions and desires for the transcendent power he craves break through and well up from the depths of his imagination. His extended poetic rapture forms one of the most powerful moments in the play:

> These Metaphisickes of Magicians,
> And Negromantike bookes are heauenly
> Lines, circles, sceanes, letters and characters:
> I, these are those that Faustus most desires.
> O what a world of profit and delight,
> Of power, of honour, of omnipotence
> Is promised to the studious Artizan?
> All things that mooue betweene the quiet poles
> Shalbe at my commaund ...
>   (A 79-87)

Placed against the rejected sacred texts, Faustus' exultation at his magical "Metaphisickes" is a stunning inversion; he is now having his own mystical experience. Yet we are also reminded of the precarious nature of his escape from Time and the normal, "heauenly" order. As a counterpoint to his previous "disputation, however, Faustus' poetic flight is enticing enough to make us indulge for a while in his capacities for invention. He is indeed lifting himself up - the expectations of his godlike power seem boundless.

> Nor can they raise the winde, or rend the cloudes:
> But his dominion that exceedes in this,
> Stretcheth as farre as doth the minde of man.
> A sound Magician is a mighty god:
> Heere Faustus trie thy braines to gaine a deitie.
>   (A 89-93)

The A-text intensifies the titanic image of Faustus and the ethopoetic nature of his striving for godhead. The B-text's "Demi-God" (B 88) seems much weaker, and the troping of cosmic "omnipotence" ("Nor can they raise the winde, or rend the cloudes") lacks entirely in B. The images he uses in this passage are very Ovidian, and Faustus' vision of power may very well echo Medea's invocation of the night in that extraordinary story of the "miracle" of Aeson's rejuvenation.[37] The idea of magic power over nature of course occupies a central place in the

Hermetic tradition, and Faustus' praise of the "Metaphisickes of Magicians" can hardly fail to establish the connection. It seems in line with the antithetical structure of Faustus' opening soliloquy that, after having rejected all orthodox traditions, he envisions his transcendence in classical and Hermetic images, the figures of a "forbidden art" with which he aspires to have "all things ... at [his] commaund." The ultimate antithesis comes as a natural conclusion at the climax of his speech: he will make himself a "mighty god."

This is the first time that Faustus uses the word "god", and although his apostasy makes the theological implications quite clear, the image he uses here still remains in the context of his classical invocation. The juxtaposition between the Christian God and Faustus' own conception of himself as a powerful "commander" is rendered explicit in the first appearance of the two Angels:

> *Good A.* O Faustus, lay that damned booke aside,
> And gaze not on it, lest it tempt thy soule,
> And heape Gods heauy wrath vpon thy head ...
> *Euill A.* Go forward Faustus in that famous art ...
> Be thou on earth as Ioue is in the skie,
> Lord and commaunder of these Elements.
> (A 102-04;106;108-09)

Faustus' "conceit" is still far too strong to allow any conception of God's judgment ("heauy wrath") to enter his mind. All his emotions are directed towards the new space he wants to inhabit and the new future he wants to control: "Ile haue ... Ile haue ... Ile haue ... Ile make..." (cf. A 114-29).

After his repudiation of Christian metaphysics and his denial of any other except his own internal viewpoint, Faustus' fantasies, as he anticipates his magic powers, betray an insatiability and

---

37 The interpolation of a more classical, pagan sensibility helps to intensify the thrust of Faustus' poetic vision, and it also underlines the earlier allusion to the Icarian flight. The analogy with Medea's invocation has often been overlooked (cf. Golding's translation of the *Metamorphoses*, VII.258-76; Marlowe also alludes to Medea in his *Elegies*, II.i.22-28).

randomness which seem to exalt the mere possibility of desiring and engendering. In a way, the long rhapsody exalts mental power over reality, defending the grand illusion of *self* ("swolne with cunning of a selfe conceit") with anxious gestures. The otherness of the object-world, and the otherness of the future, is denied by Faustus' "selfe conceit," by his narcissistic and egotistical will which is so enthusiastically directed towards the new "honor" and "blessing" that he expects from his magical enterprises. In other words, Faustus' mind invents and seeks an external world that supports his desires instead of denying them. His narcissistic self-esteem and his projections, however, display a passion that reveals and conceals at the same time.

That he may be repressing the fear that his desires could be damaging becomes obvious during the first appearance of the two Angels. He is so caught up with himself that he is quite oblivious of their presence.

> How am I glutted with conceit of *this?*

His long, programmatic speech picks up the ideas of "power," "profit," and "delight" that he had introduced earlier, and the word "this" would therefore refer to the entire magical project. His will-to-power ("Lord and commaunder of these Elements") is merely reconfirmed by the voice of the Bad Angel, and so we could say that even if Faustus actually registers the Bad Angel's insinuation, he appears so self-occupied and immersed in his book of negromancy that the stage-business around him (the Angels) becomes almost wholly detached. One cannot really say that "the conflict of conscience has begun in Faustus' soul";[38] yet Marlowe's dramaturgical use of an older convention, the stage psychomachia, seems to direct audience attention to an awareness of alternatives that are involved in mental operations, and psychic conflicts can be effectively visualized in the theatre by using representational devices of this sort: allegorical figures, con-

---

38 Campbell, *"Doctor Faustus:* A Case of Conscience," 233.

trasting postures, contrasting voices, dialogical structure, etc. Marlowe elaborates the older morality conventions, however. His Angels never argue with each other; and in their first appearance they act not so much as externalized moral-psychological forces in Faustus' mind as they reinforce, through their objectified, external presence, the gap that lies between them and Faustus' internal, egotistical perspective. If the two Angels represent a dialectic principle in themselves, they also somehow reflect the dialectics of aggression within Faustus, because one cannot overhear the efforts Faustus makes to defend his personal stance and to keep it in opposition to the Order he has negated.

This becomes more obvious during the "sage conference" with Valdes and Cornelius, his friends from the magical profession. In his address to them he boasts his revulsion against orthodox scholarship and reveals his true obsession:

>   ... but mine owne fantasie,
> That will receiue no obiect for my head,
> But ruminates on Negromantique skill ...
> Tis Magicke, Magicke that hath rauisht me.
>   (A 136-38[not in B];143)

This self-interpretation is astonishing indeed. The power of his own imagination, he says, has persuaded him at last to think of *nothing else* while he invents the grand possibilities of the "concealed arts" (A 135). The truly daemonic quality of his venture lies in his claim to sublimate his striving to become immortal by a complete and wilful negation, a misconstruction of reality, which he thinks can liberate him into the freedom of an alternate, self-sustained reality.[39] The problem with Faustus

---

39 In *Tamburlaine*, the hero's attempt to impose his central fantasy fully upon the external reality almost succeeds:

> I hold the Fates bound fast in iron chains,
> And with my hand turn Fortune's wheel about,
> And sooner shall the sun fall from his sphere
> Than Tamburlaine be slain or overcome ...
> May we become immortal like the gods. (I.ii.173-76;200)

Valdes, in a rather ironic twist, projects the master-magicicians' immortality in the form of a "canonization"(A 153).

is that he cannot invent an autonomous world for himself - and
here he stands in marked distinction to Tamburlaine. He can only
constitute a world within the given world, a kind of underground-
world which might sustain itself by the perversions and inversions
of the context in which, however, they are not beyond good and
evil but clearly defined as evil and misbegotten.

If negation is a way of taking account of what is repressed and
thus, simultaneously, a repression *and* an intellectual acceptance
of that which is repressed, it can be understood why Faustus has
entered a vicious circle. His enterprise will become an anxious
quest in the course of which he will always be reminded of the
historical context, the world, the social sphere, his human nature,
Christianity and its symbolic structures, etc. - and yet will he
ignore the futility of his negation and seek to be

> as cunning as Agrippa was,
> Whose *shadowes* made all Europe *honor* him.
> (A 150-51;my emphasis)

He craves "honor," yet does he really seek the honour of invoking shades of the dead? The image is rather ambiguous (he
will be "cunning," a second Agrippa) and ultimately disappointing
because it is imitative and, at best, merely blasphemous. It becomes increasingly clear that Faustus' projected power and fame
have to do with imitations, abstractions, shadows, "spirits" in
the "likeness" of lions, giants, and beautiful women (cf. A 154-
63). The poetry, however, is strongest precisely in those moments
when he sustains his aesthetic excitement through the ravishing
music of his mighty line. His fantasies are alluring, and we experience his anxiety and aspiration with admiring though critical
sympathy. As an audience of what Joel Altman has called the
"play of mind," we willingly grant Faustus poetic "freedom,"
and one could say that poetry, at least, opens one area of possibility for Faustus through which desire can "in fact" become
reality.

But as Valdes points out to him, his initial gesture of negation
will have to be repeated again and again. This is like saying:

you may never repent your denial, you must believe in your fantasies because they can only "create" your magical world "if learned Faustus will be resolute" (A 166).

> Valdes as resolute am I in this
> As thou to liue, therefore obiect it not.
> (A 167-68)

The problem of being "resolute" will confront Faustus repeatedly throughout the play. The "conceit" which generates his dream of magical power is the very refuge on which he will have to depend. Not surprisingly, his fixation will make him fall from the height of his vision into the depth of the nothingness that lies behind the tempting, glittering shadow-image. When Faustus, in his excitement, rushes to answer Cornelius' question, which was surely meant to be rhetorical,

> *Cor.* Then tell me Faustus, what shal we three want?
> *Fau.* Nothing Cornelius ...
> (A 181-82)

the ominous answer, "nothing," will reverberate in the short pause that follows it.

It is fascinating to see that Faustus' escape from Christian hopes and doubts, which I deduced from his wilful insistence on eternal damnation, can express itself as a hope of escape at the same time. This hope suggests that Faustus wants to determine the rules of the game; that he inadvertently drifts towards destruction and, subconsciously, embraces the image of self-destruction, becomes often visible in those moments when he is most playful and flippant:

> Then come and dyne with me, and after meate
> Weele canuas euery quiddity thereof:
> For ere I sleepe *Ile trie what I can do,*
> This night *Ile coniure though I die therefore.*
> (A 196-99; my emphasis)

Beneath the surface of these light-hearted words one can already suspect the laws of the tragedy which Faustus actually lives.

While Faustus' ravished vision of his daring flights may invite
us to speculate about the complex psychological operations that
underlie the poetry which expresses them, Marlowe can obfuscate
the rhetoric of his hero in a much simpler way by exploiting the
unique function which the comic scenes in Elizabethan drama could
have in relation to the main action. Nobody is really very happy
with the comic scenes in *Dr Faustus* as they have come down to us
in the 1604 and 1616 versions. The lack of homogeneity in the
different comic episodes, and especially the incongruous mixture
of high levels of prose with merely crude and coarse knockabout
farce, has often frustrated aesthetic and textual criticism
alike.

It is true also that I have seen a number of recent productions
of the play during which the comic scenes appeared to provoke
nothing but embarrassment among the audiences. Yet the interaction between serious tragic material and contrasting comic
entertainment was an unquestioned stage-convention in Marlowe's
time, and the popular success of *Dr Faustus* was probably partly
due to its buffoonery and spectacular "devilish" effects (fireworks, devils, pantomime, the pageant of the Seven Sins, conjuring tricks, etc.). That such sensationalism was in demand
explains why Henslowe would pay a rather large sum for the
"adicyones" of 1602. The extensions of the B version hardly im-
prove its integrity as a text, however, and the absence of gratuitous elaboration and special stage effects in A only strengthens the vitality and immediacy of focus in the 1604 version.
The earlier version in my opinion uses different levels of language quite skillfully and integrates the comic contrasts into
the main, ironic-tragic design with a number of curious, satiric
reflections. The dazzling "shows" of Faustus' rhetoric of aspiration are rhythmically intercepted by parodic "anti-shows," in
which Wagner, Robin and Rafe, the Knight, and the Horse-Courser
reduce futile heroic pretensions, through their own quasi-pretent-
ious though common-sensical clownage, to a level on which grandiose mannerism and absurd reality can flow together and reveal
the corrupting forces embodied in Faustus' quest.

If the practical jokes and comic parodies were merely there to make the vanity and absurdity of the hero's enterprise manifest, then one would have to agree with Robert Ornstein's assertion that such ironic dismantling reassures and "clarifies our perception of moral values."[40] Not all of the comic scenes may qualify for this, however, and it is even less clear to me why the middle section has been described as an unattractive, rambling clownage merely depicting Faustus' decline and transformation "from aspiring hero to despairing libertine."[41]

I would contend that the effects of satire and caricature can be rather more complex. Marlowe's dramaturgy, I think, features the hero's upward fall in a tragic design in which the comic contrasts are not merely anti-climactic, but often intensify the impression of Faustus' frustration at the limitations of human self-transcendence. The limitations of supernatural power, too, become painfully obvious to Faustus and to his audience. The triviality of the clowns' pranks and achievements may satirically emphasize the triviality of Faustus' achievements, yet the tragic predicament in Faustus' attempt to liberate himself and aspire for a more-than-common existence distances him from the low-style mimicry and obvious ridiculousness of the comic troupes, whose conventional gullibility and foolishness we take for granted. If they parody Faustus' illusions and ridicule his "fortunes," they still remain objects of ridicule themselves.

In the same way in which our aesthetic understanding of the idealized, intellectualized fixation, which drives Faustus' anxious quest to its final catastrophe, prevents us from pulling Faustus down to the level of Robin and Rafe, in the same way could the sight of the clownish pitfalls swing back our attention to a more

---

40 Robert Ornstein, "The Comic Synthesis in *Doctor Faustus*," *ELH*, 22 (1955), 169. See also Roma Gill, "'Such Conceits as Clownage Keeps in Pay': Comedy and *Dr. Faustus*," in *The Fool and the Trickster*, Studies in Honour of Enid Welsford, ed. Paul V.A. Williams (Ipswich: D.S. Brewer, 1979), pp. 55-63.
41 Ornstein, "The Comic Synthesis," 171.

disturbing form of frustration *in* the play that cannot be easily defined.

> 1.*Sch.* How now Sirra, wheres thy maister?
> *Wag.* God in heauen knowes.
> 2.*Sch.* Why, dost not thou know?
> *Wag.* Yes I know, but that followes not.
> (A 206-09)

The satiric undertones of this peculiar scene are not difficult to discern. Wagner, condescendingly proud and confident, turns the scene almost into a solo act; mimicking his teacher, the pupil manipulates logical arguments in witty trifles. But I do not know whether the irony is directed against Faustus or against anybody who asks questions that may not have a fixed answer. The mockery implied in the latter possibility goes much further and could be applied to more questions that are posed in the play.

The application of the figures of disputation and punning definition in Wagner's humorous sophistry has a bearing on Faustus' previous method of dialectic, however. After the Scholars had asked him where Faustus was, Wagner's deliberately *evasive* proposition "God in heauen knowes" tricks the Second Scholar into an "illogical" reply. Wagner then scoffs at their "error"; first, assuming that Faustus must be somewhere is logically unrelated to the proposition that Wagner does or does not know what "God in heauen" knows. Faustus never went so far as to even ask whether God in heaven knows and what the relationship between God's knowledge and man's logical enquiry may be. Secondly, Wagner rejects their testimony ("Haue you any witnesse on't?" A 216) as biased and thus invalid. He then comes round to "triumph" completely over them by a very quaint syllogism, which we could reconstruct like this:

> *Corpus naturale est mobile.*
> Faustus is a natural body.
> Therefore he is capable of moving.
> (cf.A 221-23)

That Faustus is indeed "moving" we have witnessed earlier. The question as such: "wheres thy maister?" has no conclusive answer, and Wagner can therefore mock the Scholars:

> ... then, wherefore should you aske me
> such a question.
> (A 222-23)

When he finally admits that Faustus is at dinner with the two "infamous" magicians, he perplexes the Scholars with a mock-Puritan blessing in which he inserts a blasphemous gibe at the Holy Eucharist:

> ... as this wine if it could speake, it would
> informe your worships, and so the Lord blesse
> you, preserue you, and keepe you my deare
> brethren, my deare brethren.
> (A 231-33)

The two Scholars seem seriously alarmed by the news that Faustus has dinner with Valdes and Cornelius:

> Nay then I feare
> he is falne into that damned art,
> for which they two are infamous through the world.
> . . .
> O but I feare nothing can reclaime him.
> (A 235-37;240)

Is there "nothing" that can save Faustus any more? This ominous statement is still in our ears when Faustus enters the stage to begin drawing the magical circle around himself.

Chapter Seven

MAGIC CIRCLES

>   [*Enter Faustus to coniure*]
> Now that the gloomy shadow of the earth,
> Longing to view Orions drisling looke,
> Leapes from th'antartike world vnto the skie,
> And dimmes the welkin with her pitchy breath:
> Faustus, begin thine incantations,
> And trie if diuels will obey thy hest.
>   (A 243-49)[1]

Faustus is putting his magical power to the test. It is a crucial and complicated moment, a moment in which the play begins to slant. Marlowe is forced, and one might regret his close reliance on the Faustbook, to a crossing-over. After having created the boundless, elusive visions and images of his inner yearning and after having filled the theatre with his soaring poetry, Marlowe's hero goes forward to become a practitioner. So far we have only experienced Faustus' subjective, idealized power-fantasies: a hypothetical future world built on tropes, on figurative meaning. Yielding to the powerful hunger inside him, Faustus' denial of the past and of objective truth, which was grounded on figur-

---

[1] In connection with the staging of the damnation scene, I already referred to the ambiguities involved in the diabolonian dramaturgy required by the 1616 stage-directions. At the beginning of this scene, B indicates: "*Thunder. Enter Lucifer and 4 deuils. Faustus to them with this speech*" (B 225-26). One may argue that the B-text staging is visually more spectacular; on the other hand, the rather crudely ironic overstatement of the discrepancy between Faustus' wishes and dreams and the "reality" of an encroaching, phenomenal hell seems to me aesthetically incoherent and unconvincing at this point, especially since the presence of five devils onstage (or "above") reduces Faustus' attempt to conjure them in the first place to a silly exercise. The A-text's method of pulling us into and out of Faustus' own perspective is considerably more subtle and effective.

ative language, partly collapses into the literalism of his odd, mechanical conjuration of "real" devils. He is trying to overcome the disparity between wilful words and reality, and it is clear that his attempt to leave the free space of his "conceit" and to step into and out of the gloomy magical circle is a precarious move.

One could regard the dramatization of this crossing as one of Marlowe's more complicated artistic bravadoes. Theatrical problems abound. Faustus' rebellion against accepted knowledge and against his God has a dramatic force of its own and gives us a complex psychological profile of his self-corrupting fixation. As I indicated earlier, Faustus, from his own individual point of view, can only assert the truth of his "language" of aspiration if he abolishes the other - the external, absolute language of metaphysical and theological truth. The collision of the two languages, which Faustus provokes by literalizing and applying his "Metaphisickes of Magicians" to the natural world, will create inevitable, ironic tensions. The A version, I believe, succeeds in containing a powerful, paradoxical harmony because it carefully balances poetry and the *visual*, whereas the 1616 version over-literalizes and often becomes crude in its exploitation of an old-fashioned mechanistic demonology.

Those *Dr Faustus* productions that I was able to see over the past years confronted the dramaturgical problems with varying success.[2] And this success, to a certain extent, depended on

---

[2] A revival of *Dr Faustus* is likely to present any modern director with a difficult task, yet the productions I saw impressed me with their thoughtful approaches to the textual and theatrical problems in the play. As one could clearly notice during the Ashland OSF performances, the diabolonian "entertainment" will probably remain the crux for any production mounted in our modern time. One encounters the occasional student production which tries to solve the problems by completely cutting most of the text and stage-directions and by using space differently. The Pembroke Players (dir. by Richard Spaul, Pembroke College, Cambridge, November 1979) offered a collage-version with only Faustus and Mephostophilis, the latter playing all the other parts himself. In

the choice of text. The New York CSC production, for example, gave its own interpretation of the A version; it almost completely side-stepped the problem of bringing medieval iconography on stage and largely kept Faustus' visions and struggles internalized, surrounding the protagonist with a wholly artificial world of mirages and reflecting glass balls which created an almost surreal atmosphere. The Lyric Studio production worked, even more successfully, with similar images, implicating Faustus' dreams in a pervading feeling of erotic desire for the unattainable, which was present throughout the performance. Consequently, the invocations and infernal shows remained distanced from the spectator and from Faustus himself and were vaguely intimated behind a gauze which functioned as a sort of magical box. Relying on the A version, the production managed to uphold a rigorously non-representational approach and indeed achieved astonishing effects: playing off what we got against what we expected.

The Ashland OSF production was visually the most daring and spectacular one, and part of the fascination one felt was of course also due to the fact that the play could be staged in Ashland's reconstructed Elizabethan playhouse. Interestingly, the approach was allegorical and rather unambiguously didactic, which led its director to rely on the longer B version and to emphasize an externalized, literalized diabolism. A very intricate set and a bizarre parade of devils in grotesque attires contributed to an over-explicit rendering of Faustus' magical adventures and failures. What remained of Hell in the end was a sadly harmless

---

the following, references will be mainly to (1) the Oregon Shakespearian Festival production, dir. by Jerry Turner, Elizabethan Theatre, Ashland, summer 1979; (2) the Classic Stage Company production, dir. by Christopher Martin, CSC Repertory, New York, winter 1979-80; (3) the Lyric Hammersmith production, dir. by Christopher Fettes, Lyric Studio Hammersmith, London (later transferred to the Fortune Theatre), spring 1980; (4) the Jesus College Drama Society/The Gods production, dir. by Tim Cribb, Stewart Eames, and Howard Erskine-Hill, Jesus College, Cambridge, winter 1980. Although *Dr Faustus* remains the most often performed play in the Marlowe canon, it is very rarely taken up by the commercial theatres; the most interesting work, as so often, has been done on the Fringe.

(in spite of thunder and lightning) and slightly ridiculous anachronism which was incommensurate with the brilliant expression of Faustus' suffering during his final hour.

Finally, the Jesus College production, a joint effort by the Jesus College Drama Society and The Gods (a fine name for a drama group performing *Dr Faustus*), distinguished itself by the enormous efforts that its directors had invested into a thorough analysis of the play's text. Their collaboration with Roma Gill, who has been working on her new Oxford *Dr Faustus* edition for more than fifteen years, produced results both stimulating and controversial, since Dr Gill is unwilling as yet to accept the distinct integrity of either of the two versions and continues to debate the authenticity of various parts of the plays. This gave the production a rather Janus-like face, as the opening and closing sections were based on a cut and edited version of the A playtext (supposedly the "true" original), whereas the central part, ascribed to a variety of Marlowe-collaborators, was deliberately played in the mode and mood of the B version.

As a result, the opening sequence came close to making excellent sense in the way in which A directs its intense focus on the Faustus-actor. With few props and no fireworks, with no devils and - surprisingly - no Lucifer and Belzebub at all, the opening sequence and the conjuration scene were in fact stripped of anything extrinsic to Faustus' perception; the effect was spare and extremely powerful. One must add, however, that the Faustus-actor had to struggle with one continuously "threatening" effect, an effect simply produced by the fact that the performance took place in the sixteenth-century Jesus College Chapel. The echo of Faustus' high-sounding words was thrown back from the vaults, and the dominating cross, suspended over the altar, was never quite out of sight while Faustus was trying to turn himself into a powerful magus.

The confusions that the Jesus College production, at least partly tried to avoid are of course built into the B-text. Whereas in A Faustus comes on stage simply "to coniure," informing the

audience in his soliloquy that it is night and that he will now
begin his daemonic ritual, the B stage-directions crowd the
(upper) stage with no less than five devils. Faustus would not
face the audience, as in A, but turn his back on them in order
to face the inner stage. B's stage-direction (*"Faustus to them
with this speech"*) implies that Faustus first of all joins them
on the stage and, furthermore, addresses the devils before him,
informing them that it is night (!) and, while they are before
his eyes, announces that he will try to see whether he can have
them appear. He obviously does not know what is going to happen,
since he encourages himself to "be resolute" (B 240; A 257) and
to proceed.

The Ashland production staged the scene exactly this way - and
I thought it was most awkward to say the least. These inconsistencies merely help to make Faustus look ridiculous, and if
we imagine Faustus "resolutely" muttering or declaiming Latin
phrases while his infernal stage audience gazes at him with
grinning amusement, the whole scene turns into a strange "burlesque of hell,"[3] complete with an ugly-looking monster-devil,
plenty of thunder and smoke, and a specially constructed mechanical "dragon" (B 246; not in A). This is a form of representation that logically culminates in the final "discovery" of hell
as a "vaste perpetuall torture-house" in which

> There are the Furies tossing damned soules,
> On burning forkes: their bodies broyle in lead.
> There are liue quarters broyling on the coles,
> That ner'e can die ...
>   (B 2019-23; not in A)

Furthermore, there is no stage-direction in B to indicate when
Lucifer and his four companions are to leave the stage. If we
assume that they remain present throughout the whole scene, the
conversation between Faustus and Mephostophilis about Lucifer

---

3   Following my interpretation of the B-text staging, it is a
    little easier to see why Gerald Morgan blames Marlowe for his
    "comic savaging of a popular myth" ("Harlequin Faustus," 32).

and his destiny becomes strained and artificial ("Go beare these tydings to great Lucifer."; "Go and return to mighty Lucifer" B 312;323). All this points to the conclusion that the B-text underwent a revision and expansion which, consequently, renders the crucial encounter between Faustus and the forces of evil much less subtly ironic. Daemonic power, overstated and presented in such an external and sensational manner, tends to lose all the imaginative profundity that was built into the dramatization of Faustus' progressive self-delusion. One cannot say that the B version makes no sense at all; yet the overriding objective presence of the diabolical powers undermines the complex balance that the A-text achieves in concentrating on Faustus' spiritual perversion and his ironic-tragic self-imprisonment within an evil "circle" - a circle that has a real and symbolic pertinence, while it is yet an imaginative extension of Faustus' own consciousness. What the magical circle in A symbolizes, that is in B translated into a palpable, objective "otherness" - a daemonic Order that has answered even before Faustus has begun to call.

This fascinating insight into the dialectics of evil is dramatized, in the A version, as a process of experience during which Faustus' consciousness is confronted with the paradox of a daemonic power that is created subjectively and yet re-creates and imposes itself on the creator. On the level of language, the disjuncture between constructive and counter-constructive power is already noticeable in the break-down of Faustus' imaginative poetry. After his poetic invocation of the "gloomy shadow of the earth," which re-enacts the idea of "leaping" on the level of metaphor, his speech moves into a literal hotchpotch of letters, syllables, figures, signs, and anagrams of holy names. Here is no invention any more, he is not even manipulating the symbology of his "magic art," but merely falling back on the terminology of witchcraft (and not "Witcraft", as Lever called the "art" of reason), hardly an innovative counter-culture of his particular historical period.

It is sadly ironic that Faustus' passion for power and knowledge

is now seen to rely on the "science" of hieroglyphs, a discipline
he had spared during his dialectical deconstruction of the other
sciences and the "rudiments" of which he obviously managed to
learn between dinner time and midnight (cf. A 194-99).

Faustus simply believes that "what he most desires" must be true,
and any qualms about the dangers involved are suppressed:

> Then feare not Faustus, but be resolute,
> And trie the vttermost Magicke can performe.
> (A 257-58)

It is even more ironic, however, that Faustus obviously accepts
the fact that by choosing the daemonic counterpoint of divinity
("... *inferni ardentis monarcha et demigorgon, propitiamus vos*"
A 259-62) he has to generate a behaviour ("thou hast prayde and
sacrific'd to them" A 250) determined by the Power he invokes,
which is in fact a kind of self-humiliation that he vehemently
rejected in his opening speech. It is a profound insight that
takes dramatic shape in this scene: Faustus has become enclosed
by his own "freedom." This paradox holds true on a deeper level
for the whole play: he is in submission to the values (liberation, self-damnation) that he himself sets up and creates. The
way in which this paradox surfaces, in all its fierce comic and
tragic dimensions, indicates how effective Marlowe's dramatic
technique can be.

> [*Enter a Diuell*]
> I charge thee to returne and chaunge thy shape,
> Thou art too vgly to attend on me,
> Goe and returne an old Franciscan Frier,
> That holy shape becomes a diuell best.
> (A 266-70)

Faustus rises to new heights of self-confidence and sarcastic
boastfulness. After having forgotten to specify that the devil
should appear in a pleasant shape, he surely has the laughs on
his side when he orders the mute devil to re-appear in a more
"adequate" and "holy" appearance. Beneath the joke, however,
lies the anxious wish to conceal the truth. His commands express

Faustus' pride in his new-found magical skills:

> I see theres vertue in my heauenly words,
> Who would not be proficient in this art?
> How pliant is this Mephastophilis?
> Full of obedience and humilitie,
> Such is the force of Magicke and my spels,
> No Faustus, thou art Coniurer laureate
> That canst commaund great Mephastophilis.
> (A 271-77)

From his point of view, there is reason to believe that he in fact *has* forced the devil to appear; his "heauenly words" *have* created "reality" in the way he wanted it, in a pleasant and pliant shape. Faustus feels triumphant, and his self-congratulating imagination gets inflamed by new visions of power and almost anarchic omnipotence:

> I charge thee wait vpon me whilst I liue,
> To do what euer Faustus shall commaund,
> Be it to make the Moone drop from her spheare,
> Or the Ocean to ouerwhelme the world.
> (A 281-84)

Yet Faustus' self-assurance is immediately deflated by Mephostophilis, who declares that he responds to Faustus' call only because he himself is bound by principles that govern his own nature and into which Faustus has let himself become implicated.

> I am a seruant to great Lucifer,
> And may not follow thee without his leaue.
> (A 285-86)

Faustus' furious question, "Did not my coniuring speeches raise thee? speake" (A 290), which was meant to be purely rhetorical, is answered in a way which elucidates the dangerous tangle in which Faustus has become enmeshed. Evil as such exits apart from Faustus, it transcends individual wills, and its threatening, daemonic Power only takes the *occasion* of man's internally corresponding inclination to "flye" towards him and seize control over him. In other words, Faustus' grandiose and blasphemous visions have resulted in the concurring ("per accident" or, as Mephostophilis admits, "when we heare one racke the name of

God" A 291-92) ontological-metaphysical presence of the devil. The daemonic, as Mephostophilis suggests, has existed before Faustus and will exist after him; it is *real*, a transcendent and uncontrollable mystery, even if Faustus may claim it as a mere extension or a mere fiction of his creative mind.

The fallibility of Faustus' conception of the power (and thus the confines, too) of his "art" turns into one of the predominant dramatic metaphors of the incantation scene. As I tried to indicate, the metaphorization of Faustus' subjective will-to-power, his aesthetic absorption into the most expansive projects that are conceivable within an intellectually dynamic and exploratory Renaissance culture, undergoes a precarious transition in the moment of his crossing of the magical circle. From the beginning of the play, Faustus' poetic discourse has been upholding an abstract, artificial world of the self and its fantastic dreams and fictions:

> Shall I make spirits fetch me what I please,
> Resolue me of all ambiguities,
> Performe what desperate enterprise I will?
> Ile haue them flye to India for gold,
> Ransacke the Ocean for orient pearle,
> And search all corners of the new found world
> For pleasant fruites and princely delicates:
> Ile haue them reade mee straunge philosophie,
> And tell the secrets of all forraine kings ...
> (A 111-19)

"Stretching" his imagination as far as it can go, Faustus has shaped his overassertive posture with all the "arguments" (logical or poetical, which is the same according to the Ramist understanding of "art" that Faustus so cunningly exploited in the introductory scene)[4] to which his mind found recourse.

When I speak of fallibility I refer to the particular form in which tragedy takes shape in Marlowe's play. There can be no

---

4 For a particularly interesting contemporary view on the conjunction of poetry and "method", see Gabriel Harvey, *Ciceronianus* (1577), ed. Harold S. Wilson, University of Nebraska studies in the Humanities, No.4 (Lincoln: Univ. of Nebraska Press, 1945).

doubt that from the very beginning Faustus' project of aspiration must appear duplicitous or, at least, dangerously predicated on its own discursive strategy of *self*-definition. Faustus the rhetorician, the poet, the dreamer, proudly affirms his *art*, and it lies in the nature of its aesthetic that he claims to become a "mighty god" and creator of his own projected possessions (control, power, knowledge, freedom, sensual gratification, etc.), triumphantly disregarding the equally self-evident necessities of history, of truth, of nature, and of an "external" God.

Spurning what he declares to be a world bridled by an alien law, Faustus substitutes in its stead a realm of spiritual freedom fabricated by fantasy in the shape of desire. Faustus' exaltation of his autonomy in the magical circle of the aesthetic at the same time signals its transgressive character: his leaps of the imagination entail a dual vision that must withhold the truth (that he is mortal, human, created, defined) while affirming his aesthetic principle. To state the paradox in a different way, Faustus' desire is the desire of the subject never to let itself be defined as object by others but to reach for a protective transcendence which, however, exposes more than it can protect.

If one could see Faustus' magical (or aesthetic) circle as protective, in a metaphysical sense, then one may grant him a rather modern conception of freedom (within the history of self-consciousness and anthropocentricism).[5] On one level, the essence of such freedom would be to live *like* a poet or magician or "mighty god" but not *as* a poet-magician, figuratively but not literally - to be allowed in short to live symbolically. The tragic implication of Faustus' will-to-power, on the other hand, manifests itself in the very act of his self-dramatization, his taking over the role and style of the challenger: Faustus' art wants to authent-

---

5 Cf. William Kerrigan's stimulating investigation into the new individualism of the Renaissance era, its language, and its cultural and psychological context: "The Articulation of the Ego in the English Renaissance," in *The Literary Freud: Mechanisms of Defense and the Poetic Will*, ed. Joseph H. Smith (New Haven: Yale Univ. Press, 1980), pp. 261-308.

icate itself by testing its "real" power in the external world.

When we see him searching for power and omnipotence, his determination suggests that for Faustus poetry is not simply something that reveals (or disguises) desire; it is itself a kind of acquisitive force, a power of "naming" and of imposing its will upon the external world. The expressive impatience with which Faustus' discourse overleaps the limits and determinisms contained in the phenomenal world indicates that he may be afraid of the basic emptiness of the gestures of rhetoric. While he strives to maintain a self-consciously ironic, intellectual distance between the object of his mockery and himself, he nevertheless believes in the power of his "working words" (his poetry, his "concise syllogisms," his magical incantations) to bridge the discrepancy between imagining and doing. He is willing to "embody" his conceptual, spiritual defiance, though he "die therefore." It is all or nothing.

This is the impression one gets from the methodical assertion of what Faustus calls the "proficiency" of his "art" (A 272). Marlowe's playful and eclectic use of the notion of "art," especially the polemical character of its Ramist definitions,[6] intensifies the ambiguity that underlies the panorama of intellectual and philosophical questions and confrontations brought up by Faustus' subversive ambitions. In this connection one could say that Marlowe's play certainly offers interesting perspectives on the explorative character of drama as such and on its potential for exploiting a preconceived normative order against which the protagonist can set up ideas and meanings through the "performance" of his own individual self-expressions. In a unicentric play like *Dr Faustus*, or *Tamburlaine* for that matter, the focus is inevi-

---

6 In its more radical implications, the single study of the rules of Ramus' reformed dialectic teaches the general "*ars disserendi*," a method, that is, which can externalize *all* knowledge that is latent in the mind and consider any question in any field. Lisa Jardine suggests that teachers like Gabriel Harvey who recommended Ramus to their students may be compared to their counterparts today who recommend Lévi-Strauss and Foucault: the attitude towards knowledge for

tably on the individual who holds the centre of the stage, who "makes" the meaning of the drama of his own choosing, and who struggles with meanings and values that are outside the control of his ambitious will.

The protagonist's assertion of his will and his desires is what situates him in the theatrical situation and what makes him recognizable as a particular kind of "personality." This activity has recently been described as "self-fashioning,"[7] and in Greenblatt's analysis of the generally available patterns of a "self-fashioning" culture (which he discusses, for example, in respect to rhetoric, courtliness, and strategies of Tudor absolutism), a mode of self-dramatizing can always be located as a specific cultural practice in relation to or as expression of *power*. Marlowe certainly has an uneasy relationship to the literary techniques he uses and to the ideas he explores, and the concept of power plays an important role in the "fashioning" of his heroes' tragic fortunes and their "proud audacious deeds" (cf.*Dr Faustus*, Prologue 5). However, Faustus is not Tamburlaine; his rhetoric indeed "speaks" eloquently about the possession of power. Yet the performance in the centre of the action hinges upon his "doings," and not his aesthetic self-infatuation alone.

I would grant Greenblatt the assumption that man's "longings, anxieties, and goals" have to become real somehow in order to mean anything, and part of the answer may be *power*,"whose quintessential sign is the ability to impose one's fictions upon the world: the more outrageous the fiction the more impressive the manifestation of power."[8] But such a view of a poetics of power

---

    which these authors stand is in many ways more important than the details of the texts themselves, and it is the attitude in Ramus' aggressively liberal approach to the curriculum that led the contemporaries to consider the Ramist movement as generally avant-garde and subversive. Cf. "The Place of Dialectic Teaching in Sixteenth-Century Cambridge," *Studies in the Renaissance*, 21 (1974), 58-59.
7 Greenblatt, *Renaissance Self-Fashioning*; see, in particular, the introductory chapter and the chapter on "Marlowe and the Will to Absolute Play," pp. 193-221.
8 Ibid., p. 13.

needs to be carefully balanced against the effects and limits of those representational modes that were available to Marlowe in theatrical space time.

What I earlier described as the establishing and the breaking of the "aesthetic circle" around Faustus is, in other words, nothing but the dramatic progression of the hero's rhetorical individuation from his early fantasy projections to the point where the fictions clash with the external reality upon which they sought to impose themselves. It is a sign of the immense theatricality of Marlowe's play that the clash (scene iii) can be visualized so effectively by creating the actual dynamic of Faustus' struggling along a wavering line of internal imaginings and external pressures and by relocating the intellectual and theological assumptions that underlie this struggle. When Mephostophilis appears onstage, precisely those concepts are being redefined which Faustus had rhetorically charged with his own aesthetic emphases: "power", "control", "heauenly words", the "proficiency of this art", "knowledge", "chiefest blisse", "self-shaping",etc.

The discrepancy between these emphases and what happens onstage and the irony that results from this inform the rest of the play. It is a very singular feature of *Dr Faustus* that this discrepancy is not shown through other characters or double plot devices, but is centred in Faustus himself and then extrapolated into, and dramatized in, his confrontation with the supernatural world, the uncircumscribed "Hell" which becomes quite real for him.

It is an interesting rhetorical battle that develops between Faustus and Mephostophilis. In spite of the devil's insistence that he came on his "own accord" (A 289), he is cautious enough, it seems, not to comment too explicitly on Faustus' own perception of his magical powers, but to speak only very generally about the effects of blasphemy. Throughout the dialogue he appears to be answering all questions willingly and to be obeying Faustus' orders (such as the change of "shape"). Nevertheless, Mephostophilis has no appreciation of Faustus' "art" which was the codeword for Faustus' gigantic fantasies, and he reduces it to very simple and straightforward blaspheming:

> For when we heare one racke the name of God,
> Abiure the scriptures, and his Sauiour Christ,
> Wee flye, in hope to get his glorious soule,
> Nor will we come, vnlesse he vse such meanes
> Whereby he is in danger to be damnd.
> (A 292-96)

This and the following sections of the scene are an important testing-ground for my assumption that Marlowe's Calvinist dramaturgy logically develops the conception of Faustus' self-pronounced reprobation (scene i) and underscores the theological view within which Faustus' relationship to God and the question of damnation and salvation is presented. Mephostophilis very succinctly refers to the three main principles concerning man's salvation or "chiefest blisse": God, the Saviour Christ, and the Scriptures (the latter being revealed through the working of the Holy Spirit whom Mephostophilis includes in the term "Trinitie"[A 298]). More than this is not necessary in accordance with the rigorous Protestant polemic on *fiducia*, and a mentioning of the Church, for example, could only surprise us.

At the same time, Mephostophilis is not totally straightforward but rather tongue-in-cheek: he is certainly as playful with the "art" of dialectic as Faustus when he swerves from his initial statement about the lack of faith ("abiure the scriptures, and his Sauiour Christ") of an apostate (someone who "mis-names") and suddenly claims that such a person would only be "in danger" of damnation, somebody whose soul the devil can "hope" to obtain.

Faustus is easily tricked into a stubbornly self-conscious riposte during which he goes back to precisely the same rhetorical claims that he made earlier: it is *his* proud self and *his* rebellious will that seek the right to formulate principles, to discuss "chiefest ends", to control the moral currency, and to define the nature of truth:

> So Faustus hath already done, and holds this principle
> There is no chiefe but onely Belsibub,
> To whom Faustus doth dedicate himselfe,

>   This word damnation terrifies not him,
>   For he confounds hell in Elizium,
>   His ghost be with the olde Philosophers ...
>   (A 300-05)

This dialogue asks for inspired acting. It is cruelly comic, not to say grotesque, to watch Faustus keep up a serious posture during the whole interrogation of the devil and contrive a series of astonishing and unexpected elaborations on his role of the proudly defiant blasphemer. Tone and diction of his speech, accompanied by impatient gestures, show that he is eager to get on ("But leauing these vaine trifles of mens soules, / Tell me what is ..." A 306-07). He clearly avoids discussing the theological implications of the situation as Mephostophilis has described it. And yet, he corrects the devil in telling him not to worry - he *already has* abjured the Trinity and discarded any hope in God. Such a deliberate apostasy leaves little room for doubting Faustus' view of himself as having chosen to be furthest away from the Christian principle of grace and salvation.

His own "principle", however, assumes a queer form of deviance, for while he announces his new "dedication" to his new "chiefe", Belzebub, he brushes aside the concept of "damnation" which he had deduced himself in the beginning. It is indeed a paradoxical negation, and what should appear overtly serious and terrifying to Faustus is swiftly displaced and made non-serious, trifling. He declares that he "confounds hell in Elizium," and such "confounding" metaphors are typical of Faustus' (thoroughly illogical) poetic imagination, drawn far away towards the "fables" of classical Antiquity and, conceivably, to a rendez-vous with the shadows in Homer's or Virgil's Elysian Fields. One is tempted to imagine Faustus among the perplexed crew of grave "philosophers" that wander around the dark and dreary regions of Milton's Pandaemonium:

>   In discourse more sweet
>   (For Eloquence the Soul, Song charms the Sense,)
>   Others apart sat on a Hill retir'd,
>   In thoughts more elevate, and reason'd high
>   Of Providence, Foreknowledge, Will, and Fate,

> Fixt Fate, Free Will, Foreknowledge absolute,
> And found no end, in wand'ring mazes lost.
> Of good and evil much they argu'd then,
> Of happiness and final misery,
> Passion and Apathy, and glory and shame,
> Vain wisdom all, and false Philosophy.
> (*P.L.*II.555-65)

Marlowe's dramatic dialogue, however, can stand comparison with Milton and is powerfully ironic by its own right. Faustus maintains his extravagant pose while conversing with the emissary from hell whose sincere, reliably orthodox answers create a very curious spectacle out of Faustus' own obliviousness. It seems as if Faustus has artfully and elegantly withdrawn into inverted commas (like the word "damnation"), amusedly interrogating what may appear to him a mere caricature of a devil, an instrument without a "real" theological history, whom he can use at his whim.

The speech-action, as I see it in this dialogue, implies an extremely subtle handling of the complicated role of Mephostophilis whom one could expect to stand out as a skilled tempter, wily and seductive, in command of all the stratagemata of the "father of lies." Quite on the contrary, the rhetorical provocations are all on Faustus' side, and we see him throw six short and almost condescendingly inquisitorial questions at Mephostophilis who indeed thwarts all conventional expectations, I should think, by creating a calm, sober, indulgent devil, investing all his gentle inflections and visual gestures (each syllable, each tone of voice, and lifting of the brow counts in his performance!) with the melancholia of one who knows that hell is not some fictive inferno but an irremovable part of his being.

Marlowe's dramatic style here confirms his superb imaginative control of the possibilities of his medium. He also seems to be at a certain distance from his protagonist, which allows him ironical detachment, while at the same time creating such complex allusions and reversals of role that the very aspects of Faustus' exasperating egocentricity which ought to make us remorselessly critical of him often turn out to be disarming and perplexing. Marlowe's style can surely be distinguished from

Shakespeare's in this respect, and the largest effect of this theatrical ambivalence rests on the wildly moving and shifting perspectives in the play or, in other words, on the subversive disparity between two different modes which can perplexingly divide one kind of perception or knowledge from another. The dialogue between Faustus and Mephostophilis, for example, is a typical case in point because its dramatic and theatrical effect is achieved through the very "confusion" Faustus creates with his "heauenly words": his rhetorical questions and his entire mode of argument seem to rest on his and our knowledge of what *is*, on an absolute standard and on the appropriateness of language. Yet even the most obvious theological commonplaces will not help to bridge the gap Faustus opens up between the standard responses themselves and the questions he asks and interprets for himself. His rhetorical mode has the subversive effect of transforming any value-laden word into a pun, and this can have outrageous effects since we often do not know how to respond to Faustus' "heauenly words" when they come to mean both "heauenly" and its opposite.

The reversal of role I referred to is suggested to me by the relationship between the dashing "coniurer laureate" and the "old Franciscan Frier," a son-father relationship which gains a deeply ironic quality not only through Faustus' patronizing attitude towards Mephostophilis, but especially through the significance and resonance in Faustus' own rebellious stance (rejection of God the Father) vis-à-vis a representative of the fallen angels. Mephostophilis' account of Lucifer's archetypal rebellion against his "loving God" could hardly be more ominous in this context:

> *Fau.* Was not that Lucifer an Angell once?
> *Me.* Yes Faustus, and most dearely lou'd of God.
> *Fau.* How comes it then that he is prince of diuels?
> *Me.* O by aspiring pride and insolence,
> For which God threw him from the face of heauen.
> *Fau.* And what are you that liue with Lucifer?
> *Me.* Vnhappy spirits that fell with Lucifer,
> Conspir'd against our God with Lucifer,
> And are for euer damnd with Lucifer.
>
> (A 309-17)

One can hardly distinguish the mocker from the mocked any more. Mephostophilis, who is quite rhetorical in spite of the stern, unmelodramatic tone of his expository account of the fall of the angels, echoes Faustus' question with a fine parallel construction, repeating the subordinate clause ("that *liue* with Lucifer" ..."that *fell* with Lucifer"; my emphasis) and relating his definitions to one another by ending the lines on the stressed "with Lucifer." The thrust of these parallelisms is of course quite clear: the sin of over-aspiring pride is that original sin in which, theologically, all fallen nature has its origin. Regardless of all theological explications, and whatever gnostic, patristic, scholastic, humanist, or secular re-interpretations, it is probably the most familiar story of our Western civilization and a factuality that one cannot do away with. Mephostophilis himself clearly has no illusions about the reality of God, and he even rises to unexpected pathos in his famous description of the primary "location" of hell:

> Why this is hel, nor am I out of it:
> Thinkst thou that I who saw the face of God,
> And tasted the eternal ioyes of heauen,
> Am not tormented with ten thousand hels,
> In being depriv'd of euerlasting blisse?
> (A 321-25)

I think it is wildly innovative on Marlowe's part to put such words into the mouth of the devil, and although the concept of the *poena damni* itself was not new, the theatrical implications of such a psychological concept of damnation had not been brought to life with such bold and spectacular effects before Marlowe. And it is of course Faustus himself who will experience the pain of loss; Mephostophilis, who supplies the definition, is not actually *shown* to be suffering since he is always kept at an ironic distance from his emotions.

At this point, the theological motif of the internal hell as it is formulated by Mephostophilis need not be analysed too closely; its symbolic and psychological significance for the subsequent dramatic action will become evident. I want to pay attention mainly to the theatrical implications of the motif, to the imagistic and verbal resonances it produces, and especially to the local dramatic values it assumes in its specific contexts. Whatever we might gain from doctrinal and formalist quibbles, even if one wanted to know more about the concept and iconography of hell during the 16th century,[9] we are unlikely to appreciate Marlowe's art if we continue to see certain prominent passages as isolated determinants of meaning. The intellectual ambiguity in Marlowe's images and in his language, I believe, can only be fully experienced if we appreciate the style of the dramatic dialogue between Faustus and Mephostophilis within its rhetorical coordinates and its performance-orchestration.

It is of course true that we do hear Mephostophilis' lament about the torment of deprivation; we do register the complex ironies underlying his account of Lucifer's fall; and we do understand the connections between proud aspiration, rejection of God, and eternal damnation. Most of all, we grasp the ominous allusion to the motif of loss or defeat: Mephostophilis "confesses" the loss of "euerlasting blisse," the loss of the love of God the Father. Lucifer was once "most dearely lou'd of God," and Mephostophilis once "saw the face of God." We may remember that Faustus once quoted from the book of Law, referring to the conditions under which a father may disinherit his son: "*Ex haereditari filium non potest pater nisi ...*", yet breaking off at precisely the question that plagued him most. At what point, for what cause, is a son disinherited by the father? The condition is spelled out by Faustus in his answer to Mephostophilis: "Faustus hath incurred eternall death, / By desperate thoughts against Ioues deitie" (A 333-34).

Yet all this is not the whole "truth" of the scene; the static

---

9   Helpful discussions are provided by C.A. Patrides, "Renaissance and Modern Views of Hell," *HTR*, 57 (1964), 56-67; D.P. Walker, *The Decline of Hell: Seventeenth Century Discussions of Eternal Torment* (Chicago: Univ. of Chicago Press, 1964); and Robert G. Hunter, *Shakespeare and the Mystery of God's Judgments* (Athens: Univ. of Georgia Press, 1976), esp.chap.3.

vision of traditional ethics is not the only *effect* of this dialogue. What we really *see* and *hear* is also a rhetorical show that suggests quite different kinds of motives within Marlowe's overall design, and I am here thinking of "motives" for speech-acts in the way Kenneth Burke has defined them. The motive of "style" or "rhetorical playfulness" creates such a strong dynamic in the extraordinary dialogue Marlowe devises for Faustus and his diabolical acting partner that this outrageous imposture, sustained by both actors in a beautifully straightforward manner, begins to turn in on itself and releases a second, entirely self-conscious dramatistic frame of reference - a second "reality" superimposed onto the serious tragic reality we have taken for granted.

It is perhaps no surprise to discover a remarkably uneasy relationship between the two perspectives - the theological-ethical and the theatrical - which I have proposed for the study of Marlovian drama. Theatrical notation and rhetorical style in *Dr Faustus* often rely on a different motive, on an aesthetic which testifies to a proud self-consciousness about rhetoric and connects that self-consciousness with absorbing impersonations of *roles* and a *theatrical present* that often simply forego the naive application of serious, thematic or moral, interpretative parameters. Faustus' rhetoric of paradox, his Ramistical inflation of the deconstructive "show" of the arts, or his blasphemous self-dramatization as "coniurer laureate" have taught us to expect an explosive verbal style which in a way celebrates itself and enters into a contentious marriage with the serious purposiveness of the "plot" (and the metaphysics it presupposes). Such a style links Faustus' "Tragical History" with its own self-conscious, histrionic mannerisms.[10] Although the sense of "self" in Faustus' self-created role as magus and blasphemous rebel is

---

10 My view of Marlowe's plural orchestration partly converges here with Richard A. Lanham's attempt to define the opposition of play and seriousness in Renaissance texts. See his *The Motives of Eloquence: Literary Rhetoric in the Renaissance* (New Haven: Yale Univ. Press, 1976).

even more precarious and questionable during the incantation
scene, when the audience can witness his fatal over-estimation
of his actual power, it is never to be doubted that Faustus remains incorrigibly *and* successfully theatrical. He creates and
sustains this scene, he directs and shapes the conversation with
Mephostophilis, and he is breathtakingly confident in the "vertue"
of his "heauenly words."[11] His style is outrageous; he takes
literally what was meant metaphorically, and he metaphorizes
what was meant seriously. The more outrageous the stage effects,
and the more "friuolous" (A 326) his questions and his eloquent
exhortations of the devil, the better such rhetorical play becomes:

> What, is great Mephastophilis so passionate,
> For being deprivd of the ioyes of heauen?
> Learne thou of Faustus manly fortitude,
> And scorne those ioyes thou neuer shalt possesse.
> Go beare those tidings to great Lucifer ...
> (A 328-32)

In response to Mephostophilis' confession of his "internal" hell,
Marlowe gives Faustus 18 lines to play off his heroic nonconform-
ity; in this moment it is unnecessary for Faustus to substant-
iate his "manly fortitude," but above all he can take occasion
for the display of an exuberant *style*. There is no need at all
for us to exclaim: Good Lord, Faustus, you are talking to the
Devil! Marlowe knows it and enjoys it, Faustus thoroughly sub-

---

11 The word "vertue" is an interesting Marlovian pun on the
Latin *virtus*, its philosophical and ethical connotations,
and the actual primary meaning of "virtue" during the Renaissance: "the power or operative influence inherent in a
supernatural or divine being ... [or] an embodiment of such
power ... [or] an act of superhuman or divine power" (OED,
meaning I.i.a,b,c). I find at least 9 other places in the
Marlowe canon where "virtue" is used in the sense of "power"
and "capacity," and in all these places Marlowe drives at
the more or less explicit tension between the Neoplatonic
notion of divine power and the potentially amoral notion of
Machiavellian virtù. In *Tamburlaine* Part 1, the most significant instances of this ambivalence occur during the
"banquet"-scene (IV.iv.129-32) and during Tamburlaine's
soliloquy on "beauty" (V.i.183-90). In both cases there is
a striking disparity between the virtue and nobility invoked

verts all distinctions between high seriousness and comedy that are available in an assumed "tragic" mode and enjoys it, and the audience will enjoy it too. Never mind the logical incongruities. There is no question of "To be or not to be" but more likely of "To speak or not to speak," as both Hamlet and Faustus well know. Hamlet meditates in a beautiful, poetic manner, all the time being aware that he is observed and "read" by the royal party; it is excellent "acting," and his pretended madness succeeded in fooling Ophelia, Polonius, the King, his mother, and generations of eager scholars who excavated everything we did not need to know about Elizabethan faculty psychology.

Marlowe makes his protagonist relish the same kind of self-conscious stylistic excess; Faustus mocks the devil, sets up his soul for a business transaction, and sends Mephostophilis on his way with a full catalogue of rules:

> Letting him liue in al voluptuousnesse,
> Hauing thee euer to attend on me,
> To giue me whatsoeuer I shal aske,
> To tel me whatsoeuer I demaund,
> To slay mine enemies, and ayde my friends,
> And alwayes be obedient to my wil.
> (A 337-42)

After the devil has been dismissed, the stage is all his, and Faustus can finish off the scene with a flourish:

> Had I as many soules as there be starres,
> Ide giue them al for Mephastophilis:
> By him Ile be great Emprour of the world,
> And make a bridge through the moouing ayre,
> To passe the Ocean with a band of men,
> Ile ioyne the hils that binde the Affricke shore,
> And make that land continent to Spaine,
> And both contributory to my crown:
> The Emprour shal not liue but by my leaue,
> Nor any Potentate of Germany:
> Now that I haue obtained what I desire,
> Ile liue in speculation of this Art,
> Til Mephastophilis returne againe.
> (A 347-59)

---

so expansively and the cruelty being practised onstage.

It is not at all clear what he has actually "obtaind," but it hardly matters within a matrix of a rhetorical poetic which, as I suggest, cares very little about a separate reality apart from the one its own splendid imaginings create - flying "through the moouing ayre" and packing in a puzzled audience. At the risk of being a little too emphatic about this "non-serious" dimension in Marlowe's plays, I can only urge students of Renaissance literature to think of the considerable impact the humanist revolution of learning had had on the development of rhetoric and literary form and on the emergence of a new, self-conscious exploration of vernacular prose and verse styles during the 16th century. The sophistication in the "placement" of style and rhetorical strategies in many Renaissance texts provokes the reader of More, Erasmus, Cervantes, Rabelais, Spenser, Sidney, Lyly, or Shakespeare to ponder not only *what* is said, but *how* it is said, and what effects rhetoricity can have upon the process of reading.

The difficulties one has in establishing the play's tone and genre do not make it incomprehensible. Rather, language and spectacle - in the tragic, ironic mode or the self-consciously playful and flippant mode - tend to complement each other and enlarge our sense of the highly dramatic collision that actually occurs in front of our eyes between the two authentic selves of Faustus. To me at least they seem authentic in the way in which Faustus constantly defines and re-defines what he pretends to be and what he is. During his grand visionary moments, when he is ready to give away "as many soules as there be starres" and to build "bridges" through the moving air, the play drifts towards extreme artifice and rhetorical exuberance; yet we see that Faustus' exultation can move equally powerfully to the opposite extreme, and his pretensions are torn apart by psychic torment.

But in the way in which Marlowe composes such plural orchestrations we become aware of the unstable, dramatistic Faustian personality at the core of what I would call experimental, speculative art, an art that questions, challenges, and submits, only to challenge again. Marlowe certainly goes a few steps beyond the sheer rhetorical brutality of Tamburlaine's *tour de force*; *Dr Faustus* is a much more intricate play in which Marlowe allows the counterpressures provoked by the Faustian rhetoric of aspiration to make themselves felt and to show what can be done with language and what cannot be done. Faustus' charming dialogue with the devil is an excellent theatrical show-piece, and he concludes his incantation scene with a sublime vision of power. If he overacts his role, we still admire his successful histrionic bravura. A few minutes later, the Clown end his scene with an exasperated comment on Wagner's morbid quibbles:

> God forgiue me, he speakes Dutch fustian: well
> Ile folow him, Ile serue him, thats flat.
> (A 435-36)

And he is right too. Semantic ambiguity and self-parody make the point. How foolish or wise is the Clown? And how self-conscious or unaware of the ironic echoes is Faustus when he triumphantly announces that he lives "in speculation"?

> Now that I haue obtaind what I desire,
> *Ile liue in speculation of this Art,*
> Til Mephastophilis returne againe.

Faustus in fact claims that his dream has "now" come true; and yet he speculates on his "Art", continuing to dream of the possession of what he "desires." His magic art, like his art of discoursing and fantasizing, becomes his distinctive code, an aesthetic norm or *circle* of indirection, self-protection and speculative irresponsibility. The meanings of the words he uses point into different directions; and what holds true for the ambiguities on the rhetorical surface on which he thrives also holds true for the perspectives and "speaking pictures" in the play as a whole.

The disputation between Faustus and the devil in scene iii is one of the pictures which confuse us with the different languages that are spoken; as we go further into the play, these languages of course comment upon each other and excite us

through the very discontinuities and contrasts they provoke. The
following scenes in the play exemplify this. The dialogue between Wagner and the Clown is such a comment: after Faustus'
mighty words we are transported into farce. The Clown's humorous buoyancy and commonsensical charm take us quite far away from
the Faustian ("fustian") grandiloquence, but his jokes about the
price of his soul hardly fail to remind us of the issue which is
at stake.

>   *Clo.* How, my soule to the Diuel for a shoulder of
>   mutton though twere blood rawe? not so good
>   friend, burladie I had neede haue it wel roasted,
>   and good sawce to it, if I pay so deere.
>   *Wag.* Wel, wilt thou serue me, and Ile make thee go
>   like *Qui mihi discipulus*?
>   *Clo.* How, in verse?
>   (A 370-76)

The Clown is at his best when he can boast his apparent immunity
against the intimidations and threats with which Wagner tries to
bully him into submission. Yet his most hilarious boast, namely
to "kill" Wagner's "devils" should he ever encounter them,

>   Let your Balio and Belcher come here, and Ile
>   knocke them, they were neuer so knocht since
>   they were diuels, say I should kill one of them,
>   what would folkes say? do ye see yonder tall fel-
>   low in the round slop, hee has kild the diuell,
>   so I should be cald kill diuell all the parish
>   ouer.
>   (A 406-11)

breaks down in the moment it is pronounced. We are instantly
presented with a little show of devils chasing the "kill diuell"
across the stage ("*the clowne runnes vp and downe crying*" s.d.
A 411-12), and I think it is not only the parodic effect but
above all the choreography of the sudden reversal that is very
significant for Marlowe's dramatic technique. The incredibly
thin line that the play draws between resolution and dissolution,
between boastful assertion of fortitude and instant break-down
in the face of "real" danger, is one of the conspicuous dramatic ironies which accompany Faustus' own posture, his attempts

to dramatize his rhetorical self and to transform it into more than mere "magical" showmanship.

Chapter Eight

TRAGEDY OF THE MIND: FAUSTUS AND HIS COVENANT

The paradoxical freedom which Faustus achieves in those moments in which his performance presses in one direction draws audience attention away from the contradictions inherent in his posture;[1] his rhetorical mannerisms seem so competent and so free to work their own way that the moral questions, which appeared to loom large, get deflected by the artifice. It surely makes for an extraordinary and immediate effect when Marlowe abruptly changes the direction in Faustus' third scene by capitalizing very directly on these contradictions and presenting them in a new manner:

>   [*Enter Faustus in his Study*]
> Now Faustus must thou needes be damnd,
> And canst thou not be saued?
> What bootes it then to thinke of God or heauen?
> Away with such vaine fancies and despaire,
> Despaire in God, and trust in Belsabub:
> Now go not backward: no Faustus, be resolute,
> Why wauerest thou?
>   (A 437-44)

What is left of the proud, glamorous self-confidence of the former "coniurer laureate"? While Marlowe has Faustus enter in exactly the same way as in the two earlier scenes, namely alone and in monologue, almost everything else is different in this opening. Gone is the cunning showmanship of the stylized disputation during scene i; gone is also the resolution and eagerness that characterized Faustus' attitude during the magic ritual,

---

1   John Bayley, commenting on the Dover Cliff scene in *King Lear*, makes a similar observation: "The language of tragedy does not describe events but takes them over ... Words can redeem both protagonists and audience from those events by darting off outside them, under the impetus of their own self-generative ardour, 'in the quick forge and working-house of thought'" (*Shakespeare and Tragedy* [London: Routledge & Kegan Paul,1981],

and the vigorous pace with which his imagination had run ahead
of him, producing alluring fictions for the future, has come to
an almost complete halt. The contrast between a Faustus ravished
by desire and expectation, living "in speculation" of his "art"
as he leaves the stage (scene iii), and a Faustus who comes on
to admit his insecurity and fear could not be more unexpectedly
and boldly stated. John Russell Brown's reference to Brecht's
dramaturgy may be justified here,[2] since throughout the play
Marlowe's technique of scene liaison focusses on direct, immediate effect, on expression and gestic realization of concrete
attitudes and changes of attitude, which reminds us of montage
devices used in Brecht's epic theatre. At this particular point
it is even more tempting to think of cinematic techniques, especially the sudden close-ups and rapid cuttings that are often
used to break up or telescope narrative sequence. If Faustus'
speech suggests that a change has taken place, we are not shown
why and how; we only experience the extent to which his consciousness is now assuming a different form of expression.

Since this is a crucial transitional moment in the play, I wish
to pay special attention to the text and inquire how its words
and the actions, gestures, and movements they imply come alive
in performance. If Faustus' early rhetorical virtuosity and the
tone and rhythms of his long, sustained poetic speeches[3] are
still in our ears, we will first of all notice a drastic change
in the *sound* of his verse. The verse lines, the syntax, and the
metrical design for intonation and "outward tuning"[4] are so important for the Faustus-actor at this point that one should care-

---

    p.10). See also Bayley's discussion of the incompatibility of
    the protagonist's consciousness with his situation in the
    tragic action in the case of Macbeth (pp. 184-200).
2 "*Doctor Faustus* at Stratfor-upon-Avon, 1968," in *Doctor Faust-
    us*, ed. Sylvan Barnet (New York: New American Library, 1968),
    pp. 201f.
3 Faustus' last soliloquy in scene iii has only five syntactic
    units within thirteen lines. Most of the lines are not end-
    stopped, and the flow of the blank verse is smooth, expressive
    and swelling as the syntax and rhythms lenghten into the final,
    fanciful images of his power-dreams.

fully attend to the textual impulses:

> Now Faustus must thou needes by damnd,
> And canst thou not be saued?

If we take the normal blank verse pattern as the metrical base for these lines, we can immediately hear the peculiar sound values that accompany Faustus' double-question. He begins the speech with a strong stress on "Now" (reversed foot), in a manner that is reminiscent of both the scene opening of I.iii ("Now that the gloomy shadow ...") and his final exclamation in that scene: "Now that I haue obtaind what I desire." The flow and the lyrical quality of these earlier lines, however, have gone out of Faustus' surprisingly bare and terse sentences, and apart from the self-apostrophe he uses only monosyllabic words with heavy stresses on the crucial verb forms: "must", "needes", "damnd", "canst", and "saued." Both lines are incomplete, and the very short second line[5] gains considerable dramatic force because we ought to see such a half-line as a stage-direction, indicating a pause for reflection or some stage activity (one could imagine Faustus making a few steps forward or to the side).

Since the heavy stresses draw attention to the verbs, the actor would do well to speak somewhat slowly and to build pressure towards the parallel endings of the questions: "needes be damnd / not be saued?" The parallelism, of course, creates a more complicated effect through the antithetical tension in which the speaker's thought-processes are involved for the rest of the speech and which here, for the first time, surfaces in such a shocking and seemingly insoluble form.

> ... must thou needes be damnd,
> And canst thou not be saued?
> What bootes it then to thinke of God or heauen?

---

4   Puttenham, *The Arte of English Poesie*, p. 161. The word "tuning" was meant to describe the speaker's judicious placement of stress in his delivery of dramatic poetry.
5   The line is even shorter in B: "Canst thou not be sau'd?" (B 391). In B we find a question-mark after each line (B 390-92), whereas A only ends the second and third lines with

While the words seem shockingly simple, the antithetical pattern itself certainly is not. The phrasing of the questions in the first two verse-lines and the affirmative rhetorical question or *erotema*[6] which Faustus immediately adds to them suggest that his wavering is highly ambivalent, that he invokes the contrary possibilities of damnation and salvation only to negate the assumption that these choices or alternatives actually exist for him. It is a very tricky situation, since the question is addressed to the audience as well, and the space that is opened up between the interrogative mode and the affirmative mode is so indeterminate that it is not easy to find a correct (or even obvious) answer.

The *erotema* induces us to share Faustus' perspective, and from the opening disputation we know how Faustus wishes to see himself, what he "wills", and how he interprets and defines his defiant stance. The paradox in which Faustus is implicated does not permit of mediation: he has insisted on his free will, while at the same time he set himself up against a perpetual impasse which the relationship to a deterministic metyphysic suggested to him. That he has internalized the impasse seems implied in his affirmation

> Seeing Faustus hath incurred eternall death,
> By desprate thoughts against Ioues deitie:
> Say, he surrenders vp to him his soule ...

and in the way he uses a negative formulation for his question: "canst thou not be saued?" The phrasing of the question makes it rather look like a statement, and from the immediately following rhetorical question, linked with "then", we can assume that

---

a question-mark.
6 Neither using a statement nor a simple question, Faustus' interrogative mode is here made to continue the dangerous game with language that had begun in the opening disputation. Puttenham, distinguishing a variety of rhetorical questions whose effects can be quite unsettling, defines *erotema* or "The Questioner" as "a kinde of figurative speach when we aske many questions and looke for none answere, speaking indeed by interrogation, which we might as well say by affirmation" (*The Arte of English Poesie*, p. 211).

he does not see much of a choice. The phrasing of the lines and the conjunction of the crucial verbs ("must", "needes", and "canst") are extremely subtly handled by Marlowe; although one can see why a number of editors have followed the Dyce emendation and left out the question mark at the end of line A 439 (B 391),[7] or replaced it by an exclamation mark, such modifications are already interpretations imposed upon the extant quarto texts and merely increase the editorial confusions about the A and B plays. Even John Russell Brown, who has so convincingly demonstrated that theatrical meanings depend on and originate in a careful analysis of an authoritative text,[8] fails to respond to the original quarto readings and in fact interprets Faustus' initial lines as calm, resolute statements.[9]

I should think that the first two lines rather reveal a nervous, uneasy tension, and the sense of ambiguity and suppressed emotion that lies behind Faustus' choice of words is felt in the next lines which despite of their seemingly controlled, rhythmic qualities (two almost regular verse-lines with normal stress pattern) betray a wounded, angry speaker.

> Awáy with such váine fáncies and despáire,
> Despáire in Gód, and trúst in Bélsabúb.

The antithetical thoughts and the repetition of "despaire" fit tightly within the pentameters, and yet the reversed stress on "vaine" gives that line a quickening effect which ought to indicate a rising pitch and some form of physical action: an angry

---

7 A. Dyce's 1850 edition prints the second line with a full stop. Ellis, Boas, Kirchbaum, Gill, Bowers, Maxwell and Pendry, in their respective editions of the Complete Plays, follow this practice. Barnet decides for an exclamation mark, whereas J.D. Jump (Revels Plays editor) not only leaves out the question mark but also changes the verse lining and completely disregards the original quarto readings.
8 Cf. Brown's more recent books, *Shakespeare's Dramatic Style* (1970; rpt. London: Heinemann, 1972), pp. 3-14, and *Discovering Shakespeare: A New Guide to the Plays* (New York: Columbia Univ. Press, 1981), esp. pp. 75-91.
9 "*Doctor Faustus* at Stratford," p. 202.

gesture, a raised fist. A violent gesture would express something of that stubborn wildness which seems to be taking shape in Faustus' mind; it is a mind struggling for an understanding of those unsettling thoughts which seem to have dwelled in it, which erupt and, instantaneously, have to be deflected or denigrated. Faustus' allusion to hope for salvation expresses his own mingled fear and uncertainty; it is odd that his consciousness seems suddenly to reveal something to him that he had not admitted to himself previously, and "hope", or the awareness of God, is at once displaced metaphorically by "vaine fancies." Such a negative inversion of course repeats his former categorical imperatives, yet these imperatives now show an emotional logic which is very different from his initial arrogance and "resolution" and begins to undermine his belief in himself.

> Nów gó nót báckward: nó Fáustus, bé résolute,
> Whý wáuerest thóu? O sómething sóundeth in mine éares.

The sense of expanding frustration is conveyed directly in the lengthened lines with their short, irregular rhythms and thrusts. Again, there is an initial stress on "Now", and the unusual intensity of the speech possibly asks for stresses on each word, thus shifting the style from verse to prose. Through its breathless stops and starts, turns and returns, Faustus' manner of speaking gives an immediate impression of his tension and his tendency to aggravate the very thoughts that trouble him most.

Compared to his earlier rhetorical power, to his sanguineness and playful exuberance, Faustus' discourse is now visibly less potent as the verse patterns of his speech disintegrate, and the audience can feel him losing control over the surging movement of his mind. While Faustus' confusion obviously contrasts with the surface control and bravery (his assertive "will" and "shall") which marked his earlier rhetoric, it also creates some sense that the character is shifting uncertainly around us, and we become aware how much the difference in style, as a mirror of his changing self, begins to reflect the tragic course his actions take. Again, the question of control, whether verbal,

physical or psychological, seems crucial for the passage I am
discussing.

If Faustus is beginning to doubt his commitment and his resolution
which made him crave to "resolue ... all ambiguities", the way
in which he prompts himself by using the same phrases or modals
("go not backward"; "be resolute"; "will"; "can"; "must") can only
enlarge our awareness of the terrible impasse he is caught in.
His confusion about what he "can" and what he "must" do leads him
around in circles; the nature of Faustus' self-reprobation does
not allow us to assume that the contrary impulses of "resolution"
and "going backward" offer simple choices to him. What Faustus
never expresses in words is the futility of a rebellion that his
audience knows to be dangerous, mistaken, and in any case, tragic
in its consequences. Faustus knows that his rebellion is very
"real" to him, whereas he obviously sees the possibility of return (salvation) utterly removed. At this point, the "necessity"
of defying and challenging God implies that Faustus understands
his course of action to be tragic, given his view of a vindictive
higher Order from which he tries to escape by means of a forward
flight into that space of freedom that is accessible to him. Why
does he waver, then?

> Ó sómething sóundeth in mine éares:
> Abiúre this Mágicke, túrne to Gód agáine,
> Í and Fáustus wíl túrne to Gód agáine.
> To Gód? he lóues thee nót.
> (A 444-47)

Perhaps more directly than any other passage in the play, this
central section of Faustus' monologue contains and condenses his
psychological predicament which I have attempted to explain with
the Calvinist terminology that provides such a suitable framework
for Faustus' tragedy of the mind. The monologue as a whole, as
I am trying to show, indicates a significant slip of his mask
anyway, yet it is most conspicuous that Faustus' consciousness
pours out thoughts about "God", the name he had completely avoided and left unpronounced up to this moment. Now he mentions the
name six times within nine lines, and most strongly so in the

double-line in which he expresses a sense of an intruding voice urging him to "turne to God againe." Faustus almost mechanically repeats and rehearses the suggestion which he very fleetingly entertains here. The second verse line, "I and Faustus wil turne to God againe," does not have the regular rhythm of the previous one; it is almost self-ironic that Faustus would stress the word "wil" precisely in this moment of indecision. Although it is left unclear whether Faustus is communing with an external or an internal voice, his repeating and questioning of this voice illuminates his predispositions towards what he thinks may be "real." He is clearly thinking about what he believes he is, or can do, and when he subsequently questions the possibility of turning to "God", he is very Faustian in his answer: "he loues thee not." As rapidly as the intellectual awareness of salvation opens up, so it is immediately qualified and counterstated. The incomplete line with its strong stresses and the two stoppages after "God?" and "not" again produce a heightening effect (the actor can enforce this with an anguished outcry and a pause of silence) and imply a deeper emotional involvement which is indicative of Faustus' effort to regain his psychic autonomy and control.

If his unbelief in the possibility of salvation for himself is correlative to his initial assertion of his reprobation, then it is of course consistent of him to assume that the judging God, who "loues [him] not", will inflict the inevitable punishment anyway. The question whether this is orthodox or heterodox reasoning is less significant than the dramatic impression we gain of Faustus' negative image of God and of his anxious escape from those threatening metaphysical coordinates that he finds so intolerable. His conception of a vindictive God, at the same time, is a limiting conception in itself which leaves him practically no choice.

> The God thou seruest is thine owne appetite,
> Wherein is fixt the loue of Belsabub.
> (A 448-49)

As the verse rhythms become calmer and more assured once again,

Faustus speaks two amazing lines which sound more honest than anything else he has said about himself so far, and yet the second enjambed line has a certain pathetic edge to it and a reawakened blasphemous impulse which does not connect very well with the surprising moralistic turn his first line had taken. Faustus himself, however, qualifies the unexpected self-accusation by using a rather revealing semantic and syntactical twist. Whereas *he* ought to reach out for faith and try to love God, he projects a God who does not love him and then, significantly, admits that he loves ("seruest") only his "owne appetite."

Stumbling over the problems of his relationship with God, he is evidently incapable of offering his "love," which he characteristically identifies with servitude, to anything else except his own daemonic power fantasies and the allegiance they require.

> To him Ile build an altare and a church,
> And offer luke warme blood of new borne babes.
> (A 450-51)

After the agitations of thought and feeling, and after the eventual accommodation with his self-love and the projected diabolical pact, these two lines break out in sudden cruelty and frustration. Almost as if to repress or punish his whole train of thinking, his wavering and irresolution, Faustus ends on a shrill note. And although his blasphemous parody of devotion seems to indicate that he has regained his earlier rebellious fervour, the grotesqueness of the image jars considerably with his former style. But nothing involves us more in a human consciousness than its separate moments of dejection, bitterness, and anguish, its plain and literal articulation of doubt and its manic, uncontrolled hysteria. All these different elements in Faustus' monologue, each of which evokes its own effect and demands distinct vocal and physical representation in the play-in-performance, displays the complex stylistic technique Marlowe uses to bring into focus the changing intellectual, emotional, and physical realities Faustus is now struggling with.

The prosodic and stylistic forms and the discursive or metaphorical meanings they set in motion seemed so interesting to me that I wanted to select this monologue (which stands at the beginning of two crucial scenes) as a paradigm for the dramatic techniques Marlowe employs for the development of his tragic theme. Indeed, as we move further into the play, Marlowe's dramaturgy works much more intensely towards quick, successive effects and distinct impressions which show the audience a different Faustus, a man who in his dramatic impact has lost much of his rhetorical self-confidence and his charisma as a rebellious hero. The doubts and agitations of his mind compromise him in a way that was to be expected, given the hyperbolic nature of his power fantasies. The individuality of the manner, however, in which he experiences these agitations and, more and more desperately clings to his romantic ideas, expands his sense of predicament in a different way, and it seems as if Marlowe devises a lot more stage activity for these scenes in order to exploit the dramatic conflicts between the tentative movements of Faustus' mind and the "reality" of action around it.

Marlowe is not speeding up play time, as in *The Jew of Malta* or *The Massacre at Paris*, but he intensifies activity onstage in various ways, corresponding to the tensions that build up in Faustus' consciousness. In the pact scene alone we can count no less than nine entries and exits during Faustus' presence onstage. Such entries, as with the Angels, draw attention to themselves, especially when the newly entered characters' behaviour (this holds true for Mephostophilis too) adheres to a pattern of repetitive action or when the protagonist's relationship to them undergoes significant changes.

The appearances of the Good and Bad Angels (four in the A-text, five in B), as well as those of the devils, the Seven Deadly Sins, and the Old Man, have been registered with great satisfaction by all those commentators who enlist the morality play elements on their search for coherent meaning which they will always find and then reduce to thematic statement. While symbolic action and allegorical figures in *Dr Faustus* present formal elements clearly indebted to an older tradition, it is one thing to be aware of these modes of representation, and quite another to see this legacy as controlling influence and to convert everything in Marlowe's drama to an underlying morality structure. Following in the wake of Farnham, Craig, Bevington, Battenhouse, and Cole, more recent criticism still adheres to such formulaic discussions, assuring us that an understanding of the moralities informs an understanding of Marlowe's play or, even better, that the presence of the Angels, the Seven Sins, and a "definite contest for the soul of Faustus" indicates that Marlowe's play is a morality play which only lacks "Shrift, Intercession, and Salvation although in the end the hero cries out loudly for them."[10]

To see the Angels and the other supernatural machinery in *Dr Faustus* as purely conventional and as part of a moral thesis means to take them out of their dramatic contexts where they can assume unexpected, paradoxical, and parodic qualities and lead the audience on with their very conventionality - making a joke of their pious expectations. If one asks what state of reality the Angels have and how they are used, one already asks dramaturgical questions. John Russell Brown suggests that they "should enter on either side of the stage to express visually and verbally the contrary possibilities that are available to Faustus."[11] The theatrically emphatic presence of these two figures (and their costumes which could have emblematic colours, if the director so decides) can have many effects, depending on how the actors play their parts, their entries, their movements

---

10 Hardin Craig, "Morality Plays and Elizabethan Drama, *SQ*, 1 (1950), 71. See also Sidney R. Homan, "*Doctor Faustus*, Dekker's *Old Fortunatus*, and the Morality Plays," *MLQ*, 26(1965), 497-505, and Michael Hattaway, "The Theology of Marlowe's *Doctor Faustus*," *RenD*, 3 (1970), 51-78. Structural comparisons are still fashionable, and Faustus' "progressive degeneration" and "sinfulness" have been repeatedly claimed as a convenient model for other plays. Cf. Gilles D. Monsarrat, "The Unity of John Ford: *'Tis Pity She's a Whore* and *Christ's Bloody Sweat*," *SP*, 77 (1980), 247-70
11 "*Doctor Faustus* at Stratford," p. 203.

onstage, and how they speak their lines. Their intrusion at a
particular moment and their physical positions onstage (framing
Faustus or standing behind or in front of him) may very well link
them to the protagonist and the psychological indecision we have
experienced in his monologue. It is not quite correct to speak
of a staged psychomachia, however, as the conception of psychomachia (cf. *The Castle of Perseverance, Mundus et Infans, The
Interlude of Youth*, or *The Marriage of Wit and Science*) involves
Everyman in a conflict during which the agents of good and evil
contend for dominance over him. Such a contention requests that
the allegorical personae are sufficiently explained, as it is
done in *The Castle of Perseverance*, where the actor playing
Humanum Genus begins by physically pointing out the two angels,
which have been "assigned" to him, to the audience and *explaining*
their significance.[12]

Nothing is quite so clear in *Dr Faustus*. First of all, Marlowe's
text does not unequivocally establish whether and how the Angels
interact with Faustus, how they are to speak their entry and exit
lines. During their first appearance (scene i), Faustus is so
preoccupied that he does not seem to notice them at all, and the
staging should be sensitive to this ambiguity. Their second entry
provides a decidedly odd contrast, with the Good Angel calling on
"sweet Faustus" right after the latter had burst into his violent
prophecy ("And offer luke warm blood of new borne babes"). And
Faustus' little catalogue, "Contrition, prayer, repentance: what
of them?" (A 454), sounds like a rather contrived question, particularly after we have heard him announce his new allegiance.
Again, it is not clear how one is to see this kind of interaction
between Faustus and the Angels. The text indicates that Faustus
has now entered into dialogue with them, but what they say is
merely a recapitulation of what Faustus already knows and what
he has already told us. It is hardly surprising that the Evil

---

12 Cf. *The Castle of Perseverance, ll.*27-35, in *English Miracle
    Plays, Moralities, and Interludes*, ed. Alfred W. Pollard
    (1890; rpt. Oxford: Clarendon, 1927), p. 65.

Angel's remark that contrition and repentance are "Rather illusions, fruites of lunacy, / That make men foolish that do trust them most" (A 456-57) is rhetorically congruent with Faustus' own psychological predisposition. The Evil Angel has the last word, and Faustus picks up the exit line, "... thinke of honor and wealth," as a stimulus to what we might deem closest to his own imagination.

> Of Wealth,
> Why the signory of Emden shalbe mine,
> When Mephastophilis shal stand by me,
> What God can hurt thee Faustus? thou art safe,
> Cast no more doubts ...
> (A 462-66)

There is an ominous pause after "wealth", but instead of taking off the speech falls strangely flat. The vision of power and wealth that marked Faustus' early poetry is here entertained only for a second, and then merges into a blasphemous image which is of more urgent concern to Faustus. The blasphemous intent, pointing forward to the covenant he is about to make, is most revealing in so far as Faustus' rhetorical question (another puzzling *erotema*), "What God can hurt thee Faustus?",[13] underscores the negative image of godhead he already hinted at in his monologue. Here he twists his image of an unloving God even further by admitting an underlying feeling of intense fear of God, mingled with contempt and mistrust.

His view of God as a threat, as a hostile and inaccessible Judge, is quite consistent with his attitude towards the magical power he expects from his pact with Lucifer, a power which he hopes can make him feel "safe" and protected from the threat and which would give him the space and time he craves for his ambitions. To define his antagonistic position in such terms (and here he stands at the opposite end of Tamburlaine) does hardly make it more comfortable, and Faustus' nervous attempt to reassure him-

---

13 The B-text reads: "What power can hurt me?" (B 413) and again misses out an important link in Faustus' description of his personal relationship with the God he seeks to escape from.

self ("thou art safe, / Cast no more doubts") shows how much he would wish to forget his doubts. Whatever it is that compels him, his negative conception of God is Faustus' dramatic burden and triumph; it constitutes the inescapable reality of his experience Faustus' fascination with the daemonic is of course the exact reflection of his negative interpretation of Christian doctrine, and Marlowe's play gains its dramatic force precisely from the *negativity* which imprisons Faustus and carries him towards (self-)destruction. The theological vocabulary in the play, whether it supports familiar orthodoxies or more typically Faustian blasphemies and inversions, helps to sustain the complex dialectical tensions that evolve from Faustus' rebellion and, more often than in any other Elizabethan play, draw attention to the intellectual sophistication Marlowe weaves into dramatic narrative.

Even such a relatively simple line as "When Mephastophilis shal stand by me, / What God can hurt thee Faustus?" can provoke stunning effects if we hear it spoken by a man who claims control over the supernatural agents he believes to have summoned. His trust in the Satanic protector has a superbly ironic touch, and this sense of irony will come across to the audience very directly, although it is quite likely to gain a further dimension if one recognizes Marlowe's outrageous theological punning on Paul's affirmation of divine mercy (Rom.viii.31),[14] an affirmation which Faustus turns completely upside down.

>   ... come Mephastophilus,
> And bring glad tidings from great Lucifer:
> Ist not midnight? come Mephastophilus,
> *Veni, veni* Mephastophile.   [*Enter Meph.*]
>
>   (A 466-69)

---

14 "If God bee on our side, who can bee against vs?" (Geneva). Paul's phrase echoes a topos that is pervasively present in the Psalms. The most interesting occurrences are in Ps.27.1 ("The Lord is my light and my saluation, whome shal I feare? the Lord is the strength of my life, of whome shal I be afraid?") and Ps.118.6 ("The Lord is on my syde, I wyll not feare what man doeth vnto me"). See also Psalms 124.1; 18.1-2; 62.2,6; 109.6; 118.14; and 144.1-2.

Silencing unpleasant doubts, Faustus impatiently longs for more pleasant news from the infernal world, and his use of the phrase "bring glad tidings" is just another self-consciously ironic trick of speech with which Faustus continues to confound heaven in hell. Our ears have become attuned to the jesting manner in which he employs his biblical allusions in a context which is clearly incommensurable with their original meanings, but I think it will remain a matter of contention whether we can automatically assume, as a good many ironic interpretations of the play have done, that these allusions "expose" the speaker and thus provide immediate moral comment. Even if we agree that these allusions show the basic "irony" in Marlowe's "*conception* behind the presentation of character, which is grounded on the complete and consistent inversion of values and virtues,"[15] their effect in the theatre is less obvious.

Everyone who has seen the play performed will have noticed the irreverent, almost caustic humour that is provoked by Faustus' linguistic manipulations, and in this instance the effect is heightened by the eagerness with which he expects the "tidings" from the Angel of Darkness. That this impatient expectation, expressed by Faustus' thrice-repeated call and incantation, produces a "comic" effect has escaped the attention of most commentators. The Lyric Studio production very successfully played upon the pauses that the text indicates between Faustus' first call ("come Mephastophilus"), his slightly nervous question (addressed to the audience): "Ist not midnight?", and his second call. Silence. Nothing happened. Faustus was seen pacing the foreground of the stage, repeating his calls, and finally shouting, on the top of his voice, his Latin incantation. Unnoticed by him, Mephostophilis had already silently come on stage and re-

---

15 Cole, *Suffering and Evil*, p. 125. Several critics have followed Cole's view of Marlowe's verbal and dramatic irony. Most recently, Judith Weil centred her book on the idea that Marlowe's "dark" and "oblique" allusions are a major functional element of his "prophetic style" (cf. *Merlin's Prophet*, pp. 7-21).

God. His covenant-making extends over four distinct sequences of action, from the self-wounding, the first and second writing, to the reading of the pact articles, and it is framed by his own initial conjuring act and the concluding disputation with Mephostophilis. Two further magical "shows" are staged by Mephostophilis who - immensely busy in this scene - also provides for the "chafer of fire" and the negromantic encyclopedia, symbolic offerings from the Monarch of Hell.

The pact scene is not only one of the longest and most symbolic scenes within the design of *Dr Faustus* - thus having a particular structural importance for the whole play[16] - but also reveals a highly purposeful internal organization of the modes of presentation which constitute the discursive, theatrical, thematic and symbolic dimensions of Faustus' "rewriting" of his identity ("First, that Faustus may be a spirit in forme and substance", as his first pact article reads). It is one of Marlowe's unique scenes, radically original and yet profoundly troubling because of its implications for the play.

Marlowe dramatizes the signing of the pact in such a ritualistic manner as to emphasize that it is a crucial act, the "deed" which confirms Faustus' iconoclastic posture and from which others will follow and take their meaning. The pact scene also creates a complex representation of Faustus' effort at self-dramatization

---

16 Of the A-text's total of 1517 lines, the pact scene occupies 189 lines (A 438-627), clearly dominating the first third of the play, where one could see it in the formal centre of the play's heroic upward movement, framed by the opening disputation (168 lines) and the scene of Lucifer's climactic intervention (A 628-736, followed by the pageant of the Seven Sins, A 737-807). Such a tripartite structure could very well be deduced from the plotting of emphasized scenes in the play as a whole, which would then give us the beforementioned Wittenberg triad, the middle triad (Papal, Imperial, and Ducal scenes, A 822-1265), and the final Wittenberg triad (Helen-Old Man, Scholars, and damnation scenes, A 1266-1508). Within these three tripartite phases of continuous acting, each preceded by a Chorus, one will find further significant formal devices, movements, and countermovements, which all contribute to the complex interweaving of structure and meaning; Marlowe's A-B-C design in *Dr Faustus* could be fruitfully com-

mained in the background, motionless. After another ominously long pause, Faustus seemed slowly to become aware that he was not alone onstage, made a sudden turn and stared right at his elderly partner, as if he was facing an apparition.

Mephostophilis' return marks an important point in the play since from this moment on he hardly ever leaves Faustus alone, and Marlowe further develops the curious relationship between the two as it revolves around the diabolical pact with which Faustus is invited to "buy" the "services" hell can offer. Mephostophilis, still engagingly calm and paternal, is nevertheless able to show subtle distinctions in his behaviour. At one point, he is the polite yet determined salesman ("if thou deny it, I wil backe to hel" A 477); at the next, he allows Faustus a little digression without, however, losing sight of his clear purpose ("But tel me Faustus, shal I haue thy soule?" A 486). Furthermore, he can be the skilled tempter, using his mock-innocence to gloss his plain speeches with a few rhetorical extras ("And giue thee *more than thou hast wit to aske*" A 487, my emphasis). Occasionally he will echo Faustus' own mode of reference (to actions performed "courageously"):

> ... that at some certain day
> Great Lucifer may claime it as his owne,
> And *then be thou as great as Lucifer*.
> (A 490-92;my emphasis)

The motif of the "solemn" pact begins to take shape, and Faustus is evidently willing to follow "great Lucifer's" example and to consummate his rebellion in the realm of "perpetual night."

> Loe Mephastophlus, for loue of thee,
> I cut mine arme, and with my proper blood
> Assure my soule to be great Lucifers,
> Chiefe Lord and regent of perpetual night,
> *View heere the blood that trickles from mine arme,*
> *And let it be propitious for my wish.*
> (A 493-98;my emphasis)

Faustus begins to enact the most explicit and theatrically shocking gestures of his blasphemous rebellion against the Christian which stands in a complicated relationship to the previous conjuration in the magical circle (scene iii) and to Faustus' initial assertions and imaginative projections, enunciated in what I have called his "circle of the aesthetic."

From the outset, Faustus' heretical self-persuasions, his urge to reify his will in the face of all doctrinally assumed limitations, pre-established his "role" for the drama as a would-be heroic wielder of poetic power - a kind of purely aesthetic magic which then, however, becomes progressively qualified as Faustus literalizes his idea of himself as a "sound magician" and attempts to bring about the unlikely correlation of poetic vision and practical efficacy. Faustus' imperious imagination and the transformative force it claims in its rhetorical "vaunts" (to use one of Tamburlaine's favourite words) could not have found a better *metaphor* than that of "magic," although "magic" - as a unifying symbol for man's ambition to control his own soul and the world around him - has always had a rich spectrum of potential analogies which are drawn together from several, and quite distinct, inherited traditions of speculative philosophy and popular belief in superstitious practice that inevitably involve the dangerous implications of occult power.

How much Marlowe knew of the Hermetic and Cabalistic writings is difficult to say; that he was quite well aware of the influence of these writings on the intellectual climate of the English Renaissance and, especially, on the contemporary inquiries into astronomy, astrology, mathematics, medicine, and rhetorical and poetical theory, we can deduce from textual and biographical evidence. If Marlowe indeed had a natural penchant for dissenting ideas and opinions, it should hardly be surprising to find him attracted to the relative secrecy and dangerousness of Hermetic speculation and its philosophical idealism which linked intellectual study with - to borrow Faustus' term - the "Meta-

---

pared to the similar A-B-C pattern in *1 Tamburlaine*, where it represents an escalating (and not *circular*, as in *Dr Faustus*) development of agonistic encounters.

phisickes of Magicians" and believed in the actual potency of the
magus to see beyond the literal level of things and events, to
apprehend their significance. Many passionate statements, which
underscore this radical purpose to elevate man from the status of
a pious and humble observer of God's mysteries to a manipulator
of the interacting forces of the universe, could be quoted from
the texts of such eminent, learned magi as Ficino, Pico, Agrippa,
Della Porta, Paracelsus, Dee, and Bruno. When one hears Agrippa
and Trithemius, for example, speak about "that ancient Magick,
the discipline of all wise men" as "sublime and sacred," and about
their knowledge of the "secret things" as "transcending" or "penetrating,"[17] the language of rapture and transport which invigorates their speculative endeavours strikes quite a different note
compared to the more somber, didactic and ethical tone underlying
the rhetoric of Christian humanism (e.g. Colet, Bodin, Erasmus,
More, and their Elizabethan successors writing in the theological
or pedagogic vein). If one wants to set Marlowe's use of "magic"
in the broad context of Renaissance occult theory, one ought to be
aware, first of all, of the dividing lines between several magic
traditions and popular accretions of witch lore as well as of the
confluences between them that certainly existed and perhaps most
readily appealed to the mythopoeic inventions of a writer such
as Marlowe.

It is most fascinating to ponder the role Marlowe played in mythologizing for posterity a figure whose questionable fame seemed unlikely to stand up against the religious and moral pressures at
work (demonstrated in the pitiful tale compiled by the writer of
the 1587 *Faustbuch*) and against the advancing scientific scepticism of a modern era which, after the decline of "magic," had to
give new names to the diabolic inventions it began to worship.
Marlowe certainly acted with uncanny fervour when he seized upon

---

17 The letters between Henry Cornelius Agrippa and Johannes Trithemius (written in 1510) are printed in Agrippa's famous *Three Books of Occult Philosophy*, trans. J[ohn] F[rench] (London, 1651), sigs. A2-A5.

the fable about the obscure German scholar-magician Johannes Faust almost instantaneously after the appearance of P.F.'s English translation ("newly imprinted" in the fall of 1592, which - as I believe *contra* Greg and Bowers - leaves open the possibility of an earlier date of composition for *Dr Faustus* [1588-89?], if Marlowe indeed saw the first edition of the Faustbook).[18] Passages in *Dr Faustus* and in the other plays could be cited to establish connections between Marlowe's text and occult speculation, and it is indeed interesting to see that Marlowe often travels far beyond his limited Faustbook material and displays knowledge not only of general magical practices but of more specific aspects of ritualistic and Cabalistic magic, Paracelsian alchemy, Hermetic cosmology, and Agrippan "occult philosophy." It is particularly interesting to think of the analogies between Marlowe's poetic mode and the immense pathos of rhetorical persuasion with which Cornelius Agrippa (Giordano Bruno would be another case in question) affirms the linguistic "vertue" and potency of the magus who would use his creative interpretation to "act upon" nature and seek control over divine agencies or images in order to enlarge the realm of consciousness beyond its accustomed boundaries.[19]

Agrippa's defence of the efficacy of the Hermetic language and the magus' power of intervention in the divine macrocosm takes it for granted that Hermeticism and the "sacred Canons" of normative tradition will always stand in an antithetical relationship to each other.[20] His insight, which in a way prefigures such

---

18 Apart from internal textual evidence, demonstrable by several derivative passages in *The Taming of a Shrew* and *A Looking-Glass for London and England*, early performances (c.1589) of *Dr Faustus* at the Theatre in Shoreditch are mentioned in T. M.'s memoirs in *The Black Book* (1604). See Kuriyama, "Dr. Greg and *Doctor Faustus*," 181-85.
19 Cf. *Three Books of Occult Philosophy*, Bk.I, pp. 69-70; 72-78. The only attempt to explore this field has been made by Kimberly Benston; his research into Hermetic philosophy and Marlowe's poetics presents a considerable achievement (cf."The Shaping of the Marlovian Sublime," esp. chap. 2).
20 Agrippa's praise of magic gains further significance for the Marlowe scholar if one considers the problem of how to take the tone and intention of his "recantation" in *De incerti-*

bitter self-justifications as John Dee's "Digression Apologeticall", half a century later,[21] is also an expression of his pressing concern about the status of magic which,

> whereas it was accounted by all ancient Philosophers the chiefest Science, & by ancient wise men, & Priests was always had in great veneration, came at last after the beginning of the Catholike Church to be always odious to, and suspected by the holy fathers, and then exploded by Divines, and condemed by sacred Canons, and moreover by all laws, and ordinances forbidden.[22]

If we remember that Shakespeare's Prospero is similarly defensive about his "potent art" when he declares that he had been "transported / And rapt in secret studies," "neglecting worldly ends, all dedicated / To closeness ..." (*The Tempest* I.ii.76-77;89-90), and when he sharply distinguishes himself from "this damn'd witch Sycorax" who worshipped the god Setebos and whose sorceries were "terrible / To enter human hearing" (I.ii.263;264-65), we may ask how the "myth of the magus"[23] surfaces in *Dr Faustus* and how Marlowe places his scholar-magician against the historical and literary backgrounds.

That Faustus' "art" was indeed "famous" and deeply ingrained in the popular imagination - and thus ready to be fully exploited on the Elizabethan stage - can be attested by the immensely rich and venerable traditions, from the classics on the one hand, for example, to the native tradition of medieval drama and narrative

---

tudine et vanitate omnium scientiarum et artium (1531), inasmuch as he published *De occulta philosophia libri tres* also in 1531, several years after the completion of *De incertitudine*. In its wholesale attack and indiscriminate deconstruction of all human knowledge, the latter text forms a massive rhetorical achievement, and the historical question, whether Agrippa published it as a safeguard action, is less interesting than the literary critical one, which could approach the two texts as parodic counterparts, each forming a proleptic parody of the other.
21 Cf. John Dee, "Mathematicall Preface" to *The Elements of Geometrie of the most Auncient Philosopher Euclide of Megara*, trans. H. Billingsley (London, 1570), sigs. A 1v- A2.
22 *Three Books of Occult Philosophy*, sig. A 2v.
23 E.M. Butler seems to have spent half of her life-time in pur-

romance on the other, which contributed to the portrayals of literary magicians and, even more importantly, transmitted several unmistakable motifs and plot conventions. When the Elizabethan and Jacobean stages came to full life (1590-1615), it was no coincidence that the figure of the stage magician was fairly widely used in various roles in which he could motivate plots, provide comment or contrast, become the agent of satire or simply exhibit spectacular conjuring and juggling performances to delight the audience.[24] A great deal of modern criticism that offers us new readings of old plays tends to stumble over (non-existing) interpretive problems because little attention is paid to the historical fact that playwrights like Marlowe and Shakespeare, writing for viewers and listeners in the public playhouse, had little reason not to be inclusive, not to use the freedom and flexibility of their "open" medium (to the utter dismay of the Sidneys and Jonsons) and combine lofty poetry with "merely" spectacular elements that were in popular demand. Marlowe does not hesitate to use fire-cracking devils and magical "shows," but in this case the dramatic representation of the natural and the "supernatural" is of more central significance since the hero's fantasies of power are always measurable against the ephemeral results of his practice of "heavenly negromancy."

Faustus, when he begins to "raise hell," concentrates all dramatic interest on himself, not primarily on his role as magician, but on his personality, the consciousness which is his motivating force and which enmeshes him deeper and deeper into his fictive creations. Marlowe enforces the tragic implications by means of a progressive "darkening" of his dramaturgy. The manner in which this is effected in the pact scene points to the ironic centre of

---

      suit of the profuse historical and literary traditions behind the myth. See her impressive trilogy: *The Myth of the Magus* (Cambridge: Cambridge Univ.Press, 1948); *Ritual Magic* (Cambridge: Cambridge Univ.Press, 1949), and *The Fortunes of Faust* (Cambridge: Cambridge Univ.Press, 1952).

24 Cf. Kurt Tetzeli von Rosador, *Magie im Elisabethanischen Drama* (Braunschweig: G.Westermann, 1970), and Barbara H. Traister, "Heavenly Negromancy: The Figure of the Magician in Tudor and Stuart Drama," Diss., Yale University, 1973.

the tragedy: it is as if Faustus' soaring flight of fancy had been broken off in mid-flight. If in the beginning there were the *words* of intoxicating imagination, the true (metaphorical) power of spell-binding magic, as the Hermetic magus would have understood it, the spirit is now falling away, downward, unto the literalizing plane of *deeds*, the writing of articles. My digression into the world of magical tradition may give us a further perspective from which we can reflect on the metaphorical-literal interchange that is taking place. I would contend that Marlowe very deliberately provokes his audience into watching with horrified fascination the extravagant ceremony of Faustus' "supernatural" league, while he makes it clear that Faustus is falling into the tragic gulf between "wish" ("let it be propitious for my wish") and diabolically manufactured, alienated reality. The tragic paradox of Faustus' daemonic, self-crippling act, however, is not the sole stimulus of the covenant ritual; its tenor conveys a movement compounded of psychological and physical experience (Faustus' consciousness), while its vehicle, the blood-ritual as such, is a unique stage spectacle which singles out *Dr Faustus* from all the other Elizabethan and Jacobean plays in which magic is integrated into the plot.

If we see the interaction in the play between ritual and psychological interests as one of Marlowe's main innovations in tragic form, his radical dramaturgical unconventionality is another quality that distinguishes him from other playwrights who employ similar motifs or magician figures in their plays. Of those magicians, enchanters, or wizards that trod upon the stage in romantic or satiric comedies and didactic dramas,[25] none except

---

25 Among the plays that should be mentioned are *The Rare Triumphs of Love and Fortune* (anon.,1582); John Lyly's *Endimion, the Man in the Moon* (1588); Anthony Munday's *John a Kent and John a Cumber* (c.1589); Robert Greene's *Friar Bacon and Friar Bungay* (c.1589-90)and *A Looking-Glass for London and England* (c.1590); George Peele's *The Old Wives Tale* (c.1590);Greene's *John of Bordeaux* (c.1592); Thomas Dekker's *Old Fortunatus* (1599); *The Wisdom of Doctor Dodypoll* (anon.,c.1599);Dekker's *The Merry Devil of Edmonton* (1602); George Chapman's *Bussy D'Ambois* (1604); Barnabe Barnes' *The Devil's Charter* (1607);

Greene's Friar Bacon, Jonson's wonderful charlatans, and of course Shakespeare's Prospero are anyhow central to their plays' main concerns. Much of the stage-magic, devil-play, tricks and illusions was used for the sake of spectacular effects and thrills which added a sensational touch to the performance. Even in those cases in which the magician exerts his potentially dangerous power and becomes implicated in the dramatic conflicts, the conflicts themselves are usually contained by the safe coordinates of an allegorical comedy or morality structure, which not only assert the rightness of the generally shared system of spiritual and human values but, more significantly, allow the magician to *renounce* "both substance and shadow of that most horrible and hatefull trade," as Lyly's Dipsas describes it,[26] and become reintegrated into a harmonious, natural order of society: all's well that ends well.

If we think of the interchange between scenes demonstrating the power of love and those focussing on the power of magic, as we find it in Greene's *Friar Bacon and Friar Bungay* for instance, the machinery of romantic comedy will inevitably come round to its moral conclusion by breaking the isolating, immoral, and socially disruptive energies of the magician's work and rendering them overpowered and displaced by the much larger forces of Love and Virtue - as they triumph in the customary, festive celebration of harmony and marital rites (cf. *Friar Bacon; The Rare Triumphs; Endimion*).[27] The (tragi-)comic stage and its moralist-

---

Jonson's *The Alchemist* (1610); and Shakespeare's *The Tempest* (1611). I have taken the dates of first performances from Alfred Harbage's *Annals of English Drama, 975-1700*, rev. S. Schoenbaum (London: Methuen, 1964).
26 *Endimion* V.iii.262-63. Quoted from R.W. Bond's edition of *The Complete Works of John Lyly* (Oxford: Clarendon, 1902),vol.III.
27 Similarly, Dekker's *Old Fortunatus* concludes with a hymn to Virtue ("Virtue the Victory!"), and Shakespeare, after having kept the stage under the spell of his imaginary and magical moonlight, ends all bad nightmares with the ritual blessings of "nuptial" solemnities (cf. Theseus' closing speech in *Midsummer Night's Dream*). See also Hymen's closing speech in *As You Like It* for the importance of ritual (marriage, dance, music) in the comedy-finale.

ic contrivances need such happy reformations, fusing, as it were, the double-plots and - in their extension - the proto-heroic and pastoral myths which underlie, for example, Friar Bacon's hubris and Margaret's humble, feminine virtue. While the disruptive, deceptive artifices of the Magicians fall to pieces or get silenced, a well-ordered, justly ruled nonmagical world reaffirms itself to the sound of universally harmonizing music. Greene's play, which had enjoyed its magical spectacles and self-consciously patriotic feats (Bacon's antagonist, the German magician Vandermast, is properly defeated in a contest of "negromantic spells"), turns in on itself and proceeds from Bacon's rather conventional farewell to folly

> End all thy magic and thine art at once ...
> ... it repents me sore
> That ever Bacon meddled in this art.
> The hours I have spent in pyromantic spells,
> The fearful tossings in the latest night
> Of papers full of nigromantic charms ...
> Repentance can do much.
> Think Mercy sits where Justice holds her seat,
> And from those wounds those bloody Jews did pierce,
> Which by thy magic oft did bleed afresh,
> From thence for thee the dew of mercy drops.
> (xiii.79;85-90;99-103)[28]

to a full-scale, allegorical happy ending, sublimating all previous dissonance into the projected union of Live and Fortune, presiding over "glorious England" and her healthy Fressingfields.

The point is mythical, political, as well as theological, for the concluding dramatic emblem underscores the restoration of a divine *and* human order.[29] This order gives a coherent picture

---

28 *Friar Bacon and Friar Bungay*, ed. J.A. Levin, The New Mermaids (London: Benn, 1969).
29 In the same manner, the magic spell in Lyly's *Endimion* is broken by the "divine" Cynthia, the symbolic representation of the English Queen. In Dekker's *Old Fortunatus*, Virtue even outdoes Fortune, the agent of temptation and retribution, and triumphs in the allegorical battle - finally yielding to the "true virtue" of the Queen onstage, in a clear effort at royal image-making (cf. the ending of the published Court version of 1600).

of a moral justice which transcends all misdirected purposes and to which "prayer" and, of course, "love" can appeal:

> *Henry.* But why stands Friar Bacon here so mute?
> *Bacon.* Repentant for the follies of my youth,
> That magic's secret mysteries misled,
> And joyful that this royal marriage
> Portends such bliss unto this matchless realm.
> (xvi.35-39)

Bomelio, in *The Rare Triumphs of Love and Fortune*, does not turn "mute" after his "vile blasphemous Bookes"[30] have been burnt, but breaks into a wild and hysterical frenzy which is eventually overcome by divine influence: in one of the few beautiful moments in the play, Mercury appears to "recure his woe" (1620) with his music, and Bomelio gently falls asleep, only to wake up to the final resolution of the plot through Jupiter's divine judgment. Very much unlike Marlowe's oblivious Jupiter, who is "dandling Ganymede upon his knee" (*Dido Queen of Carthage* I.i) and exults in his decadent erotic desires, the Jupiter of the 1582 Court play is attentive and providentially reconciles all quarrels: "Thus euery thing vnited is by loue" (1833). This unification, imposed upon the dramatic world (the play-within-the-play) in which Bomelio had cried out for "iust reuenge" (873) during his invocation of both Jove and Rodomantus (the "Judge of hatefull hell"), removes the dramatic tensions that had been pulling against the allegorically established order of the universe. By foreclosing all latent tragic implications and by silencing the mad Bomelio, the question of his use of magic and of the nature of his "excellent arte" (1150) is of course side-stepped and, later on, completely dropped when the play winds up its allegorical profusions.

It is interesting to see these aesthetic dissonances at work; even Prospero, who stands almost at the end of a long tradition of stage-magicians, is caught in varying moral contexts, and

---

30 *The Rare Triumphs of Love and Fortune*, ed. W.W. Greg (1582; facsimile rpt. Oxford: Malone Society, 1930), line 1356.

although he attempts a kind of "authorial" synthesis for himself and the disharmonies on his island

> But this rough magic
> I here abjure; and, when I have requir'd
> Some heavenly music - which even now I do -
> To work mine end upon their senses that
> This airy charm is for, I'll break my staff ...
> I'll drown my book   [*Solemn music*]
>   (*The Tempest* V.i.50-54;57)

and ends the play himself by merging his "heavenly music" with a plea for restoring "prayer," the play as such does not resolve the questions that arise from the ambiguous status of his "potent art" (V.i.50) which he wields much like his precursor wizards who pretend to live between the natural and supernatural worlds.[31]

Within Shakespeare's romance form there are as many ambivalent displacements at work, diffusing the disturbing implications of Prospero's "literal" magic, as we find them in Greene's *Friar Bacon*, a play which is believed to have been performed before *Dr Faustus* (and can therefore hardly be called an "anti-Faustus" play) and which has obviously shied at the problem of representing the daemonic quality of the power Bacon wants to employ so patriotically (cf. ii.57-60). If Bacon is a practitioner of black magic and can boast to have "dived into hell / And sought the darkest palaces of fiends" (xi.7-8), the implied Satanism is never actualized in a psychological or spiritual drama which would allow us to get to know this man's consciousness and his moral perception of his own stance. Using Bacon's magical feats, which are often enough farcically deflated, as an excuse for stage spectacle, Greene's uncertain authorial sensibility limits

---

31   See Barbara A. Mowat's illuminating study of the various magician figures and of the relations between the image of magic in drama and in other literary traditions: "Prospero, Agrippa, and Hocus Pocus," *ELR*, 11, no.3 (1981), 281-303. See also David Young, "'Where the Bee Sucks': A Triangular Study of *Doctor Faustus, The Alchemist*, and *The Tempest*," in *Shakespeare's Romances Reconsidered*, ed. Carol McGinnis Kay and Henry E. Jacobs (Lincoln: Univ.of Nebraska Press, 1978), pp. 149-66.

his own artistic process and shows the clumsy effects of righteous didacticism, as they emerge from the Fressingfield-Bacon double-plot and gradually dissipate characterization into a series of de-individualizing moral commonplaces.

The mystification surrounding the ritualistic conjuration of the devil and, even worse, the ritualistic signing of a blood-pact, which are avoided in almost all the other plays, are fully brought to bear upon Marlowe's drama and its relationship to the audience. No miracle of Theophilus was possible, no pious renunciation like Friar Bacon's was likely, if one brings a full-fledged Satanic ritual on the stage and thus breaks down all possibilities of regeneration that had been so deeply rooted in traditional Christian mythology. The strong mythological significance surrounding the binding devil-compact and its potentially tragic consequences is reinforced by Marlowe; fused with the rigorous Calvinist logicality which holds the play together, it can only point forward to the irrevocable destruction of the hero that was already prefigured in the wilful choices he made in the beginning. Furthermore, Marlowe's mythopoeic invention in this scene goes considerably beyond his source material; neither the elaborate conjuration ceremony nor the Satanic pact ritual are to be found in the Faustbook or P.F.'s translation. When Spies published the Faustbook in 1587, he omitted the ceremonial details on purpose, as he maintained, to make sure that they would not be abused! Such explicit conjuration rites, as one finds them in Reginald Scot's *Discouerie of Witchcraft* (1584) for example, are never met on the stage, and there is little doubt that the plays presenting a sympathetic magician, in the Bacon-Prospero lineage, would avoid staging any rituals of black magic in performance because such rites were evidently taken to be damnable by the audience.[32]

---

[32] I know of only two other plays that actually include stage-presentations of a pact with the devil, *The Merry Devil of Edmonton* (1602) and *The Devil's Charter* (1607). These later plays, however, do by no means emphasize and integrate the diabolical pact as Marlowe does and, as in the case of the Pope Alexander play, merely add it to a rich hotch-potch of crude spectacles.

It is indisputable, then, that *Dr Faustus* must have struck a new and sinister note when it put its black pact-ritual on stage, and the outrageously blasphemous thrust of the formal covenant-making with Lucifer is another one of those characteristic Marlovian "gratifications" of his original audience which almost certainly guaranteed a shocked response of a kind which a modern audience with a different (if any) religious sensibility is less likely to experience. In the same way, in fact, modern audiences often fail to appreciate the consistently Calvinist perspective with which Marlowe has buttressed the "tragical discourse" of his play. What is so astonishing about Faustus' pact-making is not only the absolute determination with which he goes about it (the Faust of the legend was rather scared and delayed the signing out of concern for the "losse of his soule"),[33] but, most conspicuously, the flagrant, demonstrative perversion of those ideas of "love", "assurance", "soul", and "wish" that traditionally adhere to the religious and sacramental relations between man and God.

"View heere the blood ... / And let it be propitious for my wish": Faustus, offering his blood "for loue of" the devil, enacts an uncanny pantomime during which the self-wounding and the drawing up of a legal "deed of gift" are transformed into a ferocious parody of Christ's self-sacrifice and the sacrament of the Eucharist in which the New Covenant is commemorated. That Marlowe wanted his ingeniously perverse parody to be seen against this background becomes unmistakable in that notorious moment in which Faustus appropriates the most solemn and momentous exclamation recorded in the Gospel to commend his spirit into the hands of Lucifer:

> *Consummatum est*, this Bill is ended
> And Faustus hath bequeath'd his soule to Lucifer.
> (A 515-16)

In the normative traditions of Christian thought, the shedding of

---

[33] *The Historie*, chaps. III and IV (Palmer and More, pp. 139-40).

Christ's blood has of course always been conceived as the decisive sacrificial act which seals the Covenant of grace that is revealed in the "New Testament" and promises man atonement, at-one-ment with God. *Testamentum* is the translation of the Septuagint word διαθήκη, and the Vulgate uses the word *testamentum* not so much in its original, technical sense (as *pactum* or *foedus*, referring mainly to the decalogue or "giving of the Law" in the OT), but to denote the saving message of the Cross and Resurrection, its new spiritual significance, in other words, as it was expressed by Christ-the-living-Word: "This is my blood of that newe Testament which is shedde for many" (Mark xiv.24, Geneva).

Both the literal and the typological senses of the Old Covenant have surfaced in many scriptural interpretations. The most interesting distinction is made between the Covenant relationship in the OT, which focussed on Yahweh as the initiator and sole Covenant maker and his people who received it as a *gift*, and the emphasis that in the NT is placed almost exclusively on Christ as the new "mediator", "servant", and "priest" who took up his prefigured role and with his blood-"ransom" (Mark x.45) atoned for man's sin and satisfied Divine justice - thus reconciling God to man and fulfilling the Father's promises.[34] Jesus' own representation of his role, his "ransom" and "covenant" sayings recorded in the Synoptics, finds its climax in the moment when he acknowledges the fulfilment of his being ("*Postea sciens Iesus quia omnia consummata sunt, ut consummaretur Scriptura, dixit ... Consummatum est. Et inclinato capite, tradidit spiritum*" John xix.28,30, Vulgate). This is recorded only in John's Gospel from which Faustus quotes.

Greenblatt, among the more provocative recent commentators, stresses the significance of Faustus' repetition of Christ's

---

34 Calvin, explicating the threefold manner of Christ's prophetic, kingly, and priestly roles, emphasizes the obedience with which Christ yields to the terrible sacrifice in order to become our "redemption, ransom, and propitiation." Not surprisingly, Calvin's exegesis is mainly based on Paul's understanding of Christ's role (cf. Phil.ii.7-8). For Calvin's view, see *Institutes*, II.16.5.

dying words, but for him it is merely a failed parodic imitation of an "archetypal act", the "culmination of Faustus' fantasies of making an end, and hence a suicide."[35] Although Greenblatt quotes the Johannine passage, he seems unaware of the theological implications of the terms Faustus uses, terms which from the beginning of Apostolic teaching had been subject to contradictory interpretations and figurative readings which in turn gave rise to various exegetical traditions (Canonical and Gnostic) up to the Reformation. Faustus' use of the word "propitious" touches very ironically upon one of the big problems that had revolved around the intellectual perception of such conflicting figures of speech as "propitiation", "ransom", "redemption", "justification", "acquittal", and "reconciliation", which were used to make sense of Christ's sacrificial act. These figures of speech, seen in their intrinsic relationship to the doctrine of God and the doctrine of salvation as they were developed later on, already reflect interpretive attitudes towards Christ's role, which would bear upon the conception of God's will (his infinite wrath, his infinite mercy) and of the relationship between Son and Father (their respective dispositions towards sinful man).

Among the "opinions and Comon Speeches" with which Marlowe evidently liked to shock his contemporaries were quite a few, cited by Baines' as well as Kyd's depositions, which referred to the Old and New Testaments. That he is said to have mentioned Moses many times, calling him "but a jugler" for whom it was easy, having been "brought vp in all the artes of the Egiptians," to seduce and "abuse the Jewes being a rude & gross people," is as interesting as the comments on Paul and Christ:

> ... all the apostles were fishermen and base fellowes neyther of wit nor worth ... Paull only had wit but he was a timorous fellow in bidding men to be subject to magistrates against his conscience ... if Christ would haue instituted the sacrament with more Ceremoniall Reverence it would haue bin had in more admiration.[36]

---

35 Greenblatt, *Renaissance Self-Fashioning*, p. 214.
36 The text of the Baines Libel is reprinted in Maclure, pp. 36ff.

In Kyd's second letter to Sir John Puckering, Marlowe is cited to have allied the apostle to Moses' "profession," namely calling Paul a "Jugler" as well.[37] The tone of these reported statements tells us more about Marlowe's temperament than about his "atheism," and the allusions themselves are perhaps more revealing if we see them related to the mode of allusion in *Dr Faustus*, where we can directly experience the intellectual ambiguities Marlowe creates by exploiting the protagonist's trenchantly blasphemous use of biblical formulations that are ambiguous themselves or, at least, point to conflicting exegetical traditions. The link between "juggling" and Moses-Christ, the two mediators of the Old and New Covenants, is too suggestive not to provoke our attention, especially if we read it in conjunction with Marlowe's view of Paul-the-"Jugler" who was also the earliest interpreter of the antitheses between the "law" (Sinai-Covenant) and the "spirit" (Christ's new Gospel) and who represented the main source for Reformation theology.

On a deeper level there seems to be a far more complicated conflation and/or juxtaposition of magical power and redemptive power implied by Marlowe's deliberate and daring decision to inscribe a blasphemous parody of the crucifixion and the New Covenant in Faustus' projection of newfound power. The particular manner of equation or analogy makes not just for a highly perverse punning on Faustus' and Christ's respective sacrifices (the "deed of gift"), but rather highlights - through Faustus' very act of denial - the inherently controversial status of the power of redemption in the play.

Yet the iconoclasm of this scene strikes deeper. Marlowe, if we can believe the remarks in the Baines Libel, did not find Christ's ceremonial institution of the sacrament particularly impressive. He was, however, interested in the Hermetic and magical tradition and seems to have been fascinated by Moses the "deceiver." Since his familiarity with classical mythology is also abundantly de-

---

37 For Kyd's letters, see Maclure, pp. 32-36.

monstrable throughout his corpus, I find it particularly tempting to see the pact scene in *Dr Faustus* as a remarkable confluence of several imaginative high-wire acts. The impact of the shocking ritual is intended in a way that reflects back on Marlowe's predilection for and peculiar fascination with the pathos of violence and the more "heroic" and esoteric qualities of an older, pagan tradition (Ovid, Lucan, Seneca) which became a source of inspiration for a kind of iconoclastic virulence that clearly marks the *Tamburlaine* plays, *The Jew of Malta*, and - to a lesser degree - *Edward II*. Often overlooked or underestimated, Marlowe's translation of Lucan's *Pharsalia* in fact brilliantly demonstrates his consanguinity with the wild pathos and rhetorical copiousness of Lucan's hyperbolic mode. Even more significantly, Marlowe obviously relished the anarchic violence and aggressive sadism which he found portrayed in Lucan's epic poem of the apocalypse of civil war. After he has painted his portrait of the diabolical hero, Caesar, Lucan describes the horror which Caesar's crossing of the Rubicon provokes, and it is in these passages in Book I that we discover Marlowe's most intense poetic idiom, a whirling, haunting crescendo-rhythm of blank verse - a verse of which Elizabethan English seemed hardly capable before Marlowe.

What strikes the reader's immediate attention in the *Pharsalia* is its tendency to evoke the macabre and the horrid, to emphasize the darker and more horrible side of magic, and to invent grisly details. I will choose the following example:

>   ... on the altar
> He lays a ne'er yok'd bull, and pours down wine,
> Then crams salt leaven on his crooked knife;
> The beast long struggled, as being like to prove
> An awkward sacrifice, but by the horns
> The quick priest pull'd him on his knees and slew him.
> No vein sprung out, but from the yawning gash,
> Instead of red blood, wallow'd venemous gore.
>   (*Lucan's First Book* 607-14)

While the main dramatic focus in the *Pharsalia* is on the struggle and the greatness of the protagonists (Caesar, Pompey), there is an equally strong interest in bold rhetorical effects of almost theatrical directness which punctuate the historical narrative and evoke gruesome scenes of sacrificial rites, witchcraft, omens, and prodigies. The strange aura of the supernatural, particularly strong in the mystical utterances of the "quick priest" who stands "amazed" at the "direful signs" of his bloody ritual (615-37), comes across in what is perhaps Marlowe's most heightened mode of writing, and - as so often in *Dr Faustus* - his tone is not devoid of a certain frivolousness.

This Lucanian strain of violent ritualism and heroic pathos - and it is the *rhetorical* mode, in which this strain makes itself so dramatically felt, that I am concerned with - is highly pertinent to Marlowe's dramaturgic concerns, and I want to see it as a significant subtext which controls some of the conflictual patterns that find such anxious expression in Marlowe's heroes. The barely repressed fury that characterizes Marlovian heroism breaks through during its movement toward crisis and forms an essential ground for tragic conflict - more essential than the overt blasphemous parodies in Faustus' pact-ritual suggest. The striking manifestation of such crises in the symbolic self-wounding of the hero, and the different meanings it can have in the context of its ritual design, could be further illuminated by means of the representational links in Marlowe's own corpus.

Since there is no precedent for Faustus' blood-ritual in the history of English drama, it may be most helpful to compare Faustus to his precursor Tamburlaine. Tamburlaine, tempter of gods, dramatizes his own agonistic and often ambiguous (the "Scourge of God") relationship with Jove and the powers of heaven, and the high energy of his hyperbolic rhetoric is very reminiscent of the Lucanian vein. While Tamburlaine's relentless, bloodthirsty conquests demonstrate the more-than-human potency he claims for himself, Marlowe very much compounds the problematic link that exists between Tamburlaine and the gods on the one hand, and between Tamburlaine and his opponents, followers, and sons on the other. The competitive relationship between son and father is one form of expression in the play, marking the ritualistic, ever-intensifying *rhetorical* and *martial* encounters Tamburlaine seeks in order to validate his vaunts. Tamburlaine uses and, in a way, needs the example of Jupiter's successful revolt as a pretext for his own intended emulation. His hyperbolic quest for supreme power, however, provokes *self*-affirming acts of violence and usurpation which are meant to initiate a principle of authority that is imagined to be *self*-engendered.

Such a conception of "self-redeeming" warfare is behind practically all of Tamburlaine's relationships, but it is especially poignant to see him turn against his own son Calyphas, whom he had encouraged to follow the same dangerous power-principle that he himself compulsively pursues.

> Villain, art thou the son of Tamburlaine,
> And fearest to die ...?
> . . .
> View me, thy father, that hath conquered kings ...
> And see him lance his flesh to teach you all.
> 			[*He cuts his arm*]
>
> A wound is nothing, be it ne'er so deep,
> Blood is the god of war's rich livery.
> Now look I like a soldier, and this wound
> As great a grace and majesty to me ...
> Come, boys, and with your fingers search my wound
> And in my blood wash all your hands at once,
> While I sit smiling to behold the sight:
> Now, my boys, what think you of a wound?
> 			(*2 Tamb.*III.ii.95-129)

Clearly designed as another theatrical hyperbole, Tamburlaine's self-wounding is a very spectacular way of demonstrating his "argument of arms" which he understands to be at the heart of all "valiant, proud, ambitious" deeds. Trying to legitimize the value and "grace" of blood, he stresses the divine status which it confers on the heroic warrior. Conceived as a glorious revolt against established authority, Tamburlaine's celebration of the life-giving, liberating force of violence confirms the principle behind his previous actions - namely to make his opponents' gore gush over the stage in a vicarious, curative blood-letting. Whether one regards it as perverse or not, from this hieratic principle almost every gesture in the two plays derives a symbolic meaning, and the unbelievable violence of the action takes on a ritual significance.

It is a very bizarre moment when the infuriated father asks his sons to "search" his "wound" so that they can "believe." Tamburlaine's parodic self-representation as a Christ-like "redeemer" (who reveals himself and blesses those who believe in him)[38] is highly ominous because a few scenes earlier Christ (!) had been invoked by Orcanes to prove Himself a "perfect God" of vengeance and to punish Sigismund the covenant-breaker:

> *Thou Christ that art esteemed omnipotent,*
> *If thou wilt prove thyself a perfect God*
> Worthy the worship of all faithful hearts,
> Be now revenged upon this traitor's soul.
> (II.ii.55-58;my emphasis)

The most suggestive visual and symbolic analogue to the scene of Tamburlaine's self-wounding in III.ii is staged four scenes later, when Tamburlaine directs his "argument of arms" against his un-believing son ("traitor to my name and majesty / ... picture of a slave" IV.i.90-91) and slaughters him in full view of his audience. Such an extreme enforcement of the Law which Tamburlaine, the God of Wrath, assumes to be a legitimate representation of universal power-struggles, cannot but provoke a shock of horror and repugnance. Yet it seems to me that the dramatization of such violent action, totally uninhibited by any moral scruples, brings us closest to the tragic implications of the impossible dream which Marlowe envisions in the second part of *Tamburlaine*.

Although Tamburlaine explains the source and essence of his

---

[38] The resurrected Christ had asked his disbelieving disciple Thomas: "Put thy finger here, and see mine hands, and put foorth thine hand, and put it into my side, and be not faithlesse, but faithfull ... Thomas, because thou hast seene me, thou beleeuest: blessed are they that haue not seene, and haue beleeued" (John xx.27,29).

struggles by referring to the law of war and "justice" (IV.i.146-48), his will-to-power is a will constrained to continuous narcissistic denials of everything existing beyond the limits of the self. Such an idea of self-fulfilment, then, is predicated on a relentless striking out against others, against unwilling parts of himself (his son), against the gods themselves.

In *Dr Faustus*, the conflicts are almost wholly internalized, and the hero's desire expresses itself mainly through his rhetorical energy and the imaginative goals which he projects and towards which he strives with the help of his "heauenly negromancy." His striving, however, involves him in acts which he cannot always displace by purely imaginative leaps. Unlike Tamburlaine, who possesses a dazzling and awesome integrity, Faustus' dream to "live at liberty" and maintain a "life exempt from servitude" (Tamburlaine's very first proclamation in I.ii.26ff.) does not fulfil itself so smoothly, although he is at great pains to demonstrate that he will try the "vttermost." Compared to Tamburlaine's voluntary demonstration of his prowess as well as of the validity (or credibility) of his "argument of arms," Faustus' wounding of his arm *must* be performed, as Mephostophilis tells him, to seal the improbable bargain, and this act of concession is at least as conspicuous as the enormous determination with which the "quick priest", to use the phrase from the *Pharsalia*, performs the sacrificial rite and assumes his "self-redeeming" role.

Interestingly, the idea that every man is his own priest is of course the logical extension of the Protestant emphasis on purely individual religious experience. Faustus' blood sacrifice is a highly ominous performance because what he claims to be carrying out is not just an aggressive act of antithetical identification, nor simply a parody of the "priestly role", but, more implicitly, a desperate act of defiance in the face of what he seems to apprehend as an inescapable law of compensation, namely that "nothing is got for nothing." If the threat is primarily embodied in Faustus' image of a vengeful God, this is, in a way, an extension of the submerged thought-processes which underlie all previous scenes and symbolically enter into the creation of the new covenant.

Whereas Faustus, throughout his ceremony of covenant-making, is insisting on his power over himself ("Now will I make an ende immediately"; "... is not thy soule thine owne?" A 513;508), the unexpected interruptions of the ritual (the congealing of his blood; the miraculous *homo fuge*-inscription on his arm) are quite troublesome to Faustus' performance of his "deed," and Mephostophilis' repeated punning on the word "deed" (meaning "legal contract", "bill", as well as "act") hardly helps to make Faustus look more successful. Mephostophilis' ironic attitude, indeed, is nowhere more detrimental to Faustus than in his deliberate punning on words like "deed", "perform", "dissolve", "heavens", etc., and in the grandfatherly compliance and patience which he is willing to show to Faustus in order to "obtaine his soule" (A 514). Depending on how it is realized in performance, Mephostophilis' behaviour is always an uncomfortable reminder that, in a way, every "act" of Faustus has its binding consequences - in relation to the old covenant he has broken and the new one he has created - and is a "deed" in two senses of the word.

Grim humour can become a strong ingredient in the physical reality of this scene, when we watch an exhilarated Faustus draw up the pact articles and read his five commandments from the scroll, while Mephostophilis is standing in the background with a grimace on his face, amusedly listening to what Faustus has to say. One begins to see that Mephostophilis seems to have his own way of interpreting the new distribution of power and the exchange of deeds and services. In order to distract Faustus from any doubts about the efficacy of his newly bought magical power, he stages the first of several flashy and inherently meaningless dumb shows. His devil-actors appear with their offerings (crowns, rich apparel), dance a little, and quickly disappear.

> *Fau.* Speake Mephastophilis, what meanes this shewe?

> *Me.* Nothing Faustus, but to delight thy minde withall,
> And to shewe thee what Magicke can performe.
> (A 527-29)

The answer is ominous indeed, and the pause after "nothing" has the same ironic touch to it as the word "performe" which to Mephostophilis does not mean "fulfil" or "realize" but rather "devise" or "contrive", with obvious theatrical implications. He will put on shows, spectacles, pageants, and use all the deceptions of which magic is capable. In a way, what is happening in front of our eyes is a reversal of roles, because it is not Faustus who emerges from the pact scene as a mighty magician, but Mephostophilis who takes over the traditional role of the producer and presenter of magical "performances."

Faustus' speeches become shorter, his questions more obsessive, and his desires remarkably less grandiose. When he finally admits to being "wanton and lasciuious", Mephostophilis does not hesitate to tease Faustus with the crude spectacle of a disguised devil who comes on stage to assault Faustus with fireworks. When the devil has left the stage, Mephostophilis mocks Faustus in a rather blatant way ("Tel Faustus, how dost thou like thy wife?" A 597) before dismissing the subject with a sarcastic hint at Faustus' mistaken sacramental "appetite":

> Tut Faustus, marriage is but a ceremoniall toy,
> If thou louest me, thinke no more of it.
> (A 599-600)

Yet he immediately proceeds to stimulate a desire for those sexual delights that Faustus can expect - "the fairest curtezans" who will be "as beautiful / As was bright Lucifer before his fall" (A 605-06). Ironic metaphorical allusions, mixed sexual identities, and optical illusions and tricks: the range of Mephostophilis' potent art of deception is impressive. Equally astounding is Faustus' tragic incapacity to understand or admit the confused relationship between himself and Mephostophilis, to see what is emerging from a contract that was to bring him absolute magical power and fulfilment of all wishes. Ironically enough,

Faustus once thought that magic could "resolve" him of "all ambiguities"; but what we see are the tensions and ambiguities that result from his (mis-)understanding of magic, and this is nowhere more obvious than in the reactions which reveal his inner state. The covenant scene is a crisis scene because ritual and blasphemy do not quite take over and glamorize Faustus or deflect from his inner conflicts but, on the contrary, provoke tensions and disruptions on their own which increase our sense of Faustus' predicament, his paradoxical shifting from affirmation ("Faustus, be resolute!") to doubt ("O thou art deceiued" A 626).

As the episode with the disguised, fire-cracking devil illustrates Faustus' world will have to be one full of visual and sensual delights and sensations, even sensations of the strangest kind, in order to be seductive enough to distract his mind from "first thoughts" which, significantly, still revolve around Hell and its location. Mephostophilis, when requested to enlarge Faustus' knowledge about the place, gives a peculiar catalogue of definitions which are more rhetorical than logical:

> Within the bowels of these elements,
> Where we are tortur'd and remaine for euer.
> Hell hath no limits, nor is circumscribed
> In one selfe place, for where we are is hell,
> And where hell is, must we euer be:
> And to conclude, when all the world dissolues,
> And euery creature shalbe purified,
> All places shall be hell that is not heauen.
> (A 565-72)

It is typical that Faustus dismisses both accounts of a limitless, inner hell as well as a physical, localized hell, countering with the extraordinary, and in the circumstances, rather hilarious "Come, I thinke hell's a fable" (A 573). Mephostophilis' calm response: "I, thinke so still, till experience change thy minde" (A 574) hits exactly the right Satanic tone of parodic agreement with which he will continue to tease Faustus. It is now, when Faustus insists on rejecting all unpleasant thoughts about "pain" and "experience" of hell as "trifles and meere olde wiues tales" (A 582), that Mephostophilis begins to refer to

Faustus' damning "deed" as an accomplished deal - governed by the idea of *justice*:

> *Fau.* Why? thinkest thou then that Faustus shall bee damn'd?
> *Me.* I *of necessitie*, for here's the scrowle,
> Wherein thou hast giuen thy soule to Lucifer.
> (A 575-77;my emphasis)

Mephostophilis cunningly appropriates Faustus' own terminology of "What wil be, shall be" and interprets their covenant as it suits himself now. This can only be one of the ultimate ironies in Marlowe's play, that the devil himself appeals to Faustus' own interpretation of divine justice (the "necessitie" of damnation) and uses the same dangerously deceptive rhetoric in order to claim that the diabolical pact is binding in eternal law.

Chapter Nine

IN THE "SUBURBS OF HELL"

> *Me.* Now Faustus aske what thou wilt.
> *Fau.* First will I question thee about hell,
> Tel me, where is the place that men call hell?

I.

Faustus' "self-redeeming" sacrifice would only be meaningful if it were to fulfil his hope in magic-as-power and magic-as-security. The following scenes do not confirm this idea, however, and the self-wounding itself becomes the meaning which Faustus, ironically, creates for himself - prefiguring his repeated, desperate gambling for the subjunctive freedom which he only sees in his negative identity. As so often with Faustus, the idea seems to be stronger than the act; his self-exalting identification with the Satanic image, *daemon est deus inversus*, may reflect his personal heroic ideal, yet it cannot serve as a magic formula to prove the efficacy of the pact. To use my favourite metaphor for the play, the *magic circle* which Faustus has drawn around himself cannot provide the security ("What God can hurt thee Faustus? thou art safe") he craves, nor can it, figuratively speaking, endow him with the perfect, godlike circularity, the transcendent harmony of interiority and exteriority, existence and essence, which would "resolue all ambiguities" from Faustus' Manichaean consciousness. Faustus' "sin" is the expression of that duality; his self-victimizing trespass is a ghostly expression of his acceptance of God as the inescapable Other and as the reminder of his own limited, incomplete humanity.

The reversals built into the play seem inevitable and artistically successful because the greater and the more daring Faustus' rhetorical gestures are, the more theatrically effective are his "circular" returns to those moments in which his desire is not quite accomplished as "deed." The audience, and, I think, audiences of all times, will understand the complementariness of both sides; they will hope and fear for the free, aspiring man as well as for the enclosed, damned man. It is not always clear, however, which side of Faustus, his freedom or his damnation, is more emphasized dramatically, and to what effect. The symbolism of spatial dimensions - heaven, hell, within, without, above, below - is certainly intrinsic to the representation of Faustus' twenty-four year journey from Wittenberg to Wittenberg, and the temporal-spatial aspects of the metaphor of the "circle" are a particularly poignant reminder of the vicissitudes of Faustus' attempted upward flight. In the pact scene and the scene that follows, Faustus begins to appear less free from the relations of time and place, possibility and necessity, and the metaphorical and the literal, than he was before. The absolute *fact* of the sinful contract, clearly overliteralized in the elaborate legalistic ceremony, rises as a fearful spectre, and it increases our sense that the "secure" magic circle of thought and possibility, of the individual self with its hopes and dreams, has begun to dissolve.

In Marlowe's source, the circle becomes quite literally a burning ring of flames, enclosing and threatening a terrified Faustus whose upward escape is blocked:

> ... his house was full of smoke, and the floore couered ouer with ashes: which when Doctor Faustus perceiued, he would haue gone vp the staires: and flying vp, he was taken and throwne into the hall ... then round about him ran a monstrous circle of fire, neuer standing still.[1]

In the play, Mephostophilis refers to the boundaries of Faustus' existence in a different, more subtle and poignant manner. It is the confinement of the "within," although represented as a spatial separation of heaven and hell, which is the truly traumatic, experiential universe the devil describes in response to Faustus'

---

1 *The Historie*, chap. IX (Palmer and More, p. 147).

question:

> *Fau.* Tel me, where is the place that men call hell?
> *Me.* Vnder the heauens.
>
> (A 562-63)

Similar to his curiosity about cosmology, Faustus' interest in the "place that men call hell" is meant to initiate a quasi-logical, scientific investigation, and it is telling how Faustus depersonalizes the form of the question in order to ward off the implications that are so obvious. Mephostophilis, who has offered to discuss all the questions Faustus will pose, strongly represents the kind of "secure" knowledge that Faustus does not want to be referred to. As the constant partner in the tenuous relationship between Faustus and the Powers of negation, he is the best reminder of the indeterminate borderline situation Faustus is caught in, suspended as he is between curiosity and knowledge, subjectivity and objectivity, concealment and revelation. Proper signification becomes difficult as long as Faustus does not recognize the daemonic presence of what he has been repressing and continues to repress ("Come, I thinke hell's a fable").

Mephostophilis' allusion to "Vnder the heauens" can be seen as another ambiguous gesture which includes the spatial dimensions of the theatre (upper stage, lower stage). The duplicitous interplay of immediate and symbolic allocations of what is called "hell" heightens the rhetorical effect of Mephostophilis' explanation, namely that hell exists at the *centre* ("Within the bowels of these elements") and yet cannot be categorically "defined." It is another one of the superb ironies in the play that Marlowe has Faustus resort to the attempt at subduing his relation/disrelation to the world of experience under the contrived Ramistical "methods" of dialectic enquiry. Faustus' desperate wish to unlimit the self almost always clashes with his attempts at "logically" debating the condition of his own reality and the larger reality that circumscribes his existence. His intention to use his logical questing as an art which in the Ramist fashion would yield a perfect closure, an order completely subject to the surveillance of consciousness, will symptomatically fail to teach safety in the face of an oppressively close, since self-engendered existence filled with anxiety. As an attempt to "abstract" an existence of such kind, to correct it by syllogistic play of invention and judgment, plausible and possible arguments, Faustus' wish to "place" hell cannot work.

> Hell hath no limits, nor is circumscrib'd
> In one selfe place, for where we are is hell,
> And where hell is, must we euer be.

Mephostophilis' striking account is of course not a logical definition but rather a kind of *reductio ad paradoxum*. Circling around "where we are," his propositions restate in conversion what, conceivably, is the terrible truth of spiritual damnation: hell has no limits, it is the awareness of negative infinity.[2] The infinite spaciousness and uncircumscribed freedom that Faustus' boundless, absolutizing dreams had bargained for turn out to exist as paradoxical enclosure for him - exiled, as he is, to a life made absolute by its confinement to the hell of *being* itself.

"To know my deed, 'twere best not know myself", Macbeth whispers in the stupefied moments after he has committed the murder and begun to realize that what was only potential in his thoughts and hallucinations has now become real, and it is Macbeth's experience of this *idea* which is in the centre of his tragedy. He does know himself, and Shakespeare's play becomes most terrifying and humanly moving in those moments when Macbeth is most private, most isolated, in his awareness of what he has lost, what it means to be exiled from the secure world of friends, company, love, and sleep.

Faustus, too, wishes not to know himself and to find consolation

---

2   The philosophical implications of the metaphor of "infinity" are of great interest since the negative concept of hell is closely related to a concept of transcendence, firmly established in 16th century Hermetic and religio-cosmological theory, which defined God as an infinite sphere whose centre is everywhere and whose circumference is nowhere. Cf. Karsten Harries, "The Infinite Sphere: Comments on the History of a Metaphor," *Journal of the History of Philosophy*, 13 (1975), 5-15.

in order to be able to endure the experience which, as Mephostophilis prophesies, will "change" his "mind." Consolation is what links Faustus more strongly to Mephostophilis because that is what the devil himself seeks: "*Solamen miseris socios habuisse doloris*" (A 482). Near the end of Webster's *The Duchess of Malfi*, Bosola reflects upon the devilish plottings of the Cardinal in a soliloquy that vividly betrays his own confusion and moral anxiety:

> The precedent's here afore me. How this man
> Bears up in blood! Seems fearless! 'tis well:
> Security some men call the suburbs of hell.
>   (V.ii.336-38)[3]

It is exactly such an experience of enabling and disabling fictions of security and consolation which Marlowe attempts to dramatize in the middle scenes of his play, and we could use Bosola's epithet to describe what is primarily the *mental* dimension of Faustus' tragedy, although he of course also enacts it physically in his spacious outward, upward, and downward travels - the restless wandering of his mind in the "suburbs of hell."

After the pact scene, the A version (the B-text inserts an imperfect Chorus from the A version) continues unbroken with the re-entry of Faustus and Mephostophilis. Since it is unlikely for all we know of Elizabethan stage practice to take two actors off the stage and bring them back on immediately, it makes good sense to assume that Marlowe did in fact adhere to the structural pattern of alternating tragic and comic scenes. Roy Erikson recently argued very convincingly in favour of moving B's clownage scene (II.iii: 743-77) forward and locating it between B's II.i and ii.[4] Although I do not agree with Erikson's preference for the 1616 text, I would follow his argument that the Robin-Rafe scene (Clown and Dick in B) logically succeeds and links up with the

---

3   Quoted from the Revels Plays edition of *The Duchess of Malfi*, ed. John Russell Brown (London: Methuen, 1964).
4   Cf. Roy T. Erikson, "The Misplaced Clownage-Scene in *The Tragedie of Doctor Faustus* (1616) and its Implications for the Play's Total Structure," *ES*, 62, no.3 (1981), 249-58.

concluding stage business of II.i and contains the basic action
required of the missing scene. Consequently, I propose to place
A 949-84 right after the final moment of the pact scene, during
which Mephostophilis presents Faustus with his marvellously inclusive magic encyclopedia:

> Hold, take this booke, peruse it thorowly,
> The iterating of these lines brings golde,
> The framing of this circle on the ground,
> Brings whirlewindes, tempests, thunder and lightning.
> (A 607-10)

Faustus had left the stage in dismay ("O thou art deceiued"), probably quite aware of the fact that he has trapped himself in an
impossible dream. Rafe the clown enters, proudly carrying the
book he has stolen and relishing the forbidden secrets he will
unravel:

> O this is admirable! here I ha stolne one of doctor
> Faustus coniuring books, and ifaith I meane to search
> some circles for my owne vse: now wil I make al the
> maidens in our parish dance at my pleasure starke
> naked before me, and so by that meanes I shal see
> more then ere I felt, or saw yet.
> (A 949-53)

The verbal and thematic links with the main action are quite obvious, and we are not unprepared by now to see the clowns attempt
their own little "heroic" deeds and show us their low-style parody versions of Faustus' conjuring in the circle. Robin's frivolous boasts about the "roaring peece of worke" that he can "easily"
accomplish (turning all the maidens "starke naked") ring a little
more ominous when he alludes to the magic circle:

> Keepe out, keep out, or else you are blowne vp,
> you are dismembred Rafe, keepe out ...
> (A 960-61)

Yet it is Rafe's answer that gives us the most memorable line of
this little scene: "Come, what doest thou with that same booke
thou canst not reade?" (A 963-64). The motif of reading or misreading books and Robin's idea that "I shal see more then ere I

felt, or saw yet" are poignant cross-references to the play's complicated treatment of vision, perception, and understanding.

Fundamental to the problem of seeing-and-understanding and seeing-and-misunderstanding is the disjunction which permeates the dramatic presentation of Faustus' magic dream from the very beginning: his vast imaginative expanse can exist, paradoxically, only within the closed and enclosing circle of magic words (which are "heavenly" and "dangerous" at the same time).[5] His will is infinite while his acts are confined to theatrical overprotesting. Looking backward into the repressed past, and looking forward into the projected golden world of power and delight, Faustus exists within the same disturbed conceptual horizon, conceiving experience in solipsistic terms and seeing appearances as an alluring screen.

The Lyric Studio production found a splendid solution to the dramaturgical problems: the idea of the desired, hypothetical yet unattainable transcendent reality[6] was amplified by the stylized artificiality that marked Faustus' eccentricities and by the stage set itself - the huge white gauze that separated Faustus from the rear stage area. Behind this gauze, functioning as a kind of magic box, invocations and magical shows were dimly glimpsed, sundry visions appeared like figures in a mirage. In another visually startling stage image, the production presented Faustus' tutor Cornelius as a blind man in a wheelchair: his dark

---

5 The most significant moment in which Faustus' "heavenly magic" and "danger" come together occurs during his ultimate conjuring act, the appearance of Helen in her "Heauenly beauty." Before she appears, however, Faustus warns the onlookers to "Be silent then, for danger is in words" (A 1290).
6 The director explained his concept in a programme note on πόθος, the Greek word for an erotic feeling of nostalgic desire, defined by Plato (*Cratylos* 420a) as a yearning desire for a distant object. Alexander the Great has often been regarded as the greatest exemplary of πόθος in Antiquity, and, as the programme note suggested, strong allusions to Alexander were built into the *Faustus* production ("He is said to have himself invented the phrase 'seized by πόθος' to account for his indescribable longing for something beyond, a longing that carried him beyond all borders in a horizontal conquest of space, a true 'space man' of ancient times ...").

prophecies sounded magnificently eerie:

> The Spirits tell me they can drie the sea,
> And fetch the treasure of all forraine wrackes,
> I, all the wealth that our forefathers hid
> Within the massie entrailes of the earth ...

The blind leading the blind, in this play of confused visions and optical illusions, is of course only one, although striking representation of the vexing ironies which Marlowe creates by means of the constantly shifting perspectives on what Faustus sees and tells us and on what the audience sees performed.

This is particularly true for the curious scene in which Faustus so drastically clashes with the infernal trinity (Lucifer, Belzebub, Mephostophilis) and which ends with the spectacle of the Seven Deadly Sins, ushering in the "comic" scenes of the play's middle section.

> *Fau.* When I behold the heauens, then I repent,
> And curse thee wicked Mephastophilus,
> Because thou hast depriu'd me of these ioyes.
> *Me.* Why Faustus,
> Thinkst thou heauen is such a glorious thing?
> I tel thee tis not halfe so faire as thou,
> Or any man that breathes on earth.
> (A 628-43)

Marlowe breaks his analogical pattern of beginning the scene of the main plot with a Faustian soliloquy and achieves an immediate effect by having Faustus and his devil-partner enter in duologue. The contrast could be seen as a symbolic visualization of the new Faustus, as he emerges from the self-wounding sacrifice - bound to the perpetual shadow of his daemon. Faustus, obviously traumatized by his growing awareness that the world is narrowing down upon him, complains to the very partner in "misery" who is ready to share his enforced solitude. While he is still able to gaze upwards and outwards and to "behold the heauens", it is not clear at all why he would speak of being "depriu'd ... of these ioyes" which he had never been able to conceive of in the first place. Yet it makes perfect sense here to speak of the return of the repressed; Faustus is responding to the dissolution of his original hopes as well as to the embarrassing, accusatory fact of Mephostophilis' presence which is, in a way, a representation of his own loss and his alienation from the "glorious" heaven to which his troubled mind, nevertheless, leads him back persistently. Howsoever we want to take his "beholding," it occurs with the skewed perspective of those who are closed in "Vnder the heauens," furthest away from the empyrean and closest to hell, as Mephostophilis had intimated earlier. His apprehension of God or of repentance seems unreal enough, given the fact that his words, ironically, are mere verbal echoes of Mephostophilis' earlier description of the pain of hell ("Think'st thou that I who saw the face of God, / And tasted the *eternal ioyes of heauen* ...?" A 322-23, my emphasis).

But Marlowe, again, manipulates our impressions and avoids a clearly identifiable situation that would exhaust the possibilities in Faustus' position. Faustus' frustration is merely intimated; it forms another change of mood - unexpected and typically eccentric in the way in which he does *not* respond to the devil's sophistic quibbles about man being more "excellent" than heaven because it "was made for man":

> If it were made for man, twas made for me:
> I will renounce this magicke, and repent.
> [*Enter good Angel, and euill Angel*]
> (A 637-38)

Marlowe immediately compounds this moment of Faustus' "resolution" by bringing on the choral voices of the two Angels, and it is again the Good Angel who has the first, and the bad Angel who has the last word. Faustus' disturbance is now unmistakable; he tells us that he can hear voices in his ears ("But feareful ecchoes thunders in mine eares") and goes on to envision his despair in images of suicide. Yet if we ask what kind of knowledge of sin Faustus actually has, we only find him entangled in unstructured emotional utterances and paradoxical evasions

> Who buzzeth in mine eares I am a spirite?

> Be I a diuel, yet God may pitty me,
> I God wil pitty me, if I repent.
> (A 643-45)

which shift the focus from the doctrinal to the psychological. His search for answers, as so often, turns inward, to the divided self ("My hearts so hardned I cannot repent, / Scarce can I name ...") and its treacherous wishing-dreading circuits. Hardly noticing the exit of the Angels, we are caught up with Faustus' meandering speech, the longest one (20 lines) given to him in the entire second Act.

Fear of damnation, desire to repent, inability to do so, the dread of wanting to do *something* - Faustus' conflict-ridden experience of what he can and cannot do again moves into the foreground and augments the central theatrical emotion of his *creating* all this out of his mind and making it a "present" that the audience shares with him. Such creating and sharing, of course, moves beyond the suggestion (the Bad Angel's) that Faustus is a "spirite"; as we observe Faustus' very human agony we feel that we - like Faustus - must hold on to the theoretical possibility of repentance and salvation. Like the Good and Bad Angels, or the Old Man and Helen, hope for escape and dread are always co-present. Like heaven and hell, radically disjoined fictive polarities can in fact become mutually sustaining correlatives, and Faustus' impassioned battling with his "deepe dispaire" is intellectually arresting and challenging enough to make us willingly grant the suspense of its conclusion.

All allusions to salvation, however, are highly tentative, poised between "if" and "may". Yet Faustus, empowered by a mind that can transform the context of death itself into an imaginative fusion of past, present, and future, suddenly rises to the sublime heights of what are surely some of the most beautiful verse lines in the whole play:

> And long ere this I should haue slaine my selfe,
> Had not sweete pleasure conquerd deepe dispaire.
> Haue not I made blinde Homer sing to me,
> Of Alexanders loue, and Enons death,

>   And hath not he that built the walles of Thebes,
>   With rauishing sound of his melodious harp
>   Made musicke with my Mephastophilis?
>   Why should I dye then ...
>   (A 653-60)

Brief and full of resonance, encapsulated by the more prosaic contemplations of Faustus' mind, those five lines in the centre of the speech (8 lines leading up to the central lines, 7 lines leading away from them) leap upward and transcend all constraints that the tragic rhetoric of loss and despair, death and limitation, had established. The evocation of the classical bards, "blinde Homer" and Amphion, and their songs of an ancient heroic past ("Alexanders loue"; "Enons death"; "the walles of Thebes")[7] are, in one sense, the movement of a momentary perception or idealized remembrance. In another sense, the exhilarating freedom of mind that is revealed in these verses, is largely an effect of the poetry itself - an essentially poetic, that is, structural effect which leaves "character" and "plot" behind and creates one of those "angelic moments"[8] John Bayley discovers in Shakespeare's tragedies.

I would add that it is certainly wrong to consider it only as a "pure" moment of formal beauty; the poetic figuration *is* operative in terms of its dramatic context because we experience its beauty precisely through our awareness that it arises from the hero's haunted imagination which in this singular moment achieves the "translation" (metaphorization) of "sweete pleasure" into a

---

[7] In a curious anticipation of the apostrophe to Helen of Troy ("I wil be Paris, and for loue of thee, / Insteede of Troy shal Wertenberge be sackt"), Faustus' metaphor of musical and erotic transport projects a scene of catastrophes in the distant past. The Alexander referred to is not the conqueror, but Homer's Paris who was in love with Oenone before he fatally encountered Helen. Wounded in the Trojan War, Paris was then carried to Oenone and died at her feet, whereupon Oenone stabbed herself (cf. *Iliad* XXIV; the Paris-Oenone story is post-Homeric and reported mainly in Lycophon, Quintus Smyrnaeus, and Apollodorus).

[8] *Shakespeare and Tragedy*, pp. 10 ff.

"secure" transcendent harmony of vision, feeling, and melodic sound. The sound and resonance of these verses, and the particular stylistic features within the framework of the blank verse, tell us a lot about the continuing fascination of Marlowe's mighty line. J.G. Lawler, in his ambitious and often diffuse meditations on "poetic structures of transcendence," contends that the particular linguistic collisions in such Marlovian passages as the one I just quoted symbolize a kind of "aspiring reconciliation point" or "nexus" of the "finite-infinite, immanent-transcendent."[9] Lawler concentrates on *Tamburlaine* and observes the fascinating undular movements of sound in Marlowe's verse, which gain their particular intensifications through the play of syllabic juxtapositions and the frequent terminal placement of Latinate or proper names. The sound-pattern in the "blinde Homer" passage is equally fascinating. The slightly altered, parallel structure of questions ("Haue not I ..."/"hath not he ...") suggest a slowly rising pitch towards the end of the second and fifth lines, and within each double line (1-2/3-4) the second line is built around the collisions of polysyllables and monosyllables ("Alexanders loue ... Enons death"/"rauishing sound ... melodious harp"). This pattern expresses its musical value especially through its strong rhythmic qualities and the consonant repetitions ("th","l","n", and, particularly, "m"), and the sound of the "m" becomes almost hypnotic in the final line which builds up its monosyllables towards the climactic, polysyllabic, outstretching "Mephastophilis."

Lawler may be right in claiming that this modulating effect and the movement from the closed monosyllabic to the open-ended polysyllabic sound conveys something of that peculiar "*longueur infinie*"[10] that is central to Faustus' ordeal, a longing that is confirmed immediately by Faustus' turning towards "diuine Astro-

---

9 Justus George Lawler, *Celestial Pantomime: Poetic Structures of Transcendence* (New Haven: Yale Univ. Press, 1979), pp. 170-82.

10 Ibid., p. 182. The expression of such longing in the stylistic structure (esp. the terminal polysyllables) is very frequent in *Tamburlaine*. Cf. the famous lines: "Is it not passing brave to be a king,/And ride in triumph through Persepolis?"

logie." I am more interested, however, in the theatrical effect
of the "rauishing sound" of poetry and its place in the continuum
of the scene. It seems to me that this brilliantly expressive
moment of Faustus' self-hypnotizing inwardness draws attention to
itself mainly as another transition (however short-lived, as we
shall see), a revealing manoeuvre of the mind's power to extricate
itself from the horrors of "deepe dispaire" and achieve sublimity
in the trance-like harmony with the ancients and with "my Mephastophilis." As a transition from dejection to a new "resolution"
it is tenuous enough, and it could have easily gone into a different direction; theatrically, Faustus' resolution ("I am resolu'd
Faustus shal nere repent" A 661) prepares the contrapuntal effect
achieved by the quite different reversal that is to follow shortly.

II.

> Come Mephastophilis, let vs dispute againe,
> And argue of diuine Astrologie,
> Tel me, are there many heauens aboue the Moone?
> (A 662-64)

Faustus' third attempt to have an "argument" with "his" Mephostophilis is particularly interesting because it opens up a topic
which lies at the opposite pole of his previous interrogations
about hell and, finally, seems to press towards the claims on
unprecedented, forbidden knowledge that he originally had. His
initial questions show that he is of course venturing upon astronomy, and not "Astrologie." The matter is different, however,
if we think of Marlowe's source; as one learns from the Spies-*Faustbuch*, Johann Faust operated on the level of astrologers,
calendar-makers, and weather-forecasters. Among the anecdotes of
his magical feats and terrestrial wanderings, there is one rather
grotesque description of a supernatural journey ("Wie Doct.Faustus in das Gestirn hinauff gefahren" chap.XXV) in a letter which
Faust writes to a fellow-scholar and in which he renders his
personal observations of the sky and the planets. Although he

appears overwhelmed by his impressions ("Ich sahe also mehr dann ich begerte"),[11] his account is a dull, miscellaneous jumble of unscientific information. It is known that P.F., in his English translation, often expanded, condensed, diverged, or interpolated whenever he felt the urge to do so, yet it has generally been overlooked that he transforms his source at a very crucial point:

> ... and we thinke that the Sunne runneth his course, and that the heauens stand still: no, it is the heauens that moue his course, and the Sun abideth perpetually in his place, he is permanent and fixed in his place, and although we see him beginning to ascend ... yet he moueth not.

Expecting to hear more, we find Faustus' discourse suddenly interrupted by the English translator's authorial intrusion:

> Yea Christian Reader, to the glory of God, and for the profite of thy soule, I wil open vnto thee the diuine opinion touching the ruling of this confused Chaos, farre more than any rude Germane Author, being possessed with the diuell, was able to vtter....[12]

P.F., however, closes what he had opened and retreats behind a paraphrase of Genesis which after a while merges again with the closing remarks of Faustus' letter. After having first brought up the Faustian "discovery" of the place of the sun in the universe, he counters it with rather safe "diuine opinion." The tension between the traditional cosmology and the one that is suppressed here (Copernicus' new astronomical speculations were published in 1543; Thomas Digges revised and expounded the theory in England in the mid-1570s) is employed for very special effects in Marlowe's handling of the dramatic dialogue between Faustus and Mephostophilis.

> *Fau.* Tel me, are there many heauens aboue the Moone?
> Are all celestiall bodies but one globe,
> As is the substance of this centricke earth?
> *Me.* As are the elements, such are the spheares,
> Mutually folded in each others orbe,

---

11 *Historia von D. Johann Fausten*, chap. XXV. I quote from H. Henning's edition of the 1587 text (Halle: Verlag Sprache und Literatur, 1963), p. 63.
12 *The Historie*, chap. XXI (Palmer and More, pp. 172f.).

>   And Faustus all iointly moue vpon one axletree,
>   Whose termine is tearmd the worlds wide pole,
>   Nor are the names of Saturne, Mars, or Iupiter
>   Faind, but are erring starres.
> Fau. But tell me, haue they all one motion? both
>   *situ & tempore.*
> Me. All ioyntly moue from East to West in 24. houres
>   vpon the poles of the world, but differ in their
>   motion vpon the poles of the Zodiake.
> Fau. Tush, these slender trifles Wagner can decide,
>   Hath Mephastophilus no greater skill?
>   (A 664-79)

Marlowe knows exactly what he is doing here. It is, of course, a moment of utmost suspense, and Faustus and his audience may obviously expect to hear revelatory, exciting news from Mephostophilis. It is clear from Faustus' tentative, cunning manner of phrasing his questions and from his emphasis on the catch word "centricke earth" that he is out to test the devil and to assert his wish for privileged knowledge that is free from the sanctions of "diuine opinion."

One probably ought to be less surprised about Marlowe's very subtle treatment of this scene than about the astonishing literal-mindedness of its commentators who by and large fail to catch the playwright's dramaturgical intentions. From the overloaded textual notes that this passage has earned by most editors, it can be deduced how startled we are meant to be by the conspicuous absence of the Copernican theory and by the inexplicable faltering of Marlowe's supposed "Renaissance scepticism." Very likely, these editorial qualms go back to Paul Kocher, who devotes an entire chapter ("Astronomy and Metereology")[13] of his book to the desperate search for a passage, a phrase, even a word that might prove Marlowe to be a "sceptic" after all. One can sense the heart-felt grief in Kocher's words, when he sums up that "one would like to be able to say that Marlowe's plays, so keenly in the forefront of religious controversy, were equally eloquent of the current issues in astronomy between the rival sys-

---

13 *Christopher Marlowe*, pp. 213-40.

tems of Ptolemy and Copernicus."[14] It seems hardly questionable, however, that the dramatic articulation of the hero's power of eloquence and power of mind in the *Tamburlaine* plays serves precisely to erase the conceptual and spatial limitations that are intrinsic to the older cosmology or "world-picture" and to represent Tamburlaine's mighty conquests as formative acts of the will: stretching beyond the limiting possibilities of an environing world and imposing on them *infinite* subjective designs.

In *Dr Faustus*, Marlowe's hero enacts the same battle of will and imagination in his own intellectual world of "ambiguities" and unpleasant "doctrines." Faustus' hyperbolic projections of his infinite "world of profit and delight, / Of power, of honor, of omnipotence" imply the same fervent attempt to break through to new frontiers of knowledge and power, although Marlowe creates a different epistemological problem for Faustus by having him pursue his desired goals with the help of "heavenly negromancy." And as we have seen, Marlowe places Faustus in a context entirely different from Tamburlaine's by formally building up a sufficiently strong, closed world of medieval order (represented explicitly by Mephostophilis' account of the traditional cosmos) and accepted doctrine (represented through the play's rhetoric of Protestant theology), in the presence of which Faustus' transgressions of ethical, logical, and metaphysical delimitation take up a more universal and symbolic meaning.

Although the religious orientation of the play makes Faustus' fatal pursuit of magic revolve around an explicitly theological axis, for which the *Good* and *Bad* Angels, Heaven and Hell, indeed represent the opposite "termines" (to use Mephostophilis' expression), Marlowe's dramaturgy uses this "terministic" reduction mainly to focus on the psychic dimension of the dialectical conflict between Faustus' aspirations and freedoms and the innate limitations and external oppositions they strive to overcome. In view of the tragic equilibrium which Marlowe sustains in the play,

---

14 Kocher, p. 213.

it would make little sense to expect him to have Mephostophilis, of all people, expound the "modern" cosmology of Copernicus and Digges or instruct Faustus in Giordano Bruno's cosmological philosophy of the infinite - thus nullifying the pressures that up to this point had been operating against Faustus' extravagant claims on behalf of magic. His disregard of the conspicuous moment in P.F.'s Faustbook suggests that he designed the argument about "diuine Astrologie" for a different purpose. Above all, it is quite consistent with his presentation of Mephostophilis that he makes him answer *less* than Faustus has "wit to aske." And it is of course a marvellous joke that Mephostophilis would give Faustus a compelling version of the old Aristotelain-Ptolemaic cosmos, that splendidly harmonious picture of the universe whose centre is the earth, enclosed within a series of concentric spheres. The devil discloses no "evil" knowledge but, ironically, presents Faustus with the most readily available commonplace notions about the old, pre-Copernican universe.

As a part of the conceptual working of the play, Mephostophilis' presentation of Christian cosmology as an authoritative map, which charts the metaphysical and physical limitations imposed upon man from all sides, regardless of his subjective stance or ethos, serves to re-emphasize once again the collision of two incompatible value-systems. Faustus' personal desires express themselves with an unpredictable and independent theatrical power, having always already denied the spiritual and intellectual delimitations provided by the play's inflexible doctrinal perspective. The doctrinal superstructure, like an immovable "imperiall" outer sphere, is always there too, however, and Marlowe very ingeniously employs the picture of the old cosmos to correlate Faustus' damnation to his temporal and spatial entrapment in a *finite universe*. (The experience of this temporal and spatial enclosure is dramatized most memorably in the final damnation scene.)

As a metaphorical construct, Mephostophilis' laconic description of the cosmos sounds not altogether different from his earlier declaration of the ubiquitousness of hell; and both accounts have ontological implications for Faustus' "place" ("All places shall be hell that is not heauen"), in so far as they presuppose a universe which in its Scholastic-Aristotelian structure denotes space or place as a function of being. A fixed centre, or "centricke earth", in turn implies a definite order of "above" and "below", and this order confers absolute values of being to all the parts and relationships among parts within it. Mephostophilis' account of the movement and direction of the planets, in other words, reflects a process of perception and empirical knowledge for which the Scholastic-Aristotelian universe presented an absolute frame of reference.

Mephostophilis' insistence on a static hierarchy of being in an ordered, intelligible, and closed universe runs of course counter to everything Faustus had exulted in: infinite imaginative space, boundless possibilities, the desired power to accomplish a multitude of things and to become a multitude of beings. On the surface, the collision is dramatized in an intriguing and subtle rhetorical duel. In a stoically patient and almost exasperatingly perfunctory manner, Mephostophilis answers Faustus' questions with "yes" or "no", a commonplace here, and a text-book quotation there. Faustus is well aware that he is only hearing "slender trifles", and at one point he cannot control his anger and proceeds to give the standard "fresh mens" answer himself. One can feel, however, that he changes his tactic after this outburst; having realized that the devil will resolve nothing of importance, Faustus assumes a similar, and even more ironic, academic attitude:

> *Fau.* Well, resolue me in this question, why haue wee not coniunctions, oppositions, aspects, eclipsis, all at one time, but in some yeares we haue more, in some less?
> *Me.* *Per inaequalem motum respectu totius.*
> *Fau.* Well, I am answered ...

Of course, he is not answered. In performance, the unresolved tension between the two actors should come across very vividly;

as the text indicates, the entire academic debate about astronomy leads nowhere and must come to appear as a complete disappointment and dead end to Faustus. The actor of Faustus should express his outburst of anger and frustration as pointedly as the subsequent effort to calm down and to prepare himself for the unexpected climax of this whole argument:

>... tell me who made the world?
>(A 690-94)

Not only is he deliberately raising a question that he knows will annoy his partner; it is also the *manner* in which he shifts within a single line from the perfunctory "Well, I am answered" to his sudden, momentous question that makes it so tremendously effective. It is obvious what an actor can do with an abrupt, unsignalled change of direction - perplexing the devil with what may have been the most important question of all for Faustus, a question that puts Mephostophilis quite awkwardly on the spot. Although the question itself is of course entirely rhetorical, since he had never denied God's existence and creatorship and in fact affirms them at this very point ("Thinke Faustus vpon God that made the world" A 701), the fact that he does ask it tells us a great deal about his frustration and his extremely uneasy relationship to the truth of what is here implicitly acknowledged.

The name of God itself remains a peculiarly strong blocking-agent ("Scarce can I name saluation, faith, or heauen"), and it seems as if he wanted to force it out of Mephostophilis' mouth ("Sweete Mephastophilis tell me"; "Villaine, haue I not bound thee to tel me anything?" A 696;698). Mephostophilis' inability to pronounce the name of God and Faustus' angry, demanding behaviour result in a furious quarrel which triggers a series of hectic, unexpected theatrical activities. When their strife culminates in mutual recriminations, the baffled Mephostophilis hurries offstage to storm back to Lucifer, and Faustus flings a phrase after him that shows how much he must have become aware of the threatening presence of his daemon:

>   I, goe accursed spirit to vgly hell,
>   Tis thou hast damn'd distressed Faustus soule:
>   Ist not too late?
>   (A 703-05)

At this point, the A-text requests the last entry of the two
Angels, and apart from their problematic echoing of Faustus'
question "Ist not too late?", there is a significant change in
the presentation of their exchange.

>   *Euill A.* Too late
>   *Good A.* Neuer too late, if Faustus can repent.
>   *Euill A.* If thou repent diuels shall teare thee in peeces.
>   *Good A.* Repent, & they shal neuer race thy skin. [*Exeunt*]
>   (A 707-10)

It is left open whether Faustus has fully perceived his mistaken
course, what he means by "too late", and how he upholds any
apprehension of the possibility of salvation. Is it too late
and not too late? Although the two Angels seem to echo precisely this logical paradox, their rhetoric purports contradictory
answers to Faustus' question, which are more ambiguous and confusing than commentators have generally assumed. It helps very
little to look for doctrinal propriety and grant the Good Angel
theological orthodoxy of expression, especially since his form-
ualtion "*if* Faustus *can* repent" ("if Faustus *will* repent" B 649,
emphases mine) is alarmingly subjunctive. From his own perspective on what is orthodox and what is not, W.W. Greg finds the
A-text's "can" unacceptable because "it is not a matter of the
possibility of repentance - that is assumed - but of the will to
repent."[15] The distinction between "can" and "will" is hardly

---

15 *Marlowe's Doctor Faustus 1604-1616*, p. 45. In his search for
discriminations between the A and B texts, Greg argues for
the "correctness" of the 1616 version on the grounds that A's
variants, such as in the case of A's "can" for B's "will",
are less valid or consistent because they lack theological exactness, propriety of expression, metrical regularity, stylistic quality, etc. Yet such exactness or propriety is often
dependent on Greg's preconceived view of the "correct" play
and its language in the first place, and his claims for the
superiority of B (cf. pp.44-46) could be easily refuted.

that unequivocal, however, because we cannot even be sure, first
of all, how colloquially the word "can" is used here and how we
are to read "will" (to "want", or simple futurity?). Moreover,
I should think that whatever the textual circumstances may be, it
is precisely the possibility of Faustus' repentance which is at
stake here and which presents the central theological problem of
the play anyhow. Superficially, the two Angels urge both the
uselessness and the effectiveness of repentance, and one could
endlessly discuss the theoretical implications of their statements in the light of contemporary doctrine. It may very well
be true that an audience will take the possibility of salvation
as an integral part of the play, at least as long as the internal
cause-end-effect structure has not been ultimately resolved, and
hold on to the idea that a penitent Faustus is conceivable or,
in the words of Peter Martyr, that "there is none so farre past
grace, but that some hope remaineth, that he may be called home
into the right way."[16]

Yet how much hope does Faustus have? With regard to the play's
Calvinist frame of reference, the question has to be related to
Faustus' private consciousness, and Marlowe's theatrical notation
clearly reinforces the ambiguity that such reference implies.
Both the Good and Bad Angels' voices should express the equivocal
and dangerous sense contained in their lines, and the actors'
physical gestures could support this. The Good Angel, on the one
hand, assures Faustus that it is never too late "if Faustus can
repent", clearly hinting at the possibility that he cannot. Such
"good" council could practically serve to intensify Faustus' fear,
because there is the vexing question, at least in Faustus' mind,
whether he can repent even if he wanted to. On the other hand,
the Bad Angel decides to discontinue his mocking counter-thrusts

---

16 *Common Places*, p. 474. Judging from the more rigorous Calvinist doctrine of repentance and grace, very little hope was
conceivable, however, and the *gift* of grace remained utterly
outside the possibilities of the reprobate. Cf. Becon, *The
Early Works*, p. 93; Calvin, *Institutes*, III.3.2; I.18.2: and
Perkins, *Workes*, I, 455-57; 468; II, 422.

and, instead, threatens him outright ("diuels shall teare thee in peeces"). For the first time, however, Marlowe changes the sequence of the Angels' lines which he had upheld so far. At this point, it is the Good Angel who has the exit line and leaves Faustus on a reassuring note. After the Angels have left, the action almost comes to another complete standstill; at least, Marlowe's dramaturgy allows for a few moments of silence, during which audience attention is re-focussed on the protagonist who is now completely alone onstage and who seems ready to make a first step out of the chaos of mixed emotions, a vital step one should think.

The result is the play's *peripeteia* - a brilliant theatrical moment which is as unexpected as it is perplexing:

> *Fau.* Ah Christ my Sauiour,
>   Seeke to saue distressed Faustus soule.
>   [*Enter Lucifer, Belsabub, and Mephastophilus*]
> *Lu.* Christ cannot saue thy soule, for he is iust,
>   Theres none but I haue intrest in the same.
>   (A 711-15)

I think it cannot be denied that such an uncanny, diabolical response to Faustus' outcry must trouble our moral sensibilities at least as strongly as it turns Faustus' expectations upside down. Max Bluestone, who has most comprehensively dealt with the doctrinal explanations this episode can afford, concludes that the infernal answer to Faustus' "heavenly" prayer enacts an oxymoron that cannot ultimately be judged in available doctrinal perspectives.[17] Most commentators have tried very hard, however, to explain away what I think is clearly meant to be a relatively cynical challenge to orthodox morality or, at the least, a consummate theatrical expression of the irreducible conflict between the tragedy of Faustus' mind and the play's doctrinal frame of reference. Those critics who take the sudden appearance of the infernal trinity "seriously," as a doctrinal statement that is to

---

17 Cf. Bluestone, *"Libido Speculandi,"* pp. 65-69.

say, have to come to terms with the fact that the Bad Angel was
right after all; it was "too late" for Faustus to repent. Kocher,
Greg, Campbell, Cole, Smith, and Westlund, among others, more or
less agree that Faustus' repentance is ineffective because he has
not really repented.[18] To remain on orthodox grounds, they have
to argue with the Good Angel ("Faustus, repent yet, God wil pitty
thee" A 641) to the effect that Christ would indeed help a truly
contrite Faustus. Yet Marlowe's text allows for the theatrical
realization of precisely such an act of contrition and repentant
prayer. The Faustus-actor could easily take his earlier lines
about God the creator and about his "distressed soule" as an implicit text-direction; the pause between the Angels' exit and
the devils' entry is long enough for him to express his remorse
by vivid gestures, by kneeling down and crossing himself, and by
placing utmost emphasis on his urgent appeal for grace ("Ah Christ
my Sauiour ..."). Dramaturgically, this moment could indeed be
transformed into a compelling representation of Faustus' emotional
break-down, his reaching out for divine grace, his submission to
Christ (it is the first time in the play that Faustus actually
names "his" Saviour).

Such an intense enactment of this moment of crisis is bound to
create an enormous amount of tension in the theatre, which would
be increased if there was a short period of absolute silence after
Faustus' anguished outcry. Marlowe carefully manipulates audience
expectation until it is at its highest peak, and it is of course
not clear at all at this moment what is going to happen, although
the Calvinist perspective in the play allows us to say, in retrospect, that the dramatic suspense in this situation is achieved
paradoxically, since there is no suspenseful situation conceivable
in view of Faustus' deliberate self-reprobation. The Calvinist
view would dispense with the circular reasoning that one must,

---

18 Cf. Kocher, pp. 108-15; Cole, p. 213; Greg, "The Damnation,"
    99; Campbell, "A Case of Conscience," 238; James Smith, "Marlowe's *Dr Faustus*," *Scrutiny*, 8 (1939), 47-48; and Joseph Westlund, "The Orthodox Christian Framework of Marlowe's *Faustus*,"
    SEL, 3 (1963), 199.

otherwise, construe in order to obscure the fact that Marlowe presents us a praying, clearly "distressed" Faustus, pleading for grace and not receiving it. Can we say, then, that Marlowe's superb *coup de théâtre* – the sudden entrance of the infernal trinity – is one of the tragedy's most provocative expressions of a strongly Calvinist-oriented pessimism? It is in fact rather ironic to ask oneself how much of a choice Faustus actually has if he cannot go "forward" without necessarily being damned, and if he cannot go "backward" either without necessarily being reminded that he is damned anyway.

"Thinke thou on hell Faustus, for thou art damnd" (A 700), Mephostophilis tells him a few minutes before "great Lucifer" appears to tell him the same again, merely putting it in a different way: "Christ *cannot saue* thy soule, for he is *iust*" (A 714, emphasis mine). In view of the play's doctrinal cosmos, in which everything is "Mutually folded in each others orbe" and "iointly moue[s] vpon one axletree", the tragic determinism which underlies these infernal utterances and is endorsed by the dramatic action comes close to making theological sense. It does so only in a very perplexing way, however, and one would want to believe that Lucifer's rhetoric ("Christ *cannot* saue thy soule") is utterly deceptive. And, in a way, so it is. While the play seems to drive very radically towards an acknowledgement of Faustus' predicament, it also pursues a radical and often subversive inconclusiveness by using dramatic spectacle to undermine the moral meanings one would normally have to rely on.

As my discussion of the performance dynamics suggests, *Dr Faustus* is a complicated and vexing play which cannot at all be seen as a world of moral judgment; it requires a method and a vocabulary that can explore its rhetorical organization and dramatic style in their complex, shifting engagement with audience responsiveness. Marlowe's use of theological, rhetorical, and logical paradoxy in the "repentance"-episode can perhaps give us an idea of the extent to which he is pushing the subversive function of spectacle. Similar to the Old Man episode, the argument about "diuine Astrologie" prepares for and leads into the crucial incident of Faustus' prayer, which I think is deliberately choreographed to arouse expectations of the kind that are fulfilled in the conversion moments of the traditional morality play or, let us say, in the renunciations of magic by the Friar Bacons and Prosperos. Marlowe, however, arouses them only to break them apart with his curious, *sprezzatura*-like gests.

> O who art thou that lookst so terrible?
> . . .
> O Faustus, they are come to fetch away thy soule.
> (A 716;718)

Faustus clearly *is* terrified. The shock of incredulity would find its strongest performance expression in Faustus' facial and gestic reactions to the unknown visitors' sudden emergence from the trapdoor, if he were to kneel upstage - directly facing their rise in centre stage. Or we may visualize Faustus kneeling downstage, facing outward. The greatest shock-surprise could be achieved if there was a slight pause after Faustus' intense prayer and if he - still in the downstage position - was unaware that the infernal trinity suddenly rises behind his back, again, conceivably, through the trapdoor from below the stage.

This is what A's stage-directions basically allow for, and most of the *Faustus* productions I saw rendered the event in a deftly marked and sinister way.[19] Less convincing in its immediate impact yet even more extravagant in its upsettingly ironic visual symbolism, the B version can suggest a different staging method that would be consistent with the paradoxical onstage presence of the devils during Faustus' conjuration in I.iii. Comparing the spatial designs of these two stage events, one could argue that Faustus' conjuration ("*Faustus to them with this speech*" s.d. B 226) could make sense in the B version, if we conjecture

---

19 The sinister aspects of this reversal scene were particularly strong in the Lyric Studio production and in the more recent Royal Exchange Theatre production in Manchester. The Manchester production was directed by Adrian Noble and ran

that the devils are present on the upper stage but not actually
seen by Faustus. If we now link this with the theatrically anal-
ogous moment of Faustus' prayer, the ironic ambiguities of the
spectacle abound, of course, but the audience will notice the
subtle division which Marlowe suggests and which the B-text elaborates in its more conspicuous dumb-shows: the audience of B
sees what Faustus himself apprehends in the actual world and also
what is "actually" happening in the supernatural-diabolical world.
B extends the impression of an elaborate infernal conspiracy
against Faustus' "distressed soule" and subordinates psychological
realism to a more cynical, anti-mimetic orientation toward a
macabre allegorization of the evil protagonists from Hell. They
appear to be omnipresent and vigilant, ready to trap the "glorious soule" they have an interest in. Mephostophilis' promise that
"experience" will change Faustus' mind can be rendered ironically
explicit if the staging emphasizes the impression that Faustus'
self-abandonment to the "suburbs of hell" has once and for all
resulted in the phenomenally enclosing ubiquitousness of the devils who could be shown to dominate all spatial levels of the
theatre.

Adapting this interpretation of the B-text as performance concept,
the Oregon Festival production gave the "prayer"-scene a sensational look. The Faustus-actor had collapsed on the platform, gasp-
ing his plea for help ("O Christ my Sauiour, my Sauiour, / Helpe
to saue distressed Faustus soule" B 652-53), when a furious-look-
ing Lucifer, dressed as a stunningly white angel, appeared "above"
in the gallery. Almost parallel to the shining Lucifer's *descent*
to the lower platform, his two companion devils appeared from
different directions: Mephostophilis slowly advanced from upstage
left, whereas right next to the sprawling Faustus the trap-door
was flung open with a bang, and an evil-faced, ugly Belzebub rose
from the smoke-filled pit. Lucifer's first lines were spoken con-
temptuously and full of subdued anger (which was in part also dir-

---

from September 17 to October 24, 1981. Cf. Russell Jackson,
"*Doctor Faustus* in Manchester," *CritQ*, 23, no.4 (1981), 3-9.

ected at Mephostophilis!); the performance came very close to suggesting that Lucifer indeed cites Christ's retributive justice at this point in order to taunt Faustus for lacking divine grace. W.W. Greg, incidentally, would have certainly appreciated this production approach since he regards Lucifer's recitation of Christ's justice as a sign of "admirable logic" which merely confirms the fact that Faustus is damned from the moment he became a "spirit in form and substance" and "took on an infernal nature." Greg, astonishingly literal-minded in this case, contradicts himself repeatedly in the course of his argument,[20] since his preference for the B version leads him to claim that B's "Helpe to saue distressed Faustus soule" must be correct whereas A's "Seeke to saue distressed Faustus soule" is doctrinally inappropriate. He glosses: "To seek to do something implies a doubtful issue: but whereas it is heretical to question Christ's power to save, it is true belief that that power is only exercised in aid of the sinner's own endeavour."[21] Greg's own logic can hardly be called admirable as he first transforms Faustus into an orthodox Christian (completely disregarding the contextual validity of Faustus' formulation in A), and then decides that Faustus' "true belief" in the proper act of repentance cannot save him anyway.

In any case, the devils in both A and B continue to make a mockery out of Faustus' belief that he in fact *had* repented ("they are come to fetch away thy soule"). It seems to me that Marlowe invests a great deal of ingenuity into the theatricality of what is basically a hopelessly paradoxical and perverse situation. Obscuring or confusing the theological issues, Marlowe's spectacle seems devised to equivocate what he in fact accepted as the working idea of his tragedy: Faustus' irrevocable self-damnation. The drama of Faustus' psychic struggle spirals towards the turning-point of the prayer and the subsequent appearance of Lucifer during which Marlowe's spectacle puzzles the audience to a degree

---

20 "The Damnation of Faustus," 98-100.
21 *Marlowe's Doctor Faustus 1604-1616*, p. 46.

where all assumptions about the turning-point become questionable, contradictory, and arbitrary. Faustus' problems double back upon themselves, begin anew, remain frustratingly unresolvable.

> Nor will I henceforth: pardon me in this,
> And Faustus vowes neuer to looke to heauen,
> Neuer to name God, or to pray to him,
> To burne his Scriptures, slay his Ministers,
> And make my spirites pull his churches downe.
> (A 724-28; not in B)

Faustus here explicitly admits to having prayed to God, and this confession also explains the horror he felt at the moment when the devils appeared to answer his repentant prayer. Expecting them to carry out the diabolic threat, Faustus is understandably cowed, and the dramaturgy of the A-text focusses all our attention on the direct, awkward confrontation between Faustus and Lucifer. Surrounded by the silently watching Belzebub and Mephostophilis, Faustus stands face to face with "great Lucifer" and learns that the devils have *not* come to fetch his soul but merely to remind him of his "promise."

Marlowe leads Faustus as well as the audience through tormenting circles of unreason, and Faustus' break-down and pathetic repentance to Lucifer is about as irrational as everything else in this spectacular scene. Lucifer's sarcastic absolution, "Do so,/ And we will highly gratify thee" (A 728-29)[22] is actually too disturbingly real, too suggestive of the world of invisible nightmare into which Faustus' confirmed allegiance to Lucifer pushes him, to become dislocated by the actual gratifications that the devils have in store. Yet Marlowe has already begun with a process of dislocation which teases and belies the tragic atmosphere of the play by its indulgence in the diabolical topsy-turvydom and by its transpositions of tone, which move away from the centre of the tragedy towards its peripheries - towards uneasy

---

22 The B-text's over-explicit reference to Faustus' "servitude" ("So shalt thou show thy selfe an obedient seruant" B 667) looks like a revisionary interpolation which has a degrading touch to it that we would hardly find in the A-text.

combinations of burlesque, melodrama, slapstick, and sheer farcical nonsense.

III.

The episodes which occupy the play's middle section, and their textual status in particular, have always posed problems for interpretation, and it may not ultimately be possible to determine how much of them was written by Marlowe, and how much of the extended B version was in fact added at a later stage (the 1602 "adicyones" by Birde and Rowley; further theatrical revisions are likely). I would be content to regard the 1604 scenes as a perfectly acceptable version of what Marlowe might have written and what was originally performed. It is also indisputable that the play, as it stands, can be given unity and coherence (if that is what we are looking for), and the middle part does not deserve the kind of dismissive apologies it usually earns by critics who complain about its triviality and the inexplicable "collapse" of the tragedy, conveniently attributed, of course, to the incompetent "collaborator."

It is as useless to condemn the "buffoonery" of the middle scenes, as it is unhelpful, I believe, to accept these sections as intrinsic in their relationship to the tragic scenes but interpret their impact as merely a symbolization of Faustus' moral deterioration and descent onto the "great stage of fools."[23] Roma Gill, who devotes her attention specifically to the comic scenes, suggests that

> Marlowe left enough pointers to indicate that the middle of his tragedy should be anticlimactic, faithful to its source in the English Faustbook and showing Faustus' in-

---

23 Weil, *Merlin's Prophet*, pp. 65 ff. Most commentators who discuss the thematic relation between the comedy and the tragedy take the middle scenes to be deflationary and see them as providing a satiric mirror in which Faustus' degradation and the stupidity of his sin can be perceived. For a more critical view of their structural significance, see Bluestone, 47f.

creasing disillusion with the vanity of his human
wishes, and frustration at the limitations of supernatural (diabolic) knowledge. Comedy was inevitable.[24]

I am interested here in the idea of the "collapse" of the tragedy and in its connections to the paradoxical spectacle of Lucifer's appearance upon Faustus' prayer. Roma Gill's contention that after this everything "should be anticlimactic" may be correct in a certain sense. The idea of the "anti-climax" seems to closely related to a moral view of the action, however; and such a view of "Faustus' increasing disillusion with the vanity of his human wishes" is not entirely supported by the playtext. And why should we think that comedy was inevitable?

I think there ought to be different ways of responding to Faustus' astronomical and cosmographic journeys, to the theatrical effects and the shows of the middle section which have tremendous variety and richness, and to the dislocation of tragic mode and tone that I already mentioned. We should not forget, either, that the play is very conscious of its symbolic use of space and time, and Marlowe interrupts the "comic" mode at least twice (A 1134-42; 1169-74) in order to present a short moment of spiritual crisis in which Faustus reflects upon his twenty-four year contract and realizes that he is inexorably advancing closer to the "finall ende" (A 1170). These short flashes of recognition point forward to the final crisis (after his return to Wittenberg) and re-introduce the theme of despair that had been suppressed in the "comic" scenes. Before his conjuration of Helen and the final *agon* lie his terrestrial and superterrestrial journeys, and the spaces represented on the stage are the courts of the Pope, the Emperor, and the Duke of Vanholt. This triad is structurally complemented by the insertion of three further incidents: the tavern scene, the Knight scene, and the Horse-Courser episode.

This short overview already shows that one can hardly speak of a structural or conceptual "collapse." As I suggested earlier, Mar-

---

24 Gill, "Comedy and *Dr Faustus*," p. 56.

lowe clearly thinks in terms of a circular pattern (which does not exclude a progressive movement in time), and Faustus' circular journey toward the catastrophic fulfilment of his damnation ends where it began, in his little "study" in Wittenberg, in his conjuring circle, where he will embrace the shadow of Helen before finally facing his irremediable estrangement from God and the painful consequences of his lost battle with life and time.

The dramaturgical emphasis on changing space and time, the rapid movement of scenes that vary greatly in spatial location and in theatrical impact, generates a sense of mixture and motion which stands in direct relation to the fact that Faustus' pact is a symbol of his circumscription, that it commits him to exactly twenty-four years of life and a definite time of death. In a sense, the entire movement and spatial sweep of the middle sections conflict with the theologically and metaphysically enclosed circuit that is alluded to by the Bad Angel's "Too late" (in the prayer scene) and by Faustus' "now tis too late" (in the farewell scene with the Scholars). These two moments of spiritual crisis mark the pivotal points in between which Faustus' adventures and pastimes inhabit the stage and, as I would suggest, represent one huge, extended paradox. It is as if Marlowe advances the Bad Angel's psychologically powerful suggestion that prayer and repentance are "illusions, fruits of lunacy, / That makes men foolish that do trust them most" to a point where he can almost literally translate it into the stage spectacle of Lucifer's shocking arrival, only to turn the whole situation around and make us slowly apprehend that this little, perverse allegory is not to be taken seriously. The very fact that Faustus' spiritual dilemma is not solved but aggravated makes itself felt only indirectly.

The impending retribution, the confirmation of God's hatred as well as the *im*possibility of repentance are denied in the very moment in which they are invoked in the prayer scene, because the tragic context of Faustus' frustration is made to merge into a context in which the infernal reality itself begins to appear awkwardly unreal, illusory, exaggeratedly theatrical.

> *Luc.* I am Lucifer, and this is my companion Prince in hell.
> . . .
> *Bel.* We are come to tell thee thou dost iniure vs.
> *Luc.* Thou calst on Christ contrary to thy promise.
> *Bel.* Thou should'st not thinke on God.
> *Luc.* Thinke on the deuill.
> *Bel.* And his dam too.
>
> (B 658;660-64)

More explicitly than in A, the B-text's arrangement of the lines calls for an overlap between the comic and the demoniac appearances of the two "companion princes." Their mimicking, stichomythic exchange initiates the farcical mood which Marlowe so brilliantly exaggerates into the bizarre scenario of the Seven Deadly Sins. In the first part of the play, Marlowe had carefully shaped the contrasting features in Faustus' relationship with Mephostophilis; Faustus' impatient, proud bumptiousness is all the more effective if seen in direct contrast with the devil's somber, dignified, and melancholy demeanour. At this turning-point, Faustus' terrified reaction to the sudden arrival of Lucifer and Belzebub contrasts equally effectively with the tone of their little mock-exhortation. There are obvious options for the director, the actors, the costume and scene designer, to produce special effects at this moment and, for example, create the impression that Lucifer and Belzebub do not particularly like each other. Both the Lyric Studio and the Oregon Festival productions came up with visually and verbally convincing portrayals of a self-divided Satanic kingdom. At the Lyric, a dissatisfied, bored dwarf Belzebub followed his master around with obvious misgivings. At Ashland, the beautiful, shining Lucifer and grubby, petulant Belzebub were equally superbly distinguished from one another, and the ironies became particularly strong when the gnomic "companion prince" announced that they had come "in person" in order to give Faustus a glimpse of the Deadly Sins "in their proper shapes and likenesse" (B 669f.).

Faustus' delighted anticipation and excitement are of course

wildly exaggerated ("That sight will be as pleasing vnto me, as
paradise was to Adam, the first day of his creation" A 733-34; B
673-74) and - as Lucifer is quick to point out - absurdly misplaced in the present circumstances.

> Talke not of paradise, nor creation, but
> marke this shew ...
> (A 735-36)

Perhaps it is even more absurd that Faustus would insist on finding the show "pleasing" while it ought to become clear that what he actually sees must be the most grotesquely farcical contrivance Marlowe was able to think of. The dramatist in fact disregards the phantasmagoria of beasts and monsters of the Faustbook and chooses to replace it with a pageant that seems to connect with a morality convention of long-standing popularity. The concept of the Seven Deadly Sins[25] had played a very important role in the art of the Middle Ages, and religious instruction as well as literary and pictorial works had for a long time exploited its inexhaustible potential for allegorical presentation. Dramatized allegories at their best (cf. *The Castle of Perseverance*, the Digby *Mary Magdalene*, Medvall's *Nature*) had integrated their abstract figures into vivid, perceptually striking and "flamboyant" spectacles, and the cohorts of the Sins in *The Castle of Perseverance* have in fact a very important role to play in the battle scenes against Mankind.[26] Later moralities, as Bevington, Potter, and others have demonstrated, began to undergo several degrees of thematic, stylistic, and structural-technical transformation, and

---

25 Cf. Bloomfield, *The Seven Deadly Sins*, chap. 7. See also David Bevington, *From 'Mankind' to Marlowe: Growth of Structure in the Drama of Tudor England* (Cambridge,Mass.: Harvard Univ. Press, 1962), pp. 114-27; 137-74; Robert Potter, *The English Morality Play* (London: Routledge & Kegan Paul, 1975), esp. pp. 6-57; and Bernard Spivack, *Shakespeare and the Allegory of Evil* (New York: Columbia Univ. Press, 1958), esp. chap. 5. For a general introduction, see Lysander W. Cushman, *The Devil and the Vice in English Dramatic Literature before Shakespeare* (Halle: Niemeyer, 1900).
26 See Michael R. Kelly, *Flamboyant Drama: A Study of 'The Castle of Perseverance', 'Mankind', and 'Wisdom'* (Carbondale:

the more presentation of character and action pressed towards the specific and practical instead of the timeless and spiritual, the more we encounter popularized, satiric types rather than generic derivations of the Seven Deadly Sins. The mid-sixteenth century moralities and homiletic tragedies on the pre-Marlovian stage had already incorporated their "vice-figures" into the dramatic structures where they - no longer engaged in a moral battle for the hero's soul - developed their own dynamics as comical, satirical, or farcical embodiments of evil, provoking audience reactions that are usually called a mixture of the hilarious and the ominous.

If extensive allegorical representation of human sins became transmuted into intensive dramatic vice-figures who would dominate the manipulation of dramatic action or activate the "comedy of evil"[27] in separate scenes of the sub-plot, a distinct world of homiletic abstraction was obsolescent in a drama that had already developed more sophisticated structural and dramaturgic techniques. It has been argued, nevertheless, that the structure of *Dr Faustus* is so determined by the traditional idea and structure of the morality play or homiletic tragedy that Marlowe's use of well-known stage conventions cannot but appeal to those expectations and responses which were part of the convention. The responses I am here concerned with need to be clarified, however, with regard to the "comedy of evil" that most critics assume to be built into the sub-plot or comic scenes of Marlowe's play. The pageant of the Seven Deadly Sins raises precisely the question whether we are in fact meant to relate such a "show" to the other scenes that contain comic material and, as Bevington suggests, are *needed* to restore "the moral balance."[28]

Southern Illinois Univ. Press, 1979).
27 Cf. Charlotte Spivack, *The Comedy of Evil on Shakespeare's Stage* (Rutherford: Fairleigh Dickinson Univ. Press, 1978). For a discussion of pre-Marlovian drama, see esp. chaps. 3 and 4.
28 *From 'Mankind' to Marlowe*, p. 255. See also Levin, *The Overreacher*, pp. 145-47; Westlund, "The Orthodox Christian Framework of Marlowe's *Faustus*," 200; and Ornsetin, "The Comic Synthesis," 165-72.

In the concluding pages, I wish to make a few suggestions which
may allow us to move beyond the reductive terminology that is involved in describing the play's middle scenes as "comedy of evil"
or as satiric mirrors of Faustus' debasement. I want to argue
that interpretations of the Seven Deadly Sins, and the Papal,
Imperial, and Ducal sequences, which are based on ideas and conventions of the morality tradition, help us as little as they
have helped us to grasp Faustus' drama of the mind or the dramaturgical strategies with which Marlowe complicates the impact of
Faustus' self-sacrifice. Instead, I wish to draw attention,
once again, to my understanding of "paradox" in the play and to
the spectacle on the stage which sustains and intensifies the
irresolvable conflict that is built into the entire Faustian
"enterprise."

If the "comic" scenes and their burlesque humour were well-definable functions of Christian homiletic tragedy, which render the
hero a pitiful, foolish, and absurdly mistaken "Doctor Fustian,"[29]
we may as well give up our hope to find anything interesting in
such a tedious moral lesson. Lucifer's ironic advice seems more
helpful in this respect: "Talke not of paradise, nor creation,
but marke the shew." Lucifer in fact announces the central concern of Marlowe's dramaturgy for the entire middle section, and
if we take Mephostophilis' earlier injunction literally, namely
to "*see* what magic can *performe*," we are already addressing ourselves to the primary importance of the play's visual language.
The Faustbook is unusually rich in potential "shows," spectacles,
and gestures - the metamorphoses of the devil, the striking of
the Pope, the ritual processions in the Vatican, the dismemberment episode (Horse-Courser), the horning of Benvolio, and the
dumb-shows of Alexander and Helen - and it is clear that Mar-

---

29 George Hunter's stimulating discussion of the "downward" and
"backward" movement of the action in *Dr Faustus* seems to suggest that the comic scenes have a dismantling effect and that
Faustus' intellectual aspirations and pretensions finally
come to his being "the leader of a troupe of clowns." See his
"Five-Act Structure in *Doctor Faustus*," TDR, 8, (1964),85-91.

lowe was ready to transform the stage into a playing field for all manner of curious and fantastic deeds. For all we know about the demands of the popular playhouse audiences and acting companies alike, there is no reason to assume that Marlowe would not exploit the transparent occasion for the pursuit of theatrical interests.

The recent production of *Dr Faustus* at Jesus College, Cambridge, made a special effort to recreate the play's central portion in the tone and atmosphere it was likely to have had in the Elizabethan theatre. I had several reservations about the production concept, but it proved to be an undeniably stimulating idea to take the tripartite structure of the text and transform the shape of the performance into three distinct sequences which were assigned as "masque - anti-masque - masque." The "antimasque" began with Lucifer's announcement of his "show", and it was done so extremely effectively that nobody in the audience would have agreed with those commentators who generally write about the play's radical descent and disintegration into boring trivia. On the contrary, with the arrival of the queer procession of Sins, the production exploded into extraordinary liveliness, colour, speed, broad humour, and carnival. The Jesus production allowed a huge new troupe of actors to burst on the stage, adding a juggler, a conjurer, and a fire-eater to the rest of Lucifer's acting company. The Sins performed their "shew" while Faustus, in a fool's hat, sat with Mephostophilis to enjoy the farce, engage the Sins in conversation, mix puns with them, and come away from the spectacle with renewed dedication to his cause. The scene had a tremendous momentum, re-vitalizing the audience and persuading them to enjoy the immediate, physical action and sensual percepts. All the succeeding episodes were played in the same inspiring mood of festive gaiety, and the audience could experience the tremendously effective shape-changing that went on while the Sins quickly disposed of one costume and slipped into the next (all parts in the middle scenes were played by the Sins, who dressed themselves at an onstage costume rack) to become Pope, Cardinal, Emperor, Duke, Alexander, Horse-Courser, etc.

This method of having the actors double the parts of the minor "characters" betrays, above all, an acute understanding of Elizabethan stage practice. Studies on the history of the English stage have amply demonstrated how versatile the Elizabethan actors were, given the limitations in personnel, staging facilities, and finances, and how fundamentally, on the other hand, these practical conditions influenced the flexibility and inventiveness of dramatists and acting companies and made themselves felt in the structural organization and performance techniques of the drama. Since *Dr Faustus* is so immediately concerned with "magic shows" and rapidly changing scenic effects, it has always surprised me that Marlowe critics hardly ever find it worth mentioning that Marlowe was well aware of the visual and dramaturgic surprise effects that the acting conventions readily granted him. The 1604 version could have been easily performed by a company of six or seven actors, one or two boy actors (taking the mute parts of Alexander, Helen, etc.), and several additional, hired men (for the Deadly Sins pageant). Since modern productions need not necessarily bring the Sins on stage together (this is what the A and B stage-directions suggest), it is possible to use extensive doubling for the Sins as well and create an intimate and startling performance with no more than eight actors altogether.

How impressive such a method can be was demonstrated by the Lyric Studio production which used a cast of eight (seven young actors, one older for Mephostophilis) and gave full scope to the actors' versatility to create a dense sardonic version of Marlowe's play. Turn by turn, one could see the actors ponder over books as serious Scholars, lend their voices to the Good and Bad Angels, become nude spirits and gravely-dressed monks, gesticulating Popes or querulous Belzebubs. Inevitably, and most successfully, the actor who had the part of the Bad Angel also impersonated "Mistress Minx" (Lechery) and, finally, reappeared as a male Helen of Troy whose icy, transvestite beauty provoked shock and amazement alike. Another tremendously effective doubling-trick occurred when the actor who had just been onstage as sinister, malicious Belzebub (played by a dwarf) returned only a few minutes later as an impressively haughty and conceited Pope.

Returning to the Cambridge Jesus production and the idea of an "anti-masque," I have to add a few critical remarks to my earlier praise. To turn the text's central part into a grand spectacle or a festive comedy might very well reflect the new momentum that the play-in-performance picks up at this point. But to put a fool's hat on Faustus' head and to suggest that the Sins' silliness is Faustus' silliness is a decisive step towards moral drama of the kind that Marlowe's text does not lend itself to. David Bevington suggests that we are meant to see Faustus' "rapt involvement in the petty and ridiculous consequences of his act," and that the Sins' "portrayal of the wages of evil" clearly epitomizes an old, venerable morality tradition in which the Seven Deadly Sins had always stood for the "comically evil side of the Psychomachia."[30] He goes on to say that the "presence of the Deadly Sins suggest that Faustus himself generically incorporates their several qualities in his ambition, covetousness, and fleshly lust. There is a trace of the Vice in his universalized acquaintance with evil...."[31] Muriel Bradbrook ventures into the world of Dunbar's poetry ("The Dance of the Seven Deadly Sins") and the tradition of English country mumming in an attempt at saving-the-appearances of the diabolical actors and at showing us that they were surely out to "combine the comic and the horrific" and provoke "terror" and "laughter" with their "horrific jesting."[32]

J.R. Brown indirectly supports this view when he claims that the Sins, even if ridiculous and offensive, "must be compelling as well so that they give 'delight' to Faustus' soul as he instinctively exclaims."[33] I should think that the Deadly Sins are every-

---

30 *From 'Mankind' to Marlowe*, p. 255.
31 Ibid., pp. 255-56.
32 Muriel C. Bradbrook, "Marlowe's *Doctor Faustus* and the Eldritch Tradition," in *Essays on Shakespeare and Elizabethan Drama in Honor of Hardin Craig*, ed. Richard Hosley (Columbia: Univ. of Missouri Press, 1962), pp. 85-86.
33 "*Doctor Faustus* at Stratford," p. 197.

thing but compelling and that, likewise, they are very far removed from "epitomizing" the moral battle that was once waged in the Psychomachia drama. Glancing backwards at the tradition does not help us; dramatic pageants of the Seven Deadly Sins were no longer used in the morality plays after the turn of the century, and those vice figures of the later moralities which were employed to particularize the Seven Sins, developed their own unmistakable qualities of aggressive scheming, plotting, and deceiving for which Marlowe's Sins will make us look in vain. To present a pageant of *all* the Sins, Sins, moreover, that are absurdly harmless and unaggressive, cannot be anything other than a spectacular trick, a parodic exhibition of a museum-piece. As Potter concludes at the end of his study of *Dr Faustus*, the characters of the old drama "are brought onto the stage, like sacred objects of a superstitious past, to be mocked and atavistically wondered at, and ritualistically destroyed."[34]

Led by Pride, the Sins walk onto the stage and present their "seueral names and dispositions" (A 738-39) in quaint, raunchy prose. Faustus does not seem to have the faintest idea what this procession of absurdities is supposed to mean.

>   *Fau.* What art thou? the fourth.
>   *Enuy.* I am Enuy, begotten of a Chimney-sweeper, and an
>   Oyster wife, I cannot reade, and therefore wish
>   al bookes were burnt: I am leane with seeing
>   others eate. O that there would come a famine
>   through all the worlde, that all might die, and
>   I liue alone, then thou shouldst see how fatt
>   I would be: but must thou sit and I stand?
>   come downe with a vengeance.
>   (A 762-68)

These walking embodiments of the Sins have such a literalized conception of what they are and turn so grotesquely funny in their accounts of their local "parentage" (especially Gluttony) that it is hardly surprising to find Faustus amused by their "sight." Costume designers for modern productions often tend to be too inspired by Hieronymous Bosch paintings (cf. Bosch's

---

34 *The English Morality Play*, p. 127.

"Seven Deadly Sins", "Earthly Paradise", etc.) and present us with Sins that have revoltingly distorted and discoloured limbs, or they turn them into Star Wars- and Tolkien-like trolls and goblins (as it was done at Ashland). But this stretches Marlowe's theatrical notation too far; the Seven Deadly Sins hardly appear "deadly" or revolting - they are simply ridiculous and absurd. In a way, Marlowe allows us to laugh at what is vulgar and absurd precisely because the object of our laughter has so detached itself from any possible relationship to theology as to be rendered completely harmless and caricatured.

At the same time, the scene is arranged as a play-within-the-play; we watch Faustus watch a spectacle that is inherently meaningless and practically irrelevant, absurd. And we notice that Faustus pretends to enjoy ("O this feedes my soule") Lucifer's delightful "pastime" so much that he exclaims:

> *Fau.* O might I see hel, and returne againe,
> how happy were I then?
> *Luc.* Thou shalt, I wil send for thee at midnight ...
> (A 799-801)

It is Faustus' exaggerated response to the pageant's sublime absurdity which leads us back to the notion of paradox. We simply do not understand what was meant by this show, and since it would be nonsense to compare Faustus with the Sins, we are left with the uneasy impression that Laucifer's distracting theatrical show was another ominous trick, and at the same time merely a distraction, meaning and signifying nothing.

It is interesting that the text does not at all enlarge on the protagonist's deception by and absorption into "his" kingdom but, on the contrary, shifts our attention immediately to the vast, open spaces of his astronomical and cosmographic explorations, paradoxically hinting at the possibility that his hopes in negromantic power and conquest were valid after all. There is no mention of "hell" any more but only of the glories that "Learned Faustus" achieves through magic and that make him famous throughout the world.

> *Wag.* Learned Faustus
> To know the secrets of Astronomy,
> Grauen in the booke of Ioues hie firmament,
> Did mount himselfe to scale Olympus top,
> Being seated in a chariot burning bright,
> Drawne by the strength of yoky dragons neckes:
> He views the cloudes, the Planets, and the Starres,
> The Tropick, Zones, and quarters of the skye,
> From the height of Primum Mobile:
> And whirling round with this circumference,
> Within the concaue compasse of the Pole,
> From East to West his Dragons swiftly glide
> And in eight daies did bring him home againe ...
> He now is gone to prooue Cosmography,
> And as I guesse, wil first ariue at Rome,
> To see the Pope, and manner of his court,
> And take some part of holy Peters feast,
> That to this day is highly solemnized.
> (A 810-15; 816-20)[35]

There is no reason to assume that the Chorus' narrative does not intend to invite us to ponder "the forme of Faustus fortune good or bad" - and the "forme" seems good in this case. We hear that Faustus has suddenly left the solitary study and conjuring circle and is "whirling round with this circumference." We hear that he mounts upward from the innermost to the outermost sphere without actually leaving a universe which is still *closed* and finite. Yet these lines convey a sense of the sweeping exhilaration of upward flights that reminds us of Faustus' earlier visions. The Chorus' admiring report gives us the impression that Faustus can accomplish marvellous feats with his magic powers. Reminiscent of Tamburlaine's Phaeton-like self-dramatization ("Holla, ye pampered jades of Asia! / What, can ye draw but twenty miles a day, / And have so proud a chariot at your heels, / And such a coachman as great Tamburlaine?"), the verbal image of Faustus' sitting in a "chariot burning bright" is so beautiful that it can be said to compensate for the limits of the stage which Marlowe was well aware of and which he had to face precisely at this moment, when he was forced to decide which of Faustus' magical

---

[35] Since the A version of the Chorus (Wagner) has a fragmented and incomplete text, I have decided to insert 8 lines (B 783-90) from the otherwise equivalent B Chorus.

feats could be put on the stage and accommodated by the available theatrical technology. I think it is quite misleading to claim that the limited resources of Marlowe's stage conveniently supplied an objective correlative to the limited deeds Faustus can perform before our eyes. The episodes of magical demonstration which Marlowe chooses for his play are clearly meant to be selective and representative of Faustus' *realization* of his earlier claims, and although Marlowe does not ultimately succeed in satisfying us, he certainly tries to sustain the tension between possibility and limitation that was built into Faustus' enterprise from the beginning.

The accounts of Faustus' supernatural journeys, cosmographic explorations, and visits to the courts of Popes and Emperors, as well as all the allusions to Faustus' growing fame made in dramatic dialogue, give us a picture of his accomplishments that must be seen side by side with those spectacles that show us a Faustus trapped in conflicts and entangled with the repercussions of those entertainments he provides. The Chorus, "his friends and nearest companions" (A 935), the Emperor, and the Duke know nothing about a debased and deluded fool; they only know that "Maister doctor Faustus" is incomparable in his "Arte", famous all over the world (Emperor); they "earnestly entreate" his "company" (Duke), or "gratulate his safetie with kinde words" (his friends), or

> ... put forth questions of Astrologie,
> Which Faustus answered with such learned skill,
> As they admirde and wondred at his wit.
> Now is his fame spread forth in euery land ...
> (Chorus 2, A 939-42, not in B)

The other picture, which speaks to us immediately through dramatized action, ought to be reconsidered too. If we look at the episode in the Vatican or at Faustus' encounter with the Emperor, we do not only find slapstick and knockabout farce. On the contrary, the text suggests that Marlowe intended to elicit an admixture of effects, calculated contrasts and rapidly alternating scenic and gestic expressions which prove that he was ready to make the most of what was dramaturgically possible. The mixture of expressions and effects and the sense of confusion and paradox that is built into these free-form, metamorphic spectacles are the most interesting and challenging aspects of Marlowe's drama, because they enhance the conflicting reactions that his hero provokes at the conceptual and rhetorical levels of his dream of magic power.

The problem of power, rebellion, and conflict, which permeates the tragic scenes, is not suppressed or disregarded in the so-called comic middle scenes; rather, it is submerged in the dramatic juxtapositions of incident with incident. And there are brilliant moments of contrast, such as between the awesome silence during the dumb-show (Alexander the Great), after Faustus has admitted that "it is not in my abilitie to present before your eyes, the true substantiall bodies of these two deceased princes ..." A 1081-83), and the immediately following noise and aggressiveness of the horning episode. In such moments we are often uncertain about how to react to the almost arbitrary reversals of tone. Taken as a whole, the emphasis is again on what Faustus does, what he can, and what he cannot do, and I would argue that Marlowe never really moves away from his hero's tragic dilemma but integrates ambivalently "comic" and serious action in such a way that the main focus of attention is on perceptual detail, visual and sensual impression, and on the emotional appeal of his spectacle. There are no "comic" middle scenes, in a strict sense, because Marlowe's visual language has a peculiar quality of shiftiness and inconclusiveness which makes it very difficult to decide what is "serious," what is "comic," and what is simply absurd. The Chorus announces:

> What there he did in triall of his art,
> I leaue vntold, your *eyes* shall *see performed*.
> (A 946-47; my emphasis)

Yet the performance of Faustus' "triall of his art" suggests different meanings, and I think one ought to allow these different meanings to exist and to complement each other. If one wants to uphold the notion that Marlowe wrote "comic" scenes, one would have to point out, first of all, what kind of humour or satiric irony accompanies those middle scenes which are not immediately identifiable as comic scenes (Pope, Emperor, Duke), and whether it is clearly recognizable who the object of ridicule is. The same question would have to be addressed to those parts of the middle scenes that are traditionally described as sub-plot scenes (tavern episode; the Benvolio scenes in the B version; the Horse-Courser episode).

The spectacle of the Pope's banquet is interesting to begin with because we can imagine the extent to which Marlowe could manipulate audience response in this case. Judging from the way the Papal court and "holy Peters feast" are mentioned in several anticipatory remarks, we can assume that Marlowe wanted to build up a "stately" scene, and the entering procession of the friars, the Cardinal, and the Pope ought to be staged with all possible regal splendour and solemnity.[36] Formal, stately movement, impressive costumes, and dignified attendance to a ceremonial banquet should set the tone for this scene. Commenting on the Old Vic production of *Dr Faustus* in 1961, the London *Times* critic writes:

> When the papal court has been gradually assembled... the scene is so impressive in its solemnity that almost any joke would seem tellingly out of place, and the final wrecking of all this grandeur by Faustus and Mephostophilis seems indeed a devilish outrage.[37]

In view of the fact that the popular Elizabethan attitude toward the papacy and its rituals was decidedly negative, one can infer

---

36 The B-text's enlarged Papal sequence (the struggle between Adrian and his rival Pope, Bruno, is in fact not based on the Faustbook but most likely drawn from Foxe's *Acts and Monuments*) presents an elaboration of A's scenario which of course greatly intensifies the spectacular stage-effects and ceremonies (the Pope's ascending the back of his "footstool" Bruno, etc.).

37 Quoted from Brown, "*Doctor Faustus* at Stratford," p. 198.

that the "invisible" Faustus' farcical wrecking of the banquet guided its satirical attack along the lines of a common prejudice. Howsoever ludicrous his antics appear, they were bound to have a sensationalist appeal that guaranteed the success of his violent smashing of the idols. Faustus and Mephostophilis seem thoroughly to enjoy their conjuring tricks, and the Vatican burlesque comes to its climax when they disrupt the friars' "holy dirge": *"Beate the Friers: and fling fier-workes among them"* (s.d. A 928). The scene breaks apart into noise, fire and smoke, and what remains is an impression of Faustus' reckless jesting and of his aggressive enjoyment of the ritual of excommunication (*"maledicat dominus"* - the curse with "bell, booke, and candle" [cf. A 909-11]) and its destruction. The threat of damnation that is evoked by the "Popish" malediction has little force to register with the audience because the entire scene becomes so farcically inflated that it is difficult to see the satire turn in on Faustus, especially since he - as actual presenter and controler of the "entertainment" - enjoys a particularly intimate and unmediated relationship with the audience.

Faustus' "triall of his art" seems to present us with a different kind of theatrical experience altogether when we move to the Imperial court in Act IV. The shift to dignified conversation in prose (between Faustus and the Emperor) and to verse (the Emperor's long monologue) is all the more recognizable after the coarse, low-level prose interlude (Robin and Rafe) which precedes this scene. The Emperor, who has heard "strange report" of the doctor's "knowledge in the blacke Arte" (A 1040-41), asks the world-renowned magician to grant him a vision of Alexander the Great,

>   Chiefe spectacle of the worldes preheminence,
>   The bright shining of whose glorious actes
>   Lightens the world with his reflecting beames,
>   As when I heare but motion made of him
>   It grieues my soule I neuer saw the man ...
>   (A 1064-68)

It may very well be ironic that Faustus plays down his magical potency and seems willing, in exchange for admiration and "bounteous reward" (A 1134), to maintain a humble attitude towards the "Potentate" he once envisioned to overrule and command. We are not sure what to make of his paradoxical behaviour, because the Emperor is genuinely impressed by Faustus' "Arte". There is indeed a certain awe and majesty attached to Faustus' conjuration of the shadows of Alexander and his Paramour which could be enlarged very effectively by a well-staged dumb-show. The Emperor's melancholy obsession with the past glory of his mighty "aunncestors" also links back with Faustus' ravished intercourse with Homer and Amphion. The most remarkable trick which Marlowe plays on his audience rests on the contradiction between what Faustus says ("such spirites as can *liuely resemble* Alexander and his Paramour, shal *appeare* ..." A 1086-87, my emphasis) and what the Emperor sees:

> Sure these are no spirites, but the true
> substantiall bodies of these two deceased princes.
> (A 1106-07)

The Emperor is overwhelmed by the "reality" of the illusionism of Faustus' magic art, and such punning on and playing with "theatrical" reality and illlusion doubtlessly added to the peculiar supernatural atmosphere that Marlowe's play must have been able to create if we can trust those legends that report of a personal appearance of the Devil Himself at one of the performances.

This sense of wonder at Faustus' magic "miracles" is shared by the Duchess of Vanholt for whom the conjuration of ripe grapes in "the dead time of winter" (A 1247) presents an inexplicable riddle. Whether or not a modern audience will find this trivial, the text itself allows no such judgment because Faustus himself shrugs off the conjuration of grapes as being only a small matter: "Alas Madam, thats nothing ... Were it a greater thing then this, so it would content you, you should haue it" (A 1242-44). This uninterrupted and unusually quiet and peaceful scene stands in marked contrast to the interruptions that occurred earlier. The Vanholt scene, in fact, is neither very good nor does it make much sense, except for the fact that Marlowe is slowing down the pace and introducing an element of quietude that links this scene with a sense of exhaustion that has already begun to surface in Faustus' "vitall life" (A 1136).

In a way, the movement of the middle episodes is not only circular in a geographic-temporal and metaphorical sense,

> Now Mephastophilis, the restlesse course
> That time doth runne with calme and silent foote,
> Shortning my dayes and thred of vitall life,
> Calls for the payment of my latest yeares,
> Therefore sweet Mephastophilis, let vs
> Make haste to Wertenberge.
> (A 1134-39; not in B)

it is also a movement back *inward*, away from the externality of his magic triumphs and strangely mixed encounters with Popes and Friars, Emperors and Knights. That his triumph and encounters provoke mixed feelings is nowhere more obvious than in the scene at the Emperor's court where the dignified movement of his wondrous magical demonstrations is harshly disturbed by the hostile Knight's persistent ridiculing and questioning of Faustus' magic power. What we see, then, is the Emperor's respect and admiration on the one hand, and the Knight's ironic detachment on the other, and as a way of resolving the conflict, Faustus decides to take revenge by horning the Knight. The horn joke is probably as crude and grotesque as the pranks Faustus plays upon the Horse-Courser. Jests about false horns, false legs, and false horses certainly appear gratuitous and hardly very funny, yet they give us another "speaking picture" of the range of Faustus' repertoire of tricks.

The spectacles mix majestic "illusions" and frivolous jokes, good-humoured burlesque and aggressive ridicule, and it will depend on the emphases given to individual moments whether the overall effect of those scenes becomes reductive irony, showing Faustus squandering his powers on trivial jokes, or whether it gives an impression of the honour, pleasure, and pageantry Faustus enjoys during his journey. I think Marlowe is not interested in exposing his hero's "clownishness"; rather, Faustus' meddling with the world always appears slightly uncertain and daemonically privileged, and the games he plays are shown to be sensational as well as occasionally absurd - frighteningly absurd.

The Horse-Courser comes back, dripping and wailing, after his straw horse had vanished underneath him in "the deepe pond at the towns ende" (A 1183-84), and he turns into an even sorrier figure when he pulls off Faustus' leg and tricks himself into a second bad bargain. The emphasis in this scene, however, is not on the Horse-Courser's momentary delusion, but on Faustus' conceit. And this conceit is on an altogether different scale.

> What art thou Faustus but a man condemnd to die?
> Thy fatall time doth drawe to finall ende,
> Dispaire doth driue distrust vnto my thoughts,
> Confound these passions with a quiet sleepe:
> Tush, Christ did call the thiefe vpon the Crosse,
> Then rest thee Faustus quiet in conceit.
> (A 1169-74)

The irony of Faustus' self-hypnotization pulls us back into the centre of the tragedy, and I would argue that the contrast in this episode is not one between Faustus and Horse-Courser but between Faustus who is "but a man condemnd to die" and Faustus who is able to deceive ("con-ceive") himself on a grandiose scale. The play's middle scenes ask for a spectacular theatrical display of the powerful seductiveness that Faustus' life in delight and pleasure (even trivial pleasure) can have. Faustus is meant to be seen "whirling round with this circumference" and creating "pastimes" that are narcotic enough to "confound these passions" which would remind him of the awful thought that the wondrous products of his conjurations cannot do anything about his condition.

The scenes of Faustus' precarious pursuit of happiness, and the potentially powerful visions that magic can afford (epitomized in the appearances of Alexander the Great and Helen of Troy), in fact insinuate that his *conceit*, paradoxically, is a necessary one, that his illusions and dreams are the only refuge left to him in a closed and finite world. Given the circumstances, his presumptive self-consolation ("Tush, Christ did call the thiefe vpon the Crosse") is quite perplexing, like so much else in this play, but what is his theological "conceit" other than that false security which one finds, again paradoxically, in the "suburbs of hell." The extraordinary availability of God's grace is another illusion that Marlowe's play has been intent on demolishing quite thoroughly.

Throughout the theatrical fireworks of the middle sections, Faustus refuses to be defeated on any other terms than those self-chosen; his magic art, too, will be "levelled" at the end. The middle scenes, however, do not simply degrade and ridicule him, as so many critical commentators have suggested to us. I rather see them as expressing, in their own way, the "forme" of his irresolvable dilemma, and what it *means* to be powerful and, at the same time, hopelessly powerless. The ultimate emptiness of all the spectacular amusements and magical exploits is the greater for their temporary satisfaction, and there is a clearly intended continuity in the action when we eventually see a mentally and physically exhausted Faustus arrive back home in his study.

As Tamburlaine feels the proximity of the "ugly monster Death", he orders a map of the world to be brought in and unrolled in front of his eyes so that he can view his conquests one more time. Then Zenocrate's hearse is brought in, and Tamburlaine is ready to sublimate the emblems of his power and of his defeat into dream landscapes which have no spatial boundaries:

> Now, eyes, enjoy your latest benefit,
> And when my soul hath virtue of your sight,
> Pierce through the coffin and the sheet of gold
> And glut your longings with a heaven of joy ...
> (*2 Tamb*.V.iii.224-27)

Faustus, too, will step into his magic circle one more time to grant the "iust requests of those that wish him well" (A 1286) and to conjure up the "heauenly beauty" of Helen before he will drown in despair, ready for the final reckoning. The innocent Scholars are literally blinded and overwhelmed by the impact of Helen's appearance, and their praise of Faustus' power is therefore quite unself-consciously ironic:

> Since we haue seene the pride of natures workes,
> And onely Paragon of excellence,
> Let vs depart and for this glorious deed
> Happy and blest be Faustus euermore.
> (A 1296-99)

Epilogue

THE FAUSTIAN ETHOS: "DESPERATE ENTERPRISE"?

Faustus, not unlike the "Scythian shepherd" Tamburlaine, sets out to break with the past and to initiate a future. He chooses his "profession" not merely by denying all the conventional "roles" he might have played but by establishing, above all, his own mode or style of ambitious wilfulness. His self-centred idealism *is* the form of his fortunes, so to speak, and he defends this "form" with the strength of the single-minded imaginative desire that lies at the heart of all the self-consuming projects with which we identify Marlowe's stage heroes.

Drunk with the vaunting energy of his "conceit", Faustus imagines the fulfilment of all his desires; his early soliloquies, in a way, become a kind of "aesthetic magic," a virtuoso performance with *words* and eloquent projections of power.

> How am I glutted with conceit of this?
> Shall I make spirits fetch me what I please,
> Resolue me of all ambiguities,
> Performe what desperate enterprise I will?

As the beginning to one of Faustus' longest and most intensive visionary speeches, this passage points, in more than one way, to the problematic nature of his wish to control nature, other men and, ultimately, his own destiny. The expression "eloquent projection," which I used above, is meant to describe what I believe to be one of the most important aspects in the dramatic representation of Marlowe's heroes: the close interdependence between rhetorical power and the power of the overreaching mind. The combination of imaginative desire and rhetorical expression in the portrayal of the hero, at the same time, bears upon the way in which Marlowe is seen to manipulate the existing resources of the theatre and the audience's preconceptions about the tragic dramaturgy of their time. The observations and interpretations that I have offered for Marlowe's plays basically concerned themselves with the effects of these manipulations; I have also tried to let the playtexts speak for themselves or, more precisely, to allow for the fact that the dramatic experience generates its own beliefs. In pointing out how Marlowe's pervasive rhetorical strategies influence the presentation of character, action, spectacle, and dramatic theme, and how they dislodge his plays from those prevailing modes of tragedy which provided, with their fixed moral boundaries, a world of absolute and secure judgment, I have been trying to address what are probably the most dynamic and spectacular components of the theatre he created. This is to say, too, that the *Tamburlaine* plays and *Dr Faustus* basically articulate the same energies and pose the same questions, even if the answers they give may seem different. And these questions determine the explorative character of Marlovian tragedy to an extent which makes the troublesome coexistence of a conventional dramaturgical practice with radical technical innovation appear inevitable, even necessary.

Both Tamburlaine's and Faustus' rebellions point to the central problem of man's relationship to his universe and to the possibilities of the will: Marlowe's heroes, as rebels and blasphemers, seek to affirm that the superior will and imagination can control reality and transcend the obstacles and the suffering reality imposes, and we can observe the successes and failures of these attempts. The perennial conflict between success and failure in Marlowe's plays does not so much expose "a tension and overstrain which Marlowe is not able to encompass within a single dramatic vision,"[1] but points to his unwillingness to reconcile the heroic ideals and rhetorical passions in his protagonists with Elizabethan ethical, political, and religious clichés. If we say that Tamburlaine's ethic of conflict leads to his dazzling fantasies of omnipotence which are both grandiose and grotesque; and if we take Faustus' blasphemous self-reprobation to be an extraordinary act of defiance which, never-

---

1 Sanders, *The Dramatist and the Received Idea*, p. 212.

theless, fails to free him from God *and* Lucifer as well as from his own self-recriminations, then we come closer to the sense of paradox that is conveyed by the almost tragi-comic confusion of possibilities that troubles Marlowe's aspiring heroes. But even though we may be invited to see Tamburlaine's king-drawn chariot and Faustus' magic circle as tantalizing images of the absurd strivings and conclusions of human beings who would be like gods, Marlowe's dramatic worlds remain too self-consciously impregnated with the disruptive energies of their heroes to allow for any simplified judgment or moral complacency about the "form" of Faustus' or Tamburlaine's "fortunes."

The vitality of Tamburlaine's hyperbolical pathos and the unusual imagistic intensity of his speeches insistently point into layers of fantasy which outpace the given world of laws and relations and explicitly deny the ethical prerogatives that govern this world. Tamburlaine's performance - his proud assaults on all authority and tradition and his undaunted valorization of his ethos of conflict - indeed possesses all the qualities that leap from stage to audience and encourage the free play of fantasy in a manner which is clearly at odds with the Christian morality that contains the dramatic action in tragedies typical of Marlowe's age. Written in a period of dogmatic faith, the tragedies of Marlowe's predecessors and contemporaries proceed from and maintain specifically religious perceptions about human destiny, and even the most secular worlds of Elizabethan tragedy press towards reconciling the tension between individual human will and spiritual norms by providing unambiguous criteria for the "right" interpretation of moral failure, of tragic culpability. If we compare *Tamburlaine* to the "mirror" tragedies produced in the Inns of Court, to the adaptations of Senecan revenge tragedy that became fashionable on the popular stage, and - most tellingly - to the imitations that were written in the shadow of *Tamburlaine* (e.g. *Alphonsus King of Aragon, Battle of Alcazar, Orlando Furioso, Wounds of Civil War, Locrine, Selimus*),[2] one can

---

[2] The anonymous *Locrine*, written around 1590 and printed in 1595

hardly say that Marlowe's drama inhabits the same "theological site", in the sense in which Derrida would use this expression.[3] On the contrary, these other plays represent the ruinous qualities of their protagonists with the forms and structures of a conventional theatrical practice, which reveal to the spectator the moral character of the action and, at the same time, reproduce cultural paradigms or master narratives such as the concept of a Providential design - of a God who enacts His will in the Theatre of the World.

This understanding of the theatre-as-microcosm comes indeed very close to H.U.von Balthasar's elaborate aesthetic model for a "Theo-Dramatik", for which "die Analogie zwischen Gotteshandeln und Weltspiel keine bloße Metapher [ist], sondern seinshaft begründet: zwischen den beiden Dramen herrscht nicht reine Diskontinuität, sondern innerer Zusammenhang."[4] The logic of von Balthasar's model of the theological stage is simple and unambiguous. On such a stage, *punishment* must be meted out upon those who violate the rules and overstep the boundaries of the divine law which overshadows human motives with its rigid eschatology and governs, so to speak, the time and the meaning of *representation* itself. And such a stage will remain theological for as long as it is dominated by ideas about divine power, retributive justice, fate, fortune, heaven and hell, etc., and for as long

---

(one year after *Selimus*, a play which is probably by the same author), is one of the most interesting imitations of *1 Tamburlaine* insofar as it demonstrates the problems its author had when attempting to revive an earlier play (*Estrild*,c.1585) and to graft the new, sensational Tamburlainean rhetoric of self-assertion onto a conventional revenge-plot, without noticing or admitting that Marlowe's conception of Tamburlaine's heroism calls into question both the ethics and the structure of earlier plays. *Locrine*'s reviser-author imitates the obvious qualities of Tamburlaine's heroic rhetoric, but clings to familiar assertions of the vanity of human actions in the unrevised sections of the original revenge-plot. For a brilliant discussion of such weak "misreadings" among Marlowe's imitators, see Peter Berek, "*Locrine* Revised, *Selimus*, and Early Responses to *Tamburlaine*," RORD, 23 (1981), 33-54.

3 "The Theater of Cruelty," pp. 234 ff.
4 *Theo-Dramatik*, p. 19.

as the tragic artist invokes such (extra-dramatic) absolutes in order to let the representation of human experience be understood on those terms that bring it closest to prevalent cultural and religious orthodoxies.

The uniqueness of the *Tamburlaine* plays, then, derives largely from the relative uniqueness of Marlowe's dramatic expression; by centring his plays around a colossus whose "working words" initiate and secure an extraordinary power of projecting the self, Marlowe shows us the aesthetic violence of spectacular conquest detached from the judgment that the feelings of Tamburlaine's victims focus in our attention. The spectacle of such unimpeded triumph over the limitations of the will unfolds an experience which produces its own space, so to speak, a space that excludes the tragic ambivalence in which all other Marlovian protagonists become fatally ensnared.

Faustus cannot manipulate his "self-conceit" in the same way as Tamburlaine because he is always too closely bound up with the attributes of the pathetic failure prefigured in Lucifer's revolt against God. The later play has its own unique place in the canon because nowhere else does Marlowe choose a subject centred explicitly in Christian myth. While Tamburlaine's ethos does not depend on an overt denial of God, Faustus' resolute will to control his world and his own destiny reveals itself, from the outset, as a desperate attempt to become "as great as Lucifer," the fiery angel and overreaching Phaeton of the Christian pantheon. What is remarkable in *Dr Faustus*, then, is the way in which Marlowe plays with and uses the very metaphysics and eschatology which had been mocked and dissolved in the *Tamburlaine* plays. But one would be insensitive to the formidable difficulties of the play if one simply concluded that Faustus is distanced into a familiar "theological space" where we can understand and no longer be troubled by his tragic fall. The actual potentialities of Faustus' performance point towards a more complex confrontation with the human problematic which lies behind Tamburlaine's use of "Tragicall Discourse." Timothy Reiss has argued that Tamburlaine is able to imagine and control a language that generates meaning and that such a successful use of language, therefore, cannot be "tragicall." Reiss concludes that Tamburlaine "is a creator of experiments that become truths ... His will, *essentially* embodied in his discourse, does dispel contradictions, doubts, all lack of coincidence between word and event."[5]

Without noticing it, Reiss in fact touches upon the essential conditions for the formation of what Oswald Spengler, in his *Decline of the West*, has called the "Faustian" ethos. Spengler's idea of the modern Faustian tradition has to do with the transition from theocentricism to anthropocentricism and the development of a new sensibility which is grounded in the "scientific revolution." On the whole, Spengler's definition of the new "Faustian" man seems to centre upon a more literal version of the Baconian idea that "Knowledge is Power." It certainly bespeaks a more literal sensibility than the one we have found in Tamburlaine's poetic assertions of his aspiring will, "still climbing after knowledge infinite." At the same time, the problematic relationship between the metaphorical and the literal in Marlowe's plays is perhaps a crucial aspect of their literary "modernity."

Marlowe's Faustus, often regarded as the prototype of Spengler's "Faustian" individual, has little success as an agent of infinity, although his rhetorical *tour de force* in the first scene and his fanciful speculations about omnipotence, infinite riches, the white breasts of the Queen of Love, and Delphic knowledge seem to promise considerable, even sensational explorations of undiscovered territory. I have argued that Tamburlaine's agonistic eloquence is a weapon with which he can "conceive" and "subdue" all difficulties that obstruct his will-to-power; the symbolic and metaphorical dimension of Part 1 affirms his claim that there are no limits of discourse for him. In Part 2, the suggestion that his world is not only one of infinite possibilities but also one of inherent limitations grows stronger the more we see Tamburlaine striving against tragic necessity (or,

---

5 *Tragedy and Truth*, p. 132.

literally, death), and the harder he finds it to impose his imagination upon his experience. In other words, the conditionality and finitude of his dramatic context are only neutralized by his extraordinary efforts to fashion a myth of epic success out of his own terribly ambivalent ethos of endless strife - an ethos which had already implied that he, too, was doomed to traverse the self-made map of his world with the circular movements of his triumphal chariot.

Faustus' magic circle, then, can be regarded as the supreme symbol for the tragic confusion that lies at the centre of this play and its double reality. If we consider *Dr Faustus* a noticeable advance over the *Tamburlaine* plays, it has to do with the fact that in *Dr Faustus* Marlowe is able to create a profoundly disturbing work which relentlessly pursues ambiguities and contradictions to their radical conclusions and enlarges the very fatality of human nature that is generally denied by the fantasy-making power of the Marlovian hero. Faustus' dream of magical omnipotence is alluring, but it only reaches us *after* he has put on a noisy disputational "show" in order to dispel the frustration which underlies his admission that he is "but Faustus and a man." Seen against the background of the Chorus' unambiguous condemnation of Faustus' overreaching self-conceit, the hero's soliloquizing could always already be understood as an aesthetic compensation for his inability to go beyond the limits of his humanity. On the other hand, the complex relationship between subjective and objective experience in the performance of *Dr Faustus* points far beyond the simple dichotomy of good and evil suggested by the routine warnings and temptations of the two Angels. If Faustus' magic circle is a grim reminder that man's striving, aspiring, and transgressing cannot alleviate the temporal anxieties out of which life is made, and that he is essentially enclosed by external limitations, it nevertheless functions as a representation of the hopes and (necessary) illusions man must have and cling to in order to be able to create the space of freedom he needs.

Faustus' magic enterprise and his diabolical pact are such an attempt to create and sustain a sense of *self* and to overcome his own inner fears and tensions. Marlowe heightens the paradoxical quality of Faustus' project by inviting us to see his wilful choice as the one and only *effective* way of creating his own "history" and his own "end." It gains its most shockingly blasphemous aspect from his readiness to indulge in the space that he opens up for himself by regarding himself reprobate and by playing with the shadow of his own personal apocalypse.

That Faustus' damnation is linked with a rigorous logic of dramatic structure does not mean, however, that it is identical with a metaphysiical logic as we know it from Shakespeare, for example. Eternal justice and moral cause-and-effect play a thoroughly insignificant role in Marlovian drama as a whole, and the constant rhetorical apostrophes to heaven and hell can become viciously ironic at times, such as in the Scholar's paradoxical advice to the damned Faustus:

> Yet Faustus looke vp to heauen, remember
> gods mercies are infinite.
> (A 1400-01)

In the same way, Faustus' theatrical performance of his rituals, whether we call them compensatory or not, is always strong and perplexing enough to support Styan's claim that "the single moral choice made by Faustus is denied and complicated by the sheer jubilation with which Marlowe invites his audience to indulge in their wicked fantasies - mocking the Pope, conjuring Helen, and so on - at the expense of the damnation of the whole house."[6]

The silent seductiveness of Helen and her effect on the ravished Faustus may indeed be the most provocative test for us too; it is a test that can resolve nothing, but it can remind us of Faustus' futile, desperate efforts to repent and his equally futile, desperate clinging to the Satanic illusion that "in hel

---

6 *Drama, Stage and Audience*, pp. 186f.

is al manner of delight" (A 798). It can remind us of the power
that such illusions must have - a power, after all, that we
have learnt to describe as imaginative freedom.

The contradictions in the text, on close examination, will not
resolve themselves in any easy moral interpretation. And the
theatrical performance of a Marlovian play will always enforce
the uneasy intersections between dramatistic and ethical motive.
The main purpose of this study has been to point toward critical
perspectives that may help to understand these intersections and
the effects they have on our experience of Tamburlaine's and
Faustus' quests for power. I have argued that these quests will
always grow out of and correspond to the problematic of a relationship with language, but Tamburlaine's success and Faustus'
failure are of course also recognizable through the form and
dramatic structure of their respective plays. The theatrical
mode that allowed Tamburlaine's endless fantasies and self-con-
firmations of his power seems diametrically opposed to the idio-
syncratic mixture of styles and tones that reflects the dialectical and psychological tensions in Faustus' dramatic world. And
these tensions remain unresolved in spite of (or, perhaps, because of) the clear and consistent use of a theological vocabulary. It is the meaning of the vocabulary, its validity and
truth, that is at stake.

When Tamburlaine, after having acted out all his violent claims
with explicit reference to the idea of God's scourge, finally
envisions his ultimate attack against the powers of heaven,

>   Come let us march against the powers of heaven
>   And set black streamers in the firmament
>   To signify the slaughter of the gods.
>   (V.iii.48-50)

he is of course still seen in control of the meaning of his metaphors. The blood-red and black colours of his conquests stand
for *his* signification of a universal doctrine of destruction and
conflict.

In *Dr Faustus*, Marlowe's visual and verbal rhetoric points into a different direction. It is not without a certain irony that the final image of the God Faustus sees ("See see where Christs blood streames in the firmament") has the blood-red colour of Tamburlainean destructiveness. Yet Faustus' magic enterprise fails not so much because the powers of heaven take revenge upon him, but because his "heauenly words" never managed to raise him high enough above the ambiguity, irony, and paradox that his daring and futile self-damnation generated in the first place.

BIBLIOGRAPHY

1. Editions of Marlowe

Complete Plays and Poems. Ed. E.D. Pendry and J.C. Maxwell. London: Dent, 1976.
The Complete Works of Christopher Marlowe. Ed. Fredson Bowers. 2 vols. Cambridge: Cambridge Univ. Press, 1973.
Dido Queen of Carthage, The Massacre at Paris. Ed. H.J. Oliver. The Revels Plays. London: Methuen, 1968.
Marlowe's Doctor Faustus 1604-1616. Ed. W.W. Greg. Oxford: Clarendon, 1950.
The Tragical History of Doctor Faustus. Ed. Paul H. Kocher. The Crofts Classics. New York: Harlan Davidson, 1950.
Doctor Faustus. Ed. John Jump. The Revels Plays. 1962; rpt. Manchester: Manchester Univ. Press, 1978.
Doctor Faustus. Ed. Roma Gill. The New Mermaids. 1965; rpt. London: Benn, 1967.
Doctor Faustus. Ed. Sylvan Barnet. Signet Classic World Drama Series. New York: New American Library, 1968.
The Jew of Malta. Ed. N.W. Bawcutt. The Revels Plays. Manchester: Manchester Univ. Press, 1978.
The Plays of Christopher Marlowe. Ed. Roma Gill. Oxford: Oxford Univ. Press, 1971.
The Poems. Ed. Millar Maclure. The Revels Plays. Manchester: Manchester Univ. Press, 1968.
Tamburlaine the Great. Ed. J.S. Cunningham. The Revels Plays. Baltimore: Johns Hopkins Univ. Press, 1981.
The Works of Christopher Marlowe. Ed. C.F. Tucker Brooke. Oxford: Clarendon, 1910.

2. Editions and Translations of Other Writers

Agrippa, Henry Cornelius. *Three Books of Occult Philosophy*. Trans. J[ohn] F[rench]. London, 1651.
Anon. *The Castle of Perseverance* (c.1400-1425). In *English Miracle Plays, Moralities, and Interludes*. Ed. Alfred W. Pollard. 1890; rpt. Oxford: Clarendon, 1927.
Anon. *The Tragedy of Locrine* (London, 1595). Ed. Ronald B. McKerrow and W.W. Greg. Facsimile rpt. Oxford: Malone Society, 1907.
Anon. *Mary of Nemegen* (Antwerpen, 1518). Ed. H. Morgan and A.J. Barnouw. Facsimile rpt. Cambridge, Mass.: Harvard Univ. Press, 1934.
Anon. *Le Miracle de Théophile* (c.1261). In *French Medieval Drama*. Ed. J. Stevens and R. Axton. Cambridge: Cambridge Univ. Press, 1974.

Anon. *The Rare Triumphs of Love and Fortune* (London, 1582). Ed.
W.W. Greg. Facsimile rpt. Oxford: Malone Society, 1930.
Aristotle. *The Poetics*. Trans. W. Hamilton Fyfe. The Loeb Classical Library. 1927; rpt. London: Heinemann, 1939.
Ascham, Roger. *English Works*. Ed. William A. Wright. Cambridge: Cambridge Univ. Press, 1904.
_____. *The Schoolmaster*. Ed. Lawrence V. Ryan. Ithaca,N.Y.: Cornell Univ. Press, 1967.
Augustine. *Confessions*. Trans. R.S. Pine-Coffin. 1961; rpt. Harmondsworth: Penguin Books, 1977.
Bacon, Francis. *Works*. Ed. J. Spedding, R.L. Ellis, and D.D. Heath. 14 vols. London: Longman, 1858-74.
Becon, Thomas. *The Catechism*. Ed. John Ayre. Cambridge: The Parker Society, 1844.
_____. *The Early Works of Thomas Becon*. Ed. John Ayre. Cambridge: The Parker Society, 1843.
Bible. *Biblia Sacra iuxta Vulgatam versionem*. Ed. B. Fischer, J. Gribomont, H.F. Sparks, and W. Thiele. 2 vols. Stuttgart: Württembergische Bibelanstalt, 1969.
_____. *The Geneva Bible*. 1560; rpt. London, 1611.
_____. *The Holy Bible, Containing the Old and New Testaments and the Book called Apocrypha*. Authorized King James Version. 1611; rpt. Oxford: Oxford Univ. Press, 1967.
_____. *The New Testament Octapla. Eight English Versions of the New Testament in the Tyndale-King James Tradition*. Ed. Luther A. Weigle. New York: T. Nelson, 1962.
Blake, William. *Jerusalem, Selected Poems and Prose*. Ed. Hazard Adams. New York: Rinehart & Winston, 1970.
Bonaventure. *The Works of Bonaventure*. Ed. José de Vinck. 5 vols. Paterson,N.J.: St. Anthony Guild, 1960-70.
Bruno, Giordano. *The Ash Wednesday Supper*. Trans. Stanley L. Jaki. The Hague: Mouton, 1975.
_____. *The Heroic Frenzies*. Trans. Paul Eugene Memmo, Jr. Chapel Hill: Univ. of North Carolina Press, 1964.
_____. *On the Infinite Universe and Worlds*. Trans. Dorothea W. Singer. New York: Henry Schuhmann, 1960.
Bullinger, Henry. *The Decades*. Ed. Thomas Harding. 4 vols. Cambridge: The Parker Society, 1849-52.
Calvin, John. *Institutes of the Christian Religion*. Ed. John T. McNeill, trans. Ford L. Battles. 2 vols. Philadelphia: Westminster Press, 1960.
Dee, John. *The Elements of Geometrie of the most Auncient Philosopher Euclide of Megara*. Trans. Henry Billingsley. London, 1570.
Digges, Thomas. *A Perfit Description of the Celestiall Orbes, according to the most Auncient Doctrine of the Pythagoreans, Latelye revived by Copernicus and by Geometricall Demonstrations Approved*. London, 1576.
Drayton, Michael. *The Works of Michael Drayton*. Ed. J. William Hebel. 5 vols. Oxford: Oxford Univ. Press, 1931.
Faustbook. *Historia von D.Johann Fausten* (Frankfurt, 1587). Ed. and introd. Hans Henning. Halle: Verlag Sprache und Literatur, 1963.
_____. *The Historie of the Damnable Life, and Deserued Death of Doctor Iohn Faustus ... by P.F., Gent.* (London, 1592). In

The Sources of the Faust Tradition from Simon Magus to Lessing. Ed. P.M. Palmer and R.P. More. 1936; rpt. New York: Haskell House, 1965.
Fraunce, Abraham. *The Arcadian Rhetorique* (London, 1588). Ed. E. Seaton. Oxford: Blackwell, 1950.
Fulke, William. *A Comfortable Sermon of Faith.* London, 1574.
Gascoigne, George. *The Complete Works of George Gascoigne.* Ed. John W. Cunliffe. 2 vols. 1907; rpt. New York: Greenwood Press, 1969.
Greene, Robert. *Friar Bacon and Friar Bungay.* Ed. J.A. Levin. The New Mermaids. London: Benn, 1969.
Greville, Fulke. *The Remains, being Poems of Monarchy and Religion.* Ed. G.A. Wilkes. London: Oxford Univ. Press, 1965.
Harvey, Gabriel. *Ciceronianus* (London, 1577). Ed. Harold S. Wilson. Univ. of Nebraska Studies in the Humanities, No.4. Lincoln: Univ. of Nebraska Press, 1945.
_____. *The Works of Gabriel Harvey.* Ed. Alexander B. Grosart. 3 vols. London: Huth Library, 1884.
Heywood, Thomas. *An Apology for Actors* (London, 1612). Ed. R.H. Perkinson. New York: Scholars' Facsimiles & Reprints, 1941.
_____. *The Hierarchie of the Blessed Angells. Their Names, Orders and Offices. The Fall of Lucifer with his Angells.* London, 1635.
Hispanus, Petrus. *Expositio magistri Petri Tatareti in summulae Petri Hyspani.* Limoges, c.1510.
_____. *Petri Hispani Summulae logicales.* Ed. I.M. Boschenski. Rome: Marietti, 1947.
Hooker, Richard. *Of the Laws of Ecclesiastical Politie* (London, 1593). Introd. Christopher Morris. 2 vols. 1907; rpt. London: Dent, 1954.
Hoskins, John. *The Life, Letters, and Writings of John Hoskins.* Ed. L.B. Osborn. New Haven: Yale Univ. Press, 1937.
Jonson, Ben. *The Complete Poems.* Ed. G. Parfitt. Harmondsworth: Penguin Books, 1975.
Kyd, Thomas. *The Spanish Tragedy.* Ed. J.R. Mulryne. The New Mermaids. London: Benn, 1970.
Latimer, Hugh. *Sermons by Hugh Latimer.* Ed. G.E. Corrie. 2 vols. Cambridge: The Parker Society, 1844-45.
Luther, Martin. *A Compend of Luther's Theology.* Ed. Hugh Thomson Kerr. Philadelphia: Westminster Press, 1943.
_____. *On the Bondage of Will.* Ed. and trans. J.I. Packer and O.R. Johnston. 1957; rpt. Cambridge: James Clarke & Co., 1973.
_____. *The Precious and Sacred Writings of Martin Luther.* Ed. John N. Lenker. 15 vols. Minneapolis: The Luther Press, 1903-10.
Lyly, John. *The Complete Works of John Lyly.* Ed. R. Warwick Bond. 3 vols. Oxford: Clarendon, 1902.
Martyr, Peter. *The Common Places.* London, 1583.
Melanchthon, Philip. *The Loci Communes.* Trans. Charles Leander Hill. Boston: Little & Brown, 1944.
Milton, John. *Paradise Lost: A New Edition. A Poem in Twelve Books.* Ed. Merrit Y. Hughes. Indianapolis: Odyssey Press, 1962.

Nashe, Thomas. *The Works of Thomas Nashe*. Ed. Ronald B. McKerrow.
   5 vols. 1904-10; rpt. Oxford: Clarendon, 1958.
Ovid. *The xv Bookes of P. Ouidius Naso*....(London, 1567). Trans.
   Arthur Golding. Ed. John Frederick Nims. New York: MacMillan,
   1965.
_____. *Ovid's Metamorphoses*. Ed. and trans. Frank Justus Miller. The Loeb Classical Library. 1916; rpt. Cambridge,Mass.:
   Harvard Univ. Press, 1976-77.
Peacham, Henry. *The Garden of Eloquence* (London, 1577). Ed. W.G.
   Crane. Gainsville,Fla.: Scholars' Facsimiles & Reprints, 1954.
Perkins, William. *De praedestinationis modo et ordine*. London,
   1598.
_____. *A Golden Chaine*. London, 1591.
_____. *A Treatise Tending vnto a Declaration Whether a Man Be in the Estate of Damnation or in the Estate of Grace*. London,
   1598.
_____. *Workes*. 3 vols. London, 1612-13.
Pico della Mirandola, Giovanni. *Oratio de hominis dignitate*.
   Trans. Elizabeth Livermore Forbes. In *The Renaissance Philosophy of Man*. Ed. Ernst Cassire et al. Chicago: Univ. of Chicago
   Press, 1948, pp. 223-54.
Prayer-Book. *The Prayer-Book of Queen Elizabeth* (London, 1559).
   Rpt. London: Griffith Farran, 1890.
Puttenham, George. *The Arte of English Poesie* (London, 1589).
   Ed. G.D. Willcock and A. Walker. Cambridge: Cambridge Univ.
   Press, 1936.
Ramus, Petrus. *Aristotelicae animadversiones libri xx*. Lutetiae,
   1548.
_____. *Commentariorum de religione Christiana libri quatuor*.
   Ed. Theophilus Banosius. Francofurti, 1576.
_____. *Dialecticae institutiones*. Parisiis, 1543 and Lutetiae,
   1547.
_____. *Dialecticae libri duo A.Talaei praelectionibus illustrati*. Parisiis, 1566.
_____. *The logike of the moste excellent philosopher P. Ramus, martyr*. Trans. Roland MacIlmaine. London, 1574.
_____. *Scholae in liberales artes*. Basileae, 1569.
Richardson, Alexander. *The Logician's Schoolmaster, or a Comment upon Ramus' Logicke*. London, 1629.
Rymer, Thomas. *The Critical Works*. Ed. Curt A. Zimanski. New
   Haven: Yale Univ. Press, 1956.
Sermons. *Certain Sermons or Homilies Appointed to be read in Churches in the Time of the Late Queen Elizabeth of Famous Memory and Now Thought to be reprinted ... Anno MDCXXIII*. Ed.
   J. Griffiths. Oxford: Clarendon, 1840.
_____. *The Seconde Tome of homelyes of such matters as were promised and Intituled in the former part of homelyes, set out by the aucthoritie of the Quenes Maiestie: And to be read in eyery paryshe Churche agreablye*. London, 1563.
Shakespeare, William. *The Complete Works of William Shakespeare*.
   Ed. Peter Alexander. 1951; rpt. London & Glasgow: Collins,1953.
Sidney, Sir Philip. *An Apology for Poetry*. Ed. Geoffrey Shepherd.
   1965; rpt. Manchester: Manchester Univ. Press, 1973.

Spenser, Edmund. *The Poetical Works of Edmund Spenser*. Ed. J.C. Smith and E. de Selincourt. 1912; rpt. London: Oxford Univ. Press, 1969.
Temple, William. *P.Rami Dialecticae libri duo, scholiis G.Tempelli Cantabrigiensis illustrati*. Cantabrigiae, 1584.
Tyndale, William. *Doctrinal Treatises*. Ed. Henry Walter. Cambridge: The Parker Society, 1848.
Webster, John. *The Duchess of Malfi*. Ed. John Russell Brown. The Revels Plays. London: Methuen, 1964.
Whitgift, John. *The Works of John Whitgift*. Ed. John Ayre. 3 vols. Cambridge: The Parker Society, 1853.
Wilson, Thomas. *The Arte of Rhetorique* (London, 1553). Ed. G.H. Mair. Oxford: Clarendon, 1909.
Woodes, Nathaniel. *The Conflict of Conscience* (London, 1581). Facsimile rpt. Oxford: Malone Society, 1952.
Wright, Thomas. *The Passion of the Minde*. London, 1601.

3. Criticism and General Reference

All journals and series that are currently on the *MLA Bibliography*'s Master List of Periodicals are cited by acronym.

Althaus, Paul. *The Theology of Martin Luther*. Trans. Robert C. Schulz. Philadelphia: Fortress Press, 1966.
Altman, Joel B. *The Tudor Play of Mind: Rhetorical Inquiry and the Development of Elizabethan Drama*. Berkeley: Univ. of California Press, 1978.
Bakeless, John. *The Tragicall History of Christopher Marlowe*. 2 vols. 1942; rpt. Westpoint,Conn.: Greenwood Press, 1970.
Balthasar, Hans Urs von. *Herrlichkeit: eine theologische Ästhetik*. 2 vols. Einsiedeln: Johannes Verlag, 1961-62.
———. *Theo-Dramatik*. Einsiedeln: Johannes Verlag, 1973.
Barber, C.L. "'The Form of Faustus' Fortunes Good or Bad.'" *TDR*, 8, no.4 (1964), 92-119.
Battenhouse, Roy W. *Marlowe's Tamburlaine: A Study in Renaissance Moral Philosophy*. 1941; rpt. Nashville: Vanderbilt Univ. Press, 1964.
Bayley, John. *Shakespeare and Tragedy*. London: Routledge & Kegan Paul, 1981.
Benston, Kimberly W. "The Shaping of the Marlovian Sublime." Diss. Yale 1980.
Berek, Peter. "*Locrine* Revised, *Selimus*, and Early Responses to *Tamburlaine*." *RORD*, 23 (1981), 33-54.
Berger, Harry, Jr. "The Ecology of the Mind." *Centennial Review*, 8 (1964), 409-34.
Bevington, David M. *From* Mankind *to* Marlowe: *Growth of Structure in the Drama of Tudor England*. Cambridge,Mass.: Harvard Univ. Press, 1962.
Bloom, Harold. *The Anxiety of Influence*. 1973; rpt. New York: Oxford Univ. Press, 1975.
———. "The Breaking of Form." In *Deconstruction and Criticism*. Ed Harold Bloom et al. New York: Continuum, 1979, pp.1-37.

Bloom, Harold. *A Map of Misreading.* New York: Oxford Univ. Press, 1975.
Bloomfield, Morton W. *The Seven Deadly Sins: An Introduction to the History of a Religious Concept with Special Reference to Medieval English Literature.* East Lansing: Michigan State College Press, 1952.
Bluestone, Max. "*Libido Speculandi:* Doctrine and Dramaturgy in Contemporary Interpretations of Marlowe's *Doctor Faustus.*" In *Reinterpretations of Elizabethan Drama.* Ed. Norman Rabkin. New York: Columbia Univ. Press, 1969, pp. 33-88.
Bowers, Fredson. *Elizabethan Revenge Tragedy 1587-1642.* 1940; rpt. Princeton: Princeton Univ. Press, 1971.
─────. "Hamlet as Minister and Scourge." *PMLA,* 70 (1955), 740-49.
─────. "Marlowe's *Doctor Faustus:* The 1602 Additions." *SB,* 26 (1973), 1-18.
Bradbrook, Muriel C. "Marlowe's *Doctor Faustus* and the Eldritch Tradition." In *Essays on Shakespeare and Elizabethan Drama in Honor of Hardin Craig.* Ed. Richard Hosley. Columbia: Univ. of Missouri Press, 1962, pp. 83-90.
─────. *Themes and Conventions of Elizabethan Tragedy.* 1935; rpt. Cambridge: Cambridge Univ. Press, 1979.
Breuer, Horst. *Vorgeschichte des Fortschritts. Studien zur Historizität and Aktualität des Dramas der Shakespearezeit: Marlowe, Shakespeare, Jonson.* München: Wilhelm Fink, 1979.
Brockbank, J.P. *Marlowe: Dr. Faustus.* Studies in English Literature, No.6. London: Edward Arnold, 1962.
Brook, Peter. *The Empty Space.* 1968; rpt. New York: Atheneum, 1980.
Brooke, C.F. Tucker. "The Reputation of Christopher Marlowe." *Transactions of the Connecticut Academy of Arts and Sciences,* 25 (1922), 347-408.
Brooke, Nicholas. "The Moral Tragedy of Doctor Faustus." *CJ,* 5 (1952), 662-87.
Brooks, Cleanth. *The Well-Wrought Urn: Studies in the Structure of Poetry.* 1947; rpt. New York: Harcourt, Brace & World, 1975.
Brown, John Russell. *Discovering Shakespeare: A New Guide to the Plays.* New York: Columbia Univ. Press, 1981.
─────. "*Doctor Faustus* at Stratford-upon-Avon, 1968." In *Doctor Faustus.* Ed. Sylvan Barnet. New York: New American Library, 1968, pp. 194-206.
─────. *Shakespeare's Dramatic Style.* 1970; rpt. London: Heinemann, 1972.
─────. *Shakespeare's Plays in Performance.* London: Edward Arnold, 1966.
Bultmann, Rudolf. "New Testament and Mythology." In *Kerygma and Myth.* Ed. Hans Werner Bartsch. London: S.P.C.K., 1953, pp. 28-41.
Burke, Kenneth. *A Grammar of Motives.* 1945; rpt. Berkeley: Univ. of California Press, 1969.
─────. *Permanence and Change: An Anatomy of Purpose.* 2nd rev. ed. Los Altos: Hermes Publications, 1954.
─────. *Language As Symbolic Action.* Berkeley: Univ. of California Press, 1966.

Burke, Kenneth. *A Rhetoric of Motives*. 1950; rpt. Berkeley: Univ. of California Press, 1969.
―――――. *The Rhetoric of Religion: Studies in Logology*. 1961; rpt. Berkeley: Univ. of California Press, 1970.
Butler, E.M. *The Fortunes of Faust*. Cambridge: Cambridge Univ. Press, 1952.
―――――. *The Myth of the Magus*. Cambridge: Cambridge Univ.Press, 1949.
―――――. *Ritual Magic*. Cambridge: Cambridge Univ. Press, 1948.
Campbell, Lily B. "*Doctor Faustus:* A Case of Conscience." *PMLA*, 67 (1952), 219-39.
Cartelli, Thomas Paul. "Marlowe's Theater: The Limits of Possibility." Diss. University of California at Santa Cruz 1979.
Cassirer, Ernst. *The Individual and the Cosmos in Renaissance Philosophy*. Trans. Mario Domandi. 1927; rpt. Philadelphia: Univ. of Pennsylvania Press, 1963.
Chambers, E.K. *The Elizabethan Stage*. 4 vols. Oxford: Oxford Univ. Press, 1923.
Clemen, Wolfgang. *English Tragedy before Shakespeare*. Trans. T. S. Dorsch. London: Methuen, 1961.
Cockcroft, Robert. "Emblematic Irony: Some Possible Significances of Tamburlaine's Chariot." *RMS*, 12 (1968), 33-55.
Cole, Douglas. *Suffering and Evil in the Plays of Christopher Marlowe*. 1962; rpt. New York: Gordian Press, 1972.
Colie, Rosalie L. *Paradoxia Epidemica: The Renaissance Tradition of Paradox*. 1966; rpt. Hamden,Conn.: The Shoe String Press,1976.
Conzelmann, Hans and Lindemann, Andreas. *Arbeitsbuch zum Neuen Testament*. Tübingen: J.C.B. Mohr, 1975.
Craig, Hardin. "Morality Plays and Elizabethan Drama." *SQ*, 1 (1950), 64-72.
Craik. T.W. *The Tudor Interlude*. Leicester: Leicester Univ. Press, 1962.
Cunningham, J.S. and Warren, Roger. "*Tamburlaine the Great* Rediscovered." *ShS*, 31 (1978), 155-62.
Cushman, Lysander W. *The Devil and the Vice in English Dramatic Literature before Shakespeare*. Halle: Niemeyer, 1900.
Dent, R.W. "Ramist Faustus or Ramist Marlowe." *NM*, 73 (1972), 63-74.
Derrida, Jacques. *Writing and Difference*. Trans. Alan Bass. Chicago: Univ. of Chicago Press, 1978.
Dessen, Alan C. *Elizabethan Drama and the Viewer's Eye*. Chapel Hill: Univ. of North Carolina Press, 1977.
Dick, Hugh G. "*Tamburlaine* Sources Once More." *SP*, 46 (1949), 154-66.
Dickens, A.G. *The English Reformation*. 1964; rpt. London: Fontana, 1978.
Diehl, Huston. "The Iconography of Violence in English Renaissance Tragedy." *RenD*, 11 (1980), 27-44.
Doran, Madelaine. *Endeavors of Art: A Study of Form in Elizabethan Drama*. Madison: Univ. of Wisconsin Press, 1954.
Dowey, Edward. *The Knowledge of God in Calvin's Theology*. New York: Columbia Univ. Press, 1952.
Ellis-Fermor, Una M. *Christopher Marlowe*. 1927; rpt. Hamden,Conn.: Archon Books, 1967.

Empson, William. *Seven Types of Ambiguity*. 1930; rpt. London: Chatto & Windus, 1956.
Erikson, Roy T. "The Misplaced Clownage Scene in *The Tragedie of Doctor Faustus* (1616) and its Implications for the Play's Total Structure." *ES*, 62, no.3 (1981), 249-58.
Farnham, Willard. *The Medieval Heritage of Elizabethan Tragedy*. Berkeley: Univ. of California Press, 1936.
Fisch, Harold. "The Pact with the Devil." *YR*, 69 (1980), 520-32.
Fish, Stanley. *Is There a Text in This Class?: The Authority of Interpretive Communities*. Cambridge,Mass.: Harvard Univ. Press, 1980.
Foakes, R.A. and R.T. Rickert, eds. *Henslowe's Diary*. 1961; rpt. Cambridge: Cambridge Univ. Press, 1968.
Foucault, Michel. *The Order of Things*. 1966; rpt. New York: Random House, 1970.
French, A.L. "The Philosophy of *Dr. Faustus*." *EIC*, 20 (1970), 123-42.
French, Peter. *John Dee: The World of an Elizabethan Magus*. London: Routledge & Kegan Paul, 1972.
Garber, Marjorie B. *Dream in Shakespeare: From Metaphor to Metamorphosis*. 1974; rpt. New Haven: Yale Univ. Press, 1975.
Gardner, Helen. "The Second Part of *Tamburlaine the Great*." *MLR*, 37 (1942), 18-24.
George, Charles H. and Katherine George. *The Protestant Mind of the English Reformation: 1570-1640*. Princeton: Princeton Univ. Press, 1961.
Gilbert, Neil Ward. *Renaissance Concepts of Method*. New York: Columbia Univ. Press, 1960.
Gill, Roma. "'Such Conceits as Clownage Keeps in Pay': Comedy and *Dr. Faustus*." In *The Fool and the Trickster. Studies in Honour of Enid Welsford*. Ed. Paul V.A. Williams. Ipswich: D.S. Brewer, 1979, pp. 55-63.
Glenn, John Ronald. "The Martyrdom of Ramus in Marlowe's *The Massacre at Paris*." *PLL*, 9 (1973), 365-79.
Goldberg, Jonathan. *Endlesse Worke: Spenser and the Structures of Discourse*. Baltimore: Johns Hopkins Univ. Press, 1981.
Greenblatt, Stephen. *Renaissance Self-Fashioning: From More to Shakespeare*. Chicago: Univ. of Chicago Press, 1980.
Greene, Thomas. "The Flexibility of the Self in Renaissance Literature." In *The Discipline of Criticism*. Ed. Peter Demetz, Thomas Greene, and Lowry Nelson, Jr. New Haven: Yale Univ. Press, 1968, pp. 241-64.
Greg, W.W. "The Damnation of Faustus." *MLR*, 41 (1946), 97-107.
Grotowski, Jerzy. *Towards a Poor Theatre*. New York: Simon & Schuster, 1968.
Gurr, Andrew. *The Shakespearean Stage 1574-1642*. 2nd rev.ed. Cambridge: Cambridge Univ. Press, 1980.
Harbage, Alfred. *Annals of English Drama 975-1700*. Rev. Samuel Schoenbaum. London: Methuen, 1964.
Hasler, Jörg. *Shakespeare's Theatrical Notation: The Comedies*. Bern: Francke, 1974.
Hattaway, Michael. "The Theology of Marlowe's *Doctor Faustus*." *RenD*, ns 3 (1970), 51-78.

Haydn, Hiram. *The Counter-Renaissance*. 1930; rpt.Gloucester,Mass.: Peter Smith, 1966.
Heilman, Robert B. "The Tragedy of Knowledge: Marlowe's Treatment of Faustus." *Quarterly Review of Literature*, 2 (1946), 316-32.
Heller, Erich. "Faust's Damnation: The Morality of Knowledge." *Listener*, 11 January, 1962, 59-61.
Homan, Sidney R. "*Doctor Faustus*, Dekker's *Old Fortunatus*, and the Morality Plays." *MLQ*, 26 (1965), 498-505.
Hope, A.D. *The Cave and the Spring*. Sidney: Rigby Ltd., 1965.
Howell, Wilbur S. *Logic and Rhetoric in England 1500-1700*. Princeton: Princeton Univ. Press, 1956.
Hunter, George K. "Five-Act Structure in *Doctor Faustus*." *TDR*, 8, no.4 (1964), 77-91.
──────. "Ironies of Justice in *The Spanish Tragedy*." *RenD*, 8, (1965), 89-104.
──────. "The Theology of Marlowe's *The Jew of Malta*." *JWCI*, 27 (1964), 211-40.
Hunter, Robert G. *Shakespeare and the Mystery of God's Judgments*. Athens,Ga.: Univ. of Georgia Press, 1976.
Jackson, Russell. "*Doctor Faustus* in Manchester." *CritQ*, 23, no.4 (1981), 3-9.
Jardine, Lisa. *Francis Bacon: Discovery and the Art of Discourse*. Cambridge: Cambridge Univ. Press, 1974.
──────. "Humanism and the Sixteenth Century Cambridge Arts Course." *History of Education*, 4 (1975), 16-31.
──────. "The Place of Dialectic in Sixteenth-Century Cambridge." *Studies in the Renaissance*, 21 (1974), 31-62.
Jochum, Klaus Peter. *Discrepant Awareness: Studies in English Renaissance Drama*. Frankfurt, Berne, Las Vegas: Peter Lang, 1979.
Kelly, Michael R. *Flamboyant Drama: A Study of* The Castle of Perseverance, Mankind, *and* Wisdom. Carbondale: Southern Illinois Univ. Press, 1979.
Kerrigan, William. "The Articulation of the Ego in the English Renaissance." In *The Literary Freud: Mechanisms of Defense and the Poetic Will*. Ed. Joseph H. Smith. New Haven: Yale Univ. Press, 1980, pp. 261-308.
Kimbrough, Robert. "*1 Tamburlaine:* A Speaking Picture in a Tragic Glass." *RenD*, 7 (1964), 20-34.
Knight, G. Wilson. *The Wheel of Fire: Interpretations of Shakespearean Tragedy*. 4th rev. ed. London: Methuen, 1972.
Kocher, Paul H. *Christopher Marlowe: A Study in His Thought, Learning, and Character*. 1946; rpt. New York: Russell & Russell, 1962.
──────. "Backgrounds on Marlowe's Atheist Lecture." *PQ*, 20 (1941), 112-32.
──────. "Marlowe's Atheist Lecture." *JEGP*, 39 (1940), 98-106.
Koyré, Alexandre. *From the Closed World to the Infinite Universe*. 1957; rpt. Baltimore: Johns Hopkins Univ. Press, 1968.
Kuriyama, Constance Brown. "Dr. Greg and *Doctor Faustus:* The Supposed Originality of the 1616 Text." *ELR*, 5 (1975), 171-97.
──────. *Hammer or Anvil: Psychological Patterns in Christopher Marlowe's Plays*. New Brunswick,N.J.: Rutgers Univ. Press, 1980.
Langer, Susanne K. *Feeling and Form: A Theory of Art*. New York: Scribner's, 1953.

Lanham, Richard A. *The Motives of Eloquence: Literary Rhetoric in the Renaissance.* New Haven: Yale Univ. Press, 1976.
Lawler, Justus George. *Celestial Pantomime: Poetic Structures of Transcendence.* New Haven: Yale Univ. Press, 1979.
Leggatt, Alexander. "Tamburlaine's Sufferings." *YES*, 3 (1973), 28-38.
Leslie, Nancy T. "*Tamburlaine* in the Theatre: Tartar, Grand Guignol, or Janus?". *RenD*, 4 (1971), 105-20.
Levin, Harry. *Christopher Marlowe: The Overreacher.* 1952; rpt. London: Faber & Faber, 1973.
Loewenich, Walter von. *Luthers Theologia Crucis.* 1933; rpt. München: C. Kaiser, 1954.
Lohse, Bernhard. *A Short History of Christian Doctrine.* Trans. F.E. Stoeffler. Philadelphia: Fortress Press, 1966.
McCanles, Michael. "The Authentic Discourse of the Renaissance." *Diacritics*, 10 (1980), 77-87.
Maclure, Millar, ed. *Marlowe: The Critical Heritage 1588-1896.* London: Routledge & Kegan Paul, 1979.
Maritain, Jacques. *Three Reformers: Luther, Descartes, Rousseau.* New York: Scribner's, 1929.
Martin, Richard A. "Marlowe's *Tamburlaine* and the Language of Romance." *PMLA*, 93 (1978), 248-64.
Matalene, H.W.,III. "Marlowe's *Faustus* and the Comforts of Academicism." *ELH*, 39 (1972), 495-519.
Miller, Perry. *The New England Mind: The Seventeenth Century.* 1939; rpt. Cambridge,Mass.: Harvard Univ. Press, 1954.
Milward, Peter. *Religious Controversies of the Elizabethan Age.* London: The Scholar Press, 1977.
Morgan, Gerald. "Harlequin Faustus: Marlowe's Comedy of Hell." *HAB*, 18 (1967), 22-34.
Morris, Brian, ed. *Christopher Marlowe.* London: Benn, 1968.
Mowat, Barbara A. "Prospero, Agrippa, and Hocus Pocus." *ELR*, 11, no.3 (1981), 281-303.
Nauert, Charles G. *Agrippa and the Crisis of Renaissance Thought.* Urbana,Ill.: Illinois Univ. Press, 1965.
Newman, John Henry. *An Essay in Aid of a Grammar of Assent.* London: Burns, Oates & Co., 1870.
Ong, Walter J. *Ramus, Method, and the Decay of Dialogue.* 1958; rpt. New York: Octagon Books, 1974.
_____. *Rhetoric, Romance, and Technology.* Ithaca and London: Cornell Univ. Press, 1971.
Ornstein, Robert. "The Comic Synthesis in *Doctor Faustus*." *ELH*, 22 (1955), 165-72.
_____. "Marlowe and God: The Tragic Theology of *Dr Faustus*." *PMLA*, 83 (1968), 1378-85.
Patrides, C.A. "Renaissance and Modern Views on Hell." *HTR*, 57 (1964), 56-67.
Poirier, Michel. *Christopher Marlowe.* 1951; rpt. London: Chatto & Windus, 1968.
Porter, Harry C. *Reformation and Reaction in Tudor Cambridge.* 1958; rpt. Hamden,Conn.: The Shoe String Press, 1972.
Potter, Robert. *The English Morality Play.* London: Routledge & Kegan Paul, 1975.
Powell, Jocelyn. "Marlowe's Spectacle." *TDR*, 8, no.4 (1964), 195-210.

Reiss, Timothy J. *Tragedy and Truth: Studies in the Development of a Renaissance and Neoclassical Discourse*. New Haven: Yale Univ. Press, 1980.
Reno, Raymond H. "The Theological Background of Christopher Marlowe's *The Tragical History of Doctor Faustus*." Diss. George Washington University 1958.
Ribner, Irving. "The Idea of History in Marlowe's *Tamburlaine*." *ELH*, 20 (1953), 251-66.
Ricoeur, Paul. *The Symbolism of Evil*. 1967; rpt. Boston: Beacon Press, 1969.
Rosador, Kurt Tetzeli von. *Magie im Elisabethanischen Drama*. Braunschweig: G. Westermann, 1970.
Salingar, Leo. *Shakespeare and the Traditions of Comedy*. 1974; rpt. Cambridge: Cambridge Univ. Press, 1979.
Sanders, Wilbur. *The Dramatist and the Received Idea: Studies in the Plays of Marlowe and Shakespeare*. Cambridge: Cambridge Univ. Press, 1968.
Seung, T.K. *Cultural Thematics: The Formation of the Faustian Ethos*. New Haven: Yale Univ. Press, 1976.
Shaw, John Mackintosh. *Christian Doctrine*. 1953; rpt. London: Lutterworth Press, 1957.
Shewring, Margaret and Clive Barker. "The Theatre-Poetry of Christopher Marlowe, with Specific Reference to *Tamburlaine*, Part I and II." Unpubl. Paper presented at the Shakespeare Institute, 28 May 1981.
Shuhmaker, Wayne. *The Occult Sciences in the Renaissance*. Berkeley: Univ. of California Press, 1972.
Snow, Edward A. "Marlowe's *Doctor Faustus* and the Ends of Desire." In *Two Renaissance Mythmakers: Marlowe and Jonson*. Ed. Alvin Kernan. Baltimore: Johns Hopkins Univ. Press, 1977, pp.70-110.
Snyder, Susan. "The Left Hand of God: Despair in Medieval and Renaissance Tradition." *Studies in the Renaissance*, 12 (1965), 18-59.
Spivack, Charlotte. *The Comedy of Evil on Shakespeare's Stage*. Rutherford: Fairleigh Dickinson Univ. Press, 1978.
Stamm, Rudolf. "The Theatrical Physiognomy of Shakespeare's Plays." *The Shaping Powers at Work*. Heidelberg: C. Winter, 1967, pp. 11-84.
Steane, J.B. *Marlowe: A Critical Study*. 1964; rpt. Cambridge: Cambridge Univ. Press, 1965.
Strype, John. *Annals of the Reformation and Establishment of Religion, and Other Occurrences in the Church of England, during Queen Elizabeth's Happy Reign*. 7 vols. Oxford: Oxford Univ. Press, 1824.
Styan, J.L. *Drama, Stage and Audience*. 1961; rpt. Cambridge: Cambridge Univ. Press, 1975.
_____. *Shakespeare's Stagecraft*. Cambridge: Cambridge Univ. Press, 1967.
Thomas, Keith. *Religion and the Decline of Magic*. 1971; rpt. Harmondsworth: Penguin Books, 1978.
Traister, Barbara H. "Heavenly Negromancy: The Figure of the Magician in Tudor and Stewart Drama." Diss. Yale 1973.
Truchet, Sibyl. "*Tamburlaine* on the Modern Stage." *CahiersE*, 13 (1978), 53-59.

Tuve, Rosemond. *Elizabethan and Metaphysical Imagery: Renaissance Poetic and Twentieth Century Critics*. 1947; rpt. Chicago: Univ. of Chicago Press, 1969.
Ule, Louis, ed. *A Concordance to the Works of Christopher Marlowe*. The Elizabethan Concordance Series. Hildesheim: Georg Olms Verlag, 1979.
Voegelin, Eric. "Das Timurbild der Humanisten." *Zeitschrift für Öffentliches Recht*, 17 (1937), 545-82.
Waith, Eugene M. *The Herculean Hero in Marlowe, Chapman, Shakespeare and Dryden*. London: Chatto & Windus, 1962.
──────. "Marlowe and the Jades of Asia." *SEL*, 5 (1965), 229-45.
Walker, D.P. *The Decline of Hell: Seventeenth Century Discussions on Eternal Torment*. Chicago: Univ. of Chicago Press, 1962.
──────. *Spiritual and Demonic Magic from Ficino to Campanella*. London: The Warburg Institute, 1958.
Warren, Michael B. "*Doctor Faustus:* The Old Man and the Text." *ELR*, 11, no.2 (1981), 111-47.
Waswo, Richard. "Damnation, Protestant Style: Macbeth, Faustus, and Christian Tragedy." *JMRS*, 4 (1974), 63-99.
Weber, Max. *The Protestant Ethic and the Spirit of Capitalism*. Trans. Talcott Parsons. New York: Scribner's, 1930.
Webster, John. "'The Methode of a Poete': An Inquiry into Tudor Conceptions of Poetic Sequence." *ELR*, 11, no.1 (1981), 22-43.
Weil, Judith. *Christopher Marlowe: Merlin's Prophet*. Cambridge: Cambridge Univ. Press, 1977.
Westlund, Joseph. "The Orthodox Christian Framework of Marlowe's *Faustus.*" *SEL*, 3 (1963), 191-205.
Wickham, Glynne. "'Exeunt to the Cave': Notes on the Staging of Marlowe's Plays." *TDR*, 8, no.4 (1964), 184-94.
──────. *Shakespeare's Dramatic Heritage*. New York: Barnes & Noble, 1969.
Wilson, F.P. *Marlowe and the Early Shakespeare*. Oxford: Clarendon, 1953.
Wine, Celesta. "Nathaniel Wood's *Conflict of Conscience.*" *PMLA*, 50 (1935), 663-70.
Wolfit, Donald and Tyrone Guthrie. *Tamburlaine the Great: An Acting Version*. London: Heinemann, 1951.
Yates, Francis A. *Giordano Bruno and the Hermetic Tradition*. London: Routledge & Kegan Paul, 1964.
──────. *The Occult Philosophy in the Age of Elizabeth*. London: Routledge & Kegan Paul, 1979.
Young, David. "'Where the Bee Sucks': A Triangular Study of *Doctor Faustus, The Alchemist,* and *The Tempest.*" In *Shakespeare's Romances Reconsidered*. Ed. Carol McGinnis Kay and Henry E. Jacobs. Lincoln: Univ. of Nebraska Press, 1978, pp. 149-66.

INDEX

acting styles, 72,86,91, 363
Acts and Monuments (Foxe), 370n
Admiral's Men, 78
Agrippa,C.,231,252, 303-4
alchemy,304
Alexander,101,333n,363, 369,371-2,374
allegory,86,114,143,181, 187,195,250,294-6, 309-10,357,359
Alleyn,E.,154
Angels,Good and Bad,174, 209,249-51,294-6, 309-10,357,359
Aquinas,T.,191,228
Aristotle,227-34,237-9, 246
Aristotelianism,30, 227-30,343-4
Artaud,A.,30
arts course,228-30
Ascham,R.,23n,230
astronomy,302,339-45, 351,379
audience-manipulation, 65,128-30,203,244,335, 349,370
Augustine,19n,28,165

Bacon,F.,231
Baines Libel,80,154-5, 315-6
battle scenes,97,118, 123
Beard,T.,82,156
Becon,T.,164,245n,347n, 357
Bible: as authority,20, 22,179,239-45; as covenant,313-16,322; Bishops' version,241n; Geneva,42,241-3; Geneva glosses,241n,242; New Testament,128n,241-3, 315; Old Testament,125, 127-8,314; Vulgate,314; -books of: Chron.,128n; Cor.,32n,190,243n,246; Dan.,182;Eccl.,225; Eph.,246;Ex.,165;Gen., 340;Heb.,243;Isa.,125, 127n,128n;John,241, 242-3,314;Num.,127n; Psalms,127,179,298n; Rev.,58;Rom.,28,127n, 241-3,298;Thess.,157n
Blake,W.,22
Bonaventure,19
Bosch,H.,365-6
boy players,363
Brecht,B.,30,286
Bruno,G.,19,303-4,343
Bullinger,H.,166n

Cabala,304
Calvin,J.,26n,157n,162, 165-6,175,182,191, 231n,239,242-4,314n, 347
Cambridge,78,229-30
Cambyses,83
Castle of Perseverance, The,169,296,359
Catholic drama,186-8, 195-6
censorship,40,155,163
Chapman,G.,307n
chariots,111-2,139-40, 142-8,379,383
choreography,34,91,98, 203-219 *passim*,283, 351
Christ,27,111,194, 217-8,240,315,349,351, 353,392; and covenant of grace,313-4; imitation of,313-5;

320
Cicero,230
Colet,J.,157n
"comedy of evil", 360-75 *passim*
Conflict of Conscience, The (Woodes),169-73
Copernicus,N.,340-4
costumes,86,91-2,101, 126,295,365,370
Cusa,N.of,231

damnation,41-2,74, 203-219 *passim*, 272-6,343,353,357, 371,384; in *Macbeth*, 56-8
dance,308n
de casibus tragedy, 85-6,120,131; and Boccaccio,85
decorum,110n
Dee,J.,303,305
Dekker,T.,307n,308n, 309n
devils,254,260-84, 294,323,352-4
dialectic,228-47, 256-7,265,329; and Ramism,229-30,267, 269,329
Digges,T.,340,343
doubling,362-4
dragons,40,263
Drayton,M.,156
dumb shows,322,252, 361,369,372

Elizabeth I,Queen, 309n
emblems,86,89,92,126, 133,139-43,155,160, 180,182,202,207n, 211,375
Erasmus,D.,231,281,

303
Everyman, 169
evil, 26-8, 53-4, 165, 266;
  as *mysterium iniqui-
  tatis*, 46, 58n, 157, 267;
  and symbolism, 26-8;
  and tragedy, 57-9, 119

Faustbook, 163, 186, 189,
  223-5, 303-4, 312-3,
  327-8, 339-40, 359, 361
Fenner, D., 230
Ficino, M., 19, 231, 303
Fortune, 84-6, 89, 110,
  115, 119, 131, 135, 143n,
  380
Fraunce, A., 66n
free will, 190-3, 222,
  292, 322, *et passim*

gallery ("above"),
  209-12, 259-62, 348-
  353
Gascoigne, G., 143
Golding, A., 25n, 102,
  140, 249n
Gorboduc, 83
Gorgias, 97n
Greene, R., 9, 80-1, 113,
  155, 230, 307n, 379;
  *Friar Bacon and Friar
  Bungay*, 308-12
Greville, F., 25-6, 231
Grotowski, J., 199, 211n,
  215-6

Hall, J., 104
Harvey, G., 80-2, 113, 155,
  230, 267n, 269n
Hazlitt, W., 79
Helen of Troy, 157-9,
  168, 175-7, 181, 195-7,
  336, 337n, 356-7, 363,
  374, 376, 384
hell, 103n, 126, 205,
  209-10, 219, 261, 263,
  271, 276-7, 324, 327-31,
  335, 344, 366, 384;
  classical, 273-4; as
  poena damni, 276, 330
Henslowe, P., 39, 254
Heraclitus, 121n
Hercules, 102-3, 107

heroism, 15-6, 21, 60,
  317-9, 327, 378; and
  Tamburlaine, 60, 77,
  79-108 *passim*, 128, 137
Heywood, T., 143-5
Hispanus, P., 228n
Homer, 273, 337, 372
homilies, 176
Hooker, R., 231n
Horace, 110n
Hoskins, J., 70n
humanism, 17, 232; and
  Hermeticism, 303; and
  rhetoric, 229-30

Icarus, 63, 139n, 157, 225,
  249n
iconoclasm, 10, 138, 141,
  155, 182n, 184n, 245, 303,
  316-7
iconography, 11, 277
invisibility, 352, 371

Jonson, B., 16, 25n, 69n,
  156, 308
Judas, 52, 181n
Jupiter, 116-7, 119-20,
  123, 139, 310, 318-9

Koran, 110-12
Kyd, T., 35-6, 80, 315-6;
  The Spanish Tragedy,
  35-6

Latimer, H., 169n
"literalism", 141-5,
  158-9, 260-9, 302, 307,
  327, 365
Locrine, 379-80
Lodge, T., 379
Longinus, 97n
Lucan, 317-8
Lucifer, 22-4, 140, 275,
  349-50, 352-4, 361, 381
Luther, 28, 157n, 164, 222,
  224, 234n; and free
  will, 190-1, 222; and
  theology of sin, 28,
  223
Lyly, J., 18, 281, 307n, 308,
  309n

Machiavellianism, 279n

magic, 247-53, 259, 297,
  316, 367-75; and Her-
  meticism, 98n, 249,
  302-7, 316, 330n; and
  poetry, 252, 264-6, 282,
  333; and tradition,
  242-9; amd witchcraft,
  264, 3o3, 318
Mahomet, 110-3
Mankind, 169
Marlowe, C.: Cambridge
  education, 66n, 156,
  229-30; dramatic
  career, 9-10, 78-80,
  154; imitations of his
  style, 78, 379-80; and
  Ramism, 73; his reput-
  ation, 9-10, 79-82, 155-
  156; and Shakespeare,
  30, 36-7, 384;
  -works: *Dido Queen of
  Carthage*, 78, 139, 310;
  Dr Faustus, 60, 63-77,
  82, 105, 128, 139n,
  151-386 *passim*;
  Edward II, 139n, 182n,
  317; *Jew of Malta, The*,
  154, 182n, 196, 294, 317;
  Lucan, Pharsalia,
  317-8, 321; *Massacre
  at Paris, The*, 40, 139n,
  234-6, 294; *Ovid's
  Elegies*, 67-70, 248n;
  Tamburlaine the Great,
  76, 78-149 *passim*, 156,
  204-5, 207, 251n, 269,
  279n, 282, 301n, 317-21,
  338, 342, 367, 381,
  378-86;
  -modern productions:
  Doctor Faustus, Classic
  Stage Company, New York
  (1979-80), 260-1; Jesus
  College, Cambridge
  (1980), 260n, 262, 362-
  364; Lyric Studio
  Hammersmith, London
  (1980), 260-1, 299-300,
  333-4, 351, 358, 363-4;
  Old Vic, London (1961),
  370; Oregon Shakes-
  pearean Festival, Ash-
  land (1979), 211n,

260-1,263,352-3,358,
366; Pembroke College,
Cambridge (1979),260n;
Royal Exchange Theatre,
Manchester (1981),351;
Stratford-upon-Avon
(1968),286n,295n;
Theatre Laboratory,
Opole (1963),199,
203-4,211n,215-6;
Tamburlaine the Great,
Old Vic,London (1951),
91,108n; National
Theatre,London (1976),
91-2,96,101,111-2,147
Martyr,P.,162n,169n,
347
Mary of Nemegen,186-8,
195
Medea,248
Melanchthon,P.,224
Milton,J.,45,193;
Paradise Lost,22,45-6,
51n,273-4
Miracle de Théophile,Le,
186-8
*Mirror for Magistrates,
The*,24,85
morality plays,24,85,
151,156,168-9,175-96,
294,339-61 *passim*,364,
379; and convention,
63-4,151-2,169,205,
250-1,294-5,360
More,T.,231,281,303
Munday,A.,307n

narcissism,45,70n,250,
321
narrative speeches,64,
367-8
Nashe,T.,80-1,104,109,
113,154-5,230
"naturalism",137,182
Neoplatonism,19n,121
Nice Wanton,169

oratory,66n,97-8
Orlando Furioso
(Greene),379
Ovid,25,67,102,140,
213,248,317

Paracelsus,303
Paris,88,89n,337
parody,10,196,254-6,
281-3,295,304n,313-6,
320-1,332,365
Paul,Saint,28,157n,190,
241-3,297-8,332,315-6
Peacham,H.,66n,69n
Peele,G.,83,307n,379
performance: dynamics
of,15,34,76-7,203,269,
350,378, *et passim*;
modern,43,91,108n,254,
260-3,322,358,363,372;
original,25,78,83,111n,
137,154,264,312-3,362;
and theatrical notation, 72,91,159-97
passim,205-6,278,293,
345,347,366
Perkins,W.,161-6,169n,
182,231n,234n,347n
Pico della Mirandola,
G.,19-20,231,303
Plato,333n
properties,72,92; *see
also* chariots,thrones
Protestantism,20,24-5,
29,232, *et passim*;
and Bible,241,314;
emphasis on inwardness,
29,173-6,190,222,321,
347; and reformed
theology,153,157-97
passim,222,342; and
reprobation,159-69,
171-3,177-80,217,
222-3,225,231n,243,
245; *see also* repentance
psychomachia,157,172,
214,250,296,365
Puttenham,G.,25n,67n,
69n,287n,288

Rabelais,F.,281
Raleigh,Sir Walter,231
Ramus,P.,73,228-47
passim,269; *see also*
rhetoric
*Rare Triumphs of Love
and Fortune,The*,307n,

308,310
repentance,179-86,
346-50,357; as morality theme,160-9,173-6,
194-5,296-7,351; in
"renunciation" plays,
308-12,351; *see also*
Protestantism
revenge plot,35-6,
379n
rhetoric: in humanist
education,66n,228,
281; in performance,
33,65,67-8,156,269,
280-1,325, *et passim*;
and poetic theory,24,
66n,302; as power,
94-5,97-8,109,377-
386; and Ramism,73,
228-9,278
Rymer,T.,24

Satan,21-2; *see also*
Lucifer
satire,355n,361,370-
371
Scot,R.,312
"self-fashioning",76-7,
94,105,116,123,270
301,319,381
Selimus,379
Seneca,23,317,383
sermons,176
Seven Deadly Sins,The,
225,334,358-66
Shakespeare,W.,25,30,
34,76-8,193,275,281,
306,308,330,337,384;
-works: *As You Like
It*,308n; *Coriolanus*,
17; *Hamlet*,16,29,36,
158,280; *King Lear*,
285n; *Macbeth*,16,
36-8,46-62 *passim*,
66,72,75-6,330; *A
Midsummer Night's
Dream*,308n; *The
Tempest*,204,305,
310-12
Sidney,Sir Philip,
16,25n,110n,231,281

spectacle,35,77,92,323,
  350,353,359,361,364,
  366,368-75,378, *et
  passim*
Spenser,E.,18,281;
  The Fairie Queene,191-
  193,245-6
symbolism,26-7,61,90,
  92n,101,120-2,127,147,
  157,195,202,225,264,
  301,327-9,351

tableau scenes,86,92,
  118,123,133,160,181,
  195-6, *et passim*
Taming of a Shrew, The
  304n
Temple,W.,230

theology,10,20,27,151-
  197 *passim*; and
  cosmology,27,157,
  162,239-47,298; and
  "dramatism", 24,32-2,
  221-2,237,275-81,385;
  and representation,
  23,27-33,124-5,137,
  153-97 *passim*, 221,
  380-1; and tragedy,
  28-9,151-3; *see also*
  morality plays; Pro-
  testantism
thrones,209-12
tragedy,22-4,30-1,35-6,
  104,108-9,130,140,169,
  186,253,267,331,348,
  356,360-1,374,378-80

verse,9,67n,78,286-94,
  317,337-40; and de-
  livery,287n,203-19
  passim; and metrics,
  69,98-9,336-8
Vice,the,359-60,364
Virgil,273
Virgin Mary,186-9,
  195-7

Wager,W.,169
Wapull,G.,169
Webster,J.,331
Wever,R.,169
Wilson,T.,66n
Woodes,N.,169-73
Wright,T.,165

Dutz, Ingold
SHAKESPEARES «PERICLES» UND «CYMBELINE» IN DER BILDKUNST
Bern, Frankfurt/M., München, 1976. 101 S.
Europäische Hochschulschriften: Reihe 14, Angelsächsische Sprache und Literatur. Bd. 34
ISBN 3-261-01865-8 br. sFr. 24.20

Die Studie schliesst sich an die bereits erschienenen Arbeiten über die Rezeption der Dramen Shakespeares bei bildenden Künstlern an und stützt sich dabei auf das Material des Shakespeare-Bildarchivs der Akademie der Wissenschaften und der Literatur in Mainz. Das Ziel ist, die Geschichte der «Pericles»- und «Cymbeline»-Illustration zu erhellen und zum Verständnis dieser beiden Romanzen beizutragen, die bisher in der literarischen Kritik vernachlässigt worden sind.

Malz, Wilfried
STUDIEN ZUM PROBLEM DES METAPHORISCHEN REDENS AM BEISPIEL VON TEXTEN AUS SHAKESPEARES *RICHARD II* UND MARLOWES *EDWARD II*
Frankfurt/M., Bern, 1982. 251 S.
Europäische Hochschulschriften: Reihe 14, Angelsächsische Sprache und Literatur. Bd. 105
ISBN 3-8204-5824-7 br. sFr. 57.–

Seit dem Beginn theoretischer Sprachbetrachtung in der Antike hat die Metapher immer wieder Interesse auf sich gelenkt. Gerade bei der Vielfalt der Theorien kann es von Nutzen sein, noch einmal ganz naiv die Frage zu stellen, was eine Metapher eigentlich ist und warum man sie gebraucht. Von den dabei gewonnenen Grundlagen und mit Hilfe einer möglichst einfachen Terminologie geht die Arbeit über zu einer Untersuchung zweier historischer Dramen der Shakespearezeit, aus denen zahlreiche Metaphern näher erläutert werden.
Aus dem Inhalt: U.a. Die Metapher als Verstoss gegen die «sprachliche Grundnorm» – Die Metapher als Pseudoerklärung – Die Metapher als Instrument des Verstehens – Blasse und anschauliche Metaphern aus *Richard II* und *Edward II*.

Verlag Peter Lang Bern · Frankfurt a.M. · New York
Auslieferung: Verlag Peter Lang AG, Jupiterstr. 15, CH-3000 Bern 15
Telefon (0041/31) 32 11 22, Telex verl ch 32 420

Lutz, Bruno von
DRAMATISCHE HAMLET-BEARBEITUNGEN DES 20. JAHRHUNDERTS IN ENGLAND UND DEN USA
Mit einer Bibliographie
Frankfurt/M., Bern, Cirencester/U.K., 1980. 230 S.
Europäische Hochschulschriften: Reihe 14, Angelsächsische Sprache und Literatur. Bd. 76
ISBN 3-8204-6661-4 br. sFr. 39.–

Die adaptive Rezeption Shakespeares hat seit den 60-er Jahren wieder einen Aufschwung genommen. Der Verfasser versucht, die vielfältigen Formen der dramatischen «Hamlet»-Bearbeitungen des 20. Jahrhunderts nach Typen zu ordnen und die einzelnen Stücke sowohl in ihrer Abhängigkeit von der Vorlage als auch in ihrer Eigenständigkeit zu analysieren. Als Ausgangspunkt dient ein kommunikationstheoretisches Modell des adaptiven Prozesses, anhand dessen die Bearbeitungen bis hin zu den zeitgenössischen Stücken von Marowitz, Stoppard, Papp und Baker dargestellt werden. Eine Bibliographie der Shakespeare-Bearbeitungen des 20. Jahrhunderts schliesst die Arbeit ab.

Rudhart, Blanca-Maria
DIE FRAUEN IN SHAKESPEARES KÖNIGSDRAMEN
Töchter der Ananke
Frankfurt/M., Bern, 1982. 388 S.
Europäische Hochschulschriften: Reihe 14, Angelsächsische Sprache und Literatur. Bd. 102
ISBN 3-8204-7034-4 br. sFr. 77.–

Die Frauengestalten in Shakespeares Königsdramen wurden in der Shakespeare-Kritik sowie in der Theaterpraxis vernachlässigt. Die Untersuchung der Frauengestalten in ihrem Zusammenspiel mit den männlichen Protagonisten offenbart ihre wichtige Funktion als Träger der Metaphorik in den einzelnen Dramen und im Gesamtkomplex dieser historischen Stücke. Erst das gründliche Verständnis der Frauengestalten und die Erhellung ihrer kulturgeschichtlichen Positionen erschliesst die Bedeutung der Königsdramen innerhalb Shakespeares Gesamtwerk.
Aus dem Inhalt: U.a. Von anarchischer Gynaikokratie zum patriarchalischen Gesetz – Werbeszenen – Ehe und Liebe – Ehe und Ehre – Die Königin. Metaphorik ihrer Doppelnatur: Herrschaft und Ohnmacht versus Schuldhaftigkeit und Unsterblichkeit – Hexerei/Magie und Politik – Töchter der Ananke: Die Bedeutung von Moira/Fortuna und Justitia/Caritas-sozio-politische, soziokulturelle Exkurse: Die Elisabethanische Frau.

Verlag Peter Lang Bern · Frankfurt a.M. · New York
Auslieferung: Verlag Peter Lang AG, Jupiterstr. 15, CH-3000 Bern 15
Telefon (0041/31) 32 11 22, Telex verl ch 32 420